WORDS AND IDEAS

SECOND EDITION

heck for abbreviations that should be spelled out (404-405)

se adverb form to modify verbs and other modifiers (316)

heck agreement of subject and verb, pronoun and antecedent (294, 306)

heck for omission or misuse of apostrophe (418)

heck for words that should be capitalized (421)

trengthen sequence of ideas; show relevance of detail (222, 261, 271)

xpression is too colloquial for its context (357)

se semicolon or period between independent clauses (432)

heck for awkward, inaccurate, inappropriate wording (339)

efine or explain abstract and technical terms (72)

evelop your point more fully — support, explain, illustrate (264)

heck dictionary for syllabication of the word (403)

ewrite the sentence to indicate what the modifier modifies (319)

heck for unemphatic, anticlimactic diction or organization (224, 380, 392)

o not punctuate as a sentence — lacks an independent clause (428)

ut items joined by "and," "but," "or" in same grammatical category (328)

heck standing of debatable usage in glossary (464)

heck for unsatisfactory forms or constructions (280)

heck for unidiomatic, un-English expression (346)

ewrite the sentence to make it clearer or more natural (381-382, 391)

heck for faulty or unnecessary capitalization (421)

xamine for logical weaknesses (92)

hift modifier into more appropriate position or rewrite sentence (317)

heck for omission or misuse of punctuation (424)

reak up into paragraphs that reflect organization (260)

void confusing or unnecessary paragraph break (260)

heck reference of pronouns (306)

void unnecessary or awkward repetition (392)

heck faulty predication, incomplete or mixed construction (321)

heck for inadequate or inappropriate subordination (386-391)

heck for shift in time or use of pronouns, shift to passive (330-333)

xpression is too slangy for its context (358-359)

heck for spelling errors (407)

se appropriate tense of verb (300, 330)

trengthen transition from point to point (240, 262)

emove deadwood (367, 389)

orrect obvious error

orrect obvious omission

se punctuation mark indicated (see reference chart, 424)

WORDS AND IDEAS

HANS P. GUTH
San Jose State College

SECOND EDITION

WADSWORTH PUBLISHING COMPANY, INC.
BELMONT, CALIFORNIA

Third printing: July 1965

L.C. Cat. Card No.: 64–11797

Printed in the United States of America

PREFACE

Words and Ideas is a rhetoric and handbook for courses whose main goal is effective student writing. It is designed to help the student overcome the basic weakness of many a student paper: a lack of substance, of conviction, of purpose. Principles of organization and of style cannot be taught in the abstract, to be applied to such materials as may come along. They must be taught to the student as the means of giving structure and form to what he knows and thinks and feels. The student must come to regard rhetoric not as the art of putting preconceived opinions into words but of discovering and shaping what he has to say. Learning to write cannot be separated from learning to observe and to think.

The first four chapters of the book provide a comprehensive and organically developed writing program.

Chapter One (Writing from Observation and Experience) addresses itself to the first requirement for successful student writing: To be authentic, the student's writing must be his own; it must derive from what he has observed, experienced, and thought. Section 1 (Observation and Description) is designed to sharpen the student's powers of observation, and to help him convey what he has observed in concrete, expressive language. Section 2 (Personal Experience), paying special attention to the substance and form of the autobiographical theme, helps the student discover his own experience as a source of material for his writing. Section 3 (Opinion) introduces the student to the central concern of the rhetoric: formulating, presenting, and supporting opinions that are more than mere hearsay or unexamined first impressions.

Chapter Two (Writing and Thinking) examines the relations between thought and language. Section 4 (Definition) focuses on the problem of saying what one means. Section 5 (Logic) relates materials dealing with critical thinking to the concerns of the student writer.

It examines basic logical processes that are at work when the writer marshals his materials; it alerts the student to the logical shortcomings of a superficial argument. Section 6 (Persuasion) examines the strategies of persuasive writing and the problems of responsibility they present; it pays special attention to the role of connotative language and the possibilities of suggestion and implication.

Chapter Three (The Writer's Attitude) deals with tone and style as the expression of the writer's attitude toward his subject and his reader. It pays special attention to the role of informality and formality, and to the role of verbal humor, irony, and satire. Chapter Four (The Writer's Sources) is an introduction to a basic discipline of concern to every competent writer—the planning and preparation of the research paper. In presenting the conventions of documentation, it follows the recommendations of the *MLA Style Sheet*.

The remaining four chapters of *Words and Ideas* make up a handbook, to be used for consecutive study, for review, or for reference. Depending on the nature of a course and the needs of students, instructors will assign materials from the handbook at different times and for differing purposes. For instance, Chapter Five (Organization) takes stock of the principles that guide the writer in developing the whole theme (Section 9) and the paragraph (Section 10). Many instructors will want to assign these sections early in the course as a preliminary survey. Others, proceeding more inductively, will prefer to assign these sections for summary and review after the students have had considerable experience with writing assignments of various kinds.

Chapter Six (Grammar, Diction, and Usage) is designed to help the student make discriminating use of his linguistic resources. Section 11 (Grammar) draws freely on both traditional philology and contemporary linguistic scholarship. Here as elsewhere in the book, it has been my aim to convey to the student not mere unexamined tradition, nor the latest enthusiasms of the author, but an understanding of the nature and uses of language, which the student can take with him from class to class and which can help to make him a more perceptive, more mature writer and reader. In the treatment of usage, my aim has been to develop in the student a respect for the conventions of written English without arbitrarily condemning as incorrect forms and constructions found daily in the speech and writing of people of true distinction. In Sections 12 (Diction) and 13 (Sentence Style), the emphasis is on relating the student's understanding of words and sentence structure to the concerns of rhetoric.

Chapter Seven deals with manuscript mechanics and spelling (Section 14) and with punctuation (Section 15). Chapter Eight provides an expanded glossary of usage (Section 16) and a glossary of grammatical terms (Section 17), new to this edition. Here as elsewhere in the book, the terminology used is, with minor variations, that familiar to teacher and student. At times, I have used a commonsense equivalent for a term unprofitably or confusingly technical. Occasionally, I have used a term from the new linguistics that seemed apt or useful. Throughout, I have tried to use terminology as a means of communicating clearly and efficiently about our subject, to keep it from becoming a barrier between the subject and the student.

The revised edition of *Words and Ideas* has been extensively rewritten and reorganized. My aim has been to make the presentation more succinct, the organization more logical, the handbook more readily usable for efficient reference. Like the original version of the book, this second edition owes much to teachers whose precepts and practices I have studied and at times tried to imitate. As with the original manuscript, I have found the criticisms of interested colleagues detailed, perceptive, and invigorating. I repeat my thanks to the readers of the original manuscript: Dudley Bailey, T. A. Barnhart, Robert W. Dent, Jack Fink, Hans Gottschalk, Harold Kane, and Paul Roberts. In the preparation of the present version, I have profited greatly from the comments of Whitney F. Bolton, University of California; Pascal Covici, Southern Methodist University; Emil Dillard, Adelphi College; Philip Durham, University of California at Los Angeles; Gerhard Joseph, Georgetown University; James Lill, Portland State College; C. F. Main, Rutgers University; and Floyd C. Watkins, Emory University. I repeat my thanks to the students who have allowed me to reproduce their themes, especially Joy Alcock, Masako Kawauchi, Carole Lebental, Virginia Lee, Earl Morris, Irving Plough, and Dean Pritchett. To the Wadsworth staff go my thanks for devoting to *Words and Ideas* time, skill, and enthusiasm beyond the call of duty.

H. Guth

ACKNOWLEDGMENTS

I am indebted to the following for permission to reprint copyrighted material:

George Allen & Unwin Ltd. for permission to use a passage from Bertrand Russell, *Mysticism and Logic.*

The American Historical Association for permission to use a passage from Carl L. Becker, "Everyman His Own Historian," *The American Historical Review,* January 1932.

The American Scholar for permission to use passages from articles by Neal W. Klausner, Joseph Wood Krutch, Donald J. Lloyd, and Philip M. Wagner.

Maxwell Anderson for permission to use a passage from his article "It Comes with the Set," *New York Herald Tribune,* September 6, 1957.

Appleton-Century-Crofts, Inc., for permission to use a passage from *A History of the English Language,* second edition, by Albert C. Baugh. Copyright © 1957, Appleton-Century-Crofts, Inc.

The Atlantic Monthly for permission to use passages from articles by Laird Bell, Saul Bellow, Paul Brooks, Curtis Cate, John K. Galbraith, Erle Stanley Gardner, Oscar Handlin, Gerald W. Johnson, Alfred Kazin, Walter Lippmann, T. S. Matthews, Charles W. Morton, Vance Packard, Leslie C. Stevens, Joseph Wechsberg, and Edward Weeks.

Bantam Books, Inc., for permission to use a passage from Clancy Carlile, "The Animal Fair," *New Campus Writing No. 2,* published by Bantam Books, Inc.

Beacon Press for permission to use a passage from "Notes of a Native Son," by James Baldwin, reprinted by permission of the Beacon Press, © 1955 by James Baldwin.

Columbia University Press for permission to use a passage from Gilbert Highet, *Man's Unconquerable Mind,* Columbia University Press, 1954.

Commentary for permission to use a passage from an article by David Daiches (*Commentary,* April 1957).

Commonweal for permission to use a passage from an article by Gunnar D. Kumlien.

James B. Conant for permission to use a passage from *The American High School Today.*

John Crosby for permission to use a passage from his article "Seven Deadly Sins of the Air," *Life.*

Dodd, Mead & Company, Inc., for permission to use a passage from Stephen Leacock, *Last Leaves,* copyright 1945 by Dodd, Mead & Company, Inc.

John Dos Passos for permission to use a passage from *The 42nd Parallel.*

Doubleday & Company, Inc., for permission to use passages from *The Summing Up* by W. Somerset Maugham, copyright 1938 by W. Somerset Maugham, reprinted by permission of Doubleday & Co., Inc.; and from "Whistling Dick's Christmas Stocking" in *Roads of Destiny* by O. Henry, Doubleday & Co., Inc.

E. P. Dutton & Co., Inc., for permission to use a passage from *Education and Freedom* by H. G. Rickover.

The English Journal for permission to use a passage from an article by Patrick D. and Mary Hazard.

Clifton Fadiman for use of a passage reprinted by special permission from *Holiday,* copyright © 1957 by The Curtis Publishing Company.

Fortune for permission to use passages from articles by Adlai E. Stevenson (October 1955) and William H. Whyte (November 1950).

Harcourt, Brace & World, Inc., for permission to use passages from S. I. Hayakawa, *Language in Thought and Action* (Harcourt, Brace & World); from Laurence Perrine, *Sound and Sense* (Harcourt, Brace & World); from *All the King's Men* by Robert Penn Warren, copyright 1946 by Harcourt, Brace & World, Inc., and reprinted with their permission; from *To the Lighthouse* by Virginia Woolf, copyright 1927 by Harcourt, Brace & World, Inc., renewed by Leonard Woolf, reprinted by permission of the publishers; and from Alfred Kazin, *A Walker in the City* (Harcourt, Brace & World, Inc.).

Harper & Row for permission to use passages from J. B. Priestly, *Rain upon Godshill* and *Margin Released;* from E. B. White, *One Man's Meat;* and from articles by James Baldwin, Bruce Bliven, Heywood Broun, Robert Brustein, Miriam Chapin, John Fischer, John W. Gardner, Robert L. Heilbroner, Jane Jacobs, Marion K. Sanders, C. P. Snow, Dr. Ian Stevenson, Philip M. Wagner, and William S. White.

Harvard University Press for use of a passage reprinted by permission of the publishers from Joseph Hudnut, *Architecture and the Spirit of Man,* Cambridge, Mass.: Harvard University Press, copyright 1949 by The President and Fellows of Harvard College.

Houghton Mifflin Company for permission to use passages from Irwin Edman, *Adam, the Baby and the Man from Mars;* and from Carson McCullers, *The Ballad of the Sad Café.*

Howard Mumford Jones for permission to use a passage from an article in the *Saturday Evening Post.*

Alfred A. Knopf, Inc., for permission to use passages from Bruce Bliven, *Preview for Tomorrow,* copyright 1953; from Robert O. Bowen, *Practical Prose Studies,* copyright 1956; from Alistair Cooke, *One Man's America,* copyright 1951, 1952; from Julian Huxley, *Essays of a Biologist,* copyright 1923; and from H. L. Mencken, *A Mencken Chrestomathy,* copyright 1949.

Little, Brown & Company for permission to use passages from Walter Lippmann, *The Public Philosophy;* from Jacques Barzun, *Teacher in America;* and from Nancy Hale, *The Realities of Fiction,* © 1962 by Nancy Hale.

The Macmillan Company for permission to use a passage from Arthur M. Schlesinger, *Paths to the Present,* copyright 1949.

Scott Meredith Literary Agency, Inc., for use of a passage from an article by Arthur C. Clarke in *Holiday,* reprinted by permission of the author and the author's agent, Scott Meredith Literary Agency, Inc.

Arthur Miller for permission to use passages from articles in *Holiday.*

The New American Library of World Literature, Inc., for permission to use a passage from Horace Coon, *Speak Better—Write Better English.*

New Directions for permission to use a passage from "Quite Early One Morning" by Dylan Thomas. Copyright 1954 by New Directions. Reprinted by permission of New Directions.

The New Yorker for permission to use a passage from James Thurber, Copr. © 1955, The New Yorker Magazine, Inc.

The New York Times and Sean O'Casey for permission to use a passage from *The New York Times Book Review.*

Oxford University Press, Inc., for permission to use a passage from Rachel L. Carson, *The Sea Around Us.*

Prentice-Hall, Inc., for permission to use a passage from Monroe C. Beardsley, *Thinking Straight: Principles of Reasoning for Readers and Writers,* 2nd ed. © 1956. By permission of Prentice-Hall, Inc., Englewood Cliffs, N. J.

Queen's Quarterly for permission to use a passage from an article by K. W. Maurer.

Random House, Inc., for permission to use a passage from Jonathan Norton Leonard, *Flight into Space,* copyright 1953 by Jonathan Norton Leonard; and for permission to reproduce entries taken from *The American College Dictionary* (Copyright 1947, © Copyright 1962) and reprinted by permission of Random House, Inc.

The Reporter for permission to use passages from articles by Robert Bendiner, Marya Mannes, and William · Lee Miller; and additional passages from articles by Michael Harrington, Lois Phillips Hudson, Ken Macrorie, Marya Mannes, William Lee Miller, George Steiner, copyright 1962 and 1963 by The Reporter Magazine Company.

Virginia Rice for permission to use passages from Paul Horgan, "Pages from a Rio Grande Notebook," *The New York Times Book Review,* copyright © 1955 by Paul Horgan.

Rinehart & Company for use of passages from *The Naked and the Dead* by Norman Mailer, copyright 1948 by Norman Mailer; from Lionel Trilling's introduction to *The Adventures of Huckleberry Finn*, by Mark Twain, in Rinehart Editions (New York: Rinehart & Company, Inc., 1948), copyright 1948, 1950, by Lionel Trilling; and from *Generation of Vipers* by Philip Wylie, copyright 1955 by Philip Wylie. All reprinted by permission of Rinehart & Company, Inc., Publishers.

Saturday Review for permission to use passages from articles by Frederick Lewis Allen, John Mason Brown, Henry Steele Commager, Elmer Davis, John Van Druten, James A. Michener, Ashley Montague, Edith M. Stern, and William H. Whyte, Jr.; and additional passages from articles by Malcolm Cowley, James K. Feibleman, Claude M. Fuess, Arthur Mayer, Liston Pope, Bertrand Russell, Hartzell Spence, Albert Szent-Gyorgyi, Harold Taylor, and Richard L. Tobin.

Charles Scribner's Sons for use of passages from Eugene Field, *The House;* and from "The Golden Honeymoon" by Ring Lardner, copyright 1922, 1950 by Ellis A. Lardner (*How to Write Short Stories*), reprinted by permission of the publishers, Charles Scribner's Sons.

Simon and Schuster for permission to use a passage from Ben Hecht, *A Child of the Century,* Simon and Schuster, Publishers; and from Clifton Fadiman, ed., *I Believe.*

The Society of Authors for permission to use a passage from Bernard Shaw, *Man and Superman.*

Edward J. Steichen for permission to use a passage from an article in *Holiday.*

Time for use of passages reprinted courtesy of *Time,* copyright Time Inc. 1958.

The University of North Carolina Press for permission to use a passage from Norman Foerster, *The Humanities and the Common Man,* Chapel Hill: University of North Carolina Press, 1946.

University of Oklahoma Press for use of a passage reprinted from *Is the Common Man Too Common?* by Joseph Wood Krutch and others, copyright 1954 by University of Oklahoma Press and used by permission.

The Viking Press, Inc., for permission to use passages from Harrison Brown, *The Challenge of Man's Future;* Carl Van Doren, *Three Worlds;* John Steinbeck, *The Grapes of Wrath;* and Lionel Trilling, *The Liberal Imagination.*

Willis Kingsley Wing for use of a passage from Sloan Wilson, "It's Time to Close Our Carnival," reprinted by permission of Willis Kingsley Wing, copyright © 1958 by Sloan Wilson.

The World Publishing Company for permission to reproduce entries from *Webster's New World Dictionary of the American Language,* College Edition, copyright 1958 by The World Publishing Company.

Yale University Press for permission to quote from Charles S. Brooks, *Chimney-Pot Papers;* and from David Riesman, *The Lonely Crowd.*

BIBLIOGRAPHY

The following books develop in detail various topics discussed more briefly in this text. Most of these books are written for the student rather than the scholar, the layman rather than the expert. In their turn, they will direct the student to specialized scholarly studies in the fields they represent.

Baugh, Albert C. *A History of the English Language.* 2nd ed. New York: Appleton-Century-Crofts, Inc., 1957. Widely used as a textbook in courses on the history of the language. Traces in detail such matters as the history of English grammar, influences on the English vocabulary, changing attitudes toward language. A comprehensive annotated bibliography follows each chapter.

Beardsley, Monroe C. *Thinking Straight: Principles of Reasoning for Readers and Writers.* 2nd ed. Englewood Cliffs, N. J.: Prentice-Hall, Inc., 1956. A thorough and systematic introduction to applied logic, with special attention to the problems encountered by the critical reader.

Brooks, Cleanth, and Robert Penn Warren. *Modern Rhetoric.* 2nd ed. New York: Harcourt, Brace & World, Inc., 1958. Contains a detailed and well-illustrated discussion of the traditional four forms of discourse: exposition, argument, description, and narration.

Bryant, Margaret M., ed. *Current American Usage.* New York: Funk & Wagnalls Company, Inc., 1962. Completed with the cooperation of eminent linguistic authorities, this book contains a full discussion of disputed points of usage. Rulings are based on the principle that "any expression is standard English if it is used by many cultivated people to communicate in speech or writing." Includes a short bibliography of published studies for each item listed.

Evans, Bergen, and Cornelia Evans. *A Dictionary of Contemporary American Usage.* New York: Random House, Inc., 1957. Discusses many difficult, confusing, or debatable terms and expressions, examining historical data, implications, and overtones that are beyond the scope of an unspecialized dictionary. Often decides questions of debated usage in favor of expressions that, though common in speech and writing, are considered objectionable by conservative readers.

Hayakawa, S. I. *Language in Thought and Action.* New York: Harcourt, Brace & World, Inc., 1949. The revised edition of *Language in Action.* An introduction to semantics, the branch of language study concerned with the relationships between words and the experiences or ideas they stand for. Good on the different purposes and effects of different kinds of language.

Jespersen, Otto. *Growth and Structure of the English Language.* 9th ed. Garden City, N. Y.: Doubleday & Company, Inc., 1956. A paperback reprint of a well-known historical survey that traces the characteristic features of Modern English to their historical origins.

Nicholson, Margaret. *A Dictionary of American-English Usage.* New York: The New American Library of World Literature, Inc., 1958. A paperback reprint of the American adaptation of H. W. Fowler's *A Dictionary of Modern English Usage.* Although based primarily on British usage, Fowler's preferences and dislikes are shared by many of his American readers.

Roberts, Paul. *Understanding Grammar.* New York: Harper & Row, 1954. A critical discussion of traditional grammatical categories and principles. Contains a seventy-page glossary of traditional grammatical terms.

—————————. *English Sentences.* New York: Harcourt, Brace & World, Inc., 1962. Like the author's earlier *Patterns of English,* a workable and eminently readable school grammar incorporating the latest developments in linguistics. An excellent introduction to the characteristic concerns and procedures of contemporary grammarians.

Sledd, James. *A Short Introduction to English Grammar.* Chicago: Scott, Foresman and Company, 1959. A scholarly and non-polemical modern grammar valuable because of its continued critical analysis of and comparison with the grammatical tradition.

Whitehall, Harold. *Structural Essentials of English.* New York: Harcourt, Brace & World, Inc., 1956. A brief introduction to structural grammar, adapting the findings of modern linguistics to the needs of teachers and students of English composition.

CONTENTS

CHAPTER TWO
WRITING AND THINKING

A CONCISE HANDBOOK

CHAPTER FIVE
ORGANIZATION

Section 13. Sentence Style   378

CHAPTER SEVEN
THE MECHANICS OF WRITING

Section 14. Mechanics and Spelling   402

CHAPTER EIGHT
GLOSSARIES

INTRODUCTION

Students often find English a confusing subject. In many other courses, there are more clearly defined ways of doing well and of going wrong. In working out a mathematical equation, for instance, there are usually one or two correct ways of doing things and three or four common sources of error. In an English course, the student's success depends on a number of things that cannot be taught once and for all: his skill and confidence in using language, his alertness as an observer and reader, the extent of his previous experience and reading. Competence in English cannot be gained in one course; it must be gradually developed over the years.

The Aims of the Writing Course. When an English course focuses on composition or written communication, what makes for successful writing cannot be summed up in two dozen simple rules, or divided into twenty lessons. At first, you may feel that the instructor's comments are unpredictable: A paper may be too slangy or too stilted, too superficial or too pedantic, too simple or too involved. At times, you may feel that not your writing but your opinions are under attack. At times, what should be a lesson in writing may seem a clash of personalities.

The point to remember is that good writing requires a range of skills, from the ability to spell *definite* or *believe* to the ability to think an argument through to its logical conclusions. To write effectively, you must become sensitive to exact meanings, and to the overtones and associations of words. You must have a command of the grammatical resources of the language. You must learn to develop

1

a point fully and systematically in a paragraph, to marshal ideas in a theme. Serious writing necessarily brings into play the personality of writer as well as reader: their opinions and preconceptions, their attitudes and emotions, their standards of truth and responsibility. A responsible writer is aware of how writing reflects thought, how words reflect attitudes and emotions. He knows how the resources of language may be abused.

A college course in composition or written communication cannot reduce effective writing to a simple formula, but it can survey some of its more important qualities. It can explain them, relate them to each other, illustrate them by examples. It can encourage the student to watch for them in his reading, and to practice them in his writing. It can show the student how to develop habits that will in the long run make his writing more thoughtful, more substantial, more readable.

Writing the Expository Theme. Courses in college composition are designed to teach the student to write **expository prose**. The purpose of expository writing is the clear and effective communication of facts, opinions, ideas. Such writing calls for accurate observation and for careful study of evidence. It calls for selection of relevant material, orderly presentation, and coherent argument. It requires adequate support of major points, clear definition of terms, and conclusions based on sound logic.

One major part of *Words and Ideas* is devoted to the study and practice of the various kinds of expository themes that you may be asked to write. The first half of the book, the **rhetoric**, examines the purposes and the sources of different kinds of writing, the strategies the writer may adopt and the procedures he may follow, the structure and the style that shape his material.

The sections in Chapter One (Writing from Observation and Experience) are designed to make you draw in your writing on what you have observed, experienced, and thought. More so than a casual observer, an effective writer has an eye for scenes, people, and events. He knows how to select the revealing detail that makes them come to life in the mind of the reader. He knows how to use graphic, specific language that enables the reader to visualize what is being described. In discussing issues and ideas, an effective writer draws on examples and illustrations from his own experience. He knows how to make his readers share in impressions and feelings that are his own honest reactions. His opinions are not mere unexamined prejudice and hearsay;

they represent the carefully considered judgment of someone who has learned to take stock of his observation, experience, and reading.

Chapter Two (Writing and Thinking) examines in some detail how we clarify our thinking on an important point, and how we can best convey our conclusions to a skeptical reader. Serious discussion can seldom make much headway without definition of important terms. Its fruitfulness depends on our willingness to consider relevant evidence and to generalize carefully, without hurrying toward premature conclusions. It depends on our ability to employ sound logic, to avoid familiar pitfalls and distractions. In presenting our conclusions in a paper, we must learn to present them persuasively without relying on devices that alienate thoughtful readers. We must be aware of common temptations to slanting and irrelevant appeals, of the resources of language for indirectness and suggestion. We must learn to convince the reader that we are not trying to bully or deceive him but honestly trying to do justice to our subject.

Chapter Three (The Writer's Attitude) examines the ways in which style expresses the writer's attitude toward his subject and toward his reader. It examines the variations in tone that keep writing from being colorless and predictable. It illustrates the range of style from the formal to the informal, the serious to the facetious, the sober to the satirical.

Chapter Four (The Writer's Sources) deals with writing devoted to the selection, interpretation, and evaluation of evidence from a range of different sources. It takes you step by step through the preparation of a research paper, acquainting you with the purposes and techniques of the library paper required in many classes in composition and of the term papers required in many other courses.

A number of basic principles apply equally to different kinds of writing and will be stressed throughout the rhetoric. Whether your writing is descriptive or autobiographical, whether you are defining a term or developing an argument, you will have to observe the following requirements:

(1) *Your writing must be your own.* It must reflect your authentic impressions, your honest attempts to work out your own answers to questions and problems. Your first task is not to follow a prescribed formula, nor to please the reader, but to write with conviction.

(2) *Your writing must be concrete.* A statement of a principle must be accompanied by specific illustrations. Generalizations must be backed up by examples; abstract terms must be anchored to concrete reference.

(3) *Your writing must have focus.* You must learn to do justice to one point at a time. Rather than merely stating miscellaneous opinions, you must limit yourself to those points that you can develop in detail and examine in their full implications.

(4) *Your writing must have coherence.* If your paper moves from one point to another, the connection between the two must be plausible. The trend of your argument must be clear to your reader.

(5) *Your writing must be responsible.* A responsible writer foregoes the dramatic impact of sweeping claims and drastic charges. He presents balanced, carefully considered views. He does not omit evidence that goes counter to his argument, nor ignore objections that might weaken his case. He respects the reader's right to examine the sources and the validity of the position he is asked to share.

The Standards of Written English. The second major part of *Words and Ideas* is a handbook for study, review, and reference. In the handbook, attention shifts from the larger questions of substance, purpose, and effect to specific problems of organization, expression, and mechanics. This part of the book summarizes the standards of written English, ranging from the requirements for continuity and adequate transition in a theme or paragraph to correct spelling and conventional punctuation. The discussions here are designed to give you an informed understanding of the writer's tools.

The standards described in the handbook are those widely observed in serious and substantial writing. Many of these standards can be justified on the grounds of clarity or economy. Often correctness of expression and clarity of statement go hand in hand. A review of punctuation can stress the way punctuation facilitates reading and clarifies meaning. Close study of sentence structure can help you to improve sentences that are logically confused because they are grammatically defective and vice versa. Close study of words can help you to avoid misunderstanding and to utilize exact shades of meaning. Many errors in mechanics, in grammar, and in word choice are "errors" because they interfere with effective communication.

To a large extent, however, the standards of written English are also a matter of convention. Conventionally, a sports shirt is appropriate to a rather informal situation, whereas a tie is appropriate to a more formal one. Similarly, expressions and grammatical constructions that pass without notice in informal speech may seem seriously out of place in a systematic argument. Few writers can afford to risk the ridicule or ill will that may attend disregard of the etiquette of written expression.

Like other conventions, the conventions of written English are subject to a certain amount of variation. Journalistic writing is more informal than scholarly writing; creative writing is more hospitable to experiment than expository writing. Over the years, educated written English has generally moved closer to the informality of speech. Nevertheless, certain features of language and of style are widely recognized as appropriate to the discussion of serious issues, to the treatment of ideas of some consequence. The advice given in this book on matters of mechanics, grammar, and word choice is designed to help you write the kind of English that is acceptable to many educated readers, regardless of region, profession, or social status.

Making Use of Criticism. The amount of evaluation and criticism that your writing receives will vary with different institutions and instructors. One function of a writing course is to break the ice, to make the student overcome his inhibitions, to help him express himself freely and honestly. Sooner or later, however, a writer reaches the point where he profits from studying the detailed reactions of a critical reader.

Regardless of when, and in what quantities, such criticism comes, you may at first have difficulty in making constructive use of it. Most of us instinctively yearn for recognition and praise. When instead we find our shortcomings analyzed or our conclusions questioned, we feel resentful and discouraged. Few people are less popular than the professional critic—the teacher, reviewer, or examiner who passes judgment on the work of others.

On the other hand, few experiences are more instructive for us as writers than the encounter with an experienced critic who stubbornly refuses to accept our own rosy estimate of ourselves. Such an encounter dramatizes for us the basic problems of communication: how to make our ideas clear, acceptable, persuasive—without meekly accepting standards that we do not share. Criticism, whether worded positively or negatively, can teach us to make our writing less open to misunderstanding, less vulnerable to attack. In later life, criticism often takes the form of reactions that are final and irremediable: a letter of application is quietly filed; a report is turned over for revision to a rival; an article is returned with a printed rejection slip attached. In a writing course, criticism is an invitation to profit from advice.

When a paper is returned to you, you may find general comments on its effectiveness and suggestions for improvement. You may find marginal comments on specific points of style. You may find symbols, like G 5b or P 3, referring you to the relevant section of the handbook for a discussion of problems of punctuation, grammar, diction, or organization. A reference chart of these symbols is printed inside the back cover of this book. You may find abbreviations like *frag* or *MM,* whose significance is explained in the guide printed inside the front cover.

Follow your instructor's suggestions concerning revisions and corrections. Treat revision not as a mechanical exercise but as an opportunity to study the strengths and weaknesses in your past performance. Try to show in your subsequent writing that you have learned to deal with problems pointed out to you in earlier papers.

Criticism has served its purpose when in your future writing you begin to anticipate the reader's reactions. Even when writing a first draft, you will tell yourself: "This paragraph is too thin. Better look for a more solid example." "This isn't the right word. How can I say this more exactly?" "This sentence is getting too involved. Let me try again." The effective writer is the one who has learned to be his own critic.

FIRST THEMES

1. Discuss and illustrate fully one important way in which the kind of English spoken in your family, or among your friends, differs from that taught in the schools.

2. What do you know about grammar? Explain and illustrate as fully as you can something that you learned in one of your previous English courses about the grammatical structure of English.

3. Discuss a recent magazine article, on a subject of general interest, that struck you as exceptionally well written, memorable, or important. Describe and evaluate as fully as you can the author's handling of his subject.

4. What did your high school English courses teach you about literature? Limit yourself to one or two important points. Use illustrations from works of literature that you have read.

5. Discuss the writings of a modern writer with whom you are familiar. What makes him "modern"? Make use of specific references to his work.

6. What kind of poetry do you know? Do you have any clear preferences or dislikes? Discuss one or two poems in some detail.

7. To judge from your own observation, what is the role of "intellectuals" in American society? What are they like, and what is their influence? Use specific illustrations.

8. Describe in detail some events or influences that helped determine your political views.

9. Have you ever had serious trouble with one of your academic subjects in high school or in college? Examine as fully and as impartially as you can the reasons for your difficulties.

10. Why do you like to write? Why don't you like to write? Explain your answer to a skeptical reader.

A COLLEGE RHETORIC

CHAPTER ONE

WRITING FROM OBSERVATION AND EXPERIENCE

1 | 1

1: OBSERVATION AND DESCRIPTION

1. THE USES OF DESCRIPTION

The first thing we ask of good writing is that it should seem real. The writer should somehow be able to re-create in words the appearance of the world around us. Rather than merely telling us *about* scenes and events, he should be able to make us see them, hear them, and feel them. To do so successfully, he must first be a receptive and accurate observer. He must learn to notice things that the tired eye of the routine observer passes over. Second, he must learn to put his observations into words. He must learn to describe people, things, and events in graphic, expressive language.

In your reading and writing, you are likely to find three main uses of accurate observation and description:

(1) **Technical exposition** occurs in reports serving a practical purpose. It provides information that will enable the reader to handle the described object or process efficiently. An analysis of a mechanism may explain its structure, its operation, and its uses. A job description may outline the most efficient procedures for performing a task.

(2) **Imaginative description** enables the reader to share in an experience by making him visualize objects, people, scenes, and events. It appeals to the reader's senses and emotions. Imaginative description may be the main purpose of a personal letter, an account of travel, a descriptive essay devoted to a memorable person or place.

(3) **Incidental description** in a narrative creates an authentic setting. It makes events seem real by providing graphic and vivid impressions of characters and scenes. Fiction, biography, historical

writing, and journalistic reports all profit from competent use of incidental description.

More generally, however, training in observation and description helps a writer make his discussion of issues and ideas concrete rather than abstract, readable rather than dull. It helps him make detail authentic, make illustrations come to life. It develops his skill in using graphic analogies and figures of speech. Prose of opinion and argument will be the more effective if the writer has first learned to do justice to sights and sounds.

2. THE NEED FOR DETAIL

When you first try to communicate sensations, words may seem a poor substitute for first-hand experience. Writing a letter to a friend while touring Italy, you give up trying to make him appreciate the aroma of the soup you are having for lunch, the sunlight playing on the profusely ornamented façade of a fourteenth-century cathedral, or the confused noises echoing from wall to wall in narrow Italian streets. Writing a letter home while on a mountain-climbing trip in Colorado, you give up trying to make your parents breathe the mountain air, see the endless pale-blue sky, or feel the reassuring tug of the rope as you are dangling from a cliff of weathered rock. However, competent writing can be as graphic as a cartoon. It can be as full of sounds and smells as a county fair.

General and Specific. The inexperienced writer, rather than re-creating his observations in detail, often merely hints at them in a vague and general way. When we ask him to tell us about the pueblos of the Mesa Verde, he says that they are "interesting." When we want to know about the performance of a world-famous Russian ballerina, he tells us that it was "enjoyable." Such words are too general to be informative; to the listener or reader genuinely interested in a subject, they are bound to appear lame, perfunctory, evasive. Every student in a writing course should declare a moratorium on the use of "interesting," "beautiful," "exciting," "impressive," and "rewarding."

A dog can wag its tail to indicate that it is pleased, but it does not have the many different and flexible signals needed to make its master share the experiences that give it pleasure. A baby can cry to show that it is unhappy, but it cannot tell its mother whether it is hungry, uncomfortable, or merely bored. If you want your own papers to show that you have graduated from the tail-wagging stage of communication, you need to observe the first basic principle of good writing: *Don't cheat your reader.* In a theme about your trip to Mexico, don't tell your reader, "The towns are full of the most picturesque little shops." Instead, make him see those shops and whatever it is that is picturesque about them. In a theme about your high school days, don't tell your reader, "I still have vivid pictures in my mind of poor student behavior." Instead, get those vivid pictures out of your mind and onto the paper in front of you.

GENERAL: We set up some improvised tables in the backyard and prepared them for the picnic.

SPECIFIC: After we had laid the planks across the marred, paint-spattered sawhorses, Mother spread a red-and-white checkered cloth over the tables we had thus improvised.

GENERAL: In the waiting room, three or four people were waiting for the bus.

SPECIFIC: On the bench, a sailor had fallen asleep waiting for his bus. A boy in a smudged T-shirt was pestering his bored mother for a dime. An old woman was diffidently surveying the two worn suitcases and the cardboard standing at her feet.

Making your writing real and tangible requires greater attention to detail than is necessary in casual everyday observation. The casual tourist can look at Indian pottery with mere passive enjoyment. The writer who wants to describe it needs to pay careful attention to shapes, ornaments, and shades of color. In fact, a writer who tries to focus on important details about a person or a piece of machinery often finds that for the first time he is really looking with both his eyes open.

Sights and Sounds. Not only should your description be detailed rather than general, but you should try to make your details concrete and tangible. In other words, you should *select details that help your reader to imagine or visualize a scene*, details that appeal to his sense of sight, hearing, taste, smell, and touch.

For example, you will not merely tell your readers that a certain instructor was "nervous." Instead, you will provide a number of details to make them visualize a nervous person. You will try to describe the way he kept straightening his tie, adjusting his glasses, shifting his weight, drumming his fingers on his notebook. If your details are authentic enough, your readers themselves will begin to feel fidgety. Your description will begin to be as vivid to them as first-hand observation. Notice how the more concrete version in each of the following pairs makes use of **sensory detail**:

GENERAL: The person walking down the path behind the house cannot help noticing the many spiders and other insects that are always present.

CONCRETE: Spiders, large black ones with red markings, stretch their webs across the path to catch the flies humming and buzzing in the afternoon sun.

GENERAL: I gingerly climbed into the open cockpit of the flimsy training plane and sat down in the narrow seat.

CONCRETE: I climbed onto the lower wing of the aircraft, being careful not to step through the thin canvas covering of the wing. I boosted my parachute-packed frame into the open cockpit and fell heavily back into the tight-fitting bucket seat.

A writer trying to make description vivid as well as concrete often prefers dynamic details to static ones. Instead of giving a frozen picture-postcard view, he will trace the changes in texture brought about by a breeze sweeping across a field of wheat or by a smile spreading across a human face. He knows that attention to change and motion can help to keep a description interesting, while perfect immobility can tire and bore the readers. He knows that effective description of persons requires attention not only to their features, proportions, and clothes but also to the way they walk, frown, turn their heads, and move their hands.

Stereotyped Description. In selecting details, you will do well to *trust your own eyes and ears.* A writer is often tempted to use descriptive phrases which he has come to associate with an object or a scene not through first-hand observation but through their frequent repetition in advertising, travelogues, or popular fiction. Thus, when assigned a topic like "Spring," the writer may automatically deliver standardized, stereotyped phrases like "balmy breezes," "sweet fragrance of cherry blossoms," "springtime riot of colors." For a reader who reads these phrases half a dozen times each spring, they have lost all power to create a vivid picture. They have become merely a tiring and roundabout way of saying "Spring is here." As they can be produced from the writer's memory with a minimum of effort, so they are absorbed by the reader without making him pay attention.

Stereotyped phrases, often called **clichés**, are necessarily general rather than specific. Their frequent repetition shows that they can be indiscriminately applied to many similar objects or situations. To the cliché expert, every mountain is "majestic Mount So-and-So," every big city a "bustling metropolis," every subtropical island an "enchanted isle." Before you can take a detailed look at the contours of a mountain or at the activities going on in a city, you may have to clear away the haze of familiar phrases.

3. ORGANIZING DESCRIPTIVE DETAIL [1]

Usually, the first thing a writer has to learn is to establish a firm grip on concrete detail. On the other hand, great chunks of miscellaneous detail tire and bewilder the reader. The writer must select and organize his details in such a way that they will give an intelligible picture, create a unified impression, or tell a coherent story. *A competent writer never merely records and reports; he constantly sorts out what he observes.* He selects what serves his present purpose.

Detail becomes significant and representative when it helps to establish a mood, make a point, or explain a process. A writer describing a football game has to prevent his description from becoming a meaningless blur. He should try organizing the countless details he observes around one **dominant impression**. If his main interest is in color and excitement, the uniforms of the band, the reactions of the crowd, the shouting of the hot-dog vendors, and the gyrations of the cheer leaders all become relevant. If his main interest is in the stress experienced by the players, he will shift his attention to the tension in the locker room before the start of the game, the exhortations of the coach, the weary faces of the players relieved during each quarter.

Often, the dominant impression supported by a number of details can be stated in a key sentence giving unity to a passage or a paragraph. In each of the following passages, describing a trip through Utah, descriptive detail supports a **major point**:

> Farther along we came to a cool moist cave beneath a great ledge of overhanging rock, like the opening of a giant clamshell. At the inmost recess, where the sloping roof came down to the dirt floor, lay a spring-fed pool, with maidenhair fern growing in the crevices above it, as it might have grown in a mist-filled mountain gorge. The contrast between the cave's microclimate and the arid heat outside under-

[1] See Chapter Five for a general discussion of organization in the expository theme.

scored the obvious fact, which we sometimes forget in the East, that *water is life.*

Fortunately, many of the Indian ruins—dwellings, storehouses for corn, ceremonial buildings—are on inaccessible ledges where they have remained largely undisturbed. As we continued down one of the canyons, we spotted several of the low redstone structures, with their neat rectangular openings, perched like swallows' nests high above us in the canyon wall. One was easy to reach, and I climbed up to explore it. The roof had long since fallen in, but the walls still stood. In the mud daubing between the stone blocks was a thumbprint that could have been made last week, the whorls sharp and clear enough to satisfy any detective who might be on that Indian's trail. But *the trail would have led back to the age of the Crusades.*—Paul Brooks, "Canyonlands," *Atlantic*

If your description of a scene, event, or process does not add up, you probably have not proceeded beyond the notebook stage of jotting down miscellaneous impressions. Your notes, whether mental or written, should be comprehensive enough so that you can discard what is irrelevant and organize the rest in a meaningful sequence. Here are some familiar patterns of organizing descriptive detail:

Chronological Order. When you are describing a process or a series of events, the least confusing way of organizing your material may be to present it in chronological order. The reader can then *follow the different stages in the same order in which they follow each other in time.* Where there are simple cause-and-effect relationships or systematic growth, chronological order will help the reader get a clear grasp of the subject under discussion. The best way of introducing a reader to ceramics may be to take him step by step through the making of a jug or a vase. Often, reconstructing the history of an object or an institution helps the reader know and understand it. The best way to describe a charitable institution may be to give a historical account of its growth. The best way to describe a castle or a cathedral may be to point out the part that was built first and then trace the various later additions.

Key Ideas. If you are trying to explain football or baseball to a foreign visitor, you might confuse him, rather than enlighten him, by taking him step by step through a sample quarter or a sample inning. You would probably realize the need for explaining the essential features of the game before a chronological account could make sense. Your success as a guide, teacher, or writer of instructions will to some extent depend on your ability to *focus on the basic principle of a thing.* Trying to explain baseball, you will do well to forget for the moment the exact dimensions of the field, the diameter of the ball, the number and the names of the players. Instead, you might start with the name of the game and explain the system by which the players progress from base to base until they return to home base to score. The additional details you give later in your paper then serve as an elaboration of a basic principle already presented.

Look for key ideas, unifying principles, distinguishing characteristics. What makes basketball different from other sports? Is it the speed of the action, the agility of the players, the lack of direct bodily contact? What makes a European city look different from an American city? What makes Japanese music sound different from Western music? A hasty answer to such a key question leads to oversimplification. A careful answer, however, can help you organize and unify a great mass of miscellaneous observation.

Order of Increasing Difficulty. A great many descriptions, explanations, and instructions *progress from the familiar to the unfamiliar, or from the simple to the complex.* In trying to introduce a student to the principle of gravity, an instructor might start from a trivial everyday manifestation of gravity, such as a pencil dropping to the floor or an apple dropping from a tree. In order to explain the workings of a steam engine, he might start from such a familiar observation as that of steam lifting the lid of a pot or blowing the whistle of a kettle. To make a student follow the intricacies of a symphony, an instructor might start by isolating a simple tune which the composer used as the main theme of one of the movements and developed in a complicated series of variations.

Analysis. Often you have to *split up a complicated subject into several simple parts.* The process of breaking up a complicated whole into smaller pieces is called **analysis.** Subjects with obvious structural, geographic, or chronological subdivisions lend themselves naturally to analytical treatment. To give a clear and systematic description of a big city, you may want to deal separately with the central business district, the slum areas spreading out from the center, the suburban housing developments, and finally the exclusive residential districts on the fringes of the valley.

In describing an automobile, as in assembling one, you will do well to deal separately with the chassis and the body—as long as you remember to put them together in the end. In describing a sewing machine, you will do well to take up different parts and operations one at a time—as long as you make sure that your reader forms a mental picture of the machine as a whole rather than of disconnected spare parts. In analysis, as in anatomy, the whole is usually more than the sum of the separate elements. Attention to a unifying purpose or over-all effect, preferably summed up at the beginning or the end of your paper, will prevent your analysis from becoming a maze of meaningless facts.

4. USING COMPARISON AND CONTRAST

Competent description makes extensive use of comparison and contrast. Often we can communicate an over-all impression of an object more easily by a brief comparison than by detailed analysis. Thus, we say that a blimp looks like a huge cigar or that a certain foreign car looks like a beetle. The most informative way of describing something often is to *show in what respect an object or situation is similar to one already familiar, or in what respects it differs*, or both. We describe a diesel engine by saying that, like a conventional gasoline engine, it utilizes the pressure exerted by exploding fuel, but that the fuel-air mixture is not ignited by spark plugs but through heat resulting from compression.

Analogy. An extended comparison bringing out the similarities between two things that may be quite dissimilar on the surface is called an **analogy**. Skillfully used, analogy is an indispensable aid in making a reader accept ideas that he considers suspect or absurd. A lecturer may want to explain the work of a famous biologist to a lay audience. He may show that the scientist, in theorizing about the evolution of man, follows a trail back through the ages just as the American Indian follows trails by using clues that are unnoticed by the untrained observer. A science teacher may be trying to explain that, applied to celestial bodies, "rest" and "movement" are relative terms. He may use the analogy of two passenger trains that meet each other at night, going in opposite directions on two parallel tracks. The traveler who watches the lighted windows of the other train go by has no way of determining which of the trains is moving and which is at rest, or whether both trains are moving at the same time. Rest and movement could be determined only by some unmoving point of reference, such as a signal light or a building visible on the other side of the track.

Trite and Extravagant Comparisons. Although useful when handled with care, comparisons lose their capacity to inform when they are used habitually. We come to accept them as conventional tags, without making the effort to visualize the object that is being offered for comparison. Conversational speech is full of comparisons that have lost their usefulness and become clichés. "Brown as a berry," "fresh as a daisy," "apple-pie order," "quick as a wink," and "clocklike precision" have lost most or all of their significance through overuse.

While *some comparisons are too trite and colorless, others are too artificial and far-fetched.* They attract too much attention to themselves and thus distract the reader from the subject under discussion. If you say that the setting sun looked like a huge candied apple descending into a sea of honey, you may put the reader in the mood for a candy bar rather than for a descriptive essay on an evening at the sea. If you say that the setting sun made the sea look like a wrinkled face full of blood, the reader is likely to forget the sunset but remember the gory picture of the blood-filled wrinkles.

5. FINDING THE RIGHT WORD

A writer cannot communicate what he has observed unless he has learned to find the right word, to use graphic, expressive language. When asked to describe a revolving door or a spiral staircase, many people start gesticulating; they find it easier to describe a circle or a spiral with their hands than with their tongues. They find that the impoverished and highly generalized vocabulary of casual conversation is too limited to identify objects and their qualities clearly and economically.

Specific Words. A writer must learn to *use words that are accurate, specific, and informative.* Many people call every second object a "thing," "gimmick," "gadget," "contraption," or "what's-its-name." The conscientious writer will use *lid, lever, valve, coil, tube,* or whatever is the proper word for the object being used.

A dictionary may describe a revolving door as "a door consisting of four vanes hung on a central vertical axle and so arranged in a wall that a person using it turns it around by pushing on one of the vanes." This definition relies for accurate and economical description of two essential parts on the words *vane* and *axle,* which not only identify the parts but give the reader definite ideas concerning their shape and function. Using expressive words is just as important in describing people and events. Instead of using an all-purpose word like *talk*, the writer will often prefer a more expressive word like *chat, mumble, coo, whisper, shout, rant, quip, orate, jeer, scold, brag, proclaim, argue, bluster, assert, drone, stammer,* or *blurt*. A word like *mumble* makes description come to life because it leads most readers to imagine a person actually mumbling; the word has visual and auditory associations. In a more general word like *speak*, all the variables of gesture, tone, and intention that make an individual speaker stand out from the rest have been smoothed over.

No matter how general, *speak* will obviously be more informative than *pontificate* to a reader who either has not encountered *pontificate* before or has encountered it but failed to pay attention to how it was used. Thus, the writer who uses specific or specialized words unfamiliar to his readers may seem to defeat his own purpose of achieving effective communication. Nevertheless, if we would always make our language conform to the lowest common denominator, it would not be long before we would all be back at the baby-talk stage. There is no reason why a reader should cease to make progress toward greater flexibility and efficiency of vocabulary once he reaches the eighth-grade level. Although it is important for the writer to be aware of the limitations of the reader, it is even more important for the reader to become aware of these limitations and to do something about them.

To emphasize the point that communication is a two-way affair, teachers of writing sometimes use the analogy of radio transmitting. If you want someone to listen to your broadcasts, you have to transmit on a wave length that he can tune in. On the other hand, if you decide that an FM frequency is more appropriate than an AM frequency for the type of program you have to offer, you may adopt it even though not every potential listener has an FM receiver. Your assumption would probably be that people will acquire FM receivers if they care enough for good music and intelligent discussion. A primary purpose of education is to provide people with the equipment they need to tune in on the knowledge and the cultural traditions of their society. A very important part of that equipment is a comprehensive and diversified vocabulary.

Technical Terminology. Even a person who seldom discusses political matters is acquainted with words like *Congress, constitution, Supreme Court, liberty, democracy*. Even a person who never discusses questions of diet is likely to be familiar with words like *calorie, vitamin,* or *pasteurized*. The political scientist, however, has to distinguish many different kinds of democracy, and the dietitian has to understand the chemical constitution of many different foods. They thus need a more specialized vocabulary than the person who merely wants to know whether a country is democratic or whether potatoes are fattening.

Each major field of interest develops its own technical terminology. The layman simply turns a knob, but the radio technician has to be able to talk about "wave lengths," "frequencies," "modulation," and "amplitude." The ordinary listener may be able to tell whether a piece of music is fast or slow, gay or solemn, complicated or simple, but a conductor has to be able to talk about "staccato," "crescendo," "syncopation," "counterpoint," and "chromatic scales."

Since technical terms may not be understood, some writers try to do without them altogether. They present nontechnical, popularized introductions to atomic energy, psychoanalysis, or English grammar. Trying to avoid technical terms, such authors are often forced to employ **circumlocution**, lengthy and roundabout description. In a passing reference to the differential, a driving instructor may well call it "that part of the automobile transmission that makes it possible for the inner wheel to turn a curve with fewer revolutions than the outer wheel." An engineering instructor whose class is studying different types of transmission would soon feel the need for the brief and unmistakable technical term.

Whenever you are discussing a specialized subject, you should be careful in using technical terms. The following suggestions can help you use such terms efficiently:

(1) *Decide how much your potential audience can be expected to know about a given field.* For instance, the average male audience will know the difference between "rare" and "well done" but not between "braise" and "sauté." The average female audience will know the difference between "clutch" and "brake" but not between "flywheel" and "differential." In college, you will ordinarily gear your writing to the level of the average college graduate, who has at least some knowledge of politics, religion, psychology, geography, music, and sports.

(2) *Keep the number of new technical terms within reasonable limits.* A writer discussing evolution will lose many of his readers if he unnecessarily keeps using such terms as "arboreal brachiators" for early man's ancestors and "predatory carnivores" for his enemies.

(3) *Use technical terms that are clearly useful in a systematic discussion of your subject, but omit those that are designed merely to impress the reader with the extent of your learning.* For instance, use the word *chiaroscuro* if you think it will fix clearly in your reader's

mind the way your favorite painters use light and shade. Do not use it merely because you want to dazzle him with your knowledge of outlandish nomenclature.

(4) *Explain or clarify all technical terms that your reader cannot be expected to know.* If a person you are talking to fails to understand "isotope" or "solipsism," he can prod you into an explanation by a blank look. But if the same person finds such terms in a paper you have written, he will either stop reading the paper or grumble while trying to find the explanation in his dictionary. Neither reaction makes for efficient communication.

Figurative Language. A vocabulary-conscious writer is careful in his use of figurative language. Figurative expressions make use of the similarities or associations between different things or ideas. However, they do not develop the comparison in detail. A compressed but explicit comparison, introduced by *as* or *like,* is called a **simile.** We are using a simile when we say that a certain proposal or comment was "like a breath of fresh air." An implied comparison that uses one thing or quality as the equivalent of another is called a **metaphor.** We are using a metaphor when we refer to politics as the "political arena." One common kind of metaphor involves **personification,** giving human qualities to objects and ideas. A writer makes use of personification when he calls the rustling sound of cars passing his own on a freeway at night "a whisper out of the throat of the night."

Everyday speech is full of metaphorical expressions. We are constantly warned not to turn back the clock, put the cart before the horse, or change horses in midstream. We are told to keep our powder dry or put our shoulder to the wheel. Unlike such familiar figures of speech, those used by a skillful writer are typically fresh and graphic enough to convey his meaning more memorably, and often more economically, than literal language can. In the following passage from a book review, each successive metaphor briefly and effectively makes an important point:

> Nabokov knows more about *the maze of language* than anyone since Joyce. His style is *a magpie's trove* of Russian, French, German, English, Middle English, and classical lexicography. He *shuffles* words with the strained nonchalance of a man *doing precarious card tricks.*— George Steiner, "Lament for a Language Lost," *The Reporter*

At their best, figurative expressions make writing concrete and colorful. They enable us to put even general impressions into words that appeal to our senses as well as to our minds. They help us translate abstract ideas into striking and memorable pictures. For instance, a reviewer may say that the film version of a novel "tiptoes" carefully around the major issues of the book. The picture of a man walking on the tips of his toes effectively communicates the idea of excessive caution. Often a good metaphor becomes the established way of conveying an idea. "Iron curtain," "cold war," and "black market" are recent examples.

An apt metaphor, like an informative analogy, requires accurate observation. The implied parallel must fit. A high government official once wrote, "Lacking the ignition of advertising, our economic engine would run at a slower pace." However, an engine without ignition would not run at a slower pace; it would just be dead.

Here are some weaknesses of figurative language that a writer must learn to avoid:

(1) Through constant repetition, many figurative expressions have become so familiar that the reader skips over them without visualizing the picture or tracing the comparison they imply. Many of them evoke a stereotyped picture rather than a fresh or informative one and as a result become clichés. *Trite metaphors have been repeated so often that like a worn phonograph record they grate on the reader's nerves.* In descriptive writing, try to do without "Mother Nature," "Father Time," "the cloak of darkness," and "the crack of dawn." Learn to recognize the metaphorical element in expressions like a "blanket" of snow, "sheets" of rain, or "shafts" of sunlight. Do not use them automatically when you want to talk about snow, rain, or sunlight.

(2) When you use more than one figurative expression at a time, the pictures they evoke should blend in a more or less harmonious whole. *Too often, a writer jumps from picture to picture so rapidly that the reader has trouble keeping up with him:*

MIXED: Our minds froze as we tried to span the years.
(The writer was not sure whether to picture the mind as a body of water, which could freeze, or as a bridge, which could span it.)

MIXED: Though Longfellow spoke of the "forest primeval," he did not mean a virgin forest where the hand of man had never set foot. (Hands do not have feet.)

(3) *Sometimes, dead or half-dead metaphors come back to life when mixed carelessly.* An editorial writer said of a government official that he "put his foot in his mouth and in doing so may have chopped off his head politically." Each of the two metaphors mixed

here is in itself violent enough, though both have been blunted by repetition. The unexpected juxtaposition of the two, however, will startle the more sensitive readers into attention. As a result, they will try to visualize a man trying to cut his head off while holding his foot in his mouth. Even when the results are less grotesque, slipshod use of metaphorical language annoys discriminating readers.

6. THE LESSONS OF DESCRIPTIVE WRITING

What, to sum up, are the lessons you can learn from descriptive writing? Descriptive writing will sharpen your powers of observation. It will make you *notice and appreciate detail.* Instead of relying on blurry general impressions of the world around you, you will learn to look closely at an individual face, a particular horse, a specific tree.

At the same time, descriptive writing will help you *develop your ability to sort out and select.* It will train you to choose what is significant and to weed out what is insignificant and confusing. In telling the story of a camping trip, you will learn to select the things most helpful to you in re-creating the more memorable moments of the trip: the sunlight filtering through branches and leaves onto a forest trail; the echo of laughter in a cathedral-like nave of big trees; the warm glow on the cheeks of campers huddled around a fire. By careful selection of concrete, significant, and characteristic detail you will give your reader the illusion of being one of the campers without making him trudge through an inventory of every tree in the forest.

Finally, descriptive writing will *develop your ability to put what you have observed into words.* A competent writer has the knack of finding the right word for something that we easily recognize but find hard to communicate. Notice how in the following passage a skillful writer uses expressive and figurative language to distinguish different kinds of laughter:

> There are four different kinds of laughter in the theater. One is the gag laugh: the *short, sharp bark* of reaction to a funny line. The second is the *nervous titter,* with an edge of hysteria, that greets a grotesquerie or a sick and special joke. A third is the *warm and rippling laughter* of an audience happily involved in the play's characters. And the fourth is commonly known as the belly laugh: *loud, released, and visceral.*—Marya Mannes, "Just Looking," *The Reporter*

Of the writing you do, and of the material you read, comparatively little will have description as its main goal. However, the lessons to be learned from descriptive writing apply to many other kinds of writing as well. Accurate observation, discriminating selection of detail, clear organization of material, and graphic, expressive language are essential characteristics of any competent writer's work. They should become second nature to you even if little of your writing is devoted primarily to description.

EXERCISES 1

A. How accurate is your knowledge of the following descriptive words? Look up those that you are not sure of: (colors) *azure, beryl, crimson, emerald, livid, maroon, ocher, sepia, tawny, vermilion;* (tastes and smells) *acrid, dank, fetid, musty, pungent, rancid, redolent, tangy, tart;* (sounds) *crackle, grate, gurgle, rasp, rustle, snarl, sough, thrum, whir;* (movements) *hover, jounce, lope, lunge, lurch, plod, plummet, quiver, saunter, slosh, totter, trudge, yaw;* (moods) *dour, ferocious, frenetic, languid, lethargic, lugubrious, morose, somber, sultry, torpid, wistful.*

B. From memory, jot down a list of words and phrases that evoke the sights, sounds, and smells of one of the following: registration day, a football game, a political convention, a rodeo, a circus, an old-fashioned revival meeting.

C. Write a well-developed paragraph (about 150 words) describing a room, a street scene, or a natural setting. Make your description mirror one predominant mood, such as gloom, happiness, loneliness, cheerfulness, anxiety, serenity, or fear.

D. What special fields of interest do the following technical terms represent? Which of the terms would you expect the average high school graduate to know? *A priori, barbican, bend sinister, brochure, calorie, camshaft, crochet, de facto, denouement, epistemology, graupel, hole in one, home run, lien, plinth, solstice, sonata, sprit, symbiosis, tachistoscope, thyroid, transubstantiation, valence, venireman, ventricle.*

E. Compile a brief list of important technical terms that you would have to use in describing the characteristic features of one of the following: this year's women's fashions, a complicated mechanism (the engine of a foreign sports car, an electronic brain), one of the traditional styles of architecture (classic, Romanesque, Gothic, baroque), a recent scientific or philosophical theory (theory of relativity, existentialism). Define and explain each of the terms for the interested layman.

F. Investigate the use of figurative language and analogy in a science or philosophy textbook. Write a brief report, providing samples.

G. Examine and evaluate the use of figurative language and analogy in the following selections. If the appropriateness of a phrase depends on the intention of the author, explain under what circumstances the passage would be effective.

1. A career is like a garden in that it, too, requires much plotting and planning, much preliminary spadework, the right seeds sown in the right soil, and a long period of careful cultivation.

2. To allow our cherished freedoms to collapse is to undermine the principle of democratic government and to plunge this free nation of ours to the doors of communism.

3. Descriptions of the average American which are based on statistical evidence tend to be portraits of a statistical meatball, with the lean and the fat all ground together to produce the average man.

4. Isolated facts do not constitute knowledge. The man who merely "plays back" what he has heard or read without any understanding of it is not truly educated.

5. Today our industrial giant, streamlined in accordance with the needs of the atomic age, stands on the threshold of a horizon of unlimited prosperity.

6. Too much economy can be as evil as unlimited spending. There is a danger that a group of economy-minded congressmen will be allowed to slash the nation's vocal cords by rendering the United States Information Agency nearly impotent.

7. In research, the mind does not move forward continuously and smoothly; it behaves like a steam shovel building a highway. Sometimes it cuts great shovelfuls from the rough embankment of the unknown; at other times it hesitates while pushing vainly against an obstacle of hidden size and weight. But eventually the roadway is leveled, and a new section is added to the highway of knowledge.

8. The really important change in Hollywood is that the creative people have the hammer hold today. The men who fashioned the industry in the image of their times are moving out to pasture. Of course the pendulum will swing wide, and many talents will fall by the wayside. The road to capital gains will be strewn with battered souls searching thirstily for a cup of profit.

9. Africa is on the brink of television, and in the fantastic giant step the Dark Continent will be hurtled from the tom-tom to the television screen.

10. Moral progress is at a low ebb and has reached the acme of stagnation. We have many outstanding religious and moral leaders, but their words of gold are falling on arid soil rather than on fertile ground.

11. The financial crises that rocked Europe after World War I harvested a breeding ground for discontent, thus providing a stepping stone for dictators and radical political philosophies.

12. Selling an international language is like selling telephones. No one will buy either unless he thinks a lot of other people will do the same.

13. In such ripe discourse as this, the syllables literally crawl with maggots of meaning for the epicure with a stomach for poetic Gorgonzola.

14. Scientific progress is a stream that owes its strength to many tributaries.

15. By taking the initiative in the current propaganda battle between East and West, the State Department has scored a bull's-eye of great magnitude.

H. Study the following passages for their use of unusual or expressive words, of sensory details, and of striking or apt figures of speech. How are the details in each selection organized? Comment on the distinctive quality of each passage and on its effectiveness as an example of descriptive writing.

1. When I call Hope a village I use a word for it which nobody there ever used. Hope was a church, a school, a blacksmith shop, one store at first and two after a while, and ten houses, in which, in fifteen years, not more than fifty persons lived. It lay at a cross-roads on the long slope of a terminal moraine in the middle of a prairie. The horizon was a circle on the plain, and the sky bent down and met it in a level line. The sun came up out of Indiana as if it were the ocean. The sunsets were sky-high and horizon-wide and rainbow-colored. The soil underfoot was as black as the nights, springing up annually into lavish corn and oats and hay, and some wheat, and along the roads and hedges into a tumult of weeds. In the hot summers they said you could hear the corn grow.—Carl Van Doren, *Three Worlds*

2. The house was left; the house was deserted. It was left like a shell on a sandhill to fill with dry salt grains now that life had left it. The long night seemed to have set in; the trifling airs, nibbling, the clammy breaths, fumbling, seemed to have triumphed. The saucepan had rusted and the mat decayed. Toads had nosed their way in. Idly, aimlessly, the swaying shawl swung to and fro. A thistle thrust itself between the tiles in the larder. The swallows nested in the drawing-room; the floor was strewn with straw; the plaster fell in shovelfuls; rafters were laid bare; rats carried off this and that to gnaw behind the wainscots. Tortoise-shell butterflies burst from the chrysalis and pattered their life out on the window-pane. Poppies sowed themselves among the dahlias; the lawn waved with long grass; giant artichokes towered among roses; a fringed carnation flowered among the cabbages; while the gentle tapping of a weed at the window had become, on winters' nights, a drumming from sturdy trees and thorned briars which made the whole room green in summer.—Virginia Woolf, *To the Lighthouse*

3. To get there you follow Highway 58, going northeast out of the city, and it is a good highway and new. Or was new, that day we went up it. You look up the highway and it is straight for miles, coming at you, with the black line down the center coming at and at you, black and slick and tarry-shining against the white of the slab, and the heat dazzles up from the white slab so that only the black line is clear, coming at you with the whine of the tires, and if you don't quit staring at that line and don't take a few deep breaths and slap yourself hard on the back of the neck you'll hypnotize yourself and you'll come to just at the moment when the right front wheel hooks over into the black dirt shoulder off the slab, and you'll try to jerk her back on but you can't because the slab is high like a curb, and maybe you'll try to reach to turn off the ignition just as she starts the dive. . . .

But if you wake up in time and don't hook your wheel off the slab, you'll go whipping on into the dazzle and now and then a car will come at you steady out of the dazzle and will pass you with a snatching sound as though God-Almighty had ripped a tin roof loose with his bare hands. Way off ahead of you, at the horizon where the cotton fields are blurred into the light, the slab will glitter and gleam like water, as though the road were flooded. You'll go whipping toward it, but it will always be ahead of you, that bright, flooded place, like a mirage.—Robert Penn Warren, *All the King's Men*

4. I had expected the Taj to be exquisite, but small and jewel-like. Actually, it is imposing and exciting in its very size. The sunlight burns white on its sleek gigantic surfaces, which imperceptibly become a rich antique yellow in the shadows. It seemed like a vast, fabulous ivory carving, set in a wonderful garden of clipped grass, roses, bougainvillea, trumpet flowers, and blossoming trees. The still pools in which it is mirrored are filled with darting fish, and from those pools dark men fill big animal skins for watering the grass and the fuchsias.

Conquerors and thieves have stolen the diamonds and other jewels with which the actual tombs were once crusted, and the looted golden doors have been replaced with carved wood; but nowhere else on earth remains such a vastness of pierced and fretted marble. And all over those gigantic sweeping surfaces, both inside and out, are inlaid patterns—lotus blossoms, poppies, lilies, and long quotations from the Koran in graceful Arabic script. Jade, lapis lazuli, agate, carnelian, onyx, and porphyry are laid into the marble with the most beautiful taste and skill to make up those flowing patterns.—Leslie C. Stevens, "The Grand Trunk Road to Agra," *Atlantic*

5. The stream wound its burrow into the jungle. Already they had forgotten how the mouth appeared in sunlight. Their ears were filled with the quick frenetic rustling of insects and animals, the thin screeching rage of mosquitoes and the raucous babbling of monkeys and parakeets. They sweated terribly; although they had marched only

a few hundred yards, the languid air gave them no nourishment, and black stains of moisture spread on their uniforms wherever the pack straps made contact. In the early morning, the jungle was exuding its fog drip; about their legs the waist-high mists skittered apart for the passage of their bodies, and closed again sluggishly, leisurely, like a slug revolving in its cell. For the men at the point of the column every step demanded an inordinate effort of will. They shivered with revulsion, halted often to catch their breath. The jungle dripped wetly about them everywhere; the groves of bamboo trees grew down to the river edge, their lacy delicate foliage lost in the welter of vines and trees. The brush mounted on the tree trunks, grew over their heads; the black river silt embedded itself in the roots of the bushes and between the pebbles under their feet. The water trickled over the stream bank tinkling pleasantly, but it was lost in the harsh uprooted cries of the jungle birds, the thrumming of the insects.—Norman Mailer, *The Naked and the Dead*

I. How effective is the following student theme? Examine its use of descriptive detail and expressive language. Examine the organization and explain its relationship to the over-all idea. Do you sympathize with the writer's feelings and attitudes? Why, or why not?

CUSTOM BALING—PLEASANT AGONY

For four years it has been my joy and sorrow to earn my livelihood during the summer as a custom baler operator. Every spring I scan the pages of the calendar in restless anticipation of the haying season. It is at this time of mid-summer harvest that I couple up my tractor and baler into a mechanical team of which I am the undisputed master and begin earning a few dollars in this supposedly profitable vocation.

Perhaps before I go any further, I should explain, mostly for the urban population, just what the term "custom baling" means and what it involves. "Custom baling" is the name given to the type of seasonal enterprise in which a farmer or some other individual with a tractor and baler at his disposal makes himself available for hire by neighboring farmers who wish to have their hay baled. The operator is paid on a piece-work basis, that is, he receives a predetermined amount of money for each bale of hay he makes.

This entire operation may seem exceedingly simple to the casual observer, but a closer look will unveil custom baling as the complex undertaking that it really is. For the money which the farmer pays for the service, the baler operator is under obligation to complete the job in reasonable time regardless of the odds. His machinery is expected to be in such dependable condition that no trouble should come from that source. The operator is supposed to be so familiar with his machinery, the topography of the field and its effect on his machines, as well as the type of hay he is baling, that he can spot trouble before it actually occurs. In short, all the farmer does in the baling operation is to reimburse the operator at the predetermined rate. The rest is up to the man on the baler.

It is he who fights to remove the rocks which were swallowed along with the hay from the innards of his machine. It is he who must take care to avoid mud holes and soft ground. If he gets stuck he must not only engineer his way out, but later he must apologize for the unsightly ruts he made in his employer's property. It is he who sits cramped under his machine in the hot sun with the chaff falling in his eyes, ears, and neck, trying to free the hopelessly ensnarled moving parts from their tangled wraps of hay. It is he who, covered with grease and dirt, must restore his machine to working condition. Often at the same time he is put into a cold sweat as he sees the sun lowering toward the west over acres of hay which he cannot possibly finish in the few short hours before sunset. In such cases custom baling is agony.

It may seem strange then that there could possibly be any room for pleasure in such a disagreeable task. Still, for every agony there is at least one pleasure. How can one adequately describe to listeners who have never had such an experience the satisfaction felt by the operator when he rises early and when going outdoors he is greeted by the sparkling freshness of the morning? When he mounts to the seat of his tractor he is about to know an experience shared only by those who love fine machinery and earn a living with it. It is the satisfaction of hearing his tractor burst into action with an authoritative roar the instant he pushes the starter button. To listen to the smooth, flawless operation of machinery which he himself has tuned to perfection is to the ears of the operator as the harmonious music of an accomplished symphony orchestra is to the lover of fine music. How, too, can one describe the sweetness which rises from the new-mown hay in the adjacent field as the operator directs his machinery into the first windrow of a new field?

It is such things as these that make custom baling something to which one becomes attached. Even an ordinary sunset acquires a special significance. As the operator heads for home with his tractor and baler, he sits relaxed at the wheel, the cares of the day left behind. Only memories of the pleasant things seem to survive in the serenity of this unique state of mind. He rides along happily tired. To him sunset is the crown of glory to an honest day's labor, the signal to forget the cares of the day and look forward to a refreshing night's rest. From his perch on the tractor he may even watch the fading glow of red in the west and quietly say to himself, "Amen."

THEME TOPICS 1

1. Assume that your reader is a high school graduate with little detailed knowledge of science or engineering. Describe a fairly complicated piece of machinery or equipment, such as a radio or television set, a gasoline or diesel engine, refrigerating or air-conditioning apparatus. Explain the principles on which it operates. Or compare two pieces of equipment to show which you consider superior.

2. Describe some type of fairly complicated work with which you are familiar. Describe it in such a way that your account can be used in

breaking in a newcomer who has not previously done this type of work. If necessary, limit your account to the most important steps.

3. Write an account of a hobby that requires a certain amount of knowledge or skill. Make your account graphic and detailed enough to convey the appeal the hobby has for you.

4. For a foreign student who has a good command of the English language but little first-hand experience with American sports, write an account of the essential features of basketball, golf, or tennis. Make your account graphic rather than drily technical, conveying some of the characteristic appeal of the game.

5. Describe in detail a change in women's fashions that you have observed since you started to take an interest in clothes. Explain technical terms that the average husband could not be expected to know.

6. Record the impressions of an observer stationed at a busy downtown intersection. Concentrate on doing justice to characteristic sights and sounds. Work toward a unified over-all impression.

7. Describe the crowd at a bus station, a country fair, a church picnic, the scene of an accident, or a political rally. Avoid the superficially weird or facetious. Work toward a unifying over-all impression.

8. Describe a city which you remember as particularly memorable, depressing, or in some other way different from what you take to be the average medium-sized or small American town. Be as specific as possible in showing your reader what the city is like.

9. To a reader who has spent most of his life in a city environment, describe the countryside in an area comparatively untouched by city civilization. Avoid stereotyped description.

10. Assume that your reader is a high school graduate whose interest in art is limited to popular music and Hollywood movies. Write a paper introducing him to classical ballet, progressive jazz, abstract painting, or some other difficult and demanding art form with which you are familiar. Explain your technical terms. Limit yourself to one or two essential features but illustrate them graphically and in detail.

2: PERSONAL EXPERIENCE

1. PERSONAL EXPERIENCE IN THE STUDENT THEME

We can write only about what we know, and what we know is derived to a large extent from what we have experienced. The successful writer seems to have selected the material for his work from a rich backlog of experiences and impressions. He has developed the patient, receptive attitude that is more essential to authentic, absorbing writing than a long life crammed with incident. What he says seems derived from what he has undergone and felt.

Obviously, a reader will respond most strongly to writing that directly relates to his own past experience. A book about a slave-labor camp in Soviet Russia may seem remote to a college student who has never seen a barbed-wire fence from the inside. It may seem powerfully realistic to a relative who was a prisoner of war of the Japanese or to a neighbor who escaped from a German concentration camp in World War II. Reacting to the suicide of the heroine in a play, we say "People don't act that way" if we have had little experience with people suffering from depression or mental illness. We say "How true to life!" if the heroine reminds us of someone we know.

However, it is only within limits that your writing can remind your readers of things they have actually witnessed or undergone. For instance, if you are appealing for a contribution to a fund for crippled children, you may try to remind your reader of a seriously handicapped person among his relatives or friends; thus reminded, he may appreciate the need for financial aid to others in similar situations. However, when you are addressing yourself to readers with different backgrounds, such direct appeals to past experience become more difficult. In writing for the student body of a large college or university or for the subscribers of a national magazine, you will have to establish contact with your readers by more general means.

When you cannot appeal to the reader's own experience, you can at least make him feel that what he reads is derived from the past experience of a human being like himself. You can make him feel that, had he been in your place, he would have come away with impressions and feelings similar to yours.

Speaking for Yourself. Giving your writing an authentic quality is partly a matter of perspective. Early in your career as a writer, *learn to speak for yourself.* Suppose you start a paper by saying "History proves that the pursuit of luxury causes the downfall of nations." Who is History? The reader will feel that a student, especially early in his college career, could have done little more than sample the masses of historical knowledge that gather dust in our libraries. How can he set himself up as a spokesman for history with a capital *H*? But suppose you start the paper by saying "A history textbook I recently read led me to believe that the pursuit of luxury causes the downfall of nations." This version sounds much less impressive. However, that a college student should be reading a history textbook seems natural and convincing.

Many students make their writing unreal because they feel that using "I think" and "I believe" would make them sound self-centered and conceited. Actually, you are more likely to sound conceited if you write as if your own opinions were necessarily true for all people and for all time.

Many familiar phrases pretend to authority more sweeping and definitive than the writer can reasonably claim. Often "It is a known fact" means "All my friends think so"; "Experience shows" means "Father tells me"; "Science has proved" means "My high school biology teacher claimed." If you present yourself as a spokesman of History, Common Knowledge, Experience, or Science, you will render your credentials automatically suspect. Talk to your reader as one limited and fallible human being to another.

Using First-Hand Experience. To make your writing seem authentic, *show that what you are saying means something to you by virtue of first-hand experience.* Notice how the account of an actual incident gives substance to the following paragraph:

> A lively street always has both its users and watchers. *Last year I was in the Lower East Side of Manhattan, waiting for a bus on a*

street full of errand-goers, children playing, and loiterers on the stoops. In a minute or so a woman opened a third floor tenement window, vigorously yoo-hooed at me, and shouted down that "The bus doesn't run here on Saturdays!" Then she directed me around the corner. This woman was one of thousands of New Yorkers who casually take care of the streets. They notice strangers. They observe everything going on. If they need to take action, whether to direct a stranger or to call the police, they do so.—Jane Jacobs, "Violence in the City Streets," *Harper's*

Notice how the following passage gains in authenticity through the mere filling in of detail from the author's experience:

THIN: I like politicians. I have spent a lot of time in their company. Mostly, I have reported their doings, but on occasion I have assisted them. On the whole, they have proved better company than any other professional group I have had a chance to know well.

AUTHENTIC: I like politicians. *Ever since I started work as a city-hall reporter in New Mexico some thirty years ago,* I have spent a lot of time in their company—*in smoke-filled rooms, jails, campaign trains, shabby courthouse offices, Senate cloakrooms, and the White House itself.* Mostly I've been reporting their doings, but on occasion I have served them *as speech writer, district leader, campaign choreboy, and civil servant.* On the whole, they have proved better company than any other professional group I've had a chance to know well— *including writers, soldiers, businessmen, doctors, and academics.*—John Fischer, "Please Don't Bite the Politicians," *Harper's*

If your own writing seems thin and colorless, try to give it substance by observing the following suggestions:

(1) *Draw on what you have personally witnessed, experienced, or undergone.* Suppose you start a paper by saying, "Man exerts great effort to attain ultimate knowledge." The reader will ask: "Do you actually know anybody who is concerned with ultimate knowledge? Can you give us a sample of ultimate knowledge so that we can see how it is different from ordinary knowledge?" You will have a much easier time if you start by discussing things you have personally observed. Talk about your brother's taking his watch apart to see what makes it tick. Mention your sister's questions about why it snows and why beetles have so many legs. Describe your father's absorption in an article about the possibility of life on other planets.

(2) *Make detailed use of your reading.* For instance, do not try to argue the need for censorship of detective stories unless you can

mention and describe some detective stories you have read. If you want to write about controversial books in public libraries, rack your brains for possibly relevant material: the story of a librarian fired from his job in your home town, a speech a college president made about book burning, your memories of John Steinbeck's *Grapes of Wrath,* a newspaper story about books withdrawn from American libraries overseas, your history professor's discussion of a book by Norman Thomas. Learn to ask "What do I know about it?" before you ask "What do I think of it?"

(3) *Look at possible subjects from a personal perspective.* When you are writing on a social, political, or cultural problem, start by asking how it affects you or people you know. If you are asked to decide whether required courses are in the best interests of the college student, take a detailed look at required courses you yourself are taking. If you are writing about the moral standards governing American business, discuss the standards of businessmen you know. Teachers in writing classes try hard to find topics that touch on some aspect of the student's experience. Examine possible topics carefully to see how they relate to things in your own background.

2. KNOWING YOUR OWN MIND

If you are trying to make your writing sound lifelike and down to earth, an excellent way to start is to write a number of papers that take stock of your own background and personality. Every writer's apprenticeship should include practice in **autobiography,** writing that gives an accounting of the writer's own life. It is not surprising that many successful professional authors keep diaries, which force them to sort out and come to terms with their experiences from day to day.

When carried beyond the collection of miscellaneous trivia, autobiographical writing can contribute much to a person's education. Most of us, as we grow up, unconsciously absorb things that seem good for us and reject those that seem undesirable. When we start writing about the people and the world around us, we need a more critical attitude. We will look foolish if we dislike our next-door neighbor for being a Republican but are not sure why we ourselves became Democrats.

Our first attempts to investigate our preferences and dislikes can be disillusioning. We may find that we have drifted into a profession or a field of study without any particular reason, or for a reason that we seldom mention in public. We may find that our political convictions are not really our own but those of our parents or of a close friend. We may discover that our opinions of the American Indian were determined by childhood books and television Westerns. Of course, it is only to be expected that we should be to some extent what our parents and teachers and friends have made us. We have neither the time nor the ability to discover by ourselves the laws of Euclidean geometry, the advantages of democracy, and the historical background of the two-party system. Our education necessarily consists to a large extent of a more or less passive absorption of time-tested traditions. Nevertheless, no matter how much we owe to our parents and teachers, we will never stand on our own feet until we begin to make our own decisions.

Such independence brings with it many responsibilities. But it also brings with it the right to point out that in some respects our predecessors could have been wrong. Autobiographical writing is enlightening because it makes us think through our own feelings and commitments, and their relation to patterns and standards to which we might have been expected to conform.

Subjectivity and Objectivity. The goal in scientific and technical writing is **objective** reporting that rules out unreliable personal elements. Science needs procedures and measurements that stay the same regardless of the thoughts, preferences, and emotions of the observer. Autobiography takes stock of the **subjective**, personal elements that the scientist and technician typically bypass in their work. Of these, the one most crucial for a writer's success is emotion. A city block is not merely a location; it is a place where people are happy or unhappy, a place that can make a reader feel lonely and unwanted or loved and secure. A person you describe is not merely a clinical specimen but a human being whom the reader can admire, fear, or despise.

In autobiography, and to a lesser extent in other kinds of writing, you must be able to do justice to the emotional dimension of experience. To make your autobiographical papers vivid and substantial, *include not merely what happened but also what you felt:* the personal qualities that make one of your relatives a warm, poignant memory; the timelessness of a childhood summer spent at the sea or on a farm; the bitterness of childish envy and disappointment; the changes wrought in a person's life and outlook by long illness.

The emotions that give human interest to your writing need not be restricted to love and fear, nor need they be laid on with a trowel. Many everyday situations have more or less subtle emotional overtones. Imagine, for instance, the annoyance with which an adolescent boy responds to the amused condescension of a grown-up sister. If, as is likely, he considers all women inherently inferior, the vain efforts to assert his innate superiority will make him an object lesson in discomfort and exasperation. Or imagine the ambition of a middle-aged high school track coach trying unsuccessfully to produce champions. If his heart is in what he is doing, he is likely to suffer from the alternation of hope and despondency that plagues ambitious people. By consciously registering the things that agitate you and the people around you during a single ordinary day, you will discover a whole spectrum of emotions in addition to the purple ones most often exploited.

Sincerity and Insincerity. When you try to give yourself and your reader an honest account of your feelings, you must *resist the temptation to tell your reader things that he would be pleased to hear.* Suppose you are writing a paper on why you plan to choose teaching as a profession. A reader who is seriously interested in you as a person will be disappointed if you merely say, "I want to teach because I love children." This sounds too much like a routine answer, like "the thing to say." If you mean it, you should provide an explanation or an illustration that will make your statement seem less secondhand. Perhaps you like the clever way young children make fools of adults, their skill in dodging embarrassing questions, their resourcefulness in making up answers that serve their own purpose. Perhaps you want to protect them because they seem helpless and easily hurt. If you do not mean it, however, you are committing a cardinal sin for a writer who wants to be taken seriously. Your writing will be insincere. The applause of the audience will have become more important than your own honest convictions.

In trying to purge your paper of insincerity, you may discover that one reason you like teaching is that it gives you a chance to influence the lives of other people. Or perhaps you are somewhat of an actor and like to perform in front of a group. Your paper should bring some of these things out into the open. If it does, you and your reader will learn something about you as a person, about teaching, and about the motives and ideals of people in general. If you examine your motives critically, your attitude toward teaching will henceforth be better informed and more responsible.

Eagerness to adopt attitudes apparently expected of you will fill your writing with **cant** phrases. In talking about teaching and teachers, you may find yourself constantly using words like *wonderful* and *enthusiastic,* simply because you have been taught to consider a highly articulate enthusiasm the mark of a good teacher. You may find your-self constantly describing your experiences as "challenging," "thrilling," and "rewarding," because you have been made to feel that admiration and prestige do not go to people with experiences that are boring, frustrating, or routine.

If a person meets "wonderful" people and has a "wonderful" time everywhere he goes, the word *wonderful* becomes automatic and meaningless. Therefore, when you are writing about experiences that are genuinely wonderful and thrilling, you should find words without such overtones of insincerity.

Cant is not always allied with optimism. A student may have come to use phrases expressing world-weary disillusionment. Instead of constantly telling his readers that "people are wonderful," he may insist that life is a farce and that all is vanity. He may delight in pointing out the greed and stupidity of his fellow men. His attitude will smack of cant if it is the result of imitation. His writing may then become just as unconvincing as that of the student who sees life through rose-colored spectacles.

Sentimentality and Convention. Through **sentimentality**, people indulge in warm and pleasant emotions at the expense of thoughtful observation. For instance, there is an obvious temptation to look with uncritical tenderness at newlywed couples, small children, and pets. A student may find himself writing about the affection and intelligence of dogs. When challenged, he may realize that his attitude has little direct relation to his own experience. He may simply have read many faithful-dog stories in popular magazines.

Much of the "real-life" drama offered on radio or television makes the listener share in the suffering of the unfortunate but concludes on a cheerful note. Sympathy for the unfortunate and the belief that there is a silver lining to every cloud allow the listener to bask in a warm emotional glow. However, these programs do not necessarily require any effort on his part to understand and alleviate suffering. People who are exposed to much soap opera and popular fiction often absorb some of this inexpensive, self-satisfied optimism into their own system. Their outlook on life may become so sentimental as to make it hard for them to face and deal with actual suffering and misfortune.

In discussing his relationships with other people, a writer often adopts **conventions** that he has absorbed without examining their appropriateness to his personality or to the circumstances. For instance, much popular fiction and most Hollywood movies rely on the convention of romantic love. Once a writer adopts this convention, it may force him to color, if not to misrepresent, his feelings in order to make them compatible with the established code. He may feel compelled to confess to love at first sight rather than to a gradual growth of love. He may allege an unconditional, overwhelming love rather than varying shades of tenderness, affection, and desire.

Sometimes every casual girl friend becomes the "one and only" woman in a man's life. In such cases the insincerity involved is fairly obvious. But even when such phrases are used sincerely, they suffer through guilt by association. The listener or reader is likely to wonder whether he is being "handed a line." The word *love* itself may make some readers think of a guitar-strumming crooner rather than of genuine emotion.

Do not allow sentimentality and convention to keep you from knowing your own mind. They handicap you as a writer because they alienate thoughtful readers. One teacher may mark your paper, "A wonderful tribute to your mother," but another may say, "Too sentimental for a weary old hand like me." Don't settle the matter by calling the first one wonderful and the second one cynical. Perhaps the second one was disappointed because instead of taking a good look at your own childhood you gave him a warmed-over story from a popular magazine.

Overdramatization. Even a writer who is trying to give an honest accounting of himself may have trouble finding the right tone. He may be embarrassed and self-conscious, using apologetic phrases like "After all, I was only a child," "This may not sound very exciting to a person who wasn't there," or "I know this sounds silly, but . . ." Trying to avoid an excessively apologetic attitude, he may go to the opposite extreme. Inexperienced writers often exaggerate for effect. They posture and pose to impress their audience. They overdramatize their experiences, making them sound impressively tragic, hectically exciting, or hilariously funny.

Overdramatization is encouraged by much reading matter intended for popular consumption. It is found, for instance, in popular journalism ("Into the vortex of the Israel crisis flew the President of the United States, his forehead deeply furrowed, his mood somber . . ."). It is equally common in advertising ("Out of the pages of history comes the stupendous story of the love that shook an empire!"). In student writing—as in advertising—the symptoms of overdramatization are often typographical: exclamation marks, dashes, ellipses, and other devices designed to create emphasis and suspense ("Finally!! We turned the corner . . . crossed the street . . . and there—partly hidden by the trees—my childhood home!!!"). Another symptom is the use of words like *extreme, absolute, tremendous, magnificent, perfect, unique,* or *superb.*

Only a thin line separates the impressive from the pretentious, the exciting from the hysterical. With mature and critical readers, exaggeration dampens rather than heightens emotion. A tragic actor who keeps clenching his fists and gritting his teeth through five long acts may strike his audience as a pathetic bogeyman rather than as a suffering human being.

When your subject calls for emotion, develop it unobtrusively, without fanfare. A statement in a low key is often more effective than one with strong emphasis. Thus, instead of referring explicitly to the sense of loneliness that he felt in the house of a dead friend, a writer said that "there are echoes now that one didn't hear before." A writer must learn to convey emotions not by proclaiming them but by making them emerge from his account of people, scenes, and events.

Obviously, some subjects call for emotion genuinely powerful or even violent. The following autobiographical passage describes the anguish of a stammering child in a school where his speech defect meets with incomprehension and ridicule:

> The word was my agony. The word that for others was so effortless and so neutral, so unburdened, so simple, so exact, I had first to meditate in advance, to see if I could make it, like a plumber fitting together odd lengths and shapes of pipe. I was always preparing words I could speak, storing them away, choosing between them. And often, when the word did come from my mouth in its great and terrible birth, quailing and bleeding as if forced through a thornbush, I would not be able to look the others in the face, and would walk out in silence, the infinitely echoing silence behind my back, to say it all cleanly back to myself as I walked in the streets.—Alfred Kazin, *A Walker in the City*

The matter-of-fact circumspection of the plumbing metaphor sets up a powerful contrast with the violence of the birth metaphor. The violent figurative language used here powerfully communicates the point that from a child's perspective nothing is more immediate, nothing more desperately serious than emotional crises of this kind.

3. ORGANIZING THE AUTOBIOGRAPHICAL THEME [1]

Finding the material for an autobiographical paper often requires some soul-searching. Arranging and presenting the material, on the

[1] For a more general discussion of organization, see Chapter Five.

other hand, may seem easy. The writer may simply determine to follow the order of events in time; to tell the story of his life, or of that
limited part of it that fits into a 500- or 800-word theme. Following a
chronological scheme, however, does not automatically solve all problems of organization.

Unity and Proportion. As the model for a paper, the story of one's
life has the disadvantage that it is formless and, in general outline,
dull. *In an autobiographical paper, even more than in other kinds of
writing, the first need is for restriction of a huge, sprawling subject.*
Only when the scope of a paper is narrow enough to allow detailed
discussion of specific persons, incidents, and problems does the ordinary person's experience become interesting. A theme that merely lists
the highlights of a visit to New Orleans or to San Francisco is likely
to reproduce the fatigue of the trip without the concrete sights and
incidents that made the trip worthwhile.

Nor is restriction of the subject merely a matter of limiting the
time span that the paper is going to cover. Themes about "My Spring
Vacation" or "A Labor Day Outing" seldom have the unity suggested
by the neat temporal limitation of their titles. The events of a week
or of a single day can be as miscellaneous as those of a month or of a
year. A paper discussing a change in Christmas customs over a period
of several decades can be more unified than the paper that assembles
the unrelated trivia of a single holiday weekend.

If failure to restrict the subject leads to lack of unity, failure to
sift out the unimportant leads to a lack of proportion. Autobiographical
writing should not be the unedited record of the past, compiled by the
camera eye of nostalgic memory. The reader absorbed in the meticulous and authentic detail of a good autobiography tends to forget how
much that would be distracting or merely routine has been left out.

Sample Patterns. Like other kinds of writing, autobiography is
weakened by a merely perfunctory chronological sequence. Chronological order becomes meaningful when it goes hand in hand with logical
or emotional unity. A given span in your life will cease to be an
arbitrary limit if it is presented as a stage in your psychological or
moral growth.

Here are some sample patterns for a successful autobiographical
theme:

(1) A theme may concentrate on *a single incident chosen to bring
out an important point*. It may deal with an episode in which an
erroneous impression is first created and then corrected, a vacation

trip that destroys a cherished illusion or fulfills a cherished dream. Many such papers derive their unity from a lesson learned, a lesson that need not be tiresomely reiterated if it emerges vividly and plausibly from the incident described. Thus, a paper may describe in detail a childish prank that misfired, with the writer concentrating on the changes from thoughtless laughter to apprehensive silence and to the beginning of a more mature attitude.

(2) A theme may owe its unity not to a central idea but to a *prevailing mood.* A writer can unify his account of a stay in a hospital or a visit to a reform school by selecting details that reflect the emotion uppermost in his mind. He can unify an episode from his childhood by re-creating a mood of sullen resentment or of excited happiness.

(3) A longer or more ambitious paper, still adhering to chronological progression from childhood to adolescence, or from adolescence to maturity, may *follow a unifying thread through a number of experiences.* It may find the common element in the author's encounters with a type of person or a kind of problem. It may trace an important gradual change in attitude: hostility yielding to understanding, prejudice replaced by sympathy, naïve trust replaced by vigorous disapproval.

(4) A paper may work out a *contrast between two conflicting influences:* a businesslike, efficient father and a sensitive, artistic mother; the foreign customs of immigrant parents and the Americanizing influence of school. Such an organization is especially effective in helping the author bring together various elements from his experience for well-focused discussion.

(5) Finally, a paper may abandon chronological order altogether and follow the order of analysis by dividing the subject into its *major logical subdivisions.* It may present, perhaps in the order of increasing importance, the three main reasons for the author's dislike of a school, or the four main attractions of his future profession.

Chronological order, even though it provides the skeleton for most autobiographical writing, is no substitute for a unifying purpose. The writer must limit himself to a subject that has inherent as well as merely external unity. He must be selective, choosing details either because they help to create an authentic setting or because they contribute to his main point. He must arrange his material so that it will lead to a satisfying climax or fulfill a promise held out in title or introduction. In short, the writer must organize as well as collect, reflect as well as reminisce.

4. THE USES OF AUTOBIOGRAPHY

What, to sum up, are the lessons to be learned from autobiographical writing? Autobiographical writing can teach you to mobilize your own resources. It can help you discover your personal experience as the most immediate, the most legitimate, and often the most interesting source of material. You may never become an authority on troop movements during the Civil War or on the behavior of subatomic particles. But nobody can question your right to act as an authority on what you have personally observed, undergone, and felt.

Autobiography thus helps a writer develop the most important single quality of effective writing: *good writing carries conviction.* Whatever good writing is, it is not the repetition of thin generalities about the values of education or the American way of life. Your writing must be something that you yourself are willing to stand up for, something to which in some way you are personally committed.

Temporarily, the readers of an article or of a book may be carried away by the writer who can argue glibly on either side of an issue. But the writer who makes a lasting impression is the one whose writing expresses his personal involvement and commitment. Good writing means recording one's own observations, pinning down one's own reactions, interpreting one's own experience, formulating one's own judgments, and making one's own mistakes. To profit from instruction in writing, you have to consider it as more than perfunctory practice. Papers dealing with personal experience can help you take your writing seriously by making you focus on some of the matters important to you in your own life.

EXERCISES 2

A. Write a one-paragraph theme describing an incident that revealed something significant about the character of a friend or relative. Sum up the point of the episode in a key sentence placed at the beginning or at the end of the paragraph.

B. Select *three* of the following general terms: *cruelty, curiosity, dignity, extravagance, forgiveness, kindness, naïveté, patience, poise, rudeness, shyness, spite, touchiness.* Write a well-developed paragraph about each, describing in detail an incident from your personal experience or observation that illustrates the quality you have selected.

C. Study the tone·and approach in the following brief excerpts from autobiographical student papers. What seems to be the major appeal or purpose of each selection? Which comes closest to carrying conviction? Why?

1. My uncle was no ordinary hypochondriac. He owned a drugstore, inherited from his father, and had been practically brought up in it. He talked to doctors and nurses every day. When some infectious disease was making the rounds, he would worry for hours over whether he had the symptoms. When he was positive that he did, his mind was in a way relieved and he went to bed. The next morning he woke up in perfect shape.

2. I am tired of watching women cater to the almighty male. A woman can't turn around today without an army of editors, writers, and psychologists warning her to beware: she may lose the king if she as much as breathes wrong! The idea is that all females should fall on their knees and knock their heads on the ground three times whenever a male comes into view. If a husband earns a living, doesn't bully his children with his fists, and smiles occasionally at his wife, he is practically a hero. A woman is supposed to spend her entire life pampering and pleasing the male, and consider herself the luckiest girl alive if he remembers her birthday.

3. Then I heard people screaming that there was a man trapped under the front tire of the other car. I found Jack, who was completely stunned by the whole event. He told me that he put on the brakes at the intersection and that the brakes had failed. He just couldn't stop the car. Within minutes the police and ambulance arrived, and the car was tediously lifted off the trapped, quiet man. I observed a girl sitting in the ambulance, and I realized that she also had been riding in the other car.

4. At first, finding a job was very difficult. There was no work for a boy nine years old anywhere. After five days of cutting school, I saw a sign in the window of a little grocery that said "Delivery Boy Wanted." When I walked through the door, I thought my heart would never stop pounding. When I told the man inside that I wanted to apply for the job, his first reaction was to look over the counter and laugh. But then he asked me a few questions and seemed to become interested. His next reaction was to go over to the sign in the window and take it down. I was so excited I wanted to scream. What would my mother say? How happy she would be! With great effort I controlled my emotions. The sweat was pouring down my back and face. Then the man said, "I hired a boy yesterday. He should be in any minute now. I guess he forgot to take the sign out of the window."

5. Any job I have ever had has been taken under duress. I am a moody, indolent, dreamy individual, and once, in a fit of pique, I quit school and wandered off to seek my soul. My parents took a dim view of the search and, becoming hungry, I found myself taking employment with the Union Oil Company, a well-fed crew. Here I found I could be moody, indolent, and dream-prone on company time.

D. The following are brief excerpts from autobiographical passages by well-known modern writers. What makes each passage graphic, effective, memorable? Show in detail how each writer uses language to re-create a setting or a scene, and to convey his feelings or attitudes.

1. I was born in a large Welsh town at the beginning of the Great War—an ugly, lovely town (or so it was and is to me), crawling, sprawling by a long and splendid curving shore where truant boys and sandfield boys and old men from nowhere, beachcombed, idled and paddled, watched the dock-bound ships or the ships steaming away to wonder and India, magic and China, countries bright with oranges and loud with lions; threw stones into the sea for the barking outcast dogs; made castles and forts and harbours and race tracks in the sand; and on Saturday summer afternoons listened to the brass band, watched the Punch and Judy, or hung about on the fringes of the crowd to hear the fierce religious speakers who shouted at the sea, as though it were wicked and wrong to roll in and out like that, white-horsed and full of fishes.—Dylan Thomas, *Quite Early One Morning*

2. Now, the First War, with its massed artillery, was the noisiest of all time; the sound hit you harder and harder as the months passed; some things you got used to—sniping and machine-gun fire if you were not entangled in the open and a sitting duck, hand bombs and rifle grenades if you had sandbags and room to dodge—but as time went on the vast cannonading, drumming hell into your ears, no matter whether it was their guns or yours, began to wear you down, making you feel that flesh and blood had no place in this factory of destruction. So in that war it was not the recruit but the veteran who began to feel he was being hammered into the ground. Every time I went back into the line, especially after being out of it long enough for my ears to be open to civilization again, I felt more and more apprehension. In that listening post I was the gallant Tommy of the home-front legends; but as time wore on I was more and more a chap who wondered what the hell he was doing there and how he could get out of it—a mouse in a giant mincing machine.—J. B. Priestley, *Margin Released*

3. I had forgotten, in the rage of my growing up, how proud my father had been of me when I was little. Apparently, I had a voice and my father had liked to show me off before the members of the church. I had forgotten what he had looked like when he was pleased but now I remembered that he had always been grinning with pleasure when my solos ended. I even remembered certain expressions on his face when he teased my mother—had he loved her? I would never know. And when had it all begun to change? For now it seemed that he had not always been cruel. I remembered being taken for a haircut and scraping my knee on the footrest of the barber's chair and I remem-

bered my father's face as he soothed my crying and applied the stinging iodine. Then I remembered our fights, fights which had been of the worst possible kind because my technique had been silence.

I remembered the one time in all our life together when we had really spoken to each other.

It was on a Sunday and it must have been shortly before I left home. We were walking, just the two of us, in our usual silence, to or from church. I was in high school and had been doing a lot of writing and I was, at about this time, the editor of the high school magazine. But I had also been a Young Minister and had been preaching from the pulpit. Lately, I had been taking fewer engagements and preached as rarely as possible. It was said in the church, quite truthfully, that I was "cooling off."

My father asked me abruptly, "You'd rather write than preach, wouldn't you?"

I was astonished at his question—because it was a real question. I answered, "Yes."

That was all we said. It was awful to remember that that was all we had *ever* said.—James Baldwin, *Notes of a Native Son*

4. The first time I needed to write anything was when I was about eight. I was sitting on the back steps of our house after a rain, staring out at the swamp, purple with loosestrife and joe-pye weed. A cat came skulking out of the long wet grass and wove its way past the steps, rubbing its sides against the rough boards. I couldn't bear it. I went back into the house, and in my journal—my "Diary. Private. Keep out!"—which had hitherto been filled only with accounts of meetings of the Four Queens Club and of swimming at Lake Pearl, I began to write, "As I was sitting on the back steps today, a cat came skulking out of the long wet grass. . . ."

With these words I was, for the first time, expressing feeling. If the writer doesn't have feeling, he is nothing, for here it is the same as belief. If the writer doesn't believe in his own fiction, he is certainly not going to persuade the reader to believe in all that imitation grass, bogus activity, and imaginary conversation. If he does have feeling for his fiction, and if he masters the tricks of conveying his feeling without interfering with it too much, a light will go up on the scene he has set, the blindfold will be snatched from his readers' eyes, and, purring with delight, they will set themselves to the willing suspension of disbelief.—Nancy Hale, *The Realities of Fiction*

E. Compare an autobiographical account published in the *Reader's Digest* or in *The Saturday Evening Post* with one published in *The Atlantic Monthly, Harper's Magazine,* or *The New Yorker.* How do the accounts compare in authenticity, candor, and intention?

F. Read two or three of the short stories of O. Henry. Describe the attitude toward life or toward people that prevails in them. Can you explain this writer's popularity?

G. Investigate current television dramas or Hollywood movies. To what extent do they bear out the familiar charge that their treatment of love is cliché-ridden and sentimental? More generally, what ideas about people—their standards and their motives—do they convey to their audience?

H. Study the advice given to people with personal or emotional problems in a question-and-answer column in a newspaper or magazine. How useful, mature, or responsible is the advice?

I. Read a number of case histories from one of the books of Norman Vincent Peale. To judge from your own experience, what is the nature and extent of the "power of positive thinking"?

J. How effective is the following student theme? Does it seem self-conscious or self-confident, authentic or overdramatized? What strategy does the writer employ in organizing the material? How effective is the selection of detail?

WHAT AM I?

When people ask where I was born, they often seem disappointed when I reply, "California." Because of my Oriental features and name, they seem to have anticipated something exotic like Japan, Siam, or at least Hawaii!! My parents were born and raised in Japan. They came to America when they were in their teens, but they have retained the language, music, and some of the customs of Japan in our home. They have reared my brother and sisters in the ways of the old country in preparation for becoming good citizens in America. Bridging the gap between home and school is sometimes as hard as trying to build a bridge across the Atlantic.

One difficulty is the transition from our home language to the school language. My father prefers to speak Japanese. Therefore, my mother refused to teach us how to speak English, because she did not want us to learn both languages poorly or to mix both in broken English. After her first week in school, my little sister came home from school and announced that she had learned a new song at school. In proud innocence she sang: "Teacher, teacher, ring the bell; teacher, teacher, go to hell." She was forbidden to speak English from then on unless she knew the *exact* meaning of her new words. She received an "A" in deportment during her first semester of school. The second semester's card, however, was accompanied by a note from her teacher ("Hideko chatters constantly") and a "C" in deportment. Evidently, she had learned to understand English.

The problems of adjustment are not usually as humorous, however. It is not just one generation's ideas against another's, but the moral standards of Japan conflicting with those of America. Dating did not exist in the Japan my parents left thirty years ago. The only respectable procedure was for a "bishakunin," a go-between, to arrange the engagement of the young couple. After that, the two principals involved were introduced and often allowed to go around together. It is strange to hear my parents saying that the time seems to have come when girls and boys will marry whomever they please, that these foolish young people should leave an important thing like the selection of one's mate in the hands of an impartial and wise elder. It is a far cry from the world of steadies, pinnings, and engagements that are so much a part of college life.

The moment I leave home, a conflict arises because the Japanese and Caucasian Americans seem to form into separate groups. In grammar school, I did not face this problem, since there were too few of us to be considered a minority group. We were considered to be individuals who had nothing special in common with each other. In high school, however, the Japanese seemed to stay together as a group. The majority of the students seemed to make generalizations about each group as a whole and to expect everyone who was Japanese to be like the others. "Oh, yes," someone would say, "I know her. She's Japanese." The sense of disinterest, of finality, and of cool classification seemed unjust to me. I rebelled against losing my own sense of identity; I didn't want to be a generalization, by any means!

I resolved to find out where I belonged by developing my interests and by following them through into whichever society they would bring me. In other words, I stopped thinking and got busy. In the four years of high school, I found that those who allow themselves to be taken over by racial bondage do not develop themselves. Their areas of interests seemed to lie only where other Japanese were active. For example, the majority of Japanese girls joined either one of two clubs—both of which had a majority of members of Japanese descent. My interests led me to join clubs of service, sports, and art as well as the other two. Others often expressed a desire to join a new club, but only if several Japanese joined together. Such conformity, to me, was like swimming in a stagnant pool.

I was happy being active in school affairs until my senior year. All went well until I began to attend parties where I began to feel like the "lone wolf" because I was the only Japanese and was always a "stagette." The latter was irrelevant because my parents would not allow me to date anyway, but the element of being irrevocably "different" entered my mind. In college, I joined a Japanese social club where I felt that I would "belong." But this kind of belonging came about through no effort of my own, but simply by virtue of being Japanese—an accident of birth. The depth of what the members had in common was apparent to the eye in a single glance.

At this time, I asked myself: "What happens to the person who is brought up in two different cultures or societies? Should he choose between the two in his adult life? What factors would influence his decision?" I think that I was frustrated for months. However, I reached the following conclusions: First, one should strive to develop the finer aspects of both cultures and their ideals; secondly, one should wear a race as he wears clothes—as just one expression of his personality. It should neither dominate nor undermine the presence of the person. It is like an attractive pin, however, that draws attention to the person.

A person with a negative attitude toward his race wraps it around himself like a huge coat. He keeps from developing the natural potentialities within because of the skin that covers them. Not to venture outside is like saying, "I wanted a different coat, but, through no fault of my own, I ended up with this one. I suppose I must arrange my other clothes to go with this coat because I can't exchange it." Eventually, that person will have a wardrobe of clothes (abilities and friends) which have one thing in common—their relationship to a coat (race) for which he had no freedom of selection.

What am I? What does it matter? To me, as with everyone else, it is *who* I am that matters.

THEME TOPICS 2

1. Discuss the role that a relative (other than your parents), or a person close to your family, played in your upbringing. Choose someone who has had a lasting influence on your outlook or personality. Avoid sentimental or stereotyped description.

2. Discuss one important lesson that your own childhood taught you about the upbringing of young children. (Was there anything in your own early training that you especially appreciate or resent? Were you spoiled, tyrannized, ignored, or treated just right?)

3. What has your own experience taught you about the causes of friction between parents and their children, or between relatives? (For instance, what is the most serious cause of misunderstanding between teen-agers and their parents?)

4. What are some of the things that make for a happy family life or successful marriage? Focus on one major factor. Avoid platitudes.

5. What first-hand observation have you had of juvenile delinquency? (What is a "juvenile delinquent" like? How does he get that way?)

6. Discuss a grade school or high school experience that in some significant way influenced your personality or changed your outlook on life. (To what extent are children influenced by things that happen to them at school?)

7. Write an account of the high school or college instructor who comes closest to your idea of an ideal teacher. Explain and defend your choice to a reader impatient with generalized or stereotyped praise.

8. Discuss contrasting influences in your family or early training. Have you encountered conflicting advice, conflicting standards, conflicting loyalties? Limit yourself to one such contrast or conflict and make use of detailed illustrations.

9. Explain an important change in your outlook—a change in attitude toward a public figure (other than athletes or movie stars); a changed attitude toward an activity, institution, or field of study; a general change in perspective as the result of work, travel, or military service.

10. Write an account of the vocation or profession that you plan to follow or that interests you most. Explain and defend your choice to a reader suspicious of public-relations prose.

3: OPINION

1. RECOGNIZING OPINIONS

In much technical writing, our main purpose is to convey information. In writing concerned with subjects of general interest, our main purpose is usually to express our opinions. This is often true even when we present our writing as a factual account, as a report. A good reporter is always more than a mere reporter. He interprets as well as reports; he reports scenes and events in such a way that they make sense. Directly or indirectly, we learn not only what he has observed but also what he thinks about it. Most of your assignments in college composition will require you to present your opinions—that is, your interpretation of and reaction to what you have observed, experienced, and read.

Inevitably, many of our opinions are tentative and superficial. We have tentative ideas on many subjects that we have never systematically investigated. Writing a paper forces us to sort out our impressions, to think through problems we had previously slighted or ignored. Writing is instructive because it makes us take stock of our opinions, causing us to reconsider and strengthen them.

Fact and Inferences. The first step toward making opinions sound and responsible is to become aware of them as opinions. A writer will not examine his opinions critically if he is convinced that he is merely reporting the facts. He must learn to distinguish between readily observable facts and the conclusions he draws from them.

Some things can be more easily verified than others. Ideally, a fact is something that you can verify by direct observation or measurement. You can see a crushed car in a ditch; you can feel an injured man's pulse; you can hear a siren wailing in the distance. If you conclude that there has been an accident, you move from fact to **inference**—that is, a conclusion produced by more or less reliable reasoning. Your inference that there has been an accident is still relatively close to the facts, though for verification you would have to depend on the testimony of others. You get further away from the facts if you conclude that the type of car driven by the injured man is unsafe, or that drivers in his age group tend to be careless. Only a research program investigating hundreds of cars or hundreds of drivers could make such a generalization plausible.

A brief survey of "facts" will probably show that most of them are inferences, resting on a more or less factual foundation. If your writing is to contribute to rational discussion, you will do well to assure a sound factual basis for the superstructure of inference. *Avoid presenting as facts inferences that are open to question:*

DEBATABLE: The voters of the fifth district expressed their resentment of Republican policies by sending a Democratic congressman to Washington.

FACTUAL: A majority of the voters of the fifth district voted for a Democratic congressman.

DEBATABLE: A comparison of homicide rates in states with and without capital punishment shows that capital punishment does not act as a deterrent to crime.

FACTUAL: A comparison of states with and without capital punishment shows that homicide statistics are not clearly affected one way or the other by the abolition of capital punishment.

The more factual your writing becomes, the more likely it is to provide a common ground on which you can meet with others to adjust differences of opinion. The less factual it becomes, the more likely it is to precipitate the kind of interchange that is mere sound and fury.

Open-Mindedness. Willingness to review the factual basis of your opinions implies willingness to change your mind. Careful, accurate thought does not exclude first guesses and tentative hypotheses. It does require that you either *confirm or modify first guesses by subsequent investigation.* The necessary adjustment may be unpleasant or unwelcome: a pet project may turn out to have been based on erroneous assumptions; a trusted leader may turn out to be suffering from delusions of grandeur. One lesson we must all learn is to reconcile our subjective preferences with a factual estimate of objects, people, and events.

Open-mindedness requires the ability to suspend judgment. Sometimes two different hypotheses both may fit the facts. There is nothing illogical in a scientist's teaching one theory concerning the nature of light on Mondays and another on Tuesdays, as long as the available evidence does not allow him to make a definite choice between the two.

Open-mindedness is not empty-mindedness. An open-minded person can make responsible decisions while at the same time realizing that he might be wrong. A critical reader will put his trust more readily in the tentative certainties of a thoughtful person than in the unconditional certainties of an unthinking one.

2. DEVELOPING OPINIONS OF YOUR OWN

When asked for their opinions on college life or freedom of the press, students sometimes have a dim feeling that they are for it. Otherwise their minds are somewhat of a blank. When writing a paper on one of these topics, they will put down a number of sentences to the effect that college life or freedom of the press is a very important subject. They will point out that it is a very important part of the democratic way of life, and that everybody should be aware of this fact. After that, there doesn't seem to be much else that could be said. Many students then pad their papers with **platitudes**. They tell the reader things that he has known since he entered the fifth grade, and that he has no need or desire to hear repeated. A writer relies on platitudes when he solemnly informs his readers that baseball is a popular sport, that the automobile is here to stay, or that ours is a complex and fast-moving age.

Finding a Subject. Reading platitudinous prose will remind you of an obvious but often ignored principle of good writing: the author should have something to say. To make an uncommunicative person talk, you can ask him a specific question about something he knows. To get started on a theme, you can try to *find a specific question that you are in a position to answer.* Ask yourself: "What are some of the questions that people I know or I myself have asked about college life? What do I know or remember that might help me to work out an answer to one of these questions?"

If you yourself are not the kind of person who asks questions, you can listen to people who do. You might read the letters-to-the-editor column of the campus newspaper or listen to a campus debate. You will soon have a supply of sample questions that, when answered adequately, can make college life less confusing. Are football players less intelligent than other students? Is student government a waste of time? Are art majors snobs? Should students live in dormitories? When does a student's social life begin to interfere with his studies? What happens to people who work their way through college?

The more specific your initial question, the better your chance of working out a definite answer. Merely writing *about* a subject may result in a catalogue of miscellaneous impressions. The freshman who writes "about" his first week on a college campus may ramble aimlessly from one thing to another. The mass of humanity swirling around him at registration, the confusing layout of the campus, a chance meeting with a hometown acquaintance, the difficulty of adjusting to dormitory food, the pleasure of finding a compatible roommate (or the disappointment of finding an incompatible one): all these are likely to merge into a blurred sequence. To give direction to his paper, he should ask a question that helps him to sort out his impressions: "What kind of advice would I give to an incoming freshman? What makes a person a good roommate? What can be done to help students find adequate housing?" He can then select those of his impressions that help him answer his question. He can reject those that do not. His paper will no longer be aimless and incoherent; it will have a unifying purpose.

Gathering Material. Whatever subject you decide to write on, your paper will not be worth serious attention unless you yourself take your initial question seriously. The answers to your questions about college life are not engraved in golden letters over the entrance to the main auditorium. You will have to work them out for yourself.

If you are writing about the intelligence of football players, start by asking yourself, "What do I personally know about football players?" Perhaps you remember the quarterback of your high school team who never opened his mouth in your English class. On the other hand, your sister once went out with a football player who was planning to go to Medical School and came close to an all-A average. Perhaps you have a chance to talk to one of the assistant coaches about the average IQ of the present team. You also ask him about the professional careers of some of his former players. You chat with him about the relationship between brains and brawn on the football field. On the way home, you compare your performance in various sports with your performance in academic subjects. You ask yourself whether the difficulties you have in geometry are in any way related to the difficulties you had in courses in physical education.

In doing all this, you are following essential advice for anyone trying to form a responsible and well-informed opinion: *Mobilize your resources of information.* You will seldom be able to write a substantial paper on the spur of the moment. Responsible writing forces you to broaden your knowledge, and to utilize and reassess what you already know.

If you have an exceptionally good memory, you may allow all the data and ideas you need to accumulate in your mind. If your memory is average, you will do well to jot them down as you go along. Some writers, like good chess players, can work out complicated relationships in their heads. Many others can see more easily how their material shapes up if they have it in front of them. Merely reading over their notes will put their minds to work interpreting and evaluating what they have collected.

Organizing Material. Even as you jot down pieces of information and tentative ideas, you will see that some of them seem to belong together whereas the connection between others is not yet very clear. In other words, even while you are collecting material, you can do a certain amount of sorting out and arranging. For instance, you will probably put all your information about smart football players into one pigeonhole and all your information about slow ones into another. Then, by comparing the two sets of data, you may conclude that on the whole football players tend to be as smart or as slow as other students, but that the slow ones have a slight edge. Here you have the organization for one major section of your paper: two paragraphs devoted to two contrasting sets of information and a third paragraph balancing them off against each other.

As you glance over your information concerning the study habits of football players, you may hit upon one possible reason that football players are slightly below average academically. They obviously cannot be out on the football field and in the college library at the same time. This realization puts you to work organizing a second major section of your paper, in which you examine the various possible reasons for poor academic performance of some of the players. One paragraph may point out how much study time a player loses through practice and through traveling to games. Another paragraph may describe how a player's physical exhaustion and nervous tension interfere with study. A third paragraph may show that, being popular, many of the players lead an active social life, which also makes heavy demands on their time.

The lesson to be learned from this procedure is that you do not apply a pattern of organization to your material from the outside: *Organize your material by putting things where they belong.* Once you know what each paragraph is supposed to do, you should have no difficulty putting the right information into the right paragraph.

Formulating a Thesis. As you sort out your material into paragraphs, you realize that your opinion on the subject you are examining has already begun to crystallize: Poor academic performance of some players does not necessarily indicate a lack of intelligence but may be a result of the way they spend their time. This sentence, summing up the result of your investigation, becomes the **thesis** of your paper. It becomes the central idea that the accumulated details elaborate and support.

You can work your thesis sentence into your paper in several ways. Your reader may benefit from it most if you make it precede most of your detailed argument, so that he can see what is coming. You can also make it emerge at the end of your argument, as a conclusion. Your reader may then be less sure of your purpose while your argument lasts, but he will at the end have no doubts about what he is supposed to remember. As you start writing a tentative draft of the whole paper, you may realize that you haven't used those of your notes dealing with your own ventures into competitive sports. Perhaps you will use them in an introduction telling your reader how you found out that a student who does well in mathematics can be all thumbs when he tries to play ball. Observing that there seems to be no direct correlation between mental and physical agility, you lead your reader up to the thesis sentence about the academic qualifications of football players.

Formulating a thesis is an excellent device for making sure that you have something to say and that you know what it is. *A well-considered thesis sentence brings a paper into focus.* Discussing the heroine of a play, you may have told your reader that she was bored and frustrated, cruel and selfish, hungry for excitement and at the same time afraid of scandal. Asked to state a thesis, you will have to make sure that the various points you have made add up to a coherent overall view. Perhaps you will arrive at something like the following: "This woman needed psychiatric care, because she was unable to adjust her desires to the limitations of her environment." You can then easily check whether you have a unified paper. You can make sure that you have covered in detail at least some of her desires, showing how they clashed with various aspects of her environment. You can make sure that you have shown how psychiatric care might solve some of the resulting problems. Or you may arrive at something like this: "She expected too much of people and as a result was inevitably disappointed." You can then make sure that you have examined several of her expectations and shown them to be unrealistic.

Each of the following passages presents and develops briefly a point that could become the thesis of a theme or article. For each of them, ask yourself what material you could supply from your own observation, experience, and reading to support, modify, or refute the point made.

(1) Under our system a student's progress up to the point of entering college has been largely automatic, as he went along from one grade to another. But at about the college level the intellectual demands on the student's capacity suggest that not all may be capable of profiting by further study. *College calls for a different kind of intellectual effort, and a more difficult one.*—Laird Bell, "Admit and Flunk," *Atlantic*

(2) The casual horrors and the real disasters are thrown at newspaper readers without discrimination. *In the contemporary arrangements for spreading the news, an important element, evaluation, is always weak and often wanting entirely.* There is no point anywhere along the line where someone puts his foot down for certain and says This is important and That doesn't amount to a row of beans, deserves no one's attention, and should travel the wires no farther. The junk is dressed up to look as meaningful as the real news.—Philip M. Wagner, "What Makes a Really Good Newspaper," *Harper's*

(3) Most of us have seen newspaper photographs of most of the prominent men and women of our time; most of us have heard them speak in newsreels. But as candid as the news photos may have been and as familiar as the newsreels may have made these voices, we have still only known such men and women at a good bit more than arm's length. *What television, with its strange public-private atmosphere, suggests* at once *is the possibility* of meeting them at armchair length, *of overhearing in our living rooms people who would not normally be found there.*—Walter Kerr, "What Good Is Television?" *Horizon*

(4) *In recent decades, planners have rarely given much thought to creating a psychologically satisfying focal point or heart for their city, town, or neighborhood.* . . . Americans in earlier centuries built their communities around a focal point. Witness Boston, with its Common and its Public Garden. Most New England towns and cities still have a clearly perceived heart, and many of the smaller, older-fashioned Midwestern towns such as Woodstock, Illinois, still do, too (and

so do a few larger cities, such as Indianapolis). But in the majority of American cities, the heart of downtown typically is the street intersection where the largest bank faces the largest department store. Downtown Dallas, Oklahoma City, Los Angeles, Sioux City, Des Moines, Milwaukee, Birmingham, and Winston-Salem seem a blur of almost indistinguishable commercial buildings.—Vance Packard, "America the Beautiful—and Its Desecraters," *Atlantic*

A thesis sentence helps you check for **relevance**. It helps you to eliminate or play down things that are not directly related to the issue under discussion. A thesis sentence claiming that football players are as intelligent as most other students focuses the discussion on the question of intelligence. It will help you realize that your picturesque description of the song girls you observed at football games may be irrelevant to your present purpose.

Revising for Clarity. In revising the first draft of a theme, first make sure that you have a clear statement of the central idea of your paper and that your supporting material is relevant to the central idea. In revising for clarity, observe the following suggestions:

(1) *Make sure that your conclusions emerge clearly from your finished paper.* Ask yourself: What is the major point that the paper as a whole is supposed to make? What subordinate idea is each part of the paper supposed to develop? Are both the central and the supporting ideas clearly and succinctly stated, or must the reader infer them for himself? If they are stated, does position and wording mark them clearly as important points?

(2) *Make sure that each point receives adequate support.* Have you shown your reader that the ideas he is supposed to accept are important to you as a writer? Have you concentrated on each of the main points in succession, trying to do them justice? Are examples and illustrations relevant to the point at issue?

(3) *Make sure to devote special care to points that the reader might find difficult or unfamiliar.* What points confused you when you first started to think about your subject? Have you made sure they will be less confusing for your reader?

The mere fact that you have presented an opinion clearly of course does not assure it general acceptance. As your instructor or your classmates read your finished paper, they will not necessarily like it or agree with it. However, their very disagreement will in a sense be a measure of your success. It will be first-hand proof that you have succeeded in saying something. It is hard to disagree with hazy generalities about the teaching of sportsmanship or the values of a college education. If your paper provokes detailed comment, it probably has meaning and point.

3. DRAWING ON THE OPINIONS OF OTHERS

Basically, you develop opinions by making up your mind about what you observe with your own eyes. In practice, however, you seldom really start from the beginning. Most of the time your observations come to you with much ready-made opinion already mixed in. In the paper about football players, for instance, some of the material you collected was first-hand observation. But you also made use of opinions that your sister and the assistant coach had formed on the basis of observations of their own.

Such contact with the ideas of others should have a stimulating and enlightening effect on you as a writer. *Other people's opinions can alert you to gaps in your information and flaws in your reasoning.* They may cause your own half-formed ideas to take more definite shape. You may not realize that you have an unconscious dislike for someone until you hear one of your friends call him "conceited" or "unfair." When hearing your own inarticulate feelings put into blunt words by someone else, you have an opportunity to review them critically and to see whether they are well founded. Similarly, the opinions of others can goad you into refuting ideas with which you disagree. Often, the most effective way of getting a student to write with conviction is to let him show what is wrong with a view he considers mistaken.

Cross-Examining Your Witnesses. No matter how stimulating, the opinions of others need to be treated with care. It is often hard to tell on what first-hand observations an opinion is based. Suppose a friend tells you that John Doe is a smart fellow. Your friend may have derived this opinion from a careful study of John's high school record and of various intelligence tests John has taken, as well as from interviews with several of his former teachers. On the other hand, your friend may have concluded that John is smart after watching him make up a good excuse for not having his English theme ready on time the day before. As a result, your friend's opinion will be of little use to you unless you probe into his qualifications as a witness.

Opinions often become instructive only after you learn something about their past history. The most enlightening question you can learn to ask is "What makes you think so?" If the coach tells you that football teaches sportsmanship, you will ask him what actual changes he has observed in some of his players. Soon you will get into the habit of preferring the opinions of people who supply detailed explanation and proof. In turn, you will get into the habit of supplying detailed explanation and proof in your own writing.

Opinions are obviously influenced by other things besides the careful collection and accurate interpretation of facts. In interpreting a statement, you will have to *distinguish between what a writer or speaker says about his subject and what he reveals concerning his own motives.* Suppose the coach tells you that we cannot make a greater investment in the young people of today than to teach them sportsmanship. You may remember that his own share of that investment amounts to ten or fifteen thousand dollars a year.

To make profitable use of the opinions of others, you often have to play the part of the amateur psychologist. You ask: "Is this man telling me that chlorophyll is good for my teeth because he cares about my teeth—or because he makes a living selling toothpaste? Is this man arguing against capitalism because he has studied the workings of various economic systems—or because his father lost the family home during the Depression?"

Comparing Authorities. As you become aware of private preferences and dislikes, you learn to look for that rare specimen, the disinterested expert. You turn for information to someone who is well qualified to discuss a given subject but has no private ax to grind. When writing about alcoholism in your hometown, you will be as skeptical of material put out by the whisky companies as of pamphlets distributed by the Women's Temperance Society. You will turn for data and statistics to investigators who are neither prohibitionists nor heavy drinkers nor employees of a brewery.

Finding impartial and well-qualified observers is not always easy. Few people are willing to finance investigations that serve no immediate purpose beyond finding out what is what. Much research is tied to some definite practical purpose, whether building a faster and more destructive missile or finding ways to educate children at the rate of fewer dollars per head. Even when research is not devoted to short-range goals, the investigator may not be truly disinterested in his search for truth. Experts are not immune to professional rivalries and to doctrinaire attachment to inadequately supported theories.

When expert and disinterested advice is not to be had, you may have to do the second-best thing. You can compare the views of different interested parties. You can note contradictions that cancel each other out and pay attention to areas of agreement. When writing a paper on teachers' salaries, you can pay attention to the arguments of teachers, administrators, government officials, and taxpayers alike. *Guard against excessive reliance on any one single source, no matter how reputable and impartial it may seem.*

Prejudices. In presenting our opinions we often come up against ideas with obscure credentials. We find that they are not the product of our own minds, nor do they come from any particular source that we can identify. We seem to have derived them from the climate of opinion in which we grew up, without examining them for their validity or even for their exact significance. The more uncertain their origin, the more thoroughly we need to investigate them before we make them definitely our own.

Perhaps you find yourself saying in one of your papers that "other people's ideas should be respected, even though different from those of the majority." To discover whether you really mean it—and to discover *what* you really mean—apply this statement to a number of specific instances. Perhaps your next-door neighbor has the opinion that every first of the month ten virgins should be sacrificed to the rain gods. You probably didn't mean to include opinions that were *that* different. Then the question becomes: "How different can these opinions be and still be respected? And what does 'respect' mean in practice? If we dismiss a teacher for his opinions on loyalty oaths or on marriage, can we at the same time respect those opinions? What is such respect good for?" As you start examining these problems, you find that your original statement covers up many questions that you have not really thought about.

Whenever you suspect that you are repeating an unexamined second-hand opinion, apply it to specific situations. Perhaps you want to say, "A teen-ager's opinions are easily swayed." Was this true in your own case? Was it true in the case of your brothers, sisters, or roommates? What were some of your opinions that were easily swayed?

Opinions adopted prior to adequate investigation are known as **prejudices** or preconceptions. A person's prejudices are most noticeable when they lead him to condemn something without due cause. However, a prejudice may be any preconceived opinion, whether favorable or unfavorable. Holding a number of such prejudices does not in itself make you a prejudiced person. Everybody necessarily has second-hand opinions on subjects which he has not had the time or energy to explore in detail. The real test of a prejudice comes when it is challenged by as yet unanswered questions or by previously unnoticed information. The prejudiced person will make short shrift of questions that interfere with his own set ways of looking at things. The unprejudiced person will feel obliged to consider such questions and to judge the issues involved on their merits. He may well decide after careful investigation that his original idea was after all sound. If so, his commitment to it will henceforth be more thoughtful and responsible, and he will be less eager than before to condemn those who do not share it.

Slogans and Proverbs. Second-hand ideas are most tenacious when they take the form of slogans. **Slogans** present ideas in capsule form, summing up a principle or an ideal in a striking phrase. Any speaker or writer can profit from the ability to summarize the essentials of his position in a simple, memorable formula. The cause of progressive education, for instance, was helped by slogans like "learn by doing" and "teach the whole child."

On the other hand, slogans easily suggest superficiality. This is what happens, for instance, when a popular writer, to emphasize that nuclear war, expanding populations, and the destruction of living space are the three crucial issues of our time, labels them "bombs, babies, and bulldozers." Above all, slogans, when repeated automatically, suggest a one-track mind. Politicians, advertisers, and educators sometimes become caught in their own catchwords. They begin to sound like tape recordings of their own past speeches.

Censor your writing for opinions that you have adopted because they came to you attractively packaged and labeled. Guard against unthinking repetition of statements like "The mind is not a muscle" and "You can't change human nature." Be wary of catchy phrases like "peace with honor," "Asia for the Asians," or "prosperity without war."

Another category of second-hand ideas with little value for serious discussion is that of **proverbs** or proverbial sayings. They often fall of their own weight when introduced into a serious argument. "Look before you leap" and "He who hesitates is lost" cancel each other out. They cannot help us decide whether somebody was dawdling, hasty, or just in time. They certainly cannot help us time our own leaps.

Avoid the kind of saying that makes you sound wise without requiring you to think about the issue at stake. Knowing that horses can be led to water but not made to drink will be of little value in discussing the role of motivation in the training of retarded children. If a saying is general enough to be thoughtlessly repeated by millions of people, it is likely to be too general to help you settle any specific issue.

4. HELPING YOUR OPINIONS TO SURVIVE

As you think about the nature and the origin of your opinions, you will begin to dispense them with less assurance. You will begin to see the difference between your tentative and superficial ideas on most subjects and your carefully worked out ideas on a few subjects to which you have given serious thought. As your attitude toward your thinking and toward your writing becomes more critical, you will begin to see the need for studying in some detail the difficulties of formulating ideas and of putting them into words.

No matter how far your study of writing progresses, you can learn some basic lessons from attempts to communicate simple ideas on everyday subjects:

(1) *Limit your scope.* Out of a multitude of miscellaneous ideas, you will have to select one, or perhaps two or three. No matter how interesting the various possible aspects of a subject, you will have to concentrate on one at a time.

(2) *Develop your points.* If one of your opinions is important enough to be stated, it is important enough to be supported and defended. If all concerned agree that insufficient attention to phonics explains why Johnny can't read, there is not much point in restating what is already well known. If the different methods for the teaching of reading are still subject to debate, there is not much point in merely asserting that your own solution is the best possible one. You will have to develop your solution in detail.

(3) *Do not take too much for granted.* A college audience is less homogeneous and less predictable than the audience at a labor-union picnic or at a Rotary luncheon. In writing for the average college student or for the average college graduate, you need to make your writing sturdy enough to help it survive doubt and dissent. Not everyone believes that Franklin Delano Roosevelt was a great President, or that free enterprise is the answer to the problems of underdeveloped countries.

(4) *Meet your reader half way.* Try to find common ground. Try to base your argument on assumptions that a reasonable reader would accept as a basis for discussion even if he disagreed with the conclusions that you aim at. An argument on the relative merits of a planned economy and of free enterprise is pointless as long as the advocates

of each system condemn the other in its entirety. The argument can make progress when those who participate can agree on some of the general aims of economic activity, such as a high standard of living for a great number of people. They can then proceed to the constructive business of judging different economic practices by common standards. Instead of denouncing each other, they can start discussing specific problems. They can talk about productivity, about the need for incentives, or about the distribution of wealth. Generally, an exchange of opinions is possible only as long as writer and reader maintain some measure of respect for each other's views and commitments.

EXERCISES 3

A. Compile a list of five specific questions that have recently been the subject of discussion or controversy on your college campus. Write a paragraph about each, summarizing the controversy or stating the principal issues at stake. Draw on the back files of the campus newspaper or on interviews with students and instructors. Your instructor may ask you to write a theme developing your own answer to one of the questions you have found.

B. Of the thesis sentences presented in the following brief passages, select the three that come closest to your own views. Then indicate for each of them what material you could supply that would bear on the point made. Indicate what tentative organization might be appropriate.

1. *Today's high schools concern themselves with too many different things, without clear priority for what is most essential.* Telephone training and driver education are made to seem as important—or unimportant—as English and Latin.

2. *Students profit as much (or more) from a summer of work, travel, or reading as from additional course work in summer sessions.* Though such experiences are less systematic than academic learning, they are educational in the sense that they broaden the student's perspective.

3. *The public schools do not fully put into practice the constitutional principle of separation of church and state.* Students, whether of Christian, Jewish, or agnostic parents, participate in Christmas plays and Easter pageants, and sing religious songs.

4. *The average high school graduate has little understanding of modern art.* Few high schools require courses in which appreciation of modern art is taught. Illustrations and advertising in magazines read by high school students show little influence of the work of modern artists.

5. *The population of the typical big city is declining in income and social status.* The unskilled and the less educated remain, while the

middle class moves out to the suburbs to find living space and better schools for the children.

6. *Newly developed suburbs and subdivisions lack a sense of community.* They lack the squares, parks, museums, libraries, and other cultural centers that in established communities provide a focus for community life.

C. Assume that you are investigating *one* of the following subjects: (1) methods of teaching reading; (2) certification of grade school teachers; (3) corporal punishment in grade schools; (4) rehabilitation of juvenile delinquents; (5) fluoridation of drinking water. In one paragraph each, explain five desirable qualifications for the authorities whose judgment you would be inclined to trust. Point out any factors that might make for bias or prejudice.

D. The following passages have been adapted from published comments on President Wilson. What accounts for such contradictory judgments on public figures whose actions are presumably well known? What do these judgments reveal about the people who made them?

1. Woodrow Wilson will be held in everlasting remembrance as a statesman who, when others thought of revenge and material gain, strove to bring nearer the day which should see the emancipation of conscience from power and the substitution of freedom for force in the government of the world.

2. Mr. Wilson in dealing with every great question thought first of himself. He may have thought of the country next, but there was a long interval.

3. Woodrow Wilson was in many respects the most remarkable figure in American politics since Jefferson. A scholar and an intellectual, unaccustomed to the hurly-burly of public life, he was nevertheless astute, hard-headed, and resourceful. A visionary and an idealist, he was at the same time the most thoroughly realistic and adroit political leader since Lincoln.

4. First it was "neutrality in thought and deed," then "too proud to fight" when the *Lusitania* sinking and the danger to the Morgan loans and the stories of the British and French propagandists set all the financial centers in the East bawling for war, but the suction of the drumbeat and the guns was too strong; the best people took their fashions from Paris and their broad "a's" from London. . . . Five months after his re-election on the slogan "He kept us out of war," Wilson pushed the Armed Ship Bill through Congress and declared that a state of war existed between the United States and the Central Powers.

5. Wilson at length chose war, but not without the gravest of misgivings engendered both by his somewhat reluctant recognition of the essentially non-ideological nature of the world struggle and by his

basic antipathy to war itself. To a less scrupulous, less self-demanding statesman, such misgivings would have brought balance and humility, but to the perfectionist Wilson, they brought only confusion and a tortured sense of guilt, which convinced him that the war must be a holy crusade to "make the world safe for democracy."

E. Which of your prejudices (if any) have been challenged since you came to college? Select three and write a paragraph about each, explaining briefly how you might have acquired it and how you became aware of it.

F. Compile a brief list of platitudes, slogans, or proverbs that you have encountered in discussions of campus life, college education, or current affairs. In one paragraph each, explain their use and their effect.

G. Study the following selections from magazine articles on American education. How does each author develop, support, or defend his opinions? How authoritative do his opinions seem? Does the selection seem partial or impartial, one-sided or balanced, responsible or irresponsible? Support your answers with detailed evidence. Formulate a thesis summing up the point of view expressed by each author.

1. Upon arriving at high school today an American youngster is faced with a bewildering choice of literally scores of subjects, many combinations of which can lead to a diploma, and many of which are far easier than physics, mathematics or a foreign language. He can study marriage, chorus or "advertising arts." In some schools he must give time to the study of safe driving and the evils of alcohol. Courses in typewriting and dancing vie for his time.

With the accident rate and the divorce rate as high as they are, a good case can be made for instruction in both driving and marriage, and there is no real reason why a youngster should not be taught dancing if the school has the extra money and the pupil has the extra time for it. But all too often the school provides courses in safe driving when it doesn't have the money for adequate courses in chemistry. The schools are becoming increasingly vulnerable to the charge that in trying to do everything for everyone, they are succeeding in doing almost nothing well.

The upshot is that many a brilliant youngster finds that his school has assumed the aspects of a carnival. In one room pretty girls practice twirling batons. The sound of cheers is heard from the football field. The safe-driving class circles the block in new automobiles lent by an enterprising dealer. Upstairs funny Mr. Smith sits wearily on a stool in the chemistry lab trying to explain to a few boys that science can be fun, but who pays any attention to him?

It is hard to deny that America's schools, which were supposed to reflect one of history's noblest dreams and to cultivate the nation's youthful minds, have degenerated into a system for coddling and entertaining the mediocre. It is one thing to establish courses of varying purpose and of varying degrees of difficulty to fit the talents of various individuals, but it is quite another to run schools in which *most* of the students avoid the tough courses—and get away with it.— Sloan Wilson, "It's Time to Close Our Carnival," *Life*

2. At Indiana University, where I am at the moment, the freshman and even sophomore courses in language and literature represent, in both content and level of teaching, what is taught in Britain two or even three years before the end of secondary education. And yet this is not altogether true. For the American freshman and sophomore has often a kind of curiosity, a provocative, uninformed but insistent "show me" attitude, an insistence on pitting his own limited experience against his teacher's knowledge, that makes the American college classroom at these levels very different indeed from the classroom of either the British grammar school or the British university.

"Why did Ulysses spend all that time in getting home to his wife after he left Troy?" a freshman asked one of my colleagues here the other day, during a lesson on the Odyssey. "If he'd really wanted to get home quickly, he would have managed it. I think he was kidding himself when he said he was so anxious to get back." This is naive, but it is not stupid, and it is not the kind of thing an English schoolboy would ask. The bright English schoolboy would mug up the standard works on the Homeric world and turn out a sophisticated essay on "Homer and the Heroic Age" based on a conflation of half a dozen books he had read in the school library; but it would never occur to him to ask whether Ulysses was kidding himself when he expressed his anxiety to return home quickly. The English schoolboy tends to relate knowledge to other knowledge, in order to form an elegant pattern (the bright essay being always the standard of achievement in the humanities); the American freshman wants to relate everything he reads or is told to his own experience. The latter as a rule has no sense of history or of form or of the *otherness* of different times and places; the former often lacks a sense of personal implication in what he studies.

To British—and indeed European—eyes, American education seems to waste some of the best learning years, at least for the brighter pupils, and to postpone until an unnecessarily late stage the essential core of education. But there is another side to the picture. The better American students are less blasé and work harder than their British opposite numbers, and by the end of their four undergraduate years have often achieved a kind of sophistication in terms of their subject which is at the opposite pole from the attitude revealed by the freshman's question about Ulysses. That kind of sophistication, which is particularly noticeable among the brighter students of literature, is consciously won by hard effort; it is (and I am talking of the best students) often the prelude to the use of specialized techniques in graduate work. The English student, building on his school training, will develop his accustomed skills with a kind of leisurely elegance and often, by the time he gets his degree, is not fundamentally any better educated than when he left school. He is likely to be less ambitious, more skeptical, less fundamentally serious than the American.

In such fields as literature, philosophy, and history, at least, the bright British student will most appreciate the lecturer who plays with ideas cleverly and suggestively, but the bright American student resents that: he wants the truth, or the right methods, and no nonsense. "Do you believe in that view of literature you were developing in your lecture this morning?" a Cornell student once asked me. I said that I did not, but I thought it was interesting to play with the idea a little and see where it led us. He replied, almost angrily, that if I did not believe the theory to be true I should not waste my own and the class's time discussing it at such length; it was sheer verbal gymnastics, and the students were there to *learn*, not to be played with. "Is C. S. Lewis's book on sixteenth-century literature a book to be read?" a graduate student asked me the other day at Indiana. I replied that it was a fresh and sometimes brilliant reading of the texts of the period, and though I quarreled sharply with some of the views expressed in it, I thought it a most stimulating book, well worth reading. "But will it give me a proper view of the period?" she persisted. "I don't know," I replied. "I'm not sure what the 'proper' view of the period is. Read it and make up your own mind about it." This answer was not regarded as satisfactory.—David Daiches, "Education in Democratic Society," *Commentary*

3. Writings about the schools always point out that "the people" wanted much of the stuff for which, perversely, others of "the people" now criticize the educators. Safety folks asked that drivers' courses be given; businessmen wanted the schools to arrange useful vocational training; fishermen suggested fly-casting practice, which turns into a course in applied ichthyology; and plenty of other-directed mommas wanted schools to teach Johnny to get along good, and never mind the grammar.

But "the people" help make our educational theory in a deeper sense. Nobody had to force Americans to want what is "practical." No intimidation was needed to get them to look for what is called new, modern, contemporary, and progressive. No educationists had to interlock in any directorate to make the American public a bit suspicious of fancy thinkers who are so busy readin' all them books that they don't even know where to find the carburetor. No "power politics" by the education fraternity was necessary to bring to the top the knowhow boys, with their "techniques" and "methods," their laboratories and work shops. This is the American inclination.

Technological proficiency and popular democracy combine to make us a nation that believes in know-how, methods, and results. Maybe they also, now and then, leave us somewhat unaware of the price and effort involved in intellectual attainment, and the distinction between that attainment and its counterfeit, especially in our crowded and hasty moods. And the crowded and hasty moods dominate many big, obvious, and powerful American influences like television, advertising, "How-To" literature, and certain phases of politics. Why should we be surprised that some of the same "practical" and "democratizing" themes turn up around the edges of our educational system? It too is a mass enterprise.

The schools, serving the whole public and inundated with floods of kids they have to take, are under some of the same pressures of number and speed and the desire for tangible results and immediate returns that mark other parts of our society. The philosophies by which these schools are guided, as they are applied not by philosophers but by the administrators and technicians drawn from this society who must keep the school system going, will tend under pressure to become thinner and more pragmatic and immediate. Perhaps the answer to that lies not in the denunciation of the educationists in which Bestor and others, including this writer, have engaged, but rather in the more vigorous and resolute effort to make the qualities important to us have a more lively position in the society.—William Lee Miller, "The Wastelands Revisited," *The Reporter*

4. The idea of the "talent search" for engineering and scientific skills, scholarship awards for high scholastic averages, special programs for the "gifted," advanced placement for special students, are all ways of meeting certain of the country's educational and social needs, but they do so not in order to build a new and more enriching social order, but to staff the manpower needs of the present conservative establishment to which science, technology, and education have now been harnessed. This is to put the cart before the horse.

The recent changes in educational practice have therefore consisted largely in new mechanical and structural arrangements for the high schools and colleges—the use of television to handle more students by the lecture method, the development of standard curricula, the consolidation of smaller schools into bigger, the proliferation of scholastic tests at every point in the system, the shift of college curricular material into selected classes in the high school, the construction of buildings and classrooms—while the central mode of education through academic credit hours, examinations, tests, grades, and competition for admission to the next stage of the educational hierarchy has become more and more dominant.

Going to high school is conceived as a way of getting into college. Going to college is a way of either getting into a graduate school or into a satisfactory place in the business system. In the process, the purpose of education as a means of recreating the culture and renewing its social ideals has been lost in the shuffle.

The intellectual freedom of the student is accordingly inhibited, not so much by specific legislation, but by the requirement that he submit to one kind of success symbol, one kind of academic achievement, and one set of subject matter taught and learned in one particular way—lectures, textbooks, examinations, grades. The control by the college and the society over the student is gained through administering grades and awarding credits. Thus the student cannot find in his education a means of achieving his spiritual, moral, and intellectual maturity, since that is not a concern of the educator. If the student does not play the system and win the requisite grades, no matter how sterile and irrelevant the courses, or how talented he may be, he is blocked from the professions and the higher vocations. He therefore submits to the system and lives a double life, while his real education goes on outside the curriculum.—Harold Taylor, "Portrait of a New Generation," *Saturday Review*

THEME TOPICS 3

Formulate a thesis sentence that states the main point of your theme.

1. Was your high school training adequate preparation for the kind of work you are expected to do in college? Limit yourself to one major area or subject.

2. What are the accomplishments or merits of student government? Is it make-believe or does it serve real functions? Examine one of its functions or contributions in detail.

3. Do different kinds of sports call for radically different aptitudes, or is there such a thing as the "all-around" athlete? For instance, do basketball players need more intelligence than football players? Limit yourself to one such contrast or comparison.

4. Is there any truth to charges that athletic competition between high schools promotes rivalry, rowdyism, and other undesirable traits? Take an impartial look at the evidence from your own observation and experience.

5. Do women make better grade school teachers than men? (Are women better suited than men to teach children of grade school age?)

6. Are there any characteristic differences between college teachers and high school teachers? Do they differ in teaching methods, attitude toward students, attitude toward their work? Limit yourself to one major aspect of the teacher's task.

7. Weigh the advantages and disadvantages of being a member of a fraternity or a sorority.

8. Is a part-time job an asset or a handicap? How does it affect a student's education, his social life, his general outlook?

9. Would students be better off if there were no required courses? What is the value of the required courses you yourself have to take?

10. Does the problem of anti-intellectualism exist in the high schools? If it does, who or what is responsible for it? Draw on first-hand observation and experience.

CHAPTER TWO

WRITING AND THINKING

4: DEFINITION

1. THE NEED FOR DEFINITION

Until we examine the way language works, we usually assume that words have definite, permanent meanings. We feel that, as long as our grammar and punctuation are adequate, what we are trying to say should be obvious to all people of good will. However, when dealing with issues of some consequence, we soon learn that different people use the same words in widely different ways. As a writer found when he set out to explain what the term *excellence* means in education:

> . . . "excellence" is a curiously powerful word—a word about which people feel strongly and deeply. But it is a word that means different things to different people. It is a little like those ink blots that psychologists use to interpret personality. As the individual contemplates the word "excellence" he reads into it his own aspirations, his own conception of high standards, his hopes for a better world. . . .
>
> It isn't just that people have different opinions about excellence. They see it from different vantage points. The elementary school teacher preoccupied with instilling respect for standards in seven-year-olds will think about it in one way. The literary critic concerned with understanding and interpreting the highest reaches of creative expression will think of it in a wholly different way. The statesman, the composer, the intellectual historian—each will raise his own questions and pose the issues which are important for him.—John W. Gardner, *Excellence*

Once a writer realizes that such differences exist, he will feel obligated to make clear what his *own* vantage point is, what ideas and aspirations *he* reads into a term. The first step is to become aware of the types of words that are most likely to need such narrowing down; that is, words in need of definition.

Vague Words. On close inspection many common words turn out to be vague. They cover a great deal of ground and may have to be narrowed down for the purpose of precise and reliable communication. *Weather,* for instance, is a convenient general term when we are trying to indicate whether it is pleasant or unpleasant to be outdoors. But the meteorologist concerned with accurate evaluation and prediction has to make distinctions between wind, temperature, humidity, cloudiness, degree of precipitation, and other factors that together determine atmospheric conditions.

Like the person training to be a meteorologist, the person training to be a competent writer needs to realize that *familiar terms are often too inclusive to be useful in detailed discussion.* For instance, the argument that a person should have a "well-rounded" education is so vague that it can be used to justify inclusion in the curriculum of anything from finger painting and baby care to Chinese philosophy and Inca music.

Relative Words. *Many words are inherently relative; they cover a range of meaning.* Their significance varies with the context in which they appear. "Hot" may mean 95 degrees or 9,500 degrees; a "large" sum of money may be $500 or $500,000. Often we have to specify degree or amount more precisely than such relative words do. The reader should not have to ask: Exactly how rich is "rich"? Exactly how cold is "cold"?

Similarly, we often have to make clear the extent or the limitations of "freedom," "responsibility," or "unselfishness." Failure to spell out such limitations can lead to dangerous misunderstanding. A school board, for example, may declare that a teacher should feel free to discuss controversial issues. The teacher will feel that he is being given exceptional elbow room until he is told: "The American tradition is not controversial." Since the American tradition is concerned with representative government, constitutional safeguards, freedom of speech, equality before the law, and individual initiative, the teacher may feel barred from discussing many major political or social issues.

Ambiguous Words. The more comprehensive the words we use, the more elusive their exact meaning is likely to become. If we have trouble with a simple word like *hot,* we will have to be even more careful with words like *democracy* and *social justice. Many terms that* *we take for granted have several different, and at times contradictory, meanings.* Words with a possible double meaning are **ambiguous.** They are ambiguous, that is, unless a writer makes it clear which of the possible meanings he has in mind.

For instance, the English word *honor* throughout its history has had two major meanings. One is implied in the expression "to honor a person"; this meaning centers on recognition, esteem, prestige, reputation. The other is implied in an expression like "an honorable person"; this meaning centers on the person's own standard of conduct. We might call the first "external" and the second "internal" honor. The first is used in "honor roll," a list of students honored by a school. The second is used in "honor system" or "school code of honor," which appeals to the students to behave honorably. The difference in meaning becomes clear when a student is found to have acquired his school honors dishonorably, through cheating on examinations. As a result, when we read "A man's honor is his most important asset," we may not know whether external or internal honor is meant.

Many words that cause cruel misunderstanding and bitter controversy belong in this category. To some people, the term *justice* implies that the strong, the intelligent, the competent should be rewarded: "Let the best man win." To others, it implies that the weak and disadvantaged should be allowed to share in the good things of life. Because of the fundamental ambiguity of the term, mere insistence that "justice be done" will not resolve the differences between the conflicting points of view.

Specialized Terms. Finally, *much serious writing relies for precision on the specialized use of terms that have a more general meaning in everyday use.* In popular journalism, for instance, the term *tragedy* usually means "disaster," any event involving fatal loss or great suffering. A drama critic is likely to use the term in its more technical sense of "a serious play having a disastrous or unhappy ending." He will probably restrict the term further by setting up more specialized criteria. He may specify a certain type of plot and define tragedy as "a play about a great man who brings about his own downfall by choices inherent in his character." He may apply the term only to a play with definite philosophical implications—for instance, a play that raises questions about a moral order or divine plan behind all existence. Much of the difficulty the layman has in reading scholarly studies and technical reports is due to his lack of training in observing the exact implications of terms used in a limited technical sense.

Like other good things, definition can be overdone. No one will expect you to define *spoon* as "a utensil for eating" or *clock* as "a device for measuring time." No one will thank you for making fine distinctions where they are not needed. But few discussions of cultural, political, or moral questions can be profitable without careful definition of important terms.

2. THE SEARCH FOR CONCRETE REFERENCE

The general principle for successful definition is one that applies to all successful writing: *Anchor the general to concrete reference.* Give substance to abstract terms by relating them to people, places, and events. Notice how the writer in the following example uses the first paragraph of an essay to anchor the general term *work* to her account of a character who throughout the essay serves as an example of what hard, lifelong work means:

> Whenever I think of the word "work" I first think of my Aunt Clara. Next I think of the hymn we used to sing so often in our North Dakota village church: *Work, for the night is coming,/ Work in the noonday sun./ Work, for the night is coming,/ When man's work is done.* The logic of those verses has always eluded me, but their meaning has always been mysteriously clear, perhaps because I knew my Aunt Clara and so many others almost like her. Because I knew my Aunt Clara I am astounded at the number of people who seem to think of work as an abstraction—like Truth or Beauty.—Lois Phillips Hudson, " 'Work, for the Night Is Coming,' " *The Reporter*

When a term covers much ground, and is used in many diverse situations, anchoring it to concrete reference may require some careful thought. For instance, many students who accept *liberty* as a basic democratic concept find it difficult to give a clear and coherent account of what liberty means in practice. Asked for a definition, they may say that it means "freedom to do as you please" or "freedom to follow the dictates of your own conscience."

Suppose I volunteer for an experiment designed to test the validity of such a definition. I start to build a cigar store in front of my house and am stopped by the city zoning commission. I go out deer hunting and am driven from the woods because the season does not start until December. I lie down on a bench in the city park and am arrested for vagrancy. Meanwhile, I am compelled by threat of fine or imprisonment to do many things that I am not at all eager to do. I am made to pay taxes to the city, to the county, to the state, and to the federal government. I am forced to comply with the city's elaborate system for complicating traffic. If there is a war, I am taken from my family and sent out to face hardship, injury, or death.

Obviously, *liberty* does not mean "freedom to do as I please." The city fathers, the forest ranger, and the policeman stand ready to prevent me from realizing desires that I consider quite harmless. They would take rather serious measures if I should please to abduct children or to place a time bomb in the mayor's desk. I then try to work out a definition of liberty by doing what I should have done in the first place: I examine various societies and institutions that I would call "free" to see what they have in common. I then compare them with societies and institutions that I would call "unfree" to see how they are different. For instance, I visualize the inmates of a jail in Aberdeen, Scotland, and compare them with those of a jail in Vladivostok, Siberia. I compare the circumstances of my arrest for vagrancy with those of my uncle's arrest in Shanghai in 1951. I review what various courses in history and political science have taught me about different political systems.

Upon surveying the data I have collected, I am likely to conclude that any society imposes limits upon the freedom of its members. In some societies, however, these limits seem clearly defined and intelligible, whereas in others they are vague and susceptible to astonishing interpretations. In some societies, these limits are established through a complicated process of gradual adjustment and compromise. In others, they change overnight to suit the whims of those in charge. In some societies, these limits are established to facilitate the pursuit of happiness for an overwhelming majority. In others, they are based on the taboos, prejudices, or personal interests of a small number of influential people.

After investigating some of these differences, I may come to define *liberty* tentatively as "freedom under law" or "freedom compatible with the common goals of the community." Expanded and sharpened, my definition may finally call for

> freedom within limits that are clearly defined and that are established through a system of gradual adjustment and compromise enjoying the support of the majority of the people.

This definition may not prove to be generally acceptable. However, it will effectively bring us to the point where "liberty" makes a difference in practice. It will prove relevant, and perhaps enlightening, in many situations where questions concerning liberty arise.

3. FORMULATING AND SUPPORTING DEFINITIONS

The most reliable way of arriving at an adequate definition is to start from the concrete situation where the term occurs. We arrive at a definition of *horse* by determining what all the horses we have seen have in common and what makes them different from mules, cows, unicorns, elephants, and donkeys. Since this procedure involves serious thought, we may be tempted to look not at a horse but at a dictionary. There we find a conveniently definitive description:

> A graminivorous quadruped of the genus *Equidae*, distinguished from other species of the genus by excessive elongation of the metacarpus and the metatarsus and by a mane and tail of coarse hair.

Dictionary Definitions. A dictionary definition provides the layman with an exact and detailed account of a term, based both on a knowledge of technical subject matter and of the history and use of words. Nevertheless, excessive reliance on dictionary definitions raises questions more serious than an occasional overdose of polysyllabic terminology. Suppose you are asked to write a paper on some problem of maladjustment. You start by saying,

> The *New American Standard Dictionary* defines adjustment as "the process of fitting individual or collective patterns of activity to other such patterns made with some awareness or purposefulness."

Your reader is likely to ask: "How is this definition related to your own knowledge and interpretation of adjustment? What does it mean? Why do you accept this definition rather than some of the other possible ones? Can you think of any concrete cases that this definition seems to fit? Can you think of any cases that it does not fit?"

These questions are not designed to discourage you from making as full and frequent use of your dictionary as possible. However, *to make effective use of a dictionary definition, you have to relate it to your own investigation of the subject.* You have to show why you accept the definition, or how it needs to be modified.

Often a dictionary definition will make you think about some important points that you had not previously considered. If *free enterprise,* for instance, is defined as "a minimum of government regulation of business," you may start thinking about whether, why, how, and when regulation is necessary. An effective paper may use a dictionary definition as a point of departure and then proceed to expand and qualify it.

Importance of Context. As you will discover, important terms and phrases used by an author may not be in the dictionary at all or may be defined in a way that does not agree with the way the author uses them. Terms like *liberalism, materialism,* or *idealism* have a long and confusing history. You will have to pay close attention to what a writer is saying to find out what kind of "liberalism" he has in mind. The same is true for many less ambiguous words. "Moral laws" are not, as some students seem to think, laws dealing with the sale of liquor and with curfews for teen-agers. But the twenty entries under *law* in your dictionary might not by themselves help you to find a more adequate definition. You will have to observe how and where the phrase is used. Perhaps the author has been discussing conscience and individual responsibility rather than legislators and policemen. *Law* is then likely to stand not for a written law but for an unwritten standard of behavior based on custom or personal conviction.

The meaning of a term depends to a large extent on the context in which it appears. The word *honor* used in a speech about the Civil War is likely to mean something like the prestige or glory of a nation. The same word used in a sentimental novel is likely to mean the innocence or virtue of the heroine.

As a result, you can often do without definition when the meaning of an otherwise confusing term is clear from the **context** in which you use it. There is no need to define *conservative* in the following sentence: "The present owner, being an extremely conservative man, still follows the daily routine first instituted by his father." But suppose you are saying, "Powerful conservative forces are at work in American society." Here *conservative* needs to be carefully defined. It may mean "dedicated to the preservation of law and order," "irrationally attached to outmoded conventions," or perhaps "cautious in spending public funds."

Formal Definitions. One general lesson you can learn from dictionary definitions is to sort out the parts of a definition into two types of information. First, you can list things that classify the term to be defined as a member of a group, or **class.** Second, you can list characteristics that distinguish the term to be defined from other members of the same group. Thus, a formal definition of *horse* first places horses in the general category of four-legged mammals that have solid hoofs and feed on grass or grain. It then points out characteristics that distinguish horses from such other animals in the same general category as zebras and mules. Here are some examples of formal definition:

TERM TO BE DEFINED	CLASS	DIFFERENTIATION
An autobiography	is the story of a person's life,	written by himself.
Oligarchy	is a form of government	in which power lies in the hands of a few.
A martyr	is someone who suffers persecution	for refusing to renounce his faith.

When both the class and the distinguishing characteristics are well chosen, formal definitions are efficient and useful. Careful choice of the class may by itself clarify a confused argument. For instance, a debate concerning free enterprise is likely to profit from general agreement that free enterprise is not "a form of government" but "an economic system" or "an economic theory." Careful choice of the differentiating qualities can effectively exclude things or ideas that a term might mistakenly be thought to include. For instance, revolutionary communism is excluded by a definition of evolutionary socialism as "a political movement that aims at bringing about government ownership of the means of production, *using peaceful or constitutional means.*"

Several precautions have to be observed if a formal definition is to be informative. Check your definitions for the following shortcomings:

(1) *The class in which a term is placed may be too inclusive to help narrow down a general area.* Classifying a cello as "a musical instrument" is less informative than classifying it as "a string instrument of the violin family." Classifying an epic as "a type of literature" is less informative than classifying it as "a long narrative poem."

(2) *The definition may place the term in a group without supplying adequate differentiation.* Defining *Puritanism* as "the religion of the Puritans" makes it clear that we are dealing with a religion but does not tell us what kind. Defining *tragedy* as "a play concerned with a tragic situation" clarifies the meaning somewhat but leaves the key term undefined. Definitions that repeat the key term in a slightly different guise we called **circular definitions**. Their circularity is often less immediately obvious than in the preceding examples. Take, for instance, the familiar definition of *liberty* as "the right to do whatever does not interfere with the liberty of others." Only on second thought do most readers realize that "liberty of others" is vague unless *liberty* has already been defined in some other way.

(3) *When distinguishing characteristics are stated, they may not*

adequately differentiate between things that are similar or closely related. This is the weakness of a definition of *patriot* as "a person who promotes the best interests of his country." This definition does not exclude the person who serves his country for the sake of gain or personal glory. Adding the words *zealously* and *unselfishly* to the definition would make it more discriminating.

(4) *A definition may be too restrictive.* A definition referring to a *senator* as "an elected representative of a state" would exclude the minority of senators who are not elected but appointed. Defining *patriot* as "a person who wholeheartedly supports his country's policies" would exclude many patriotic persons who criticize or oppose unwise policies.

(5) *Instead of enumerating the characteristics of the term to be defined, a definition may offer a synonym, another term covering approximately the same area of meaning.* Synonyms are useful when they provide a familiar equivalent for an unfamiliar or difficult term, such as "double meaning" for *ambiguity*. But a writer makes little headway if he explains that by *just* he means "right in action or judgment" and by *equitable* "fair or equal." Substituting one set of familiar general terms for another does not help a writer pin down the exact meaning he intends to give to flexible and elusive words.

(6) *What looks like a definition may actually be only a partial description or a tangential observation.* Many statements that use an "is" or "means" are not intended to define but to comment on some aspect of a term whose definition is already known. Such a comment is George Bernard Shaw's remark that "martyrdom is the only way in which a man can become famous without ability." To feel the edge of this irreverent observation, the reader has to rely on his previous knowledge of what *martyrdom* means.

Helps to Definition. Like other general statements, *definitions often need the support of examples.* Suppose you define *liberal arts* as "academic studies whose value is primarily cultural rather than professional or vocational." This definition will not become meaningful unless you discuss in detail some sample subjects and their cultural value. Notice how the author of the following passage, after first making a general distinction between different kinds of freedom, gives us a series of graphic examples of what freedom means in everyday life:

> A man's free condition is of two parts: the instinctive free-ness he experiences as an animal dweller on a planet, and the practical liberties he enjoys as a privileged member of human society. The latter

is, of the two, more generally understood, more widely admired, more violently challenged and discussed. It is the practical and apparent side of freedom. The United States, almost alone today, offers the liberties and the privileges and the tools of freedom. In this land the citizens are still invited *to write plays and books, to paint their pictures, to meet for discussion, to dissent as well as to agree, to mount soapboxes in the public square, to enjoy education in all subjects without censorship, to hold court and judge one another, to compose music, to talk politics with their neighbors without wondering whether the secret police are listening, to exchange ideas as well as goods, to kid the government when it needs kidding, and to read real news of real events instead of phony news manufactured by a paid agent of the state.*—E. B. White, *One Man's Meat*

At the same time, the first part of this passage reminds us that successful definition often requires adequate distinctions between different meanings of the same term. The same is true for different meanings of terms that are closely related. More frequently than other general statements, *definitions depend for reinforcement on comparison and contrast.* One major section of an essay on "liberal education" may explain in what respects it resembles "general education"; another major section may explain how it differs from "vocational education." Often a large part of an **extended definition** is taken up by an explanation that A is *not* B, that it is *not* C, and that, though it overlaps with D to some extent, it is *not* D either.

Historical information can help to explain a term's present meaning. For instance, a cultural historian may be discussing the influence of Puritanism on life in nineteenth-century America. In defining *Puritanism,* he might start from the efforts of seventeenth-century Puritans to go beyond their fellow Protestants in restoring Christianity to what they considered its original purity. Seen from this perspective, the Puritan's strictness of standards and austerity of behavior will fit into a meaningful context. Many of the terms used in previous illustrations—*freedom* and *free enterprise, liberal arts* and *liberal education, tragedy* and *epic*—cannot be fully defined without reference to their historical background. Here is the way one writer puts the term *freedom* in historical perspective:

> The eighteenth century was the matrix from which most contemporary ideas of freedom have come. As Carl Becker pointed out, "the eighteenth century was the moment in history when men experienced the first flush and freshness of the idea that man is master of his own fate." The American and French Revolutions testify to the extent and passion of this conviction. Men were to be freed from coercive institutions—from tyrannical government and dogmatic creeds—by

their own efforts. Had not Rousseau declared that man is naturally good but is corrupted by institutions, and is born free but is everywhere in chains? Men were to be freed from superstition, and Voltaire's iconoclastic wit did a great deal to accomplish this purpose. Men were to be freed from autocratic government: the contents of the American Bill of Rights reveal that government was regarded as the chief danger to individual liberty.—Liston Pope, "Does Faith Impair Freedom?" *Saturday Review*

The philosopher, the literary critic, and the sociologist often reinforce definitions with historical material. *The scientist, the engineer, and the businessman frequently supplement definitions with information about causes, effects, and functions.* Often a scientist is interested not so much in a definition as in directions showing how a given phenomenon can be experimentally produced or what functions it can be made to serve. A physicist may decline to comment on what "matter" *is* but talk freely about how it behaves.

4. CLARIFYING VALUE JUDGMENTS

Lack of definition raises especially serious problems in judgments of value. *When you express approval or disapproval, praise or blame, your reader will feel entitled to a clear statement of your standards.* Undefined one-word labels like *propaganda, rationalization,* or *unrealistic* will make your writing sound hazy and opinionated. *Propaganda,* for instance, may mean "clever spreading of lies," but it may also mean "effective presentation of the truth." *Rationalization* may mean "trying to find excuses"; it may also mean "trying to find a rational explanation." Before you can meaningfully use the term *unrealistic,* you have to explain what you think reality is like and what you would consider a satisfactory attitude toward it.

Words such as *good, fair, wholesome, inspiring, ridiculous, challenging, practical,* or *absurd* often mean little until we find out about the standards of the person who uses them. One writer may use the word *evil* in discussing smoking and the use of lipstick; another, in discussing the imprisonment of fellow citizens without due process of law. The word *evil* thus covers a great variety of things that are objectionable, if at all, for different reasons. The reader will feel entitled to a clear explanation of what the objection is in each case. If the idea of a manned space platform seems practicable to one scientist and absurd to another, the two men very likely have different standards of practicality and absurdity.

The ambiguity of undefined value judgments is most obvious in discussions of entertainment and art. By saying that a movie or a concert was "enjoyable," you may convey a great deal to a friend who knows what kinds of things you enjoy. But you will tell the uninitiated reader little except that you had a good time. If he wants to know whether the movie is good by his own standards, he will ask for a much more detailed and more clearly defined evaluation. A person who calls a television program "the best of the year" may mean "the most exciting," "the most amusing," "the most thought-provoking," "the most convincingly acted," or "the most coherently written." If he works in the field, he may mean "best for attracting sponsors" or "best suited to the possibilities of the medium."

A basic difficulty in defining such terms as *freedom, democracy,* and *justice* is that they bring into play our personal preferences and values, our personal vision of a good and decent life. Therefore, the most instructive discussions of such terms are often those that frankly recognize the role of personal commitment. Notice how the following definition of democracy gains in authenticity and sincerity by reflecting freely the author's private doubts and aspirations:

> Democracy isn't a beloved republic really, and never will be. But it is less hateful than other contemporary forms of government, and to that extent it deserves our support. It does start from the assumption that the individual is important, and that all types are needed to make a civilization. . . . The people I admire most are those who are sensitive and want to create something or discover something, and don't see life in terms of power, and such people get more of a chance under a democracy than elsewhere. They found religions, great or small, or they produce literature and art, or they do disinterested scientific research, or they may be what is called "ordinary people" who are creative in their private lives, bring up their children decently, for instance, or help their neighbors. All these people need to express themselves, they can't do so unless society allows them liberty to do so, and the society which allows them most liberty is a democracy.— E. M. Forster, *I Believe*

The more sincere we are in applying our moral and aesthetic standards, the less likely we are to feel the need for stating them explicitly. However, *truth, beauty,* and *goodness* do not become meaningful until we explain what makes a statement truthful, a picture beautiful, and an action good. Through careful definition of such terms, we can clarify, strengthen, and, if necessary, modify our standards.

5. USING DEFINITIONS TO ADVANTAGE

When we first start thinking about language, we usually feel that the meaning we ascribe to a word is its "real" meaning, that this real meaning is obvious and beyond cavil, and that to tamper with it is both frivolous and futile. As we gather experience, we sometimes go to the opposite extreme. We conclude that words are "just words," that anyone can define any word in his own way, and that attempts to give a term a generally binding meaning are necessarily misdirected.

Neither view prepares us to meet the problems we encounter when trying to make ourselves understood. In practice, we have to know what ideas the reader is likely to connect with a given term and what ideas we ourselves want him to attach to it. The more the two differ, the more explicit we have to be in stipulating the meaning we ascribe to the term, and the more concerned we have to be with making that meaning plausible. If we use a word in an unconventional way, we have to convince our reader that our use of it is apt, convenient, or historically justified. We have to *keep a stipulated meaning clearly in view to prevent inconsistency and confusion.*

In itself, definition is not an argument but merely a preliminary step toward an argument. It is a means of making clear both to ourselves and to our readers exactly what we are trying to say. Careful definition prevents arguments from bogging down in verbal confusion. It protects people from agreeing in theory and disagreeing in practice.

The space a writer devotes to definition varies greatly for different subjects and different kinds of writing. At one extreme, an author, in one brief sentence, illuminates his interpretation of an important term. An example is the educator who defined *education* as "a lifelong discipline of the individual by himself." Another example is the philosopher who defined *individualism* as the conviction that "everyone should paddle his own canoe, especially on the high seas." At the other extreme, an author defines a term like *liberalism* by tracing its history, examining its associations, distinguishing it carefully from similar or related terms, and giving detailed illustrations of its use. Between the two extremes is the writer who, while infrequently using a formal definition, makes a constant effort to keep his key terms stable and meaningful.

EXERCISES 4

A. In one sentence each, rewrite the following definitions to make them more exact or more informative. Explain what made the original version inexact or uninformative.

1. A barometer is an instrument used in predicting the weather.

2. Classical music is the type of music played in concert halls.

3. A cat is a small domestic animal with soft fur.

4. Tyranny is rule by a tyrant.

5. Jazz is a form of strongly rhythmic music played by Negro musicians.

6. Islam is the religion of the Moslems.

7. A strike means that workers leave their jobs in order to get higher pay.

8. An alien is a person born in another country.

9. To lie is to say something that is not true.

10. A plebiscite is a method of giving the public a voice in political decisions.

B. State as briefly and as accurately as possible the difference between (1) murder and manslaughter; (2) blasphemy and sacrilege; (3) a trade and a profession; (4) tactics and strategy; (5) a college and a university; (6) a democracy and a republic; (7) intuition and instinct; (8) a revolt and a revolution.

C. In a paragraph of at least 150 words, explain the most essential feature of *one* of the following: "conscience," "love," "integrity."

D. The following passages define terms of special interest to students of language and literature. Examine and compare the methods of definition employed. Comment on the clarity or adequacy of each passage.

1. Sophistication is the quality that results from wide experience and mature observation. The sophisticated person both feels and thinks, but he does so with an attitude which is generally accepted as sound by the world. Sentimentality is, in a way, the opposite of sophistication, for it is an unreasonable appeal for emotion. The sophisticate accepts emotion as a natural part of life and controls it; the

sentimentalist is carried away by emotion and over-emphasizes what that emotion deals with.—Robert O. Bowen, *Practical Prose Studies*

2. An inference, as we shall use the term, is *a statement about the unknown made on the basis of the known*. We may *infer* from the handsomeness of a woman's clothes her wealth or social position; we may *infer* from the character of the ruins the origin of the fire that destroyed the building; we may *infer* from a man's calloused hands the nature of his occupation; we may *infer* from a senator's vote on an armaments bill his attitude toward Russia; we may *infer* from the structure of the land the path of a prehistoric glacier; we may *infer* from a halo on an unexposed photographic plate that it has been in the vicinity of radioactive materials; we may *infer* from the noise an engine makes the condition of its connecting rods. Inferences may be carelessly or carefully made. They may be made on the basis of a great background of previous experience with the subject matter, or no experience at all. For example, the inferences a good mechanic can make about the internal condition of a motor by listening to it are often startlingly accurate, while the inferences made by an amateur (if he tries to make any) may be entirely wrong. But the common characteristic of inferences is that they are statements about matters which are not directly known, made on the basis of what has been observed.—S. I. Hayakawa, *Language in Thought and Action*

3. I am not sure that I can draw an exact line between wit and humor. Perhaps the distinction is so subtle that only those persons can decide who have long white beards. But even an ignorant man, so long as he is clear of Bedlam, may have an opinion.

I am quite positive that of the two, humor is the more comfortable and more livable quality. Humorous persons, if their gift is genuine and not a mere shine upon the surface, are always agreeable companions and they sit through the evening best. They have pleasant mouths turned up at the corners. To these corners the great Master of marionettes has fixed the strings and he holds them in his nimblest fingers to twitch them at the slightest jest. But the mouth of a merely witty man is hard and sour until the moment of its discharge. Nor is the flash from a witty man always comforting, whereas a humorous man radiates a general pleasure and is like another candle in the room.

I admire wit, but I have no real liking for it. It has been too often employed against me, whereas humor is always an ally. It never points an impertinent finger into my defects. Humorous persons do not sit like explosives on a fuse. They are safe and easy comrades. But a wit's tongue is as sharp as a donkey driver's stick. I may gallop the faster for its prodding, yet the touch behind is too persuasive for any comfort.—Charles S. Brooks, *Chimney-Pot Papers*

4. Snobbery is not the same thing as pride of class. Pride of class may not please us but we must at least grant that it reflects a social function. A man who exhibited class pride—in the day when it was

possible to do so—may have been puffed up about what he *was,* but this ultimately depended on what he *did.* Thus, aristocratic pride was based ultimately on the ability to fight and administer. No pride is without fault, but pride of class may be thought of as today we think of pride of profession, toward which we are likely to be lenient.

Snobbery is pride in status without pride in function. And it is an uneasy pride of status. It always asks, "Do I belong—do I really belong? And does he belong? And if I am observed talking to him, will it make me seem to belong or not to belong?" It is the peculiar vice not of aristocratic societies which have their own appropriate vices, but of bourgeois democratic societies. For us the legendary strongholds of snobbery are the Hollywood studios, where two thousand dollars a week dare not talk to three hundred dollars a week for fear he be taken for nothing more than fifteen hundred dollars a week. The dominant emotions of snobbery are uneasiness, self-consciousness, self-defensiveness, the sense that one is not quite real but can in some way acquire reality.—Lionel Trilling, *The Liberal Imagination*

5. Image, metaphor, and symbol shade into each other and are sometimes difficult to distinguish. In general, however, an image means only what it is; a metaphor means something else than what it is; and a symbol means what it is and something more too. If I say that a shaggy brown dog was rubbing its back against a white picket fence, I am talking about nothing but a dog and am therefore presenting an image; if I say, "Some dirty dog stole my wallet at the party," I am not talking about a dog at all, and am therefore using a metaphor; but if I say, "You can't teach an old dog new tricks," I am talking not only about dogs but about living creatures of any species, and am therefore speaking symbolically.—Laurence Perrine, *Sound and Sense*

E. Examine and evaluate the following tentative definitions of *sportsmanship*. Which of the definitions would be most useful to you in working out your own definition of the term?

1. Sportsmanship means playing a game according to the rules and obeying the instructions of the referee. If a player does not obey rules, he is penalized.

2. Sportsmanship is applauded by crowds at boxing events when the boxer allows his opponent to stagger to his feet before being smashed to the canvas again.

3. Sportsmanship is the quality of wanting to let another fellow have a chance. It is parallel to the ideal embodied in the Ten Commandments. Religion teaches a way of life that will always have the sportsman as a part of it.

4. Sportsmanship is the ability to get along with one's fellow man and at the same time oppose him. It enables a player to congratulate an opponent who has just handed him a crushing defeat.

5. The American athlete is known for his high sense of sportsmanship. Sportsmanship is hard to explain, but most people recognize it when they see it. It means being friendly, fair, just, and sincere.

6. Sportsmanship is a luxury. The gentleman hunter who hunts for amusement can afford to observe a sportsmanlike code in shooting animals. The hunter who has to find food for a starving family cannot afford to be particular about his methods.

7. Sportsmanship is the quality of being sportsmanlike. A sportsman, in other words, is the person who adopts a standard of sportsmanlike behavior and lives up to it.

8. Sportsmanship is the willingness to live up to the established traditions of a sport. Through the years, a certain kind of conduct has come to be expected of the players. A player is unsportsmanlike when he violates the traditions of the sport.

9. The most important ingredient in sportsmanship is courtesy. Consideration and restraint make the difference between a courteous player and a ruffian.

10. Sportsmanship means playing not in order to win but for the love of the sport. The sportsman who plays primarily for profit or for personal glory is not a sportsman in the true sense of the word.

F. What are the problems of definition suggested by the following passages? How would you deal with the terms that cause difficulty?

1. Southern Democrats are not really true Democrats at heart. For years they have opposed programs advocated by Democrats representing the Northern and Western sections of the country.

2. The trouble with my high school teachers was that they used absolutely no psychology. They tried to argue recalcitrant students into changing their ways, instead of cracking down.

3. A student-body president who is working against the best interests of the student body should resign. Our own student-body president reached that point when he came out openly in favor of the administration's plan to de-emphasize football. If this plan is accepted, the prestige of the college is bound to suffer, and every student and alumnus will be affected.

4. The college administration has definitely taken its stand on the side of reaction and against the forces of progress. It has been an outstanding characteristic of progressive American society that it has made available a college education to ever increasing numbers of students. Nevertheless, the administration has decided to reduce the number of freshmen to be enrolled next year by raising admission standards.

5. At its last meeting the local school board decided that an "enriched" and accelerated program would be set up for children who show ex-

ceptional aptitude for academic work. The community should reject this program as undemocratic.

6. One kind of inflation is caused by the law of supply and demand. Prices go higher in a time of shortage because demand exceeds supply. The other kind of inflation is caused when people are paid higher wages without producing more. To distinguish between these two kinds of inflation is to distinguish between a natural law and a man-made condition.

7. Theft means taking things that belong to others. The businessman who inflates prices for the sake of excessive profits takes what belongs to me as surely as the thief who picks my pockets.

8. I was surprised to see that a prominent teachers' organization opposed a bill requiring the removal of obscene publications from school libraries. The organization claimed that the bill could be used against books of educational and cultural value. Since when have obscene books contributed to the culture of a nation? There is more than one way of sabotaging a nation, and placing undesirable literature in school libraries is one of them.

9. Large-scale killing of civilians by atomic warfare is a crime. Political and military leaders responsible for atomic attacks on civilians should be brought to trial as war criminals.

10. Insanity means a serious derangement of the mental faculties. Anyone who is deranged enough to commit murder must be considered at least temporarily insane.

G. Study the following extended definition of *courage*. Describe in detail the technique employed by the author. Point out features that add to or detract from the effectiveness of this student-written paper.

COURAGE

The word *courage* has the power greatly to stimulate the imagination. All one has to do is to see the word in print or hear it spoken to be prepared for an account of stirring deeds of bravery and selfless sacrifice. Because of this immediate appeal to the emotions, we often pay little attention to causes that effect courage in a person or in animals. I believe that human courage and animal courage are completely different, both in nature and origin.

First I would like to consider courage in man and offer some ideas about what human courage is and why it manifests itself in man. Imagine that you are witnessing a hunter stalking a wounded lion in dense brush. It undoubtedly takes great courage to hunt lions, and even more so under the conditions I have described. Let it be presupposed that the hunter is fully aware of the possible consequences of hunting lions and, further, that the hunter is one of that vast group of people who show a marked antipathy toward being eaten by a lion. Why is he there at all, especially if he realizes that lion-hunting is not conducive to longevity? If the hunter is responsible for the lion's being wounded in the first place, it is possible that he is acting to conform to a hunter's code that forbids leaving a wounded animal to suffer. However, in addition to the influence of the hunter's code there is a strong chance that other pressures are holding the hunter on the trail of the lion.

If the hunter were to lose his nerve and break off the hunt, he would have to face up to the fact that he had lost his nerve. Even with the anesthetic of rationalization this would be a painful blow to his ego. In addition to self-esteem, there are the love of excitement and the desire for the acclamation that is accorded someone who has killed such a formidable beast as a lion. Add to these the awareness that his friends would censure him should he show fear in the face of danger and you can see that the hunter is more or less pushed along by these combined pressures.

Let us turn to the lion who lies a few yards deeper in the brush licking his wounds and waiting for the hunter to get just a little closer. Since the instant the lion was slammed to earth by the impact of the hunter's bullet, he has been bathed in agony, and this agony has fanned his instinctive spark of hatred for man into a blazing inferno. Why does the lion wait for the hunter when he could run and avoid the possibility of another wound or perhaps death? It is clear that the lion does not have the same reasons for being there that the man has. The reason for the lion's ambush is his instinctive hatred for man and his instinctive fear that if he doesn't kill the man, the man will kill him. Whatever "courage" the lion has is strictly the result of instinct.

While the word *courage* might be used to describe the actions of both hunter and lion, the motives behind their actions are quite different. The basic difference between animal courage and human courage is that animal courage is purely of instinctive origin, while courage in man is a result of many factors that lie mostly outside of himself. These factors consist of the attitudes of his friends, the ideals he pursues and the codes he conforms to, and his particular desires or appetites. All these combine to produce the attribute we call "courage."

THEME TOPICS 4

1. Explain your idea of a "tactful" person, a "perfect gentleman," a "snob," or a person "who knows the score." Use detailed illustrations.

2. Can one draw a clear line between the "amateur" and the "professional" athlete? (For instance, are college football players "amateurs" in the true sense of the word? What is the true sense of the word?)

3. Can college students be called more "mature" than high school students? (What are some of the characteristics of "maturity"?)

4. Write an extended definition of *one* of the following: "fair play," "tolerance," "open-mindedness." Defend your use or interpretation of the term and give detailed illustrations of what it means in practice.

5. Explain your idea of a "selfish" person, an "idealist," or a "cynic." Use detailed illustrations from your own experience.

6. Write an extended definition of *one* of the following: "free enterprise," "the welfare state," "individual initiative," "economic security." Defend your use or interpretation of the term and give detailed illustrations of what it means in practice.

7. What is the difference between a "liberal" and a "conservative"? (Do the two terms overlap in any way? What are the most characteristic distinctions?)

8. Can one draw a clear line between ideas that are merely new or foreign and ideas that are "un-American"? (How and by whom should the term *un-American* be defined?)

9. Can one draw a clear line between the "radical" and the "responsible citizen"? What are some of the difficulties involved?

10. Explain what you mean by a "good actor," a "good play," or a "good book." Limit yourself to one or two essential characteristics and illustrate each fully.

11. Explain the difference between "highbrow" and "lowbrow" art. Limit yourself to one or two essential criteria and illustrate them fully.

12. What is the difference between "genius" and "talent"?

5: LOGIC

1. WHY LOGIC MAKES A DIFFERENCE

People with similar experiences often disagree on the lessons to be drawn from them. Your classmates may come from the same section of the country, read the same textbooks, and subscribe to the same newspapers as you do. Yet on many issues their opinions may differ from yours. One reason for such disagreements is that some people think more clearly and more accurately than others. They are more competent than others in the use of **logic**; that is, the system according to which the mind sorts out, digests, and interprets information.

Superior logical ability, like superior mathematical ability, is probably as much a matter of heredity as of training. However, in logic as in mathematics, a number of basic principles are generally accepted. Most of them are within the reach of everyone with average intelligence. A club will hardly elect as treasurer someone who cannot do simple sums. A reader will hardly attend to a discussion of serious issues by a writer who is unaware of elementary principles of logic.

At the same time, sound logic is not something we cultivate merely to escape the censure of the critical reader. Straight thinking helps us deal with our own confusions and perplexities. It helps us order our impressions, test our tentative conclusions, clarify our convictions. The ability to marshal ideas in a theme cannot be separated from the ability to think through a problem in orderly and systematic fashion.

2. HOW TO GENERALIZE SOUNDLY AND EFFECTIVELY

You will occasionally hear someone call a statement a "mere generalization." If he wishes to discredit the statement, the charge that it is a generalization is scarcely enough. "People who eat strychnine usually die" is a mere generalization. It merits serious consideration nevertheless. No one can go about his daily affairs without relying on generalizations of all kinds. The difficulty that concerns you as a writer is not that generalizations are generally unreliable but that some are more reliable than others. If you want a generalization to survive in the rough-and-tumble of critical discussion, you have to show that it is a general conclusion derived from a careful study of whatever evidence or information was available.

To generalize means to extract the common element from a number of different situations. A group of educators studying high school curricula may find that the senior class in the first high school they visit is, among other activities, reading *Macbeth*. In the next school, a senior honors section is scheduled to read *Macbeth* later in the year. In the third or fourth school visited, the senior class is studying *Hamlet*. If this pattern persists, the educators' final report will generalize that high school seniors in the area visited usually study a Shakespeare play, often *Macbeth*. This process of drawing general conclusions from individual observations is known as **induction**, or inductive reasoning. To be reliable, generalizations have to be formulated according to the principles of sound induction.

Hasty Generalization. *The basic logical weakness of much student writing is the excessive scope of many of its generalizations.* Our minds tend to be far ahead of the evidence actually collected. We talk to Professor Smith and find that he is a Democrat. We talk to Professor Brown and find that he is a Democrat. We talk to Professor Miller and find that he is a Democrat. Meanwhile, our minds have already jumped to a sweeping general conclusion: "All professors are Democrats." It costs us an effort to revise our conclusion to read: "Some (three, to be exact) of the college professors I know are Democrats." As more and more information accumulates, we can replace the *some* with *many* or even with *a great many*. Only on the basis of very comprehensive statistical information can we claim that the "majority of them" or "most of them" are Democrats. Only rarely are we entitled to a generalization containing words like *all, nobody, everything,* or *nothing*.

In revising your papers, look for sweeping generalizations that would profit from cautious rewording:

SWEEPING: Armenians are an exceptionally gifted people.
CAUTIOUS: A number of Armenians have done exceptional work in music and art.

SWEEPING: Americans are the most generous people on earth.
CAUTIOUS: Over the years, Americans have given impressive support to private charity and to such government programs as foreign aid.

Even when generalizing on a fairly large scale, an effective writer can gain the confidence of his readers by careful wording. Notice how the author of the following passage presents his generalizations as tentative first impressions, how he explains terms that might prove misleading or offensive:

> American women are particularly conspicuous to the European observer. *They strike him first* as being *generally* better groomed and better dressed than their European sisters, *even if* they rarely show individual and critical taste. *Then they strike him* as being more sure of themselves than are the women of any other nation, even those of Northern Europe. *There seems to be* little hesitation and shyness, even in a very young American girl. American women, to the European, *may even seem* "tough," *not in the sense that* they are vulgar in any way, *but in the sense that* they are both resilient and forthright. These are qualities which the European is accustomed to find only among men.—Gunnar D. Kumlien, "America: Image and Reality," *Commonweal*

The more complicated the subject with which we deal, the more tentative and limited our generalizations necessarily become. Long-range trends in the cost of living, the relationship between information and entertainment in a large metropolitan newspaper—these are fairly complicated subjects. Nevertheless, after reasonably detailed investigation we can write on them with assurance. Whatever assurance we may be able to muster becomes much less well founded when we discuss intentions and motives. When we talk about what goes on in other people's minds, we can seldom go beyond cautious speculation. We all have some ideas about why the last Presidential election turned out as it did. But only a mind reader with an electronic calculator at his disposal could give a definite answer.

Sampling. Concrete examples are an indispensable aid to effective and foolproof communication. But as one occurrence does not set a trend, so one example does not prove a point. Ideally, a generalization is sound if it fits all the known facts and if all apparent contradictions can be satisfactorily explained. Obviously no one can show any such thing in a short paper. The best you can do is to *expand your examples and illustrations until your reader begins to feel that you have presented a fair sampling of the evidence.* Notice how the author of the following passage provides a solid array of examples to substantiate his original generalization:

> *Americans* are a sententious people and *are taught at an early age to moralize.* They learn it in Sunday school. They learn it from Poor Richard—at least they did so in my time. In Chicago during the twenties we were filled up with Poor Richard: "Little strokes fell great oaks." "Plough deep while sluggards sleep." These formulas seemed true and sound. Longfellow, whom we had to memorize by the yard, was also strongly affirmative: "Life is real! Life is earnest! And the grave is not its goal." And finally there was "The Chambered Nautilus": "Build thee more stately mansions, O my soul."—Saul Bellow, "The Writer as Moralist," *Atlantic*

Usually the evidence you provide is only part of the evidence you have collected, which in turn is only part of all the evidence actually relevant and available. But though your examination of the evidence cannot be exhaustive, at least *your sample must be representative.* When asked to find out the number of words in a 300-page book, we select perhaps five or ten sample pages. On each page we count the words in perhaps five or ten sample lines. We then multiply the average number of words per line by the number of lines per page and by the total number of pages. Though this method is usually satisfactory, you can easily see how it could go wrong. If 100 pages are taken up by graphs or pictures, or if some parts of the book are set in smaller type, the estimate needs to be adjusted accordingly.

Adequate sampling is equally important when you generalize about people. You cannot base general conclusions about the attitude of college professors toward their students on your observations of a Latin professor about to retire, a part-time Greek instructor, and a graduate student who plans to teach Hebrew. You will have to consider teachers of language, of science, of home economics, of engineering, of physical education. You will have to consider Democrats and Republicans, young men and old men, instructors at large universities and at small colleges. Your sample will have to be representative. A small sample, carefully chosen to represent men of different opinions and backgrounds, can be more reliable than a large sample that confines itself to one fairly homogeneous group and ignores other groups, whose members might have quite different attitudes.

Levels of Generalization. The way to make generalizations sound and meaningful is to anchor them firmly to the first-hand experience from which they are derived. Make it a habit to provide at least some concrete detail with every general statement you make. Even one example or illustration is better than none: "My father is a mechanical wizard; only last night, for instance, he repaired the wiring in our electric toaster." "History 21 is a difficult course; two of my friends failed it last year."

Once you adopt this habit of translating the general into the specific, it is likely to bring about a general downgrading of your generalizations. *Many student papers move on such a high level of abstraction that the writer has trouble getting down to earth.* He says, "My father is a wonderful man" when he means "He let me use our new car over the weekend." He says, "Farm income is deteriorating" when he means "My uncle has been complaining about the price of hogs." When there is such an obvious gap between the general and the specific, a concrete example may not support the generalization but rather deflate it. Notice how the original generalization in the following example becomes more obviously untenable the closer the writer comes to first-hand observation:

VERY GENERAL: The younger generation has no morals.
LESS GENERAL: Students are careless in their conduct.
LESS GENERAL: College students present a casual appearance.
LESS GENERAL: Freshman girls dress casually.
SPECIFIC: Betty wore shorts to class.

The various levels of generalization form a pyramid. There are countless concrete, factual observations at the bottom ("My feet are blistered"). There are a limited number of sweeping general pronouncements at the top ("Man is born to suffer"). At the bottom of the pyramid, Betty, like millions of her kind, goes about her daily business. Seen from a more elevated point of view, she loses her individual identity and fits into the general category of "girl." Soon she joins her brothers and boy friends to appear under the more inclusive heading of "mankind" or "humanity." As the categories become fewer and more comprehensive, she is included under "organism." At the very top of the pyramid, there is still a trace of her in an all-embracing term like "life" or "creation."

Some writers are most at home on the ground level, talking about individual human beings. Others are most at home in the clouds, generalizing about life and existence. The most instructive kind of writing often occupies the space between, presenting generalizations large enough to be of general interest and yet limited enough to be firmly tied to individual instances.

3. THE USES AND ABUSES OF DEDUCTION

The generalizations produced by inductive reasoning are indispensable in day-to-day living. They tell us how to react and what to expect. They enable us to predict the behavior of people and of things and to anticipate correctly the consequences of our own actions.

Induction and Deduction. In the absence of reliable generalizations, life becomes a matter of constant experiment. As long as we have not arrived at general conclusions about which mushrooms are edible, our cooking will have to proceed by the trial-and-error method. If we survive, the mushrooms we ate were edible. If we become ill, they probably were not. As long as we have not arrived at general conclusions about what animals make good transportation, we will have to test the suitability of each individual horse and donkey. On the other hand, once we develop sound general notions about mushrooms and animals, we simply establish what category each specimen belongs in. If the animal is a horse, we more or less confidently expect that it will be suitable for riding. Our reasoning proceeds somewhat like this:

> All the horses that I have observed were suitable for riding.
> This animal seems to be a horse.
> Therefore, this animal should be suitable for riding.

When fully and explicitly stated, such an argument, proceeding from two initial assumptions to a conclusion, is called a **syllogism**. The statements representing what we already know or assume are called **premises**. *Syllogistic reasoning deduces conclusions that are implied in, or follow from, accepted premises.* The common term ("horse") that accounts for the partial overlapping of the two premises and thus makes a conclusion possible is called the **middle term**. Here are some formal syllogisms, with the middle terms italicized:

FIRST PREMISE: All *members of the Pegasus Club* are English majors.
SECOND PREMISE: Claire Benton is a *member of the Pegasus Club.*
CONCLUSION: Claire Benton is an English major.

FIRST PREMISE:	No *round-headed Irishmen* are eligible to join the Phi Beta Gamma Fraternity.
SECOND PREMISE:	I am a *round-headed Irishman.*
CONCLUSION:	I am not eligible to join the Phi Beta Gamma Fraternity.

FIRST PREMISE:	Only *seniors* can be elected to the student court.
SECOND PREMISE:	Gerald is not a *senior.*
CONCLUSION:	Gerald cannot be elected to the student court.

In contrast to the generalizing, inductive kind of reasoning, the process of applying general knowledge to specific instances may be called deductive reasoning, or **deduction**. Induction and deduction so defined are obviously two different sides of the same coin. Once you have established inductively that students who don't know how to spell fail their English courses, you can apply this general knowledge to your own case and predict that you will fail your English courses unless you learn how to spell. Accurate deduction makes generalizations pay off; it helps you to convert your general knowledge into solutions to specific problems.

The basic model for the kinds of reasoning here described is that of simple progression from concrete observation to general conclusion to specific application. In a third major type of reasoning, inductive and deductive reasoning interact, but according to a somewhat more complicated scheme. When we try to explain a state of affairs, when we construct a **hypothesis** to account for a set of phenomena, we often model our reasoning on the following example:

> The house across the street has shown no signs of life in some days;
> Some rolled-up, rain-soaked newspapers lie on the front steps;
> The grass needs cutting badly;
> Salesmen who ring the doorbell get no answer; . . .
> > *Therefore:*
> > The people across the street are away on a trip.—Monroe C. Beardsley, *Thinking Straight*

Each of the original observations here is interpreted as an instance of a generalization of the type "Some houses show no life because the owner is away"; "Some lawns remain uncut because the owner is away"; and so on. Since a number of generalizations of this kind intersect, we assume that their common element provides the clue to the present instance. How reliable a hypothesis is depends on our caution and skill in correlating relevant observations, and on our determination not to ignore clues that point in unexpected directions.

Faulty Deduction. Faulty deduction is hard to detect. True or acceptable premises tend to establish a climate of assent. Once a reader has found that he agrees with a writer on two or three initial points, he is predisposed to keep on saying "yes" as the writer starts drawing conclusions. Both as a writer and as a reader you will have to be alert enough to say "no" when an argument proceeds from sound premises to dubious conclusions. Not every argument that has a *therefore* in it is necessarily logical.

Just as we have to be cautious in working out generalizations, so we have to be careful in applying them to specific instances. For instance, there is a difference between "*All* pacifists read Gandhi" and "*Only* pacifists read Gandhi." The first version does not exclude the possibility that not only pacifists but also many other people who are *not* pacifists read Gandhi. It does not mean that every person who reads Gandhi is necessarily a pacifist. "*All* communists attend party meetings" does not rule out the possibility that party meetings could also be attended by reporters, FBI agents, social scientists, and other persons hostile or indifferent to communism.

In applying a generalization to specific instances, pay careful attention to its scope. It may apply to some members of a group but not all, to all members of the group and no one else, or to all members of the group and possibly members of other groups. *Assuming the premises to be true,* the following arguments would result in the following justified conclusions:

FIRST PREMISE: Some redheads are passionate.
SECOND PREMISE: Horace is a redhead.
CONCLUSION: Horace *may or may not be* passionate.
                    (The likelihood that Horace is passionate will be the stronger the greater the percentage of passionate people among redheads.)

FIRST PREMISE: All redheads are passionate.
SECOND PREMISE: Horace is a redhead.
CONCLUSION: Horace is passionate.
                    (A quality ascribed to *all* members of a group applies to each individual member.)

FIRST PREMISE: All redheads are passionate.
SECOND PREMISE: Horace is passionate.
CONCLUSION: Horace *may or may not be* a redhead.
                    (Horace shares *one* quality with all members of the group "redheads," but that does not make him a member of the group.)

FIRST PREMISE:	Only redheads are passionate.
SECOND PREMISE:	Horace is passionate.
CONCLUSION:	Horace is a redhead.
	(Horace has a quality possessed *only* by redheads; it therefore identifies him as a member of the group.)

FIRST PREMISE:	No redheads are passionate.
SECOND PREMISE:	Horace is a redhead.
CONCLUSION:	Horace is not passionate.
	(A quality *ruled out* for all members of a group is necessarily ruled out for each individual member.)

FIRST PREMISE:	No redheads are passionate.
SECOND PREMISE:	Horace is not a redhead.
CONCLUSION:	Horace *may or may not be* passionate.
	(When both premises are negative, neither an affirmative nor a negative conclusion can be drawn.)

Logicians sort out arguments such as these into two types. The first is the true syllogism, in which a definite conclusion *necessarily* follows from the premises. If the premises are true, and the logical operations valid, the conclusion is necessarily true. The second type leads to a merely *probable* conclusion; it allows a degree of more or less reliable prediction. In your writing, you will seldom work with generalizations that start with "all" or "no" and thus can function as the first premise in a true syllogism. More typically, you will be concerned with what conclusions you can reasonably draw from generalizations neither all-inclusive nor all-exclusive.

Faulty Premises. Even when the logical operations in an argument are valid, the results will be unsound if the argument starts from unreliable assumptions. *Any argument based on previous knowledge can be only as accurate as that previous knowledge itself.* If our generalizations about horses ignore the fact that some horses are unsuited for riding because of temperament or lack of training, the most accurately constructed deductions will not protect us from being thrown into a ditch by a bucking bronco.

When your readers find one of your arguments unconvincing, the flaw may be not in the way you have conducted the argument but in what you have taken for granted. Critical readers will not accept without question such premises as "Football promotes unselfishness," "High taxes cause inflation," or "The voters can be trusted to detect insincerity." Before you make such statements the basis of a deductive argument, you should carefully examine, qualify, and support them.

Hidden Premises. Often some of the assumptions on which an argument rests are not stated. The reason may be that writer and reader tacitly agree on basic convictions or common goals. Sometimes, however, the reason is that the writer does not realize what is involved, or that he does not feel prepared to defend his premises once they are brought out into the open.

An argument based on hidden premises frustrates the reader. He may feel that something is wrong, without being able to put his finger on what it is. To find his bearings, he might outline the argument something like this:

PREMISE: Jones is a fascist.
CONCLUSION: Don't listen to him.
(HIDDEN PREMISE: Fascists are not worth listening to.)

PREMISE: That camera was made in Japan.
CONCLUSION: I won't buy it.
(HIDDEN PREMISE: Cameras made in Japan are not good buys.)

Fruitful discussion often depends on our willingness to bring hidden assumptions into the open. For instance, a student may object to the discussion of family relations in sociology classes on the grounds that some of the students "may be hurt." He writes, "Somebody might say something which could be painful to students from unhappy homes." The unstated assumption here is that educational experiences should not be painful. The assumption deserves explicit statement and support.

Equivocation. *Often the generalizations that serve as the basis of deductive arguments are not formulated precisely enough to be applied to specific cases without error.* For instance, we might agree that famous symbols of patriotism should be preserved in museums. We might also agree that General X is a symbol of patriotism. However, that does not mean that the general should be in a museum. The term *symbol* has changed its meaning from "symbolic object" in one statement to "symbolic figure" in the other.

An intentional shift in the meaning of key terms in order to deceive or mislead is known as **equivocation**. A political speaker may be equivocating when using a versatile word like *radical*. In one sentence, *radical* may mean "a person who wants to destroy all law and order"; in the next sentence it may mean "a person who advocates a revision of collective-bargaining laws." In an argument over social security, *weak and helpless* may mean "sick and disabled" in one sentence and "able-bodied but temporarily out of work" in another. The best protection against errors resulting from fuzzy terminology is careful definition of key terms.

Misleading Statistics. Of the various generalizations whose bearing you may misinterpret, the most deceptive ones are those given to you in the form of statistical data. Statistical figures have something solid about them and are a powerful tool of persuasion. However, unless you interpret them cautiously, they may lead you to conclusions they do not justify.

Suppose a set of statistics indicates that the average income of the twenty families living in Blueberry Park is $10,000—a figure that is said to represent an increase of 100 per cent during the last two decades. If you read them hastily, these figures might conjure up a picture of twenty well-to-do families. However, the figures themselves do not exclude the possibility that nineteen of the twenty families earn $2,000 a year and live in shacks, while the twentieth family earns $162,000 and lives in a mansion on the hill. In that case, it would be no contradiction to say that the average income is $10,000, but that the average family makes only $2,000. *Average,* in other words, does not always mean "typical." The reported increase offers similar problems of interpretation. It may be an increase in dollar earnings, which could be largely nullified by a corresponding increase in the cost of living. It could be an increase in actual purchasing power as determined by the cost of basic commodities.

In basing logical arguments on statistical figures, you need to know exactly what kind of information your figures provide and how that information has been arrived at. You can often test the reliability of a set of statistics by the willingness of the statistician to discuss the exact implications and limitations of his data. When looking for a statistical survey of audience reactions to television programs, you will do well to choose one that tells you how many people were interviewed and what social and cultural groups they represented. You may further want to know whether the questions encouraged impromptu reactions or carefully considered evaluation, whether they presented *either-or* choices or made allowance for different shades of enthusiasm and disapproval. Before you make use of the data provided by an intelligence test, you will try to find out what kinds of intelligence the test measures and what measurements it applies. If the results of the test are described in terms of norms, medians, and percentiles, you will make sure that you understand the technical terms before you start quoting any of the figures.

◄ **Circular Arguments.** Some arguments, though they have the appearance of moving from premises toward a conclusion, in fact merely tread water. Consider the following example:

> True ability will always assert itself.
> A man of true ability sees to it that his talents are recognized.
> Therefore, true ability will not want for recognition.

The supposed conclusion, except for differences in wording, is identical with the initial premise. We gather at the very beginning that the speaker is not going to label as "true ability" the abilities of a man who cannot gain recognition for his talents. What accounts for this position we are not told. The supposed argument makes no contribution toward showing that such a way of labeling ability is helpful or reasonable. It moves in a circle; it leaves us exactly where we started.

Many would-be arguments merely reiterate the initial assumptions of the speaker or the writer. Though they are futile from the point of view of logic, they may nevertheless produce results. Some people judge the validity of an idea by the persistence with which it is repeated. Psychologically, "what I tell you three times is true"—though not with an audience trained to look for evidence, and to evaluate the logic brought to bear on it.

4. GUARDING AGAINST PSEUDO-LOGIC

Through the centuries, writers have catalogued the ways in which the human mind strays from the path of sound logic. A number of logical errors, of common fallacies, recur in the reasoning of people of widely different backgrounds and convictions. Many of these errors are the result of **short-cut thinking**. Most people are impatient with complicated and detailed explanations, with elaborate arguments pro and con. They readily turn to someone who can give them a forceful and simple answer. Often, the simple answer is not the right one.

Other errors result from an even more basic tendency of the human mind. The person with preconceived ideas and strong convictions will naturally look for arguments that support his own point of view. Instead of using logic as a means of arriving at the truth, he will assume that he knows the truth and put logic to work to support it. Logic then ceases to enlighten and clarify; it becomes a means of advancing pre-determined ideas and interests.

Post Hoc Fallacy. One common error occurs when we argue about causes and effects. It is sometimes called the *post hoc* fallacy, since it results from a confusion of "after this" and "because of this." *If one thing happens first and something else thereafter, the second is not necessarily a result of the first.* That a tornado hits a community after an H-bomb test in the Pacific does not mean that the test caused the tornado. That Chinese foreign policy changes after a speech by the American Secretary of State does not mean that the speech caused the change in policy. That a young man proposes to a girl *after* he learns of her wealth does not mean that he proposed *because* he learned of her wealth.

We tend to look for immediate, tangible causes for an event and naturally seize first upon anything striking or extraordinary that preceded it. Often the real causes of events are less simple and less close to the surface. Often, of course, something does happen both after and because of something else. However, that there actually is a cause-and-effect relationship needs to be established by careful investigation. If the world's weather charts show a deviation from customary patterns after two or three H-bomb tests in a row, the meteorologist will launch a detailed study. To arrive at a sound conclusion, the investigator would have to take into account cases where H-bomb tests were *not* followed by tornadoes, where speeches by the Secretary of State were *not* followed by changes in Chinese foreign policy.

Like the weather, psychological, economic, and political conditions are usually influenced by a variety of causes. Thoughtful readers will distrust the quack who has a simple answer for all problems and look for the expert who takes a balanced view. When they read about what can be done to help underdeveloped nations, they will be reassured if the writer first of all recognizes that the poverty of backward nations "is the product of a plurality of causes":

> . . . Few poor countries are without a minority of exceedingly rich. And it is difficult to understand why an Andean or Middle Eastern peasant should seek to enhance his income by irrigation, improved seed, or acceptable livestock when he knows that anything in excess of subsistence will be appropriated by the landlord, tax collector, moneylender, or merchant. *Yet* the world has much poverty without evident exploiters. In India and Pakistan there are millions of small landowning peasants who are very poor but whose poverty cannot be related to the enrichment of any landlord, moneylender, tax collector, or other visible oppressor.

. . . Low income allows of no saving. Without saving there is nothing to invest. Without investment there can be no economic advance, and so poverty is self-perpetuating. *Yet* in several countries of the Middle East, as also in South America—Venezuela is particularly a case in point—oil provides a rich source of revenue and capital is not scarce. But the vast majority of the people remain exceedingly poor.— John Kenneth Galbraith, "The Poverty of Nations," *Atlantic*

Such an ability to go from "on the one hand" to "on the other hand" does not prevent a writer from deciding which causes are most important, or what remedial action is most urgently needed. A writer should be able to make up his mind, and to present his conclusions vigorously and effectively. However, he should make up his mind by weighing relevant possibilities, not by ignoring all but the most superficially obvious.

Arguments from Analogy. Just as there is a difference between *after* and *because*, so there is a difference between *similar* and *alike*. We often rely on **faulty analogy.** If two things are alike in two or three respects, it seems only reasonable to expect that they will be alike in others. If we remember shifty-eyed, red-haired Johnny, who struck his math teacher and had to be placed in a detention home, we become wary of Ronny, who is also shifty-eyed and who also has red hair.

Partial analogies can be valuable when used for explanation and illustration. When we try to explain something that is complicated or abstract, we compare it to something the reader already knows. For instance, we might compare the human brain to a telephone switchboard or to an electronic calculator. The switchboard analogy, for instance, could explain how the brain sorts out the many incoming impressions and establishes relevant connections. However, we should also point out some of the things that make a brain different from a machine. For instance, a brain is not produced in a factory, its components are not half so well known, it is largely self-directing, and it suffers from quirks and ailments more mysterious than a short circuit.

One of these quirks of the human brain is its tendency to make too much of the similarities of things and to play down their differences. Because we expect an Irishman to be like one or two other Irishmen we know, we don't make enough of an effort to judge him on his own merits. However, *two things that share two or three or four characteristics cannot be assumed to share any number of others.* Two Irishmen may have a great deal in common. They may both have been born in Ireland, exposed to Irish folklore as children, and instructed in the Catholic faith. At the same time, they may differ widely in other respects: the one may like Irish folklore, the other sneer at it; the one may be a devout Catholic, the other an agnostic; the one may be easygoing, the other serious.

To use an analogy to advantage in your own writing, make sure you realize where it breaks down. Show your reader in what respects analogous situations are similar and in what respects they are dissimilar. Suppose you are writing a paper on the relationship between business experience and government employment. You say:

> Our nation is in a way a big business. To prevent businesses from failing one has to have qualified business executives. So why not give high offices in the federal government to business executives qualified to deal with business problems?

The analogy you have in mind will become instructive if you follow up both similarities and differences. You can point out such assets of the business executive as training in organizing and coordinating many different activities, in selecting and directing personnel, in handling legal and financial problems, or in maintaining good public relations. On the other hand, you can point out that unlike most businesses government is owned and run by and for the customers. There is one vote per head rather than per share. And whatever the main purpose of government may be, it is not financial profit or giving employment to its employees.

Oversimplification. One common cause of erroneous conclusions is the *either-or* or **black-and-white** approach. Whatever isn't black isn't necessarily white, but may be green, beige, ochre, violet, or scarlet. Whatever isn't red or pink isn't necessarily true-blue. *Fruitful argument usually requires a comprehensive grasp of differences of kind and of degree rather than a choice between clear-cut alternatives.*

The *either-or* fallacy often manifests itself in the belief that there are two sides to each issue, and that by looking at both of them we can arrive at a sound conclusion. Such an approach easily leads to oversimplification. Looking back at the Spanish Civil War, most observers agree that it was more than a simple question of "Democracy versus Fascism." The struggle was in various ways complicated by the role of the Catholic church, of the Spanish monarchist tradition, of many different shades of democratic thought, and, above all, of the Communist International. After the end of World War II, the simple slogan of "Democracy versus Fascism" soon proved deceptive to observers of events in the Soviet-dominated countries of Eastern Europe. There are many similar alternatives: "Conservatism versus Liberalism," "Social-ism versus Free Enterprise," "Censorship versus Freedom of Thought," "Traditional versus Modern Education."

The appeal of a thoughtful writer often lies in his ability to re-examine and redefine such oversimplified contrasts in order to make us see the underlying, more complex relationships. Here, for instance, is Walter Lippmann discussing the familiar distinction between "straight news" and "editorial comment":

> It is all very well to say that a reporter collects the news and that the news consists of facts. The truth is that, in our world, the facts are infinitely many and that no reporter could collect them all, no news-paper could print them all, and nobody could read them all. We have to select *some* facts rather than others, and in doing that we are using not only our legs, but our selective judgment of what is interesting or important, or both. . . .
>
> Because we are newspapermen in the American liberal tradition, the way we interpret the news is not by fitting the facts to a dogma. It is by proposing theories or hypotheses, which are then tested by trial and error. We put forward the most plausible interpretation we can think of, the most plausible picture into which the raw news fits, and then we wait to see whether the later news fits into the interpretation.
> —"The Job of the Washington Correspondent," *Atlantic*

Simplified alternatives appeal to us because they make us feel that we have a firm grip on our subject. Being able to divide many confusing items into two or three main categories makes us feel that we have a clear over-all view of what is going on. However, not everything that is simple and clear is necessarily logical. For instance, suppose you are discussing the motives of business executives who come to Washington to work for the government. You set up three possible categories: They enter the government for the sake of money, for the sake of prestige, or for the sake of wielding influence in favor of their former businesses and associates. You then write a paper demonstrating that most of the businessmen coming to Washington stand to lose rather than to gain both money and reputation. After thus eliminating these first two possibilities, you then conclude that the third one must be true. Actually your paper proves no such thing. There may be a fourth, a fifth, and a sixth possibility which you have not mentioned. One such possibility is that they feel obligated and qualified to serve their country.

Supporting Foregone Conclusions. The kinds of short-cut thinking just reviewed may lead astray someone seriously looking to answers for his questions. Other kinds of reasoning are kept from being productive by the basic purposes they are made to serve. One of the habits that can make discussion sterile is excessive devotion to the spirit of debate. Competitive debating is an exciting pastime. In many high schools, the debating team does an invaluable job of transferring to intellectual activity some of the excitement and prestige usually monopolized by athletics. Nevertheless, when it places excessive emphasis on competition, debating can develop attitudes that hinder rather than help responsible communication.

Competitive debating puts the cart before the horse if it makes the debater look for evidence to fit his conclusion rather than for a conclusion to fit his evidence. *Discussion becomes unproductive if the participants decide beforehand not to change their minds.* At the same time, debating often puts a premium on mere verbal virtuosity. It may dazzle and overwhelm the listener instead of making him think.

Closely related to the spirit of debate is the promotional or advertising habit. We often find ourselves praising or attacking things while suspending our own independent judgment. Not only the debater but also the advertiser or the publicity agent may start with a ready-made conclusion. He may then put his resources of language, logic, knowledge, and imagination to work supporting it. The public-relations director of a college may be fully aware of the financial, organizational, and intellectual problems of education. In his official capacity, however, he may spend most of his time celebrating the virtues and achievements of his Alma Mater. A tourist may be quite critical of shortcomings of his countrymen when at home. Abroad, he will spend much of his time defending and praising his country.

Many essay contests invite the contestant to support a predetermined point of view. Suppose your instructor is informed of an essay contest offering prizes ranging from a $400 fall wardrobe to a $1,000 scholarship. The contestants are asked to write on "The Influence of Manufacturers' Brand Names on Better Retailing." Unless the little word *better* is left out, your instructor may hesitate to announce the contest in his classes. In effect, the student is promised $1,000 for eloquently supporting a foregone conclusion—namely, that the influence of brand names on retailing is to the good. There is an important difference between "Tell us *why* you liked our new product" and "Tell us *whether* you liked our new product." The second version treats you as a responsible adult entitled to his own choice.

Rationalization. The debater and the advertiser are sometimes accused of a lack of sincerity or integrity. But even when we are at our most sincere, we may follow a procedure very similar to theirs. If a question arises about an idea or an institution dear to us, few of us pause to re-examine or reassess its merits. Rather, we hurry to its defense. We put our brains to work finding arguments and evidence in its favor. Psychologists call this kind of mental activity **rationalization**. *Much of our so-called reasoning consists in the spontaneous defense of prejudices and preconceptions.*

When the issues under discussion are of great concern to us, rationalizations are hard to avoid. A mother whose child did poorly on an intelligence test is more likely to claim that the test is unreliable than a mother whose child did well. Such claims may be based on careful investigation, and the person who makes them may be ready to adjust his findings in the light of new evidence. Often, however, they are based on a desire for reassurance or self-justification. If so, they may keep us from looking for adequate solutions to important problems. A habit of praising and glorifying her child may keep a mother from taking the corrective steps necessary to prevent the child from becoming a failure. A habit of rationalizing his scholastic inadequacies may keep a student from finding out what is wrong and what he can do about it.

5. DEVELOPING HABITS OF STRAIGHT THINKING

Awareness of common logical errors is indispensable insurance against elementary blunders. However, when carried to excess, it may immobilize thought altogether. When a student first becomes aware of the imperfections of many familiar arguments, he may conclude that any idea he might adopt is bound to involve a logical flaw. Like a man finding himself on thin ice, he may refuse to move another step. He may decide that the safest course is not to commit himself, to suspend judgment on all issues that present a choice among several alternatives.

Such complete skepticism is of course impossible in everyday life. A businessman has to make decisions, even though his estimate of market conditions can never be absolutely foolproof. If his guesses are intelligent guesses, he will, with luck, be more often right than wrong. A voter can never be sure about the qualifications and intentions of a political candidate. He will nevertheless vote for the most attractive or the least objectionable one. In making up our minds, as in all other aspects of life, we can never eliminate error and chance. What we can do is to cultivate mental habits that make for truth and accuracy, not in each individual case, but in the long run and on the average.

Some of the habits that make for straight thinking may be summed up as follows:

(1) *Be prepared to change your mind.* Pursue possibly important questions, and examine possibly relevant evidence, even when they go counter to your original assumptions or your present tentative conclusions. When investigating any subject of importance, you are bound to discover things you did not know, problems you were not aware of.

(2) *Take your time in formulating conclusions.* A thoughtful person has explored a range of examples and evidence before formulating a carefully limited generalization. He develops his argument step by step, paying attention to the soundness of his assumptions and the validity of his inferences.

(3) *Distrust the simple answer.* Gross oversimplification is the stock in trade of the demagogue. Few problems in education or politics are limited and clear-cut enough to permit simple solutions. Few social or cultural ills can be cured by a single drastic remedy.

(4) *Examine your views for consistency.* Although a rational person may be slow to arrive at conclusions, he takes them seriously once he has adopted them. He does not make a generalization and a few minutes later contradict himself. If his salary is paid out of city taxes, he does not charge that city taxes are too high when he pays his taxes and complain that city taxes are too low when he picks up his paycheck. If you change your mind while writing, you will have to revise what you have already written to make sure there is no inconsistency. Do not claim on page 1 that the chief cause of highway accidents is lax law enforcement only to assert on page 3 that the chief cause of highway accidents is careless driving. Make clear from the beginning that there are several important causes and, if possible, show how they are related.

Absolute consistency is a quality of a calculating machine rather than of a mere human being. In your own writing, you will be able to move toward greater consistency and greater regard for the requirements of logic without much danger that you will go to superhuman extremes.

EXERCISES 5

A. What kind of evidence would you need to support the following generalizations? Point out generalizations that are difficult or impossible to support.

1. Women are poorer drivers than men.

2. Most high school graduates know little or nothing about the history of British rule in India.

3. Teen-agers smoke to prove that they are grown up and mature.

4. The quality of motion pictures put out by Hollywood producers has improved over the last five years.

5. The crime rate among Americans of Oriental descent is lower than among the rest of the population.

6. Businessmen tend to support the Republican party.

7. Grade schools used to be more effective in teaching reading.

8. College teachers are more impersonal than high school teachers.

9. Any condition that causes a child to be tense interferes with learning.

10. Americans form new friendships more easily than Europeans.

11. The American farmer is worse off than he was ten years ago.

12. Television has had a bad effect on the morals of children.

13. Capital punishment does not have a deterrent effect on crime.

14. A person who is hungry will do anything to obtain food.

15. Wives are never satisfied with their husbands' income.

B. Identify the logical shortcomings of the following arguments.

1. The establishment of a universal language is a difficult problem. Man has solved many other difficult problems, such as that of flight or of harnessing atomic energy. Therefore, man will succeed in establishing a universal language.

2. John Q. Doe is opposed to infant baptism. He must be an atheist.

3. George is above the national average in intelligence. He is below the national average in reading ability. Therefore, the school's system of teaching reading must be defective.

4. The X Company produces a battery additive. The additive has enjoyed a steady sale for many years. Therefore, the battery additive must be effective.

5. Neighbor A has had trouble with a Brand X washing machine. Neighbor B has had trouble with a Brand X washing machine. Obviously, Brand X washing machines tend to be defective.

6. College students are interested in learning all they can while in college. Unlike high school, college is not required by law; therefore,

a person who goes to college is going because he desires to further his education.

7. A white man is better than Africans, because he is a member of a superior race.

8. Last winter, Grandmother suffered from rheumatism. Her rheumatism disappeared after she started drinking rhubarb juice. Therefore, rhubarb juice is a remedy for rheumatism.

9. Today, columnist Y criticized the Democratic leadership in Congress. Columnist Y must be a Republican.

10. Last semester I disagreed with my history teacher's opinion of Thomas Jefferson. I received a failing grade in the course. The teacher failed me because I contradicted him.

11. A law is passed by the majority of the people before it becomes a law; therefore, everyone should obey the laws.

12. In periods of rapid expansion, the American economy gorges on time payments and capital investment. It needs to chew this cud sufficiently before it resumes eating. Therefore, recessions are a natural and organic part of the business cycle.

13. After two world wars, every American realizes what General Sherman meant when he said, "War is hell." I firmly believe that nobody in America desires a war. Therefore, the oil companies that are promoting a price war by selling gasoline at cut-rate prices are going against the desires of the American people.

14. Statistics are unreliable as a means of determining public opinion. After careful tabulation of the answers on more than 1,200 questionnaires, I have concluded that 70 per cent of those questioned felt that statistical opinion polls misrepresent public opinion.

15. Where there is smoke there is fire. If a public official comes under attack for stealing public funds, it is a good sign that some kind of wrongdoing has been committed. Officials accused of dishonesty should be removed from their jobs before they can do any further harm.

C. Point out the strengths or weaknesses of the logic employed in the following excerpts from newspaper columns, magazine articles, letters to the editors, congressional newsletters, and similar sources.

1. Every teacher should have previously served an internship as a house-to-house salesman, if only for six weeks. For salesmanship is much alike, whether of insurance or magazine subscriptions, or of ethical ideas from the pulpit, or of educational concepts from the schoolteacher's rostrum. Therefore, schools should stress former sales training on the part of new teachers as much as advanced degrees. For such salesmanship actually pays richer dividends in the classroom.

2. With her A.B. in hand, tomorrow's college graduate should be encouraged to enter a profession and to stick with it even if this involves postponing motherhood and eventually delegating some of its responsibilities. The delusion that every woman must be a chambermaid, cook, and nurse—in addition to any other work she may do—is archaic. It makes no more sense than insisting that a research chemist take time out to wash the test tubes and scrub the lab floor. Women, like men, should give their highest skills to a society which badly needs them.—Marion K. Sanders, "A Proposition for Women," *Harper's*

3. Many high schools have tried detaining students after school as a means of enforcing discipline. However, in deciding how effective detention is, educators might consider the questions suggested by the following syllogisms: Detention is implemented as a disciplinary measure to curtail offenses committed by chronic offenders. The chronic offender has little or no respect for the school and what the school attempts to do for him. Therefore, the discipline imposed by detention has little or no effect upon the chronic offender. Furthermore, the most effective punishment is direct punishment meted out nearest to the time an offense has been committed. Detention is delayed indirect punishment served at least a day or more after an offense has been committed. Therefore, detention is not effective.

4. Eighteen-year-olds should be allowed to vote. Take for example a young couple that married when they were about seventeen or eighteen. They should have some say about the political future of the country their children will grow up in. These young people have the right to want their children to live in a democratic country. They want each child to have the same freedoms and privileges that they themselves enjoy.

5. A biological axiom explains that progress is made only through differences. The breeders of race horses succeed only because some animals are born different from the ordinary. The same is true of roses or potatoes or grapefruit—or thinkers! If we all tend to think, or to appear to think, the same way, under compulsion or from any other motive, the laws determining intellectual evolution cease to operate. —Claude M. Fuess, "The Perils of Conformity," *Saturday Review*

6. Haven't we advanced farther and faster than any other nation in the past one hundred and eighty years? Isn't our standard of living the highest in the world? The answer is *yes,* even though every four years violent claims are made to the contrary, and disaster is foretold by one of our temporarily unseated politicians. Since we are governed under a two-party system and since we enjoy the highest standard of living under this system, it certainly follows that attempts to form a third major party in the United States should be discouraged.

7. A Democracy, unlike a Communist government, is only as strong as the combined *individual* strength of its people. Strength, like muscle, can be built only through exercise. Moral strength comes from the exercise of our religious and parental training through prayer and practice. Physical strength comes not from watching a steamshovel move dirt but from shoveling it ourselves. Strength of any kind is improved through exercise. Can anyone name one major proposal which has come before Congress this year that is not a transfer of responsibility from ourselves to federal government? Can anyone deny that today there are more individuals and local governments following the easy course to the federal treasury than ever before? I can't help feeling that we are growing soft and weak from lack of exercise.

8. We can do something about that all too prevalent attitude that intellectual honesty requires emphasis upon our national mistakes and downgrading our attributes. There are those who feel that promoting instinctive patriotism is intellectually dishonest. They contend that if Democracy is good, it should survive the injection of doubt. This may be true for those who possess mature judgment. Certainly any American has the right to question our system and the obligation to seek its improvement. But to think that a student, for example, has such judgment at the start of the learning process is to ignore psychological reality. A young mind must first be taught to believe in something before it can intelligently doubt. To stifle unquestioned pride in our heritage and love of our flag is to deprive this, the greatest of all nations, of men and women who will understand and urgently rededicate themselves to the ideals of Democracy.

D. Examine in detail several examples of weak logic that you have discovered in your own writing or in your own reading. Point out their shortcomings and explain how they might be revised.

E. State as fully as you can the hidden premises or unstated assumptions in a political speech, an editorial, or a letter to the editors of a newspaper or magazine.

F. How effective is the following student theme? How adequate is the writer's selection and interpretation of statistical material? To what extent are the writer's conclusions justified by the evidence? How effective are the organization and the over-all approach of the theme?

NO VACANCY

Last weekend, I went to a picnic with the girls from the women's co-op where I live. We were joined by the members of a newly formed men's co-op. We engaged in an impromptu football game and happily charred hot dogs and marshmallows. We finished the afternoon singing around a dying fire. The high point of the afternoon, for me, came when I did a vaudeville routine with one of the boys. The boy, by the way, is a Negro.

This fact was of no great interest to me until I chose to look into the attitude which college students in general have toward minority groups.

I made a personal survey of forty students at the college I attend and found that ninety per cent of them would theoretically live in a house with a member of a minority group. Three-fourths of those I questioned said they would share a room with a member of a minority group. Ninety-eight per cent said they would attend a party where members of minority groups were present. The same percentage said they had close friends who are members of minority groups. However, when I studied the results of a survey of one thousand students, which was compiled by a Student Housing Survey Committee last spring, I found the results were less favorable. According to the report of the committee, approximately one-third of the student body would refuse to share a room with a colored student and fourteen per cent would refuse to share a room with an Oriental.

The ladies, it seems, take top honors for prejudice. On the question "Would you share a room with a Negro girl?" more than forty per cent of the girls indicated they would refuse. Twenty per cent of the males said they would refuse to share a room with a Negro boy. The reason for the higher percentage of women students who would refuse may be that their parents usually take a more active part in choosing their housing accommodations than those of the men students. Even more of the house-holders who rent rooms to students said they would discriminate. Forty-eight per cent of them said they would refuse to rent rooms to members of racial minority groups.

According to the advisor of the College Religious Council, an attempt was made to have only non-segregated houses put on the approved housing list. This attempt failed because the housing office personnel stated that many students would be unable to live at school if only non-segregated houses were on the approved list. These students' parents would not permit their children to live with those of minority races.

In reading the "Letters to the Editors" column of the college daily, I found two students who felt that investigating housing conditions for minority groups was creating "much ado about nothing." However, after reading letters by Negro students describing their attempts to find housing, I feel that there has been too little ado. One Negro student describes how he and his wife looked at over a hundred apartments without finding one available to them. Their final solution to the problem was to live respectively in the YMCA and the YWCA. Another student states that he put a deposit down on an apartment and later received his check back in the mail with a note which he describes as saying, "It would be better for all concerned if you found someplace to live with your own kind."

I have learned of many other cases where students of minority groups have experienced much the same sort of rebuff. However, in social matters, most of the students I talked to seemed willing to accept minority group members as equals or at least near equals. Most of those I interviewed also seemed to feel that there is little need to worry about a racial problem at their college.

Before investigating this problem for myself, I too had the comfortable feeling that discrimination against races was something which was reserved for the Southland of the United States. Granted, the racial minority problem at colleges in other parts of the country is not as serious as it is in the South. However, it is foolish to believe that no problem exists. There is not much sense in acting like the little boy who breaks the cookie jar, then closes his eyes and pretends it never happened. As long as one-third of the students of a fairly representative college freely admit that they are racially prejudiced we can hardly boast of a truly democratic respect for all individuals, regardless of race, creed, or color.

What is the answer? It would be fine if we could make racial prejudice stop existing just by saying that it is not right. Obviously, this can not be done. For the present at least, we must face the fact that some students will discriminate. It is impossible to force them not to discriminate.

There is a practical solution, however, to one phase of this problem. Why not establish more cooperative houses for those students who are not prejudiced? This would give members of minority groups better housing than they now have. It would also help to improve racial understanding. I have found that when I learn to know a person as a person I tend to forget that he is a member of a racial group. This is, I think, a start in the right direction.

THEME TOPICS 5

A. Rely on inductive procedures in working out the following assignments:

1. Explain and support a general conclusion you have reached about a group of people or a type of person. For example, develop a generalization concerning first-generation Americans, students successful in campus social life or campus politics, art majors, or local politicians. Avoid stereotyping and hasty generalization.

2. It is sometimes charged that newspapers give a distorted picture of everyday life because the events of ordinary lives are not newsworthy. Examine the treatment of local news in several issues of your local newspaper to see whether or not it overemphasizes the unusual. Does it do justice to what is typical about life in your community?

3. Discuss what you consider the major reason for the popularity of a television show or a type of motion picture. Use detailed illustrations.

4. Americans are often said to think of themselves as open, generous, and motivated by sympathy for the underdog and a concern for justice. To what extent is this estimate of the American's image of himself borne out by current newspaper and magazine editorials, speeches, letters to the editors, and material from similar sources?

5. Explain and support a general conclusion you have reached about the status of racial or ethnic minority groups in your hometown or in the schools you attended before coming to college.

B. Rely on logical argument in supporting your answers to the following questions:

1. Should a newspaper represent the opinions of its journalists, its publishers, its advertisers, its readers, or the general public?

2. Should comic books be subject to censorship? (What are some of the things that make it difficult to find a generally acceptable answer to this question?)

3. Should a college provide facilities for political speeches and debates? If so, does the college have a right to bar allegedly undesirable or controversial speakers?

4. Should eighteen-year-olds have the right to vote? (How valid are some of the familiar arguments both for and against allowing them to vote?)

5. Should instructors in political science classes remain politically neutral? (Can or should a political science teacher maintain an objective or scientific attitude toward current social and political problems?)

6. Should state or federal authorities subsidize promising American artists? (What are the advantages and disadvantages of government support for artists?)

7. Should high positions in the federal government be entrusted to businessmen? (Should business executives be appointed in preference to people with other backgrounds? What would be the advantages or disadvantages of such a policy?)

8. Should socialist books be on the book shelves of public libraries? (What are the reasons for removing or retaining such books?)

6: PERSUASION

1. KNOWING YOUR READER

Not everyone who can draw sound conclusions from available evidence knows how to present those conclusions to advantage. An orator whose logic is good may be speaking before empty benches, while an orator whose logic is poor may be speaking to overflow crowds. A book developing important truths about American foreign policy may go unnoticed, while a book marred by superficialities and misconceptions may influence great masses of readers. Not everyone who thinks clearly and accurately knows how to persuade.

The art of persuasion is the art of making ideas, suggestions, and advice palatable. *A writer who wants to persuade must know his reader.* He must know what information he has to fill in, what prejudices he has to overcome, what arguments he has to refute. He must have some understanding of the reader's motives and preferences; he must anticipate emotional reactions. As far as possible, he will avoid arousing doubts and antagonisms not directly relevant to the issue under discussion.

The basic difficulty in persuasive writing is the temptation to use one's knowledge of the reader to manipulate the reader's reactions. Doing justice to one's subject is not always the most effective way of influencing an audience. As a result, instead of giving his honest convictions, and an accurate and fair account of his subject, the writer is tempted to put down whatever will have the desired effect. When a writer depends on his readers for a living, for influence, or for prestige, catering to their expectations may radically alter the quality of his writing. If his readers are unwilling to accept the unvarnished truth, he may feel compelled to gloss it over or evade it. If they are impatient with the ordinary, he may cater to their desire for the sensational. If a balanced account does not convince them of the superiority of his product or his point of view, he may resort to exaggeration and unfounded claims.

A writer must ask himself to what extent he will allow the needs of persuasion to override personal conviction. People have different views on what constitutes a permissible or necessary departure from strict truth. In our daily social contacts, we all recognize that some compliments and expressions of interest are polite rather than candid. In political life, many people reluctantly agree that a good candidate should not injure his prospects by an unbending refusal to humor the voters. Many businessmen feel that with the best of intentions they cannot substitute informative discussion of merchandise for high-pressure advertising.

From the point of view of effective writing, however, one general observation applies regardless of how strictly or how flexibly you interpret the requirement for candor and truthfulness. A critical, informed person will resent writing that has too obvious a design on the reader. A publisher will not make friends among educated readers by an advertisement like the following:

> First of all, you want the big new novels everyone's talking about. Deeply *emotional* novels that "carry you away" to the penthouse apartments and skyscraper office suites of Manhattan . . . the luxurious villas of ancient Rome . . . the meadows and gardens of England.

An experienced reader will resent the pretense to excitement, the calculating appeal to immature tastes, the overuse of attention-getting typographical devices.

You can antagonize critical readers simply by trying too hard to persuade. The more intelligent and the better informed your readers are, the more likely they are to feel insulted by techniques of persuasion that rely on ignorance or gullibility. They do not like to be wheedled, bullied, or threatened. An appeal to fear had better be well grounded. Flattery had better be subtle. Skillfully used, persuasive techniques can help your writing get all the attention and consideration it deserves. Used indiscriminately, they can make the reader dismiss your writing as brash and unscrupulous.

2. AVOIDING DISTORTION

Most writers feel that their ideas, no matter how meritorious, will not prosper unless they are dressed up to advantage. As a reader, it is part of your job to separate reliable information from the simplifications, exaggerations, and embellishments that an author uses to make you adopt his point of view. As a writer, it is part of your job to keep the same persuasive devices from discrediting you with readers who object to being misled.

Rhetorical Exaggeration. Children early learn to rely on exaggeration in trying to get the attention or assistance of adults. A little girl, pushed away from the drinking fountain by a boy she dislikes, may come crying to her teacher, trying to convince both the teacher and herself that she was badly hurt.

In trying to attract the attention of an audience, we find it difficult not to act like the little girl. We feel that the louder we shout, the easier it will be to convince our listeners that somebody did something wrong. We assume that the more solemnly we preach, the sooner our readers will feel that we have a point. Editorials, speeches, and advertisements are full of **superlatives**, expressions that make absolute a claim to superiority or singularity: "the biggest," "the best," "the greatest," "the most colossal," "the most unheard of," "the most inspiring"; "available now for the first time," "threatening us with utter extinction," "fatal to our most cherished institutions," "unparalleled in recorded history." Sooner or later we learn to discount at least some of these exaggerations.

The more experienced and the more intelligent an audience is, the more likely it is to look through the more obvious distortions. The real-estate salesman who uses terms like "tremendous values," "unique opportunities," and "once-in-a-lifetime savings" in advertising a housing development will ignore them when he himself buys a house. Instead, he will try to find out what grade of materials was used, whether the sewer assessments have been paid, and whether the neighborhood is going to be industrial, residential, or commercial. He will compile all the information which a customer needs to make an intelligent decision, but which an advertiser seldom provides.

Since in college you write for a relatively well-informed audience, you will do well to *purge your writing of exaggerated claims*. If you feel the need to blow off steam, do so in your first draft. Then, in revising it, trim down all statements that seem extravagant when read in a more sober mood:

EXAGGERATED:	The mayor's program for urban reconstruction is diametrically opposed to the best interests of the business community.
BALANCED:	The mayor's program for urban reconstruction does not pay sufficient attention to the interests of downtown businessmen.
EXAGGERATED:	The bald truth is that railroads are being starved to death through government regulation.
BALANCED:	The railroads lack adequate funds for modernization and expansion because of the government's failure to approve higher rates.
EXAGGERATED:	The American Aspirin Company is gratified to announce the climax of its relentless search for the absolute truth about pain relief.
BALANCED:	The American Aspirin Company is gratified to announce a number of new findings about pain relief.

Slanting. Though parallel in effect to exaggeration, **slanting** is more subtle in method. A writer can slant his material by consistently selecting from several equally true statements the ones most favorable to his cause. A lawyer defending his client may describe him as a veteran, a home owner, and a father of three children. A lawyer representing the plaintiff may describe the same man as an ex-convict, a man twice divorced, and a heavy drinker. Both descriptions may be quite truthful, but each creates an entirely different picture.

In persuasive writing, a slanted selection of evidence may make the reader draw conclusions not justified by the facts known to the writer. Such slanting is hard to detect and hard to resist. Its insincerity or inaccuracy lies not in what the writer says but in what he omits. Thus, an article about a college campus may describe expensive modern classroom buildings and ignore the temporary wooden structures around the corner. The article may be quite factual in what it does describe; it just happens to create a wrong impression.

Parallel in effect is verbal slanting, illustrated in the familiar example of the pessimist, who calls a bottle half empty, and the optimist, who calls it half full. Verbal slanting helps steer the reader's reactions in much effective writing:

> Enterprising shopping centers are setting up day nurseries. So are bowling alleys. This gives the nation's ten million *female bowlers* a considerable edge over the seven million *working mothers.*—Marion K. Sanders, "A Proposition for Women," *Harper's*

This passage basically appeals to a sense of fairness, the feeling that a mother who works should enjoy at least the same privileges as a mother who is free to pursue sports or entertainment. In an impartial examination of the issue, however, the two groups of women would have to be described either as *"female bowlers"* and *"female workers"* or as "bowling *mothers"* and "working *mothers."*

Similar kinds of slanting are possible in the use of analogies and figurative language. A writer may wish to show that the aim of education is not acquiring knowledge but learning how to think. He may say that education is not to be compared to the filling up of an empty pot but rather to the lighting of a fire. A pot is something banal and profoundly uninteresting, whereas a fire is bright, alive, and intriguing. As a result, the comparison, though apt, is likely to prejudge the question of how much knowledge a student needs in order to have something to think *about.*

Like exaggeration, *slanting ceases to persuade as soon as it becomes obvious.* In attacking the dangers of one-man rule, do not limit your examples to notorious tyrants and demagogues. If your reader thinks of the less evil examples first, you have put him in the position of attorney for the defense. In using comparisons and figures of speech, try to keep your reader from saying "Yes, but . . ."

Appeals to Emotion. The heightening achieved through exaggeration and slanting makes it possible for the persuasive writer to release powerful emotions. Admiration, love, joy, and fear are typically our response to an overwhelming impression, a clear-cut situation, a drastic turn of events. A writer who wants to move men to action will often through simplification appeal to their passions rather than to reason. Passionate appeals can move men toward decision in times of crisis; they can strengthen morale in times of danger. Like Thomas Paine in "The American Crisis," a writer may appeal to love of freedom and fear of oppression, to the desire for glory and fear of infamy, to love of country and hatred of its enemies:

> The summer soldier and the sunshine patriot will, in this crisis, shrink from the service of his country; but he that stands it NOW, deserves the love and thanks of man and woman. Tyranny, like hell, is not easily conquered; yet we have this consolation with us, that the harder the conflict, the more glorious the triumph. What we obtain too cheap, we esteem too lightly: 'tis dearness only that gives everything its value. Heaven knows how to put a proper price upon its good; and it would be strange indeed, if so celestial an article as FREEDOM should not be highly rated.

The great power such appeals can exercise invites abuse. Every day we hear appeals to our love of freedom that are designed to promote someone's private profit or ulterior purpose. But even when employed in good faith, appeals to emotion tend to prejudge issues; they interfere with the kind of inquiry on which sound decisions must be based even in times of stress. Learn to recognize some of the more commonly abused emotional appeals:

(1) *Beware of responding to flattery, and beware of substituting flattery for argument in your own writing.* Advertisers often work with statements like "Women know values," "Discriminating buyers prefer Lusterol," "Men of distinction drink Sunlight soda water." Such statements are not well-deserved recognition of discriminating customers but an attempt to ensnare undiscriminating ones. Political candidates assure the public that they have "faith in the intelligence of the American people." Such assurances flatter the voter, but they do not help him decide whether the candidate's program is sound.

(2) *Be skeptical of appeals to fear, and hesitate to employ them to sway the reader toward your way of thinking.* Some people represent every minor departure from their own views as a national disaster. Too often and too rashly they predict runaway inflation, large-scale depression, or totalitarian tyranny. As their audience learns to disregard their shouts of alarm, they may find their warnings ignored not only when they are inappropriate but also in times of real danger or distress.

(3) *Do not cheapen such ideals as love of country by invoking them in support of every minor project or conviction.* A pamphlet that praises the use of phonics in the teaching of reading (as opposed to the "whole-word" method) as part of a "soundly American" education (as opposed to "education for socialism") shows that the author lacks an elementary sense of proportion and responsibility.

These warnings are not meant to imply that all your writing should be coldly unemotional. They are designed to make you guard against appealing to emotions that keep your reader from making responsible decisions. As one authority on logic observed,

> It would be a mistake to condemn, or even to mistrust, all discourse that appeals to our emotions. A statement can arouse emotions and still be true. Some facts are delightful and some are damnable. But to get at the truth about anything you have to do something more than feel strongly about it. And that is why it is necessary to recognize these emotional appeals. For if they do not paralyze clear thinking, they make it very difficult. As the immortal John J. McGraw (who was occasionally known to take offense at umpires' rulings during the thirty years he managed the Giants) once remarked, "When a man sees red, it's not likely he sees much of anything else."—Monroe C. Beardsley, *Thinking Straight*

Evading the Issue. The skilled controversialist tends to shift ground whenever hard pressed. In a general discussion of government subsidies to farmers, the subsidies granted commercial airlines can serve as a basis for comparison. But suppose the discussion has been narrowed to the effect of government subsidies on the production of surplus crops. In that case, the person who suddenly asks "But what about the airlines?" is evading the issue.

One popular technique for evading the issue is the argument **ad hominem**, directed "at the person." It diverts attention from the merits of ideas to the merits of their advocates. Instead of refuting an economist's analysis of economic trends, his opponents may manage to let us know that his wife is suing him for divorce or that his brother recently failed in business. Resorting to such tactics is the persuasive writer's equivalent of hitting below the belt.

In evaluating issues and ideas, distrust your likes and dislikes for the personalities who represent them. You may be impressed by pictures of a political candidate rushing to the sickbed of his father or playing baseball with his sons. These impressions do not illuminate the candidate's qualifications for public office. At any rate, your liking or admiration of the person will not persuade a critical audience of the soundness of his program. If a man's appearance, background, or conduct is relevant to a discussion of his views, be prepared to explain the connection in detail.

3. THE POWER OF EMOTIVE LANGUAGE

Suppose that in writing a theme you have made the point that majority rule or fraternity hazing is a tradition. You can now continue, "I approve of this tradition" or "I disapprove of this tradition." Immediately, you will have to show *why* you approve or disapprove of it. On the other hand, you may want your reader to share your approval or disapproval without your examining the issue on its merits. You may then act as though the very fact that majority rule is a tradition decides whether or not the reader should approve of it. You will say, "Majority rule is *a time-honored tradition,*" if you favor it. You will say, "Majority rule is *just a tradition,*" if you are opposed to it. This procedure may save you the trouble of starting a long argument—unless an alert reader asks, "How exactly does time honor?" or "Why did you use the word *just* in this sentence?"

Part of the secret of persuasive writing is skillful use of language—often in ways of which the reader is unaware. Language serves other functions besides explicit statement. While seeming to convey information, language can at the same time convey the writer's preferences and dislikes. The propagandist or the advertiser relies heavily on **emotive language**, language making extensive use of words charged with attitudes and emotions. Emotive language is effective as a means of persuasion because it suggests attitudes without submitting them to critical examination. *The reader who wants to make up his own mind must learn to distinguish information and argument from suggested attitudes.*

Tracing the attitudes and judgments of an author is relatively easy when he expresses them in belittling or praising modifiers. As an alert reader, you should note such modifiers as *merely, finally, great, notorious, biased, honest,* or *wholesome.* These are like labels, telling you "This I like," "This I don't like," "This I admire," "This I am trying to make ridiculous," or "This I think came too late to do any good." Once you become sensitive to such labels, you will expect the author to explain and defend them. When he speaks of a "wholesome spirit of competition," you will examine the appropriateness of the label by asking, "When, where, how, why, and for whom is it wholesome?" When he speaks of a college heavyweight champion as a "fine young man," you will ask, "Which of his qualities or achievements do you think highly of, and by what standards do you judge them?"

Denotation and Connotation.[1] The very words used to name an object, describe an event, or paraphrase an idea may be colored by the writer's or the speaker's attitudes. Pairs like *cur* and *man's best friend, politician* and *statesman, war hero* and *militarist* can be applied to the same individual by different writers or speakers. In discussing the meaning of the words concerned, we can therefore separate the hard-core, objective meaning from that part of the meaning which expresses the attitudes, preferences, or emotions of the person who uses them. The objective meaning of a word is often called its **denotation**. The attitude or emotion it suggests is often called its **connotation**. While the denotation of both *cur* and *man's best friend* may simply be "dog," *cur* has unfavorable or derogatory connotations, *man's best friend* has flattering or complimentary connotations. *A difference in connotation is typically a difference in the attitude of the observer rather than in the nature of the thing observed.*

The power of words to suggest varying attitudes with a minimum of explicit statement is most obvious in fields like politics, where atti-

[1] See also D 1b.

tudes differ widely. When a public official is accused of dishonesty, his opponents say that he has been "exposed," while his friends say that he has been "smeared." When the same official is cleared for lack of sufficient evidence, his opponents say that he has been "whitewashed," while his friends say that he has been "vindicated." To indicate that its foreign policy is changing, the administration calls it "dynamic" and "alert," whereas its political opponents call it "aimless" and "confused."

From the broad range of possible terms, the political propagandist will select those with either favorable or unfavorable connotations. He knows that most of us associate the word *statesman* with public-spirited wisdom and the word *politician* with crafty and often self-seeking manipulation. *Bureaucrat* makes us think of red tape and of incompetent officeholders meddling with the public's business; *public servant* makes us think of somebody looking out after our own best interests. In a discussion of a road-building program, the phrase *government funds* makes us think that we are getting something for nothing, while the phrase *taxpayers' money* makes us feel that the money is coming out of our own pockets. We feel encouraged when a proposal for disarmament is called a "hope for a better future"; we shrink from it if it is called "wishful thinking."

Some words are so strongly charged as to evoke an almost automatic response. If a writer refers to the killing of John Doe as the "murder" of John Doe, the word *murder* will cause an almost automatic reaction of horror, disgust, and violent disapproval. If he speaks of the "execution" of John Doe, the killing will sound respectable and official. If he refers to it as "administration of justice," most readers will feel reassured. To "liquidate" one's political opposition makes killing sound businesslike and scientific; "exterminate" or "eradicate" makes it sound as though one were getting rid of vermin. Goebbels, minister for propaganda under Hitler, made the killing of political prisoners sound reassuring by announcing that certain elements had been "rendered harmless."

Interpreting Emotive Language. Just as it is in the interest of the campaign manager and of the public-relations expert to exploit emotive language, so it is in your interest as a reader to recognize and to make allowance for it. To maintain a clear view of people and events, you need to track down the objective meaning of words and to separate it from the attitudes and emotions that the words imply. For instance, the words *constitution* and *constitutional* have a strong emotional coloring. They suggest pride, approval, assurance that things are regulated for the best. A careful reader will not let this feeling of approval spill over into his attitude toward provisions of a state constitution that were adopted in a spirit of partisan spite. The mere fact that a provision is in a constitution does not make that provision wise or just. *Alien, foreigner,* and *un-American* may evoke suspicion and uneasiness; they may inspire a compensating eagerness to be kind, understanding, unprejudiced. However, they often need to be treated as dispassionately as "originating outside the continental United States" or "coming from another part of the world."

You will find that it is not easy to brake your impulse to cheer an idea when it is stated in flattering terms and to boo it when it is stated in unflattering ones. One possible precaution is practice in matching corresponding complimentary and derogatory terms in order to neutralize whatever unexamined attitudes they may suggest. For instance, examine the relationship between alternative terms describing familiar human qualities: *courageous—reckless; loyal—servile; tolerant—indiscriminate; devout—sanctimonious; realistic—cynical.* Or pair the "plus words" and the "minus words" for familiar political ideas: *democracy—mob rule; leader—demagogue; freedom fighter—subversive; conciliation—appeasement; grant-in-aid—handout.* Such pairing of related terms, like the confrontation of contradictory witnesses, will remind you of your responsibility to draw your own conclusions.

Another helpful precaution is to chart the emotive expressions typical of a writer in order to prevent them from subtly subverting your own better judgment. Many journalists and public figures habitually use one set of terms when reporting the activities of their favorite "statesman," another set of terms when reporting those of an opposition "politician." Statesman knows, understands, is aware of, is firmly convinced; Politician guesses, theorizes, speculates, or suspects. Statesman gravely points out, forthrightly declares, bluntly states, eloquently sets forth; Politician excitedly sputters, theatrically proclaims, brazenly alleges, or stridently asserts. Statesman consults with his advisers, reaffirms basic convictions, makes decisions, and finds solutions; Politician listens to his cronies, hunts for issues, jumps to conclusions, and gets bright ideas. Statesman presents a sound program, guards basic rights, and works for the good of the nation; Politician indulges in Utopian dreams, caters to special interests, and plays politics. Statesman shows his skill in facing the realities of political life; Politician demonstrates his political deviousness and lack of candor. When exposed to such consistent verbal slanting, even an alert reader will have to remind himself that the difference between Statesman and Politician may be all in the words of the reporter.

Once you learn to make allowance for it, emotive language will cease to mislead and become instructive instead. *When skillfully interpreted, emotive language provides valuable clues to preferences and commitments that a writer does not openly admit.* A man who represents himself as an impartial observer will often reveal his sympathies and affiliations by the words he uses to identify issues and personalities. An editorial writer who speaks of "labor strongmen," "labor politicians," and "union bosses" is not likely to be a champion of organized labor. The parent who refers to "warming a youngster's tail" is less likely to be a foe of corporal punishment than the parent who refers to "beatings administered to children."

Changes in vocabulary are often a symptom of changes in attitude. Changing moral standards are reflected in gradual shifts from *vicious* to *antisocial* to *maladjusted;* from *perversion* to *abnormality* to *deviation;* from *modest* to *shy* to *inhibited.* Paying attention to the values implied in such words is one way of reading between the lines.

Variable Connotations. In your writing, emotive language will be as much of a problem as in your reading. The connotations of words are more unstable and more unpredictable than their denotations. *A word may have different associations for different readers.* To some readers, the term *progressive* suggests an outlook in keeping with the demands of the modern world; to others, it suggests a tendency toward newfangled ideas and addle-headed schemes. If your reader's attitudes are different from yours, emotive language may produce a short circuit rather than assent.

This power of emotive language to short-circuit discussion is most obvious with words expressing strong feelings of disapproval and contempt. In moments of emotional stress, we are tempted to employ **invective**, more popularly known as name-calling or abuse. If you talk about "dyed-in-the-wool reactionaries," conservative members of your audience might reconsider some of their conservative ideas. More likely, their ideas will be so dear to them that they will feel personally insulted. Even those who are *not* conservative may not be impressed. Terms like *reactionary, radical, fascist,* and *communist* have so often been used as ignorant abuse that they have lost their power to influence a thoughtful reader.

Invective, like swearing, provides an outlet for emotional tensions. When we are angry at motorists who dump eggshells, beer cans, and waste paper along scenic highways, we derive strong satisfaction from an article attacking "rampant slobbism," "careless boobs," and the "spreading desecration of the American landscape." Even such an article, however, is likely to owe its more lasting effects not to invective but to more substantial means of persuasion. Compare the following two passages by the same writer:

> . . . Acquisition of new parkland has not kept pace with population growth, and in many cities the planners have been *stealing* land from existing parks for projects with higher priority, such as superhighways and parking lots. The newer the metropolitan area, the more likely it is to be short of a *decent minimum* of greenery. I suppose Los Angeles has a park somewhere, but I have never seen it.

> . . . Much of Denver's beauty comes from trees that were planted and parks that were established more than forty years ago. I would say, on the basis of having very recently viewed some of the jam-packed, look-alike houses now springing up on the north side of Denver, that *not much is being done to make the city beautiful forty years hence.*—Vance Packard, "America the Beautiful—and Its Desecraters," *Atlantic*

In the first passage, the term *steal* will strike as unfair many people who are aware of the conflicting pressures and interests that planning commissions must reconcile. The second passage, by contrast, does without abusive language; instead, it effectively appeals to a sense of obligation that many readers will share: We enjoy the fruits of the investments by earlier generations, and we should make similar investments to benefit our children and grandchildren.

Need for Objective Terms. Even when you feel strongly about a subject, your readers will want to feel that you respect their judgment enough to give them a chance to make up their own minds. They will welcome emotive language that helps transform a dry treatise into a lively and emphatic piece of writing. They will respect emotive language that is the sincere expression of strong convictions. But they will resent emotive language if you consistently use it to prejudge issues and to prevent rational appraisal.

If you are interested in a meeting of minds, *develop the habit of toning down the emotional implications of the language you employ.* You can often keep a discussion focused on the issues at stake by substituting neutral terms for words that are complimentary or derogatory. For instance, you can learn to keep irrelevant associations out of references to other people by studying alternatives like the following:

COMPLIMENTARY	DEROGATORY	NEUTRAL
public servant	bureaucrat	government employee
financier	speculator	investor
law officer	cop	policeman
legislative consultant	lobbyist	spokesman of group interests
stage personality	ham	actor
manufacturer's representative	huckster	salesman
labor leader	union boss	union official
captain of industry	tycoon	successful businessman
investigator	spy	detective
captive	jailbird	prisoner

Even a writer who is trying to present an objective argument or a scientific report sometimes has trouble with emotionally weighted words. A psychologist describing typical or frequent behavior may inadvertently use terms which, contrary to his intention, suggest approval or dislike. *Healthy* would imply strong approval; *normal* would be taken to imply approval by many readers; *mediocre* sounds negative and implies that to be average is not good enough. However, the systematic procedure and the careful attention to detail of a scientist's report can do much to cool off emotions that a word would ordinarily arouse. Similarly, a dignified and objective context can do much to neutralize the derogatory implications of *politician, socialism, lobbyist,* or *vagrant.* A word that can be used to incite violent disapproval may in a different context be ironic, neutral, or only mildly derogatory. Even a word suggesting strong feelings may be fully justified by the evidence or by the explanations that accompany it.

4. THE POSSIBILITIES OF SUGGESTION

Emotive language makes people respond to unexamined, almost automatic associations. It conveys praise and blame in such an indirect way that they become hard to evaluate and to challenge. Reliance on association and indirectness is also characteristic of other common means of persuasion.

Illogical Associations. A writer often finds it easier to connect people and ideas with the thought of something undesirable than to show what is wrong with them. He knows how easily we form unconscious associations. For instance, we see a Western in which the villain wears a mustache. We read a novel about a gambler who wears a mustache. We see pictures of Adolf Hitler wearing a mustache. Then, a family moves in next door, and the new neighbor turns out to be wearing a mustache. We suddenly have the uncomfortable feeling that the man is a villain. The mustache, through no fault of its own, has become a symbol of villainy.

Many writers make use of such symbols of villainy and heroism, pain and pleasure, ugliness and beauty to influence their readers. Writing a commercial for a breakfast cereal, they associate the product in the customer's mind with a popular athlete. Advertising a deodorant, they associate it with domestic bliss.

Two other common sources of favorable associations are the prestige of science and loyalty to country. Magazine advertisements often use scientific-sounding terms and pictures of white-clad people working in laboratories. Few of these advertisements give a scientific evaluation of the product being advertised. Their purpose is to associate a commercial product with qualities characteristic of noncommercial research: objectivity, dedication to human welfare, amazing discoveries. Political candidates and spokesmen for political organizations link their proposals with symbols of patriotism: the Pilgrims, George Washington, Thomas Jefferson, Abraham Lincoln.

It is of course possible that a speaker who quotes Thomas Jefferson has studied Jefferson's life and works and is convinced that Jefferson's ideas are relevant to twentieth-century problems. But obviously some orators who refer to Jefferson in their speeches have never read him. Many people associate with great men not to profit from their wisdom but to borrow from their prestige. However, a critical reader is not easily impressed by references to famous or learned authorities. He knows that Lincoln's name, for instance, has been invoked in support of different and mutually contradictory programs.

In trying to bolster your own ideas, *use references to people widely respected or admired not as evidence that your ideas are true but as evidence that they are worthy of consideration.* In a paper attacking censorship, you may well wish to point out that the President of the United States said on such and such an occasion that censorship is bad in principle. This shows that the President agrees with you, but it does not show that he is right. You will still have to present arguments against censorship, whether they be the President's or your own.

Indirectness. By relying on emotive language and on subconscious associations, a writer can avoid explicit assertion and thus protect himself against explicit criticism and refutation. As a result, indirectness has become second nature to many people and, like the protective coloring of the chameleon, may be used without malice. *Much use of language exploits the difference between statement and implication.* Suppose a senator calls an enterprise undertaken by the Secretary-General of the United Nations "a failure by any standards that Americans can use." This statement implies that those who consider the enterprise a success are not good solid Americans. Mentioning two things together can suggest a causal relationship: "He is Irish and drinks a great deal" (because he is Irish?). The mere fact that something is mentioned at all can suggest that it is newsworthy. "Salvex is now 100 per cent pure" suggests that purity is important. "Salvex now contains *three* active ingredients" suggests that impurity is important.

Implications can cause bad feelings because the author is usually ready to accept responsibility for what he states but not for what he suggests. The investigator who admonishes a witness to tell the truth seldom admits that he is trying to make the witness look like a liar. The congressman who says "Most college professors are loyal, competent Americans" is seldom prepared to substantiate charges against that minority of college professors who, by implication, are disloyal and incompetent. Suggestion thus becomes **innuendo**, a means of insinuating things that the writer or the speaker is unable and unwilling to defend.

Implied charges of this kind are often left deliberately vague, so that the victim has little chance to refute them. "Scientist So-and-So associated with communists" might conceivably damage So-and-So's career and reputation. However, it may mean many different things: He may have met a communist or two at a cocktail party. He may have had long arguments with communist fellow scientists. He may have associated with communists in planning legal activities, such as fund raising, strikes, or propaganda campaigns. He may have associated with them in planning illegal activities, such as revolution or espionage.

The hints a writer throws out vary in subtlety. For instance, an editorial writer may have been blaming the opposition party for being too friendly toward a foreign power. His last sentence reads, "If we listen to these people, we may be engulfed by disaster, without so much as a Trojan horse for a souvenir." The **allusion** to a "Trojan horse" is designed to make you remember that in the war against Troy the Trojans were tricked into dragging into the city a huge wooden horse left by the Greeks outside the city walls. At night, Greek soldiers hidden in the horse emerged as a fifth column, opened the city gates, and made possible the destruction of Troy by the rest of the Greek army. "Who," you ask, "are the enemy soldiers, the enemy's fifth column, in the editorial I just read?" That's easy. They are the people in the political party attacked by the writer. Not that he would say such a thing outright. Nevertheless, the idea is there, floating between the lines, seeping into the minds of unwary readers.

Rhetorical Questions. Special instances of the possibilities of suggestion are **rhetorical questions**, questions with built-in answers. *A rhetorical question makes it sound as though the decision is left up to the reader, while at the same time it is worded in such a way that only one answer is possible.* "Would you deprive your wife of a convenience that is essential to her health and peace of mind?" "Would you recommend a teacher who doesn't care whether his students succeed or fail?" It is hard to answer "yes" to such questions. If you answer "no," however, it sounds as though the responsibility for the point of view being developed is just as much yours as the writer's.

An occasional rhetorical question can serve to dramatize an important point. However, when rhetorical questions are used to cover up a scarcity of good arguments, they easily become annoying. Do not try to settle difficult issues by simply inquiring: "If the government can send an eighteen-year-old boy to war, can it deprive him of the right to vote?" or "Can a law that goes against the desires of millions of citizens be called just and fair?" An impatient reader is likely to reply: "Well, can it? If not, why not?"

5. PERSUADING THE CRITICAL READER

Many of the most familiar techniques of persuasion have overtones of deception or insincerity. As a result, they easily antagonize thoughtful readers. The writer who values the respect of the more critical members of his audience will do well to follow the example of the old-fashioned merchant who relies less on advertising than on the quality of his product. The critical reader will prefer a sound if unspectacular paper to a flashy and irresponsible one. Nevertheless, of two equally sound and responsible papers, he is likely to prefer the one that is more persuasively written.

Effective persuasion, like other aspects of effective writing, is as much a result of practice and experiment as it is of following a set of specific instructions. However, in revising a persuasive paper, you might make use of a check list summarizing the essential features of persuasive writing somewhat as follows:

(1) *Consideration for the reader's background, interests, and preferences.* A policeman's view of people living in slums is likely to differ

from that of a social worker. A businessman's view of taxes differs from that of a city employee. Where possible, a persuasive writer takes such differences into account. He shows his willingness to enter the reader's frame of reference—not by adopting the reader's opinions, but by showing that he is aware of them and that he is taking them seriously.

(2) *Full discussion of whatever is startling, controversial, or difficult.* A writer throwing out a multitude of unexpected or original ideas can stir up discussion, suggest possibilities, impress his readers. He seldom produces lasting conviction. To be effective, persuasion needs to concentrate on driving home one major point at a time.

(3) *Willingness to identify doubtful conclusions and open questions.* A writer addressing critical readers weakens his position by pretending to omniscience. He should not feel obligated to have a ready answer on every aspect of a complicated problem. If conflicting evidence prevents clear-cut conclusions, he should say so.

(4) *Serious consideration of possible objections.* To many readers, a writer's handling of adverse evidence is a touchstone of his sincerity and competence. He should show that he has thought of possible objections and has found a satisfactory way of dealing with them. By taking this precaution, he makes it harder for the reader to resist his arguments and for the critic to find fault with them.

(5) *Full and impartial discussion of the testimony of reputable and disinterested authorities.* Readers become suspicious when a writer pretends that he is the first one who has anything worthwhile to say on a subject. Though necessarily varying in extent with the scope of a given paper, the consideration of relevant testimony by important authorities gives the writer an opportunity to demonstrate his knowledge of the subject as well as his open-mindedness and fairness.

EXERCISES 6

A. Examine the differences in attitude suggested by the changes in the wording of the following passages.

1. Jones was a portly man with a healthy glow in his cheeks.
   Jones was a stout man with a ruddy complexion.
   Jones was a pudgy man with a complexion like a boiled lobster.

2. Last night, vandals defaced a patriotic monument by smearing yellow paint over a statue of the Father of Our Country.
   Some youngsters out for a lark last night painted a yellow mustache on a weather-beaten statue of George Washington.

3. Simon withdrew from college because he had difficulty keeping up with the pressure of college work.
Simon flunked out of school because he was unable to do the assignments.
After one semester on probation, Simon dropped out of college.

4. An economy-minded legislature has called a halt to additional spending.
A penny-pinching legislature has refused to appropriate adequate funds.
The legislature has cut the budget submitted by the governor by approximately 3 per cent.

5. John studies little and often quarrels with his classmates.
John needs to improve his study habits and his relations with other children.
John, in addition to being lazy, is a constant troublemaker.

6. Former prisoners were continually spied upon even after their return to civilian life.
Ex-convicts were kept under surveillance after their release from penal institutions.
Criminals were carefully watched as a potential menace to society.

7. Her father was unemployed and received relief payments from the County Welfare Department.
Instead of working, her father lived on goverment handouts.
Her father was out of work and had to accept help from the county.

8. The school board fired Mr. Smith for insubordination.
The school board dismissed Mr. Smith for refusing to answer questions about his home life.
The school board deprived Mr. Smith of his job for resisting their attempts to pry into his private affairs.

9. The pollsters concluded that the public is fed up with oversized cars.
Of 3,000 persons interviewed, 57 per cent felt that this year's models are too large.
The survey indicated a trend toward customer preference for more compact cars.

10. The governor made an exception to his principle of official rectitude by allowing John Smith to continue in office.
The governor compromised standards of official integrity by condoning John Smith's misconduct.
The governor refused to turn his back on a trusted subordinate involved in legal difficulties.

B. The following passage is addressed by Don Juan to the Devil in Act III of George Bernard Shaw's *Man and Superman.* Explore as fully as you can the common core and the contrasting connotations of each pair of words. Which words have unfavorable connotations for Shaw (or Don Juan) but favorable connotations for you, and vice versa? How do you explain the difference? To judge from the description here provided, who are the Devil's friends?

Pooh! Why should I be civil to them or to you? In this Palace of Lies a truth or two will not hurt you. Your friends are all the dullest dogs I know. They are not beautiful: they are only decorated. They are not clean: they are only shaved and starched. They are not dignified: they are only fashionably dressed. They are not educated: they are only college passmen. They are not religious: they are only pew-renters. They are not moral: they are only conventional. They are not virtuous: they are only cowardly. They are not even vicious: they are only "frail." They are not artistic: they are only lascivious. They are not prosperous: they are only rich. They are not loyal, they are only servile; not dutiful, only sheepish; not public spirited, only patriotic; not courageous, only quarrelsome; not determined, only obstinate; not masterful, only domineering; not self-controlled, only obtuse; not self-respecting, only vain; not kind, only sentimental; not social, only gregarious; not considerate, only polite; not intelligent, only opinionated; not progressive, only factious; not imaginative, only superstitious; not just, only vindictive; not generous, only propitiatory; not disciplined, only cowed; and not truthful at all: liars every one of them, to the very backbone of their souls.

C. Examine and evaluate the techniques of persuasion used in the following selections. Pay special attention to the use of emotive language.

1. The editorial policy of the campus daily seems to be directed by a Mid-Victorian Sunday school teacher with an inferiority complex. As a result, this chicken-hearted, lily-livered, weak-minded, professor-parroting, know-nothing, do-nothing, say-nothing fish wrapper refuses to take a stand on anything (assuming that it is capable of such). Any news with the magic word "instructor" in it gets top coverage, while other news, no matter how important, is put on the back page under the obituaries. Why this lack of backbone? Is it because the editors do not realize that the world has changed since 1870, and that tomatoes aren't really poisonous? Open up your eyes, student journalists of the Daily! It's hard to see unless you do.

2. Heywood Broun once said, "A case of sorts could be made for censorship if you imagine the job being administered by the wisest man in the world." The extent to which American censors fall short of this standard can be partially indicated by a look at the cross-examination of Police Captain J. Ignatius Sheehan in the case of "The Game of Love," as reported in *Chicago* for February, 1956. At that time it was Sheehan's function, assisted by five widows of police offi-

cers, to decide what the citizens of Chicago should see or hear on the picture screen. Here are some excerpts from the cross-examination:

Q. Have you taken any courses subsequent to your high school?
A. No, sir.
Q. How many literature courses did you have during high school?
A. I don't remember.
Q. How many books on an average do you read a year? . . . A dozen, two dozen?
A. No.
Q. It is less than that?
A. Yes.
Q. How many plays do you attend each year?
A. Very few.
Q. Would you say one or two?
A. No.
Q. . . . Do you attend the art exhibits in Chicago?
A. No.
Q. Do you read the book review section of . . . any newspapers?
A. No, sir.
Q. Are the members of the board required to have any special qualifications?
A. No, sir.
Q. Are any of them writers or recognized in other forms of art?
A. I wouldn't know.
Q. . . . Do any of them have any special literary qualifications?
A. I wouldn't know. . . .
Q. . . . In the course of events is the producer of the film ever called in to explain ambiguities in the film?
A. No, sir.
Q. Is the distributor ever called in?
A. No, sir.
Q. Are other people's views invited, such as drama critics or movie reviewers or writers or artists . . . ? Or are they ever asked to comment on the film before the censor board makes its decision?
A. No, sir.—Arthur Mayer, "How Much Can the Movies Say?" *Saturday Review*

3. Business colleges deserve far more praise than they have thus far received in American education, for they operate on the eminently practical theme that colleges should be able to pay their own way. Business colleges thus do not beg for money from state legislatures. Nor do they panhandle from alumni and big business corporations each June for funds to bail them out of their red ink. Furthermore, they practicalize education, and their pupils are sufficiently adult to glean all they can of such vital teaching. American liberal arts education is still far too impractical. But business colleges get down to brass tacks and also teach students a greater respect for our American free enterprise system.

4. Down the aisles of the supermarket—the soups, the cars, the dog food, the bras, the cigarettes, the beers, and the wienies—*Life* pushes its cart of Moral and Spiritual Values, nudging its customers to lift their eyes to the hills while they reach for a Pepsi. As *Life* initiates them into the majesties of Rembrandt and the immortal attributes of art and beauty, it subjects them to a graphic nightmare of crass layouts of a blaring and brazen carnival of sales. As it urges Americans to think, to discriminate, to improve, as it appeals to the national intelligence, it permits this same intelligence to be abused week after week and page after page by banal and blatant appeals to the purse. As it claims to "strengthen *Life's* graphic presentation"— and it did indeed make a vain attempt in recent months to keep "islands" of editorial matter intact—it still seems unable to stem an ever-increasing encroachment of advertising matter that makes the magazine, in fact, a graphic mess.—Marya Mannes, "The Intruders," *The Reporter*

5. Deficit financing never accords with the public weal. Government spending in excess of tax revenues and the resulting inflation both indicate either ignorance or neglect of duty on the part of the legislators and executives responsible. Clearly, inflation is always reprehensible, for it surreptitiously robs every bank depositor and every owner of bonds, notes, or mortgages of part of his property. Indeed, it is an especially pernicious type of theft, for it even filches away the pensions going to the disabled or decrepit and the life insurance accumulated through the years by thoughtful and considerate men for the protection of their loved ones. Therefore, to prescribe inflation as a remedy for recession indicates that the person doing so is either an economic illiterate or a knave.

6. For many decades, American retailers have given savings stamps which their customers can redeem for merchandise. Savings stamps have become a tradition as truly American as fireworks on the Fourth of July and turkey on Thanksgiving. Though there are thoughtless people who attack savings stamps, the wise customer realizes the advantages savings stamps offer and the place they occupy in the American economy. When you trade with merchants who show their appreciation by giving savings stamps, a veritable bonanza of America's finest merchandise awaits you—absolutely free. Mom can get just about anything she wants for home decorating and equipping. Dad can get those do-it-yourself tools or sports needs. The youngsters can save for toys, sports equipment, bikes, and many other "musts" for happy children.

7. Television and the compliant squealing audience have created another illusion: the television world of children—a world of frenetic activity, perpetual din, adult innuendo, and children's home permanents. The child is exploited in many ways to create this nightmare world: the curried child performer appears on adult programs; real live

children attend a nursery "school" whose curriculum is largely brand-name toys for Mommy to buy—today!; rows of dutiful "Hey, Kids!" sit watching hard-sell commercials punctuated only briefly by the vulgar antics of an unfunny clown and some unimaginative puppets. Having been thus shouted, cajoled, seduced, and bribed into his role as amplifier for adult pitchmen, the child is fit for nothing more demanding in his non-working hours than crude old cartoons and new slapstick shorts.—Patrick D. and Mary Hazard, "Art Linkletter Says the Damndest Things!" *The English Journal*

8. Crest deodorant beauty bar is a truly unique bath and beauty product. Before you take your first Crest bath, we would like to tell you just a few things about Crest . . . a few of the reasons why it's so wonderfully different. Open the luxurious foil wrapper and notice first of all the delicate pastel color . . . smell that fragrance of fine perfumes. Then, step into your Crest bath and see how billows of rich lather appear almost like magic. And Crest is so wonderfully mild . . . so gentle to your complexion . . . leaves your skin clearer, fresher, cleaner. After your first Crest bath, you'll discover the new sensation of "feeling really clean." You see . . . Crest leaves your skin free of the unseen sticky film that all ordinary soaps leave. Perhaps most wonderful of all . . . you'll find that Crest's amazing new deodorant action helps keep you fresh and protected all day. That's because Crest's wonderful new deodorant ingredient destroys odor-causing bacteria all over your body.

D. Select a piece of writing which shows that the writer's emotions are aroused. For example, choose a newspaper editorial, a political speech, or a letter to the editors of a newspaper or magazine. Discuss and evaluate the methods of persuasion used. If your instructor desires, provide a copy of the selection you discuss.

E. Discuss and evaluate the techniques of persuasion illustrated in all or portions of a famous document from American history. Choose a document like the Declaration of Independence, Thomas Paine's *The Crisis,* one of James Madison's contributions to *The Federalist,* or a selection from the speeches and writings of Daniel Webster, John C. Calhoun, or William Lloyd Garrison.

F. Read the editorials of two nationally known magazines over a period of several weeks. Select magazines representing two clearly different points of view. Compare the purposes and methods of the editorials.

G. Study samples of advertising for a nationally known product or company. Examine and evaluate the methods of persuasion used.

H. The following pair of student themes represents different versions of the same paper written by the same author. Examine in detail the differences in approach and in development. Which version is more persuasive?

If its persuasive effect depends upon the audience, describe the kind of audience with which it would be effective. Which version is harder to write?

[Version A]   BARNUM WAS HALF RIGHT

When Phineas T. Barnum, the father of the American circus, said that there was a sucker born every minute he was only *half* right. There are actually two born every minute. I have arrived at this startling conclusion by simply dividing the number of suckers by the number of minutes and finding that either twin births among suckers are extremely common or the birth rate Barnum referred to has soared like everything else.

My technique for counting suckers is really rather simple. All you've got to do is stand near the door of a bar. You'll be rewarded with a veritable flood of them as they stampede to swill their favorite panacea for everything—alcohol in one disguise or another.

Please do not be too critical of our guzzling friends, because to the majority of them this type of behavior is completely necessary. Without the crutch of alcohol life would be very unpleasant for them. While they sit in their dim, stale-smelling bars life is sweet indeed. Here is a refuge from all trouble. Even the worst kind of trouble is soluble in alcohol, and it is a grave situation indeed that cannot be dissipated by a fifth or so of bonded trouble-obscurant. Do not misunderstand me. Drinking is not a confirmed habit with these people. Any one of them can quit drinking any time he feels like it. Most of them are sure they can stop because they have done so at least half a dozen times, sometimes for as long as a whole week!

In observing the bartender you will immediately notice how friendly he is. You will soon learn that the bartender's name is Al or Louis (all bartenders are named Al or Louis) and that all the male customers are named "Mac," while all the females are known as "Honey." This is very handy, since it does away with having to remember cumbersome names like Joe and Mary.

This place really has "atmosphere." In fact, if you wished, you could just about hack off a hunk and take it home with you. Stale cigarette smoke hangs from the ceiling like a cloud and nearly obscures all vision above waist height. This poor visibility is handy for the barkeep, since it relieves him of the necessity of washing glassware and enables him to salvage half-finished drinks from the more comatose patrons while they are wandering around in quest of the rest room or television set.

Before too long one of the customers of this converted phone booth will decide to go home, and, being much too drunk to walk, he will, of course, drive. His departure is a signal for much back-slapping and well-wishing, and no one seems to notice that "good ol' Mac" has his hat on backwards and has been trying to light the wrong end of a cork tip cigarette for the last five minutes. Mac lurches to his car and collapses gratefully behind the wheel. We never find out if Mac makes it home safely, because he turns the wrong way down a one-way street and is soon lost to view. Chances are, though, that the siren heard shortly thereafter is the signal to enter Mac's name on the traffic fatality rolls.

If Mac is dead who is to blame? Is it the portly church-going manager of the distillery that distills Mac's hooch? Is it the man who delivered it? Or is it Al, the bartender? Some would go so far as to blame the lobbyist for the liquor interests whose job it is to buy and sell legislators and their products. Probably the fact nearest to the truth is that you and I are responsible for Mac's death. As long as we sit idly by and do nothing but make airy assertions about drinking in general and drunk driving in particular we must bear the indictment for the death and destruction that occur when gasoline and alcohol are mixed. Don't wait too long to take some positive action! "Mac" may take you with him!

[Version *B*]   IS IT WORTH IT?

No argument is as apt to be met with a cold countenance and hot words as is the argument in favor of temperance. Any argument that could possibly result in the reduction of a person's pleasurable sensations is likely to be met with something less than enthusiasm, but this matter of temperance ranks among the most powerful of alienators. It is not my intention to provoke a heated argument but to offer some ideas that might have been overlooked in the discussions that invariably arise when the subject of temperance is broached. The crux of the question of temperance is the rather wide variance of opinion about what·is morally right or wrong. Since the moral aspects of temperance are certainly complex, I will not touch upon them at all but rather will discuss the purely practical side of the question of whether or not drinking is worth the trouble it causes.

The prime argument of those people who wish to ignore the fact that alcoholic beverages damage their body and impair its functions is that the body involved is theirs. While this could be contested on theological grounds, it seems plausible enough from other points of view. From the practical standpoint, what a person does to his body is more or less his own business. However, this argument would be valid only if there were only a half dozen people on earth, all of them separated by long distances. Unfortunately, no one of us can really say that his actions do not affect someone else. So it is with those who drink. The person who takes "one too many" and then runs down a pedestrian is not being very realistic if he believes his drinking affects no one but himself. I do not contend that all drinkers have accidents, but the AAA reports that the chances of having a wreck increase about ten times when one drinks before driving. Further statistics show that six of every ten wrecks involving a fatality are due to someone's use of alcohol. Those few tenths of a second of delay in the reflex of a person who has been drinking are magnified in the distance a speeding car can cover in them. Since a car going 60 m.p.h. is traveling 88 feet per second, even the slightest hesitation could be disastrous under certain conditions. It would seem that as far as progress in the automotive field is concerned, the efficiency of automobiles has outstripped that of drivers.

The danger caused by the drunken driver is just one of many to be considered in an argument for temperance. Many homes are broken up because of alcoholism. Alcoholics Anonymous reports that one out of every sixteen people who take their first drink today will become a confirmed alcoholic. To put it bluntly, there is very little good to be found in the use of alcohol. If you doubt that alcohol can destroy a person just visit the skid row in any major city. You will come away with a new respect for the potency of this common substance. We certainly wouldn't expose a fine watch to hydrochloric acid, but perhaps we do something very similar when we expose the intricacies of body and character to the effects of alcohol. When I consider all the disadvantages of drinking and compare them with the advantage of being stimulated for a short while, I cannot help asking, "Is it worth it?" I don't think so.

THEME TOPICS 6

1. Write two different accounts of an incident involving members of a group of which you are not a member, such as students of a rival college, college teachers, policemen, members of a minority group, foreigners, or politicians. In either version, use only details that to the best of your knowledge are factual or true. Make one version flattering by the selection of favorable details. Make the other unflattering by the selection of unfavorable details.

2. Write two different accounts of a person, a place, or an event. Use roughly the same details and information in both. In the first version, try to create a favorable impression by selecting words with favorable connotations. In the second version, try to create an unfavorable impression by selecting words with unfavorable connotations.

3. Attack an institution, custom, or practice of which you disapprove. For instance, you might attack labor unions, English courses, big business, congressional elections, final exams, unchaperoned parties. Write two versions, one an overstatement of your case designed to sway readers who are poorly informed and impressionable, the other a balanced argument acceptable to readers who are well informed and critical.

4. Select a current social or political issue about which you have strong feelings. For example, you might choose desegregation in the public schools, high taxes, the role of pressure groups, inequities in the treatment of ex-servicemen, projects for urban renewal, federal aid to education. Present your position in two different versions. In the first version, make use of nonrational means of persuasion, such as name-calling, slanting, unfavorable comparisons, insinuation. In the second version, make use of rational means of persuasion, such as sound logic and evidence directly relevant to the issue.

5. Advertise a product, a service, or a project that you know well. Provide two versions, one addressed to a prospect who is poorly informed and impressionable, the other addressed to a prospect who is well informed and critical.

6. Argue your position on one of the following questions. Make your presentation as persuasive as possible while avoiding persuasive devices that would alienate critical readers.

a. Does the United States have a moral obligation to help newly independent countries establish democratic governments?

b. What should be our attitude toward outstanding political leaders in the nation's past? Is there a middle ground between uncritical glorification and overcritical debunking?

c. Should the principle of the separation of church and state be observed to the point of banning from public schools prayer, bible reading, religious songs, Christmas or Easter programs?

d. Can a good patriot support world government? Can one be loyal to his own country and to the ideal of world government at the same time?

e. Should past membership in a totalitarian political organization be considered sufficient grounds for barring a person from public office?

CHAPTER THREE

THE WRITER'S ATTITUDE

7: TONE AND STYLE

1. SETTING THE RIGHT TONE

A piece of writing may be precise or vague, concrete or abstract, logical or illogical, direct or indirect, coherent or rambling. All these qualities help to determine a writer's **style**, the characteristic manner of expression that makes treatments of the same subject sound and feel different from each other. However, style depends on factors beyond the expressiveness of the individual word, the soundness of a logical argument, the coherence and comprehensiveness of treatment. Often a reader is influenced not so much by the substance and soundness of what he reads as by the tone in which it is presented.

Tone and Attitude. **Tone** reflects the attitude of the writer toward both his subject matter and his reader. In speaking to a friend in need of help, we can give essentially the same advice in a tone of nagging insistence or in a tone of quiet encouragement. Similarly, a writer can vary his tone to express indifference or concern, patience or resentment, gaiety or gloom. In a discussion of a community project, he can adopt the coaxing tone of a kindergarten teacher or the curt, impatient tone of someone pointing out the obvious and letting his readers make their own decisions.

To a certain extent, tone is, and should be, the natural expression of the writer's feelings. Much writing that is powerful and memorable is animated by spontaneous anger, genuine enthusiasm, or righteous indignation. Nonetheless, *a writer has to be able to control tone in accordance with the purposes he is trying to achieve.* A book reviewer, for instance, will produce quite different results depending on whether he adopts a tone of crude sensationalism ("the shock-by-shock confessions of a sorority girl") or a tone of judicious evaluation ("a sensitively told story of college life").

Formal Writing. In expository writing, the most obvious differences in tone are due to the level of formality or informality on which the writer moves. At one pole is the dignified, impersonal, carefully polished style most appropriate to the **formal** discussion of serious issues. At the other pole is the chatty, personal, improvised style most appropriate to **informal** letters among friends. Your own writing in college will generally stay closer to the former extreme than to the latter. *In technical reports, in themes of opinion and argument, and in scholarly discussion, a relatively formal style is usually the most appropriate choice.* In autobiographical writing, in accounts of travel, and in essays devoted to personal impressions, a relatively informal style is often appropriate, with the degree of informality depending on the intentions of the writer.

A formal style owes its distinctive quality to a number of features, some more essential than others. Its vocabulary tends to be more extensive, more discriminating, and more technical than that of everyday English. Unlike their equivalents in parentheses, the words in the following list are likely to appear only in relatively formal writing: *arduous* (difficult), *felicitous* (appropriate), *incongruous* (queer), *indigenous* (homegrown), *lucid* (clear), *precarious* (risky), *serene* (peaceful), *spurious* (false); *frivolity* (silliness), *jeopardy* (danger), *leisure* (free time), *unison* (harmony), *virtuosity* (skill); *abound* (have plenty of), *beguile* (seduce, cheat), *compel* (force), *rejoice* (be glad).

Closely related to the scope of vocabulary is the range of **allusion** and comparison. A writer cultivating a formal style is likely to draw freely on references to history, literature, the fine arts. He may expect his readers to know what a "Utopia" is, what "Napoleonic airs" are, or how an "interregnum" comes about. He may not stop to explain what the disadvantages of a "Pyrrhic victory" are, or how it feels to be stretched on a "Procrustean bed." He will expect his readers to know the difference between a virtuoso and a dilettante, a symphony and a sonata.

The sentences of formal writing are usually more elaborate, or at least more carefully planned, than those of ordinary conversation. Where an informal paragraph might have five or six separate or loosely coordinated sentences, a formal paragraph might have two or three compact sentences making ample use of subordination. In informal writing, a minor point or a short comment might appear in a sentence by itself; in formal writing, it might appear as a parenthetic observation in another sentence. An informal sentence often uses the one-subject-one-verb pattern; a formal sentence often uses series of grammatically parallel elements.

In matters of usage, formal writing often shows the standardizing influence of editing designed to make it generally acceptable to a large body of educated readers. It is likely to observe closely the traditional distinctions between *who* and *whom, like* and *as, can* and *may, if he was* and *if he were.* Magazine articles and books, like student themes, often become more formal in diction and in grammar in response to the criticisms of editors, reviewers, and teachers.[1]

The organization of a paragraph or of an essay written in a formal style is likely to be systematic. Formal writing is usually easier to outline than informal writing. It is likely to arrange several subdivisions of a topic in the most logical order and then adhere to it rather closely. The subdivisions themselves are often clearly labeled ("The first major objection that arises is that . . ."; "the second reason for making this change is that . . ."). **Transitions** are likely to be explicit, signaled by relatively heavy connectives like *however, nevertheless,* and *moreover.* Within paragraphs, both parallel and antithetical ideas are likely to be lined up in parallel constructions.

Finally, formal writing often does without the subjective *I* and the direct *you.* Writer, reader, and humanity at large may merge in the impersonal *one* ("One cannot but agree with the writer who said . . ."; "one should also remember that . . ."; "one tends to idealize the events of his childhood"). Formal arguments and discussions, even when they include personal comment, will on the whole maintain an objective, detached tone; conclusions and opinions will keep close to the evidence presented.

Informal Writing. The kind of informal style that you will have use for in college-level writing is not the shirt-sleeve informality of much advertising and much popular journalism. Though easygoing and relaxed, *an informal paper can have the thoughtful, well-mannered quality of polite conversation.* Informal writing of this kind may make occasional, but by no means undiscriminating, use of the folksy, **colloquial** phrase. It occasionally uses **slang**, usually in tongue-in-cheek fashion.[2] Its range of reference and allusion is likely to be that of patio, garage, and playing field rather than that of library or study. Its sen-

---

[1] See Chapter Six for more detailed discussion of variations in diction, grammar, and sentence style.
[2] See D 3.

tence structure and its punctuation are sometimes suggestive of the pauses, ramblings, and afterthoughts of speech. Its unity derives less from step-by-step development than from the continuity of an underlying mood. It tends to be subjective; it makes room for personal impressions, reminiscences, and whims. It often tells the reader as much about the author as about his subject.

The following three selections move from a relatively formal to a relatively informal style:

> (1) Of escapes from the pressure of an increasingly mechanized life to occasional outbursts of excitement or triviality there is much to be said. At least it may be said for them that they are natural, perhaps needful, refuges from a world whose tightly woven days would otherwise be unbearable. It is perhaps a sad commentary on the angular and constricted lives we lead that we should have to seek such lurid or futile ways to peace. But it is not to be wondered at that, living in such a world of routine, we should plunge ever so often into the loud nonsense of inane parties, wallow in the absurd pathos and comedy of the screen, or fall enraptured victims to successive crazes of bootless puzzles and dull games. We may be forgiven our excursions to musical comedies without wit or music, and conversational evenings without humanity or ideas. The contemporary citizen is vexed beyond his own realization by the humdrum unthrilling pressure of his days; he craves naturally now and then an opportunity to be trivial, irresponsible, and absurd.—Irwin Edman, *Adam, the Baby and the Man from Mars*

This selection, while concerned with trivial amusements, is scholarly and formal in style. Its vocabulary, though not pretentious or bookish, departs enough from the level of everyday language to be reserved and dignified: *needful, enraptured, excursion, vexed.* Its metaphors are fresh and expressive rather than familiar or amusing: "tightly woven days," "angular and constricted lives." Sentence structure departs from the ordinary by inversion ("Of escapes . . . there is much to be said") and by frequent use of parallelism ("plunge . . . of inane parties, wallow . . . of the screen, or fall . . . of bootless puzzles and dull games"; "excursions . . . without wit or music, . . . evenings without humanity or ideas"). Throughout, the use of the impersonal passive reinforces the tone of dignified detachment ("it may be said," "it is not to be wondered at," "may be forgiven").

> (2) It happens to be a fact that all classic works without exception deal directly or indirectly with problems of conduct. That is their great virtue for school use. Not that they teach a plain goody-goody morality, but that they show and discuss and solve dilemmas that a

shipping clerk or an athlete can be made to understand. For this understanding, the discussion of any classic *must be superficial*. If you dive below the surface with your pupil you drown him. Certain teachers are always terrified of superficiality; they seem to think other teachers will scoff or that the dead author will scold. Let them remind themselves that their colleagues' profundity would strike the great author as either surface scratching or pedantry; and let them remember that for every reader there is a time when a given book is being read for the first time—Jacques Barzun, *Teacher in America*

This selection illustrates an urbane and discriminating kind of informality. It uses the conversational phrase ("it happens to be a fact that . . ."), the occasional colloquialism ("goody-goody morality"), the informal *you*. Its metaphors have a homely, familiar quality ("if you dive . . . you drown him"; "surface scratching"). Its sentences, on the whole, are shorter, more abrupt, and more emphatic than those in the preceding selection ("That is their great virtue for school use"). However, the author does not *limit* himself to the familiar, the simple. His vocabulary ranges beyond the conversational: *terrified of superficiality, scoff, colleagues' profundity, pedantry*. His sentences are deliberate and effective; they repeatedly become insistent ("show and discuss and solve"; "let them remind themselves . . . let them remember . . .").

(3) If television is ever to amount to anything of cultural importance, it should rid itself of the idea that it's the motion picture industry, the book business or the stage. It's a big, new art form of its own. It was radio's lack of standards that led to that dizzy lunacy known as the giveaway program. Radio programs gave away washing machines, Cadillacs, $1,000 bills, houses—everything, in fact, except women. I could never quite understand that lone omission. If Bert Parks had thrown a beautiful 18-year-old babe into the jackpot of *Stop the Music,* even I would have stayed home and listened for the telephone. But he wouldn't. Some faint moral scruple—or conceivably fear of the Federal Communications Commission—stayed the broadcaster from this final depravity. The Roman emperors who gave the populace bread and circuses—which is what radio was imitating with its giveaway programs—also threw in sexual orgies, and it always seemed to me inconsistent of the broadcasters not to follow through with the thing. I brought this to the attention of several vice presidents, but they failed to see any humor in the suggestion. They also failed to see anything wrong with the giveaway program, which shows where a lack of moral standards leads.—John Crosby, "Seven Deadly Sins of the Air," *Life*

This selection illustrates the kind of distinct informality that would be inappropriate in a more serious, more objective, less personal context. There is no doubt about the literacy and skill of the writer, suggested by such phrases as "faint moral scruple" or "stayed . . . from this final depravity." However, his style is in keeping with his brash, no-holds-barred attack on his subject. The tone of the passage is set by the colloquial phrases ("amount to anything," "follow through with the thing"), the slang expressions ("babe," "jackpot," "threw in"), the informal contractions ("it's," "wouldn't"). Overstatement runs wild ("dizzy lunacy," "sexual orgies"). Sentence structure ranges from the short half-sentence ("But he wouldn't.") to the overloaded last sentence, with its parenthetical *which*-clause reaching halfheartedly for an antecedent. On the one hand, serious students of the mass media might object to the writer's flippancy; on the other hand, readers who would not otherwise interest themselves in the subject might be attracted by the writer's treatment of it.

2. HUMOR, IRONY, AND SATIRE

Among the elements that contribute to the informality of a writer's tone, humor deserves special attention. Humor can help attract a reader, break down his reserve, soften the impact of unpleasant truths. It is a means of overcoming distrust. People feel relieved when they see a grin on the face of a policeman (or of a professor); they tend to be suspicious of people who look as though it hurts them to smile.

A writer who lacks a sense of humor often lacks a sense of balance. A piece of writing seems to lack proportion when it treats the most solemn and the most trivial matters with the same deadly seriousness. There is something reassuring about the detachment that enables a writer to perceive whatever might be ridiculous or amusing about his subject or about himself. Some of the most readable writing we encounter combines a basic seriousness with occasional touches of dry wit:

> There is another possibility to be taken account of, which is that of manufacturing food chemically. There seems no good reason why we should continue to grow our food laboriously in soil and allow ourselves to be dependent on the vagaries of sun and rain. Why not make beefsteaks in factories? And flour in workshops? I dare say that food made in this way would not taste very nice, but in time people would get used to it and a little "real" food would still be produced for wedding feasts and the banquets of Heads of States. Some very rich men would occasionally issue invitations saying in one corner, "Decorations will be worn" and in the other corner "Real peas."—Bertrand Russell, "The Next Eighty Years," *Saturday Review*

Obviously, a writer has to be skillful in managing what wit he can muster. Humor is relative. *More so than other aspects of writing, it depends for its effectiveness upon the tastes, interests, and standards of the reader.* For instance, much humor exploits the unexpected or incongruous. Such humor can effectively point out, and perhaps correct, shortcomings. Often, however, such humor exploits disabilities and misfortunes that are beyond the control of their victims. Jokes about morons, foreign accents, and physical infirmities are likely to be funny in a cruel or thoughtless way. Many readers will resent ridicule directed at suffering or misfortune, even when they are in no way personally concerned. They will suspect the writer of a lack of human sympathy, or at least of a lack of tact or good taste.

Verbal Humor. *The writer who wants to be serious without being dull is likely to make at least some use of verbal humor.* He will use unexpected yet appropriate twists in his choice and arrangement of words. He may employ the antithetical effect of contrasting ideas lined up in parallel grammatical form:

> This is an age of *big words* and *little work*.
> Nearly *everybody talks, many can read,* and *some listen*.

He may make use of **paradox**, an expression that at first seems absurd but then turns out to contain a valid point. "When peace breaks out" is an example of a paradoxical phrase. We usually speak of war, rather than peace, as "breaking out," but on second thought we may agree that in a period of constant international tension the arrival of genuine peace would be as momentous as the outbreak of open war. Similarly, a bachelor may startle us by mentioning the possibility of "committing matrimony." The term *commit* is usually applied to crimes rather than to something as legal and respectable as marriage. On second thought, we would realize that to the speaker the thought of marriage is as abhorrent as the thought of crime is to others.

Similar in effect to paradox is the practice of reviving a trite phrase by modifying it in an unexpected way. A publisher, referring to unsold books returned to him by booksellers, might complain that his stock is "gone today and here tomorrow." A writer might list a number of relevant and important questions but go on to say that "space and ignorance" do not permit his answering them.

Witty phrasing can serve to make a serious point striking or memorable. However, some devices of verbal humor tend to give a flippant tone to a passage as a whole. One such device is the **pun**, a play on words that makes one word suggest two different but equally appropriate meanings. For example, a reporter may speak of pollsters "*galluping* from door to door"; a columnist may speak of contemporaries leaving "footprints on the sands of *Time*." When allowed to run wild, both paradox and pun become mannerisms, habitual stylistic devices used without regard for their appropriateness.

Irony and Sarcasm. Many uses of humor go beyond the witty formula or the clever phrase. Of these, **irony** is probably the most pervasive and the most important. The most common kind of irony makes use of statements that mean the opposite of what they seem to say. A student is likely to be ironical when he says, "I just love to write my English themes!" or "How I enjoy dormitory food!" Several things help to make such irony obvious: the pained look on the student's face, the knowledge that students often have a prejudice (however unfounded or unfortunate) against English themes and dormitory food.

Unable to rely on gestures and on facial expression, *the writer using irony has to make context, wording, and over-all tone suggest his ironical intention.* Suppose he says, "Bill's political ideas happened to correspond exactly to those of the employer he worked for at a given time." The wholeheartedness of Bill's agreement with his employers, combined with the opportune changes in his convictions, is obviously *not* a coincidence; the word *happened* is therefore being used ironically.

The uses of verbal irony are varied, and some are harder to recognize than others. **Sarcasm** is a bitter or insulting kind of irony; it is often inspired by resentment or contempt. **Understatement** achieves an ironical effect by belittling something that is of serious importance to the speaker, as when a man with double pneumonia says, "I don't feel quite as sprightly as I might wish." In the following passage, a familiar point gains fresh impact through vast understatement:

> Among the enterprises currently attracting the energies of man, one of considerable moment is his effort to launch himself across space. A second, less grand, less costly, *but perhaps not less important,* is the effort to improve the position of *those who will stay behind.*—John Kenneth Galbraith, "The Poverty of Nations," *Atlantic*

Similar in effect to verbal irony is **irony of situation**. Not only the writer's statements or opinions but also the details and events he describes may go counter to expectation. For instance, he can ridicule what is pompous by placing the pretentious next to the trivial. He can point out the shabby rear of a building with an imposing façade, or he can emphasize the gaudy medals on the chest of a small-time dictator. An easy prey of this kind of irony is the person whose theory points one way and whose practice another: the traffic-safety expert who has an accident or the marriage counselor whose wife sues for divorce.

Irony and sarcasm, like all humor, require discrimination on the part of the writer. Sudden shifts into irony are likely to confuse the reader—if they don't escape him altogether. Ironic exposure of the shortcomings of others easily becomes routine debunking. It may seize upon surface defects in order to belittle real merit.

Satire. When you make systematic use of humor, irony, or sarcasm to attack something you disapprove of, you are employing **satire**. Satire criticizes shortcomings by holding them up to ridicule and scorn. For instance, you may use satirical exaggeration. In a paper entitled "The Quick and the Dead," you might say of the gentleman hunter, "Death awaits anything foolish enough to place itself in front of his gun, be it a cow, mule, fellow hunter, or even, in rare instances, a deer." By exaggerating the occasional failure of the inexperienced hunter to aim at a legitimate target, you would emphasize and ridicule his lack of competence. Satirical exaggeration is the stock in trade of satirists like Mark Twain and George Bernard Shaw:

> A work of art? It has no invention; it has no order, system, sequence, or result; it has no life-likeness, no thrill, no stir, no seeming of reality; its characters are confusedly drawn, and by their acts and words they prove that they are not the sort of people the author claims that they are; its humor is pathetic; its pathos is funny; its conversations are—oh! indescribable; its love-scenes odious; its English a crime against the language.—Mark Twain, "Fenimore Cooper's Literary Offenses"

A satirical paper is most effective when it clearly implies the positive standards by which its target is judged. For instance, a paper on hunting, no matter how merciless in its attack upon hunters, can have a constructive purpose. The reader can be made to realize that the author is, indirectly, setting up two basic requirements: minimum competence in the handling of firearms, and a respect for human life strong enough to keep the hunter from firing at just anything that moves.

By clarifying your standards, you will be able to avoid the most common defect in student-written satire: lack of focus. A satirical description of a hike, for instance, can concentrate on incidents that illustrate inconsiderate or thoughtless behavior. It can dwell on the hiker who is suddenly consumed by an unquenchable thirst, and on his companion who consistently finds the scenery inferior to that in the Black Forest or that in the Kize-Kazuyo Mountains. Other incidents, though amusing, could obscure the target of the satire. The alarm clock that goes off late and the sudden rainstorm might help to create a hysterical slapstick atmosphere, but they might also keep the reader from getting the main point: a cooperative enterprise will be a success only if everyone learns to subordinate some of his personal whims and complaints to the common good. In preparing a satirical paper, ask yourself: Does my paper have a definite point? Or am I merely taking potshots at miscellaneous abuses? A satirist who fails to ask such questions easily becomes a kind of court jester, whose barbs nobody takes seriously.

Limitations of Humor. Whether you use humor in a few incidental touches, or whether you make it part of your basic strategy, it creates special problems of appropriateness and consistency. Humorous anecdotes are inappropriate in a funeral sermon, just as whistling is inappropriate in church. How far a writer goes in making his writing humorous or satirical is a matter of taste—both his own and that of his readers. Some uses of humor, however, are certain to strike a false note:

(1) *The strained facetiousness by which a writer seems to apologize for taking up a serious subject.* Some writers seem unable to refer to themselves, to their readers, or to their country without a would-be humorous variation: "Yours truly," "the gentle reader," "these Yew-nited States." They overwork the facetious circumlocution, which substitutes an impressive roundabout phrase for a simple everyday word: a toothbrush becomes a "denture scrubber"; women become "the female gender"; a dog's tail becomes a "caudal appendage."

(2) *A tone of contemptuous, sarcastic familiarity.* Some papers address the reader in the tone of a parent addressing a misbehaving and not very bright child. Beware, for instance, of condescending or bullying questions put directly to the reader: "I believe in honest government. How about you?"

(3) *The kind of flippancy that results from discussing serious or solemn subjects in racy, colloquial language.* Suppose that in answering an examination question, you write: "Poor Othello finally blows his top when he sees Cassio fondling Desdemona's hanky." If the person so unceremoniously discussed is, like Othello, a figure of considerable dignity, your reader is likely to feel that you are not taking the material—and the examination—seriously.

3. DEVELOPING A STYLE OF YOUR OWN

Many students are too preoccupied with elementary problems of writing to think of cultivating a distinctive, personal style. Even those who are not, however, sometimes find less encouragement than they expect. Concern for style as style may lead to a straining for effect, to an artificial "literary" quality. A desire for originality may lead a writer into mannerisms that attract attention but that often also *distract* from what he has to say.

Distinctive Styles. The following passages illustrate some of the strengths and weaknesses of expository writing with a distinct style:

> In CBS's *Gandhi,* the scrawny, jug-eared little man in the white loincloth looked as Author John Gunther once saw him: an inscrutable "combination of Jesus Christ, Tammany Hall, and your father." Fuzzy images from old films showed the gentle ascetic all but engulfed by the worshiping, hysterical throngs on the mass pilgrimage to the sea to carry out a plan of passive resistance during the British salt monopoly. There was the shrewd lawyer-diplomat putting his hand over an inquisitive British reporter's mouth or quipping on arrival in London in 1931: "You people have your plus fours. These are my minus fours." In the best sequences, faded with age, there was "your father"—with metal-rimmed spectacles, a big, near-toothless grin, the dollar watch dangling from the dhoti—who tenderly encircled a little girl with a garland of flowers that she had brought for him.—*Time*

This passage illustrates a sophisticated and very successful kind of journalism whose trademark is its slick, bright-eyed quality. The tone is irreverent and ironical ("jug-eared little man"; "big, near-toothless grin"). The account owes its graphic quality to a selection of striking external detail ("the white loincloth," "the dollar watch dangling from the dhoti"). It owes its dynamic quality to its habitual exaggeration of the dramatic ("worshiping, hysterical throngs"; "all but engulfed"), heightened by contrast ("gentle ascetic"). The "little girl" keeps the exotic scene from escaping beyond the scope of ordinary human interest. There is a smattering of brief, striking quotations—too short to give an insight into the speaker's character, too simple to require careful interpretation, but either startling ("Jesus Christ, Tammany Hall, and your father") or witty ("minus fours"). Even a demanding reader may find this passage clever and entertaining. He is likely to ask, however: "If something genuinely profound or complex comes along, is *Time* style adequately equipped to deal with it?"

In pre-movie days, the business of peddling lies about life was spotty and unorganized. It was carried on by the cheaper magazines, dime novels, the hinterland preachers and whooping politicians. These combined to unload a rash of infantile parables on the land. A goodly part of the population was infected, but there remained large healthy areas in the Republic's thought. There remained, in fact, an intellectual class of sorts—a tribe of citizens who never read dime novels, cheap magazines or submitted themselves to political and religious howlers.

It was this tribe that the movies scalped. Cultured people who would have blushed with shame to be found with a dime novel in their hands took to flocking shamelessly to watch the picturization of such tripe on the screen.

For forty years the movies have drummed away on the American character. They have fed it naïveté and buncombe in doses never before administered to any people. They have slapped into the American mind more human misinformation in one evening than the Dark Ages could muster in a decade.—Ben Hecht, *A Child of the Century*

This passage illustrates a deliberately "tough" style, marked by a boisterous disregard for standards of refinement, politeness, or tact. Its tone is that of a heavy-handed facetiousness ("tribe of citizens," ". . . that the movies scalped"). It produces the effect of **caricature** by a combination of habitual extreme overstatement and heavy invective ("business of peddling lies," "rash of infantile parables," "flocking shamelessly," "buncombe in doses never before administered to any people"). Its vocabulary is an uncouth mixture of slang ("unload . . . on the land," "tripe," "slapped into the American mind"), faintly archaic tags ("a goodly part"), slightly outlandish phrases ("hinterland preachers"), and facetious neologisms ("picturization"). Many readers find this kind of writing both invigorating and entertaining, in a beer-garden sort of way. However, they will not discount the possibility that the writer might be as indiscriminate in his judgments as he is in his choice of words.

The radio has made sentimentality the twentieth century Plymouth Rock. As a discipline, I have forced myself to sit a whole morning listening to the soap operas, along with twenty million moms who were busy sweeping dust under carpets while planning to drown their progeny in honey or bash in their heads. This filthy and indecent abomination, this trash with which, until lately, only moron servant girls could dull their credulous minds in the tawdry privacy of their cubicles, is now the national saga. Team after team of feeble-minded Annies and Davids crawl from the loudspeaker into the front rooms of America. The characters are impossible, their adventures would make a saint spew, their morals are lower than those of ghouls, their habits are uncleanly, their humor is the substance that starts whole races grinding bayonets, they have no manners, no sense, no goals, no worthy ambitions, no hope, no faith, no information, no values related to reality, and no estimate of truth. They merely sob and snicker—as they cheat each other.—Philip Wylie, *Generation of Vipers*

This passage, though it resembles the preceding selection in its reliance on overstatement and invective, has a more exasperated, more serious tone. It has some of the profuse, passionate eloquence of the moralist denouncing and belaboring his fellows. It owes its insistent, emphatic quality to the skillful use of repetition and parallel grammatical structure. Starting with a brief, concise statement of the key idea, the paragraph warms up until it launches into the sustained parallelism of the last but one sentence. It keeps piling up resounding abstractions that, though they overlap somewhat in meaning, reinforce each other's emotional impact ("goals," "ambitions," "hope," "faith," "values"). Reading a book written in this style is like frequenting a Turkish bath: not everyone likes the steam and the heat. If a writer becomes intensely emotional about a minor annoyance, his readers will hardly trust him to be calm and judicious about things that are genuinely threatening or frightening. Assuming that the writer is carried away by *words* rather than by sincere emotion, his readers may well consider him too glib to be trusted with a serious subject.

Learning from Others. *The best protection against an artificial or exaggerated style is a constant concern with doing justice to one's material.* Meticulous stylists build up their reputation by searching, not for the unusual word, the colorful word, or the startling word, but for the *right* word. They learn to choose words and phrases, not for their surface sparkle but for their capacity for setting the right tone, reflecting the right shade of emotion, creating an authentic setting, or conveying a precise shade of meaning.

Some writers have a native gift of phrase, a knack for finding the inevitable, illuminating way of putting ideas into words. Most people, however, have to train their powers of expression through careful listening and reading. They read a magazine article and stop to repeat an apt quotation or a striking phrase. They start reading a short story and are caught up by its arresting first sentence. They become aware of the strong pull of personal emotion under the objective surface of a systematic argument, or of the continuity of basic purpose in an artlessly rambling essay.

Attentive reading of other writers' work will help you develop your sense of what makes expression appropriate and effective. What it is that makes the style of an essay adequate is often hard to put into words. Many writers rely on a sense of fitness rather than on rules or instructions. They feel that a piece of writing fails to "come off," and they keep tinkering with it until it does. A word sounds strained, a metaphor doesn't fit, a conclusion is too obvious. The writer tightens a relationship here, cuts out a phrase there, not because of theories he has about stylistic effects but because as a result his work reads better, seems more finished. To help your own sense of fitness develop, you can learn to pay attention to stylistic effects in the work of other writers.

EXERCISES 7

A. How formal or informal is the style of each of the following passages? Take into account such factors as diction, range of allusion, sentence structure, and degree of objectivity. How appropriate is the style of each passage to its subject matter?

1. My first affection for the University of Michigan was due, simply, to their accepting me. They had already turned me down twice because my academic record (I had flunked algebra three times in my Brooklyn high school) was so low as to be practically invisible, but the dean reversed himself after two letters in which I wrote that since working for two years—in a warehouse at $15 a week—I had turned into a much more serious fellow. He said he would give me a try, but I had better make some grades. I could not conceive of a dean at Columbia or Harvard doing that.—Arthur Miller, "University of Michigan," *Holiday*

2. Above Albuquerque begins the lyric grace of the river in its richest passage of the pastoral life. Where life is fed by water, the landscape here recalls the opulence and grandeur and occasional vistas of order in the image of classical country painted by Nicolas Poussin, who left so many celebrations of grove and meadow, shady leaf and column of light, reflecting stream and stepped mountain and composed bodies. There is more than a reminder here, there is a real likeness. It is a likeness of grace and plenty in the midst of dramatic nature; nourishment in the desert; bounty summoned by the most ancient of agricultural rites out of the most inscrutable of antiquities; cool for the heated, slaking for the parched, food for the hungry, rest for the weary, ease for the eye blinded in the unimpeded sun.—Paul Horgan, "Pages from a Rio Grande Notebook," *The New York Times Book Review*

3. Then there is another hazard—the hazard of owning a camera that is just too complicated for the beginning photographer. It's really

advisable to have a simple camera. That leaves him free to have fun. Whether he's an artist working with a camera or an amateur working with a camera, the instrument must become a part of him. He must be just as free as you are with a fork when you're eating mashed potatoes. You don't sit down and figure out how you should hold the fork; you do that unconsciously.

Worrying about technique is inhibiting. There was a time, during a very weak period in painting, when Sargent had such an influence, when long, suave brush strokes were considered important. It amounted to a closed system, and that's always pernicious. Today in modern painting they put it on with a trowel, they put it on with their feet, they drip it out of a can, they do anything with it. It's unimportant. It's what the fellow *feels* about the thing, what he has to give, what he sees, what he experiences, that counts.—Edward J. Steichen, "The Living Joy of Pictures," *Holiday*

4. Yet even apart from such lonely geniuses there are other surprises in the history of thought, phenomena almost as unexpected and almost as inexplicable. There are men who express the age and the milieu in which they were educated, but who, by the intensity of their imagination, the sweep of their knowledge, and their astounding versatility, rise high above their era and their neighbors, so that they inhabit both time and eternity at once. When we analyze their minds we can identify nearly all the component elements, tracing this to family and that to school and the other to social climate, and yet the compound is far more than the sum of all these elements: richer, intenser, different in quality as a diamond is different from carbon. Shallow thinkers often fail to understand that this qualitative difference occurs again and again in the realm of the intellect. That is what leads some critics to deny that Shakespeare could have written those plays because he was only a middle-class provincial youth who went from a small-town school to become an actor: they expect the real author to be someone calculable, like the university-trained lawyer and statesman Bacon, or a witty and graceful young nobleman with the learning and worldly experience of the Renaissance in his very blood. But they are wrong. They are making the elementary error of believing that, in the world of the mind, two and two make four.—Gilbert Highet, *Man's Unconquerable Mind*

5. Einstein knocked out space and time, as Rutherford knocked out matter. The general viewpoint of relativity toward space is very simple. Einstein explains that there is no such place as *here*. "But," you answer, "I'm here; here is where I am right now." But you're moving, you're spinning around as the earth spins; and you and the earth are both spinning around the sun, and the sun is rushing through space toward a distant galaxy, and the galaxy itself is beating it away at 26,000 miles a second. Now, where is that spot that is here! How did you mark it? You remember the story of the two idiots who were out fishing, and one said, "We should have marked that place where

we got all the fish," and the other said, "I did; I marked it on the boat." Well, that's it. That's *here.*—Stephen Leacock, *Last Leaves*

B. What is the characteristic tone of each of the following passages? Is it indulgent, impatient, angry, nostalgic, bitter? Is it humorous, ironical, sarcastic? What is its effect on the reader?

1. The present state of things on the planet earth would be rather a puzzle to an observer from another planet. If he landed in the United States, the most conspicuous animals in sight would be automobiles, and if he examined these vigorous hard-shelled creatures, he would find that each contains one or more soft, feeble organisms that appear notably helpless when removed from their shells. He would decide, after talking with these defenseless creatures, that they have no independent existence. Few of them have anything to do with the production or transportation of food. They need clothing and shelter, but do not produce them for themselves. They are dependent on their distant fellows in thousands of complex ways. When isolated, they usually die—just like worker ants that wander helplessly and hopelessly if separated from their colony.—Jonathan Norton Leonard, *Flight into Space*

2. Have women a special aptitude for teaching English? If I think they have—and I do—it is because, of all those who struggled to instruct the runt I was, I remember most affectionately three who taught me English. The first was a little sparrow of a woman and so nicknamed by the school; she taught us public speaking. The whole grade would line up before her, hands on diaphragms, and with mouths thrust forward like feeding robins, we would follow her lead as between sucks of breath we audibly pushed the vowels out of our centers in short explosions: "a!"—"e!"—"i!"—"o!"—"u!" The Sparrow could achieve the most amazing explosions for so small a person, and she was so earnest about it that we never thought to giggle. To make sure that our bellows were in working order, she would pass down the line adjusting our hands to the proper spot and urging us to "Force it out! Force it out!" She taught us to enunciate, and although we had small liking for the poems she made us memorize, the exercise of learning them by heart and spouting them aloud taught us, without our knowing it, the beauty of the vowels and the rhythm of good English.—Edward Weeks, "The Peripatetic Reviewer," *Atlantic*

3. Like many other people, I am allergic to bankers. When I get in front of a barred cage I somehow feel as though I were inside one. It doesn't help me much, either, to put me instead before a desk, or a long flat counter. I sit there and brood about bankers: what right have they to look so neat and tidy, when my hair is flying, my collar points are waving in the breeze, and my shoes are scuffed? Why should the bankers be able to do mental arithmetic so fast and so accurately, and to keep their pencils so nicely sharpened, when mine are always

broken? At such a time I am in no mood to hear the banker's invariable reply to a request for a loan, which in substance is, "Do you need it? If you need it, you can't have it."—Bruce Bliven, "Erma, the Automatic Banker," *Harper's*

4. As more and more people have painful reason to know, the press has a nasty kind of power, the same kind of power a bully has; that of hurting somebody smaller and weaker than himself. An individual's only defense against the press is the law of libel, but considerable harm and much pain can be caused without going so far as to commit an actionable libel. Journalists themselves generally have a horror of being interviewed, "written up," or even noticed by the press; they know too well from their own experience how inept and cruel a distortion the result is likely to be—even in photographs—which, in the lying phrase, "cannot lie."—T. S. Matthews, "What Makes News," *Atlantic*

5. We should behave towards our country as women behave towards the men they love. A loving wife will do anything for her husband except stop criticising and trying to improve him. That is the right attitude for a citizen. We should cast the same affectionate but sharp glance at our country. We should love it, but also insist upon telling it all its faults. The dangerous man is not the critic, but the noisy empty "patriot" who encourages us to indulge in orgies of self-congratulation.—J. B. Priestley, *Rain upon Godshill*

C. Study the satirical techniques used in the following passages. For each passage, describe the different possible reactions of different kinds of readers.

1. As advertising men by the tens of thousands bring their wiles to bear to stimulate sales of products, we are seeing a massive straining for greater impact. Some months ago a distiller sent a photographic team to the edges of the Sahara Desert in order to obtain a photograph of a martini-filled glass in a setting which would suggest dryness. The photographers faced a crisis when, in searching the fruit markets of Cairo for a sliver of yellow lemon peel to go with the drink, they discovered that lemons sold in Egypt are green. This problem was solved when they arranged for a yellow lemon to be flown over from Italy.—Vance Packard, "The Growing Power of Admen," *Atlantic*

2. One of the difficulties of crowding so much honor and tribute into the calendar is that there is a good deal of overlapping, some of it a little trying to respectful people who want to do the right thing. Is it possible, for example, to give due recognition to Jewish Book Month when right smack in the middle of it you have to celebrate National Long Underwear Week and Holiday Eggnog Time? Not to mention the fact that November also happens to be National Contact Lens Month. Or consider the predicament of the man who starts out

on a Monday to observe National Weight-Watchers Week, sponsored by the "Lite Diet" bread people, only to find that Thursday marks the beginning of Kraut and Frankfurter Week, a festive rite presided over by the National Kraut Packers Association.—Robert Bendiner, "Fifteen Weeks Hath September," *The Reporter*

3. The propaganda for cigarettes on the airwaves is transcribed ecstasy on a 24-hour basis, with its hymn of jubilation over the latest filter, the new cigarette, or the old cigarette with its newly discovered richer-milder-smoother-finer—where have we heard those words before?—qualities. The hymn fades suddenly into the voice of the high priest, who repeats in the voice of hysteria the inanities of the ritual: Don't miss the fun of smoking. Smoke *real*. Smoke modern. Smoking is a pleasure. Togetherness. Be a real American. Come along with the rest of us. Don't be an outsider. Smoke, smoke any old thing just so long as you smoke something and don't try to be so different from other folks.—Charles W. Morton, "Accent on Living," *Atlantic*

4. If a man, being ill of a pus appendix, resorts to a shaved and fumigated longshoreman to have it disposed of, and submits willingly to a treatment involving balancing him on McBurney's spot and playing on his vertebrae as on a concertina, then I am willing, for one, to believe that he is badly wanted in heaven. And if that same man, having achieved lawfully a lovely babe, hires a blacksmith to cure its diphtheria by pulling its neck, then I do not resist the divine will that there shall be one less radio fan later on. In such matters, I am convinced, the laws of nature are far better guides than the fiats and machinations of medical busybodies. If the latter gentlemen had their way, death, save at the hands of hangmen, policemen and other such legalized assassins, would be abolished altogether, and the present differential in favor of the enlightened would disappear. I can't convince myself that that would work any good to the world. On the contrary, it seems to me that the current coddling of the half-witted should be stopped before it goes too far—if, indeed, it has not gone too far already. To that end nothing operates more cheaply and effectively than the prosperity of quacks. Every time a bottle of cancer oil goes through the mails *Homo Americanus* is improved to that extent. And every time a chiropractor spits on his hands and proceeds to treat a gastric ulcer by stretching the backbone the same high end is achieved.—H. L. Mencken, *A Mencken Chrestomathy*

5. The new fashion, on the contrary, is to see God everywhere and at least potentially succoring everyone in his secular pursuits— except, of course, Communists and fellow travelers. Today the idea of partnership with the Divine is no longer seriously contested, except perhaps in a few last strongholds of resolutely negative thought. Everywhere else it is expanding and triumphing prodigiously. In Dr. Peale's books we find God everywhere, lending a hand in the most mundane occupations. We find Him helping to sell vacuum cleaners and run-

ning a beauty parlor; we find Him on the football field, the athletic field, and out on the golf links; above all, we find Him in the business office, helping the enterprising to get ahead in the world. For nothing succeeds better in business, Dr. Peale assures us, than "effecting a merger with God." God is everywhere in the universe, the source of all energy, like a cosmic battery that any believer can plug into with the live wire of faith. . . .

In the "dynamic" religion that we are being promised for tomorrow no ascetic discipline or special humbleness will any longer be required. It will be a hot-water bottle kind of piety with none of that gritty old morality in it. It will be a brand of faith that has been synthetized, vitaminized, homogenized, and capsulized, and it will be as ready-made for effortless consumption as that magically bleached, cottony, crustless, already sliced white bread which is the symbol of the modern American's massive superiority over the pagan bushwacker.— Curtis Cate, "God and Success," *Atlantic*

D. Describe in detail the characteristic tone and style of *one* of the following: the section entitled "Cinema" in *Time;* the section entitled "Notes and Comment" in *The New Yorker;* the section entitled "The Editor's Easy Chair" in *Harper's;* the section entitled "Trade Winds" in the *Saturday Review.* Pay attention to diction, sentence structure, figurative language, use of humor, attitude toward the subject and toward the reader. Provide illustrations.

E. Study several selections from the writings of a contemporary American humorist, like James Thurber, S. J. Perelman, or Max Shulman. Describe the characteristic features of the type of humor he employs.

F. Study the use of satire in the comic strips of such cartoonists as Al Capp, Walt Kelly, or the contributors to *Mad* magazine.

G. The following student theme is indebted to the tradition of the "personal" or "familiar" essay, a type of informal writing distinguished by its tone of pleasant, easygoing discussion, often with serious undertones. Describe in detail the tone and style employed by the author.

BE GONE, WOMAN!

Modern society, at least the serious or businesslike part of it, is still a man's world—a world forbidden to women on the assumption that women are frivolous. History does not record the emotions of Eve when she was expelled from Eden, but any girl growing up in today's society cannot help sharing her probable state of mind. There is a wound, tender to the touch; a sense that an important door was closed long before one became wise or strong enough to knock. It helps very little to reflect in private that women are frivolous because they are reared in a frivolous way.

It begins early. Brother, still in diapers, is buttoned into comfortable, practical rompers. (Rompers make the fifteen or twenty changes a day rather complicated, but after all, he's a *boy.*) Sister, on the other hand, is compelled to struggle around in starched dresses, tender knees taking the brunt of every experiment in locomotion.

By the time the siblings are ten, even more significant warpings have taken place. Sister's natural interest in mud-puddles and tree-climbing has been strongly discouraged; Brother's similar bent is still tolerated. Brother has been encouraged to think artificial guns, trains and planes are essential and desirable elements of play, and dolls are despicable; Sister, on the other hand, has been induced to think just the opposite. The resultant cleavage of values shows up in the divorce statistics of our great nation.

When Sister reaches puberty, Nature throws her a final curve, one from which she seldom fully recovers. Now, all that she has been taught by precept and pressure seems confirmed. She really *is* here on this planet for the express purpose of procreation and nothing else. So, clutching her lipstick and comb, she is chivvied through algebra and geometry and taught to screech the grand old school song while Brother performs on the field of sports. It may or may not occur to her that nothing she can ever do in the course of her life will command such public response unless she becomes a famous actress or a lady wrestler. The passage of time usually reveals these possibilities to be remote.

In her twenties, if Sister completes her education and enters a business or profession, she discovers that she must be truly exceptional to excel. Otherwise, only the crumbs that fall from the table set for males can be hers. Brother may get by with luck and pomposity; Sister cannot.

Long after she marries and has children the pattern of her society and what it has done to her may emerge, to burn in her mind like an evil star. She may have brought healthy children into the world, she may have been active in various community enterprises, she may have been a creditable wife, a fastidious housekeeper—but she has been wedded to inevitable frivolity since the obstetrician announced to her mother, "It's a girl!"

THEME TOPICS 7

1. Write a humorous account of your difficulties in adjusting to college life. If you can, give your paper a serious undertone, stressing things you have learned about yourself or about college.

2. Write a satirical attack on features of college life that you think could be improved. Try to employ a type of satire that will appeal not only to students but also to teachers and administrators.

3. Write a satirical paper attacking a type of behavior, or some feature of contemporary American society, of which you disapprove. Avoid excessively trivial subjects. Make your paper effective and acceptable for a fair-minded, well-informed audience.

4. Write a satirical paper that relies primarily on irony, such as ironical praise of something you condemn or easy mock solutions for difficult problems.

5. Write a parody (that is, a satirical imitation) of a type of speech, lecture, or editorial that annoys or amuses you.

6. Study the manner and technique of an author who has attracted your notice because of his distinctive style. Modeling your style on his, write a composition on a subject of your own choice.

7. Write an informal essay designed to give your reader some insight into your personal interests, preferences, or dislikes.

8. Write a composition that gives free rein to your imagination and creative ability.

CHAPTER FOUR

THE WRITER'S SOURCES

8: THE RESEARCH PAPER

1. CHOOSING A SUBJECT

A competent writer draws heavily on personal observation and experience. However, even in dealing with subjects of general interest, he often needs more detailed evidence than he can supply from memory, more comprehensive information than he can assemble by looking up relevant facts in books he has on his shelf. In dealing with technical or scholarly subjects, he must know how to employ the appropriate techniques of research and scholarship. *Every writer must learn to assemble, interpret, and correlate material from a variety of sources.* He must learn to build on the work of previous investigators. He must present his findings in such a way that they will be accepted as the result of detailed and comprehensive exploration, conducted by a competent and responsible observer.

As a student working on a research paper or library paper, you labor under special pressures. The scholar and the scientist accept false starts, unsuccessful experiments, and inconclusive investigations as part of their daily routine. As a student writing a research paper, on the other hand, you need to produce definite results in a limited time. The result of whatever research you do is supposed to be a substantial and coherent paper. Your first task, therefore, is to select a subject that you can profitably treat within the time and with the materials at your disposal.

Obviously, you will avoid subjects for which you are completely unprepared. For instance, recent developments in the natural sciences or in medicine make interesting subjects, but most of them call for a knowledge of mathematics, physics, or chemistry that many college freshmen do not have. If you can, try to start from a foothold of previously acquired knowledge. If you grew up in the South, you might be prepared to investigate the ideas or the influence of a Confederate leader like Jefferson Davis. If your home state is known for its Indian reservations, you might profitably investigate the cultural traditions of an Indian tribe. A research paper, like any other paper, will profit from your ability to relate your subject to your previous interests, your previous experience, your previous reading.

On the other hand, many subjects of general interest provide fruitful topics for a paper of this kind. A research paper will give you a chance to focus on a familiar idea and to assess its validity or significance. For instance, you might trace the concept of "rugged individualism" in the speeches and writings of Herbert Hoover. Or you might compare Mahatma Gandhi's concept of nonviolence with Western ideas of passive resistance.

As you select your subject, make sure that it will allow you to observe a number of basic requirements for a successful paper:

(1) *The paper should center on one limited aspect of a general subject.* If it is designed to establish a thesis, it should concentrate on establishing one or two main points. Avoid subjects that would lead you to compile miscellaneous information. Many research papers are unsuccessful because they cover too much ground. They are too broad in scope, too shallow in treatment. Restrict your general subject area until you arrive at something that you can explore in detail. "The early history of American universities" is a general subject area; "the training of Puritan divines at Harvard" is a specific subject.

(2) *The paper should show that the author has made detailed use of several different sources.* Avoid subjects that would tempt you to summarize preassembled information from one main source. Avoid subjects that are conclusively and satisfactorily treated in a textbook or in an encyclopedia. By definition, a research paper is more than a condensation of easily accessible material. Whatever points you make should require careful sifting and comparing of evidence from different, and possibly conflicting, sources.

(3) *The conclusions elaborated in the paper should stay close to the evidence actually presented.* Avoid subjects whose discussion might bring into play a large measure of partisan allegiance, personal preference, or individual taste—or be prepared to make a special effort to be objective. Your admiration for a presidential candidate and your distaste for Western-style music are likely to hinge on psychological factors that are beyond the scope of the ordinary library paper.

Here are some general areas for research:

1. The past history and future prospects of English spelling; reasons for its irregularity; causes that led to standardization; attempts at spelling reform.

2. The history of dictionary making; the principles and practices of lexicographers like Samuel Johnson or Noah Webster; the history of the *Oxford English Dictionary;* problems of lexicography.

3. The nature and history of Basic English; the purposes it was designed to serve; arguments for or against its use; the obstacles it encountered.

4. The state of foreign-language teaching in American public schools; arguments for and against the study of Latin; current trends toward increased study of foreign language; public-school offerings in Russian and other languages not often taught.

5. The need for an international language; the arguments for or against such projected world languages as Esperanto or Interlingua; the obstacles encountered by advocates of an international language.

6. The history or the extent of the censorship of imaginative literature in the United States; standards applied by critics, courts of law, civic groups; legal means and indirect pressures at the disposal of would-be censors.

7. The early history of some outstanding American universities or colleges; the philosophical, religious, or political motives of their founders; the purposes, vocational or otherwise, for which the institutions were originally intended; the educational principles of their founders or of their original faculties.

8. The education or the reading of a prominent early American; books that influenced Washington, Jefferson, Franklin, or Madison; the influence of the classics or of contemporary trends of thought.

9. The present state of the American theater; the extent, quality, or reception of theatrical activity; the role of professional companies, amateur groups, drama festivals; economic and social status of actors and playwrights.

10. Religious trends in the United States; the growth of Catholicism, the spread and influence of evangelistic movements, the prospects for closer association of the various Protestant denominations, tendencies within American Judaism; interest in religious subjects among high school or college students.

2. USING THE LIBRARY

One aim of a research assignment is to make students realize that a college library is a mine of information and ideas. In a college library, every imaginable subject is covered by books, articles, and reports that are often the result of painstaking and comprehensive study.

Encyclopedias. Whatever your subject, you can start by looking it up in an encyclopedia. A general encyclopedia is a survey of reliable information in every field of study. It is written for laymen, usually with a minimum of technical terminology and of editorial bias.

The *Encyclopaedia Britannica,* as its name implies, is exceptionally full in its coverage of various aspects of British life, such as the British monarchy. Although you would normally consult the most up-to-date edition, you will sometimes find references to the earlier Eleventh Edition, which contained a number of valuable scholarly articles not retained in later revisions.

The *Encyclopedia Americana,* like the *Britannica,* is compiled with the help of outstanding authorities in academic and public life.

The *New International Encyclopaedia* is an older work of comparable standing (now out of print). Each of these major encyclopedias is supplemented annually by a yearbook dealing with the events and discoveries of the preceding year.

The one-volume *Columbia Encyclopedia* provides a bird's-eye view of many subjects that the more comprehensive encyclopedias treat in greater detail.

Bibliographies. At the end of many encyclopedia entries you will find a short bibliography, a list of important books and other sources of information. The encyclopedia may suggest only very general books, but these in turn will often contain more detailed bibliographical listings or direct you to book-length bibliographies. Any general survey of a subject is likely to provide information about more detailed studies. College textbooks in education, history, or language often provide a short bibliography at the end of each chapter.

Take up first those books that a bibliography labels "standard," "indispensable," or "the best introduction" to your subject. If the bibliographies you have consulted merely list books without evaluating them, take up those that are most frequently mentioned. Study their tables of contents, prefaces, introductory or concluding chapters. Find out what each book is trying to do and whether all or parts of it would be useful for your project.

The *Book Review Digest* contains short selections from book reviews written shortly after publication of the book reviewed. These are often sufficient to give you an idea of the intention and importance of books on subjects of general interest.

Periodical Indexes. When writing on a current problem, you may have to rely primarily on articles in both general and technical magazines. Often a well-written magazine article is the most convenient survey of and guide to information on a subject. Often magazine articles contain detailed discussion of points treated very briefly in available books. Since the card catalogue of your library lists magazines but not individual magazine articles, you will have to locate the latter in the so-called periodical indexes. These are published in monthly or semimonthly installments and then combined in huge volumes, each listing articles for a period of one or more years.

The *Readers' Guide to Periodical Literature* indexes magazines written for the general reader. If you are writing on American policy in the Far East, the *Readers' Guide* will direct you to speeches by government officials reprinted in full in *Vital Speeches of the Day* or in the *U.S. News and World Report*. It will direct you to detailed discussions of American foreign policy in such magazines as *Newsweek* or *The Reporter*.

The *International Index to Periodicals* lists articles in technical or scholarly magazines. If you are writing on the status of the American Negro, this index will direct you to articles in sociological and psychological journals. For a paper on cancer research, it will direct you to articles written by outstanding authorities.

Poole's Index to Periodical Literature lists articles published between 1802 and 1906. For instance, it can help you find contemporary reviews of Noah Webster's dictionary or of the novels of James Fenimore Cooper.

Whatever index—or bibliography—you use, read its introductory pages and study its list of abbreviations. Otherwise you may not be able to make sense of its condensed contents. Study the list of the periodicals indexed—it may not include a magazine that you have seen mentioned elsewhere and that you know to be important. Look at sample entries to study the listing of individual articles (usually by subject) and the system of cross references.

Specialized Reference Works. Every major area, such as education, history, or art, has its own specialized reference guides: yearbooks, specialized encyclopedias, dictionaries of names and technical terms, general bibliographies. To find specialized reference works relevant to your research project, turn to Constance M. Winchell's *Guide to Reference Books,* including the supplements bringing it up to date. It lists the standard sources of information for all major fields of study and contains many helpful hints for the inexperienced research worker.

Biography. One type of library project that is often assigned in writing classes is the biographical or quasi-biographical paper. In addition to the biographical entries in the major encyclopedias, most libraries have ample material for this kind of project.

Who's Who in America, a biographical dictionary of notable living men and women, provides a brief summary of dates and details on important contemporaries.

The *Dictionary of American Biography* contains a more detailed account of the lives of important persons. (The British counterparts of these two volumes are *Who's Who* and the *Dictionary of National Biography*.)

The *Biography Index* is a guide to biographical material in books *and* magazines. By consulting both recent and earlier volumes, you can compile a comprehensive bibliography of material on the married life of George Washington or on the evangelistic campaigns of Billy Graham.

Literature. Courses that stress reading and discussion of imaginative literature may include a library project on a subject from literary history—an author's schooling or early reading, recurrent themes in the books of a well-known novelist, the contemporary reputation of a nineteenth-century American poet.

The fifteen-volume *Cambridge History of English Literature* and the *Cambridge Bibliography of English Literature* provide comprehensive information about English authors and literary movements.

The Spiller-Thorp-Johnson-Canby *Literary History of the United States*, with the bibliography published as its third volume, lists as its contributors an impressive and representative roster of contemporary American literary scholars.

Harper's Dictionary of Classical Literature and Antiquities is a comprehensive scholarly guide to Greek and Roman history and civilization. (Robert Graves' *The Greek Myths* and Edith Hamilton's *Mythology*, both available as paperbacks, provide an introduction to famous names and stories.)

Current Events. A number of special reference guides are useful for papers on a political subject or on current events.

Facts on File (published since 1941) is a weekly digest of world news, with an annual index. It gives a summary of news reports and comments with excerpts from important documents and speeches. It can serve as a convenient review of day-to-day happenings in politics, foreign affairs, entertainment, sports, science, and education.

The *New York Times Index* (published since 1913) is a guide to news stories published in the *New York Times*. By looking up an event or a controversy in either one of these indexes, you can ascertain the approximate dates for relevant articles in newspapers and magazines.

The annual index to the *Monthly Catalog of the United States Government Publications* lists reports and documents published by all branches of the federal government.

Sifting Evidence. The collecting and ordering of relevant information, though a basic requirement, is only one limited aspect of research. Research starts when we stop taking things for granted. An inexperienced writer often shows an uncritical acceptance of other writers' views. He tends to accept statements as factual or true on the say-so of a single source: "The teaching of grammar has no appreciable effect on a student's writing" (because Professor X says so). "Economic rivalry between Germany and Great Britain was the primary cause of World War I" (because a book I have just read developed this theory).

An experienced writer will accept such conclusions, if at all, only after comparing and sifting the conflicting evidence offered by different authoritative sources. When he is in doubt, he will prefer the testimony of those best qualified to judge. He is likely to consider such points as the following:

(1) Is the author an *authority on his subject* or merely a casual observer? If you can, find out whether a book was written by an economist whose specialty is Russian agriculture or by a columnist who spent four weeks surveying Russian agriculture from the windows of a train.

(2) Does the author have an *established reputation in his field?* Keep an eye open for comments on the background and the scholarly competence of authors you are reading, or on the reputation of institutions and organizations with which they are connected.

(3) Does the publisher of the book or magazine represent a *tradition of scholarly and serious work?* Does he have a reputation to maintain? Know whether your material comes from a university press or from a popular book club, from a technical journal or from a mass-circulation magazine.

(4) Regardless of the reputation of the author and the publisher, *is the present work a thorough and carefully documented study* or a sketchy, improvised survey of the topic? Is it short on opinion and long on evidence, or vice versa? Does it weigh the findings of other authorities, or simply ignore them?

(5) Does the author settle important questions by *referring to primary sources*—that is, legal documents, letters, diaries, eyewitness reports, transcripts of speeches and interviews, reports on experiments, statistical surveys? Or does he rely exclusively on *secondary sources*—other authors' accounts and interpretations of primary materials?

(6) Is the work *recent enough to have profited from current scholarship?* If it was originally published ten or twenty years ago, is the current version a revised edition? Consider the possibility that an author's views may have been invalidated by new findings and changing theories in a rapidly expanding field of study.

3. USING BIBLIOGRAPHICAL INFORMATION

As soon as one of your writing projects requires extensive use of printed sources, you will realize the usefulness of systems of description and classification that help you to identify and to locate books. You will have to be able to interpret at least some kinds of bibliographical information—that is, information about books that describes their origin, authorship, publication, content, and other matters of interest both to the librarian and to the general reader.

Library Catalogues. Your research projects will ordinarily be geared to the resources of your college library. Its central card catalogue is a complete alphabetical index of the materials available to you.

In most card catalogues, the same book is listed several times: by *author* (under the author's last name), by *title* (under the first word of the title, not counting *The, A,* or *An*), and by *subject*. Often, a card lists the several major *subject headings* under which the book can be found. For instance, a catalogue card for a sociological study of a town in the Middle West may carry the following notation concerning various headings under which it is listed:

1. U.S.—Social conditions. 2. Cities and Towns—U.S. 3. Cost and standard of living—U.S. 4. U.S.—Religion. 5. Social surveys. 6. Community life.

Subject cards can direct you to many books that are relevant to your topic. You have to be flexible and persevering, however, in looking for subject headings under which books on your topic might be listed. Books on progressive education, for instance, might appear under *Education—Aims and Objectives,* under *Education—Experimental Methods,* or under *Educational Psychology.* For books on the Civil War, you would probably start checking under *U. S.—History—Civil War,* but you might also find relevant books under *U. S.—History—Military,* under *Slavery in the United States,* or under *Abolitionists.*

A card for a general-interest book brought out by a commercial publisher will look something like this:

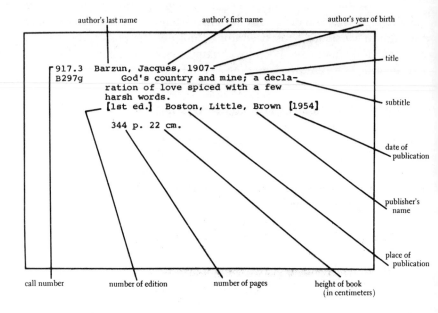

author's last name
author's first name
author's year of birth
title
subtitle
date of publication
publisher's name
place of publication
call number
number of edition
number of pages
height of book (in centimeters)

917.3
B297g

Barzun, Jacques, 1907–
    God's country and mine; a decla-
ration of love spiced with a few
harsh words.
    [1st ed.] Boston, Little, Brown [1954]

344 p. 22 cm.

Such cards contain several kinds of information that can help you to decide whether the book described is of interest to you. After the *full name of the author,* you will find the *date of his birth* and, if applicable, of his death. After the title of the book, you will find *the number or description of the edition.* If the catalogue lists both the original edition and another one marked "2nd ed." or "Rev. ed.," you will generally choose the one that is most nearly up to date and most nearly represents the author's final judgments or opinions.

Occasionally, the *name and location of the publisher* can be a clue to the nature of a book. For instance, a book published by one of the numerous university presses is more likely to be a scholarly and specialized study than a book published by a commercial publisher. The *date of publication* is especially important for books on scientific, technological, or medical subjects, since new scientific discoveries can rapidly invalidate old theories.

The standard catalogue card contains several other items of immediate interest to you. The *number of pages,* with the number of introductory pages given as a lower-case Roman numeral, can indicate whether you are concerned with a short pamphlet or a full-scale treatment of the subject. If the book contains *illustrations* or a *bibliography,* the card will carry a notation to that effect. Of the minimum information contained on the standard catalogue card, the only item that will seldom be of any use to you is the height of the book, given in centimeters.

Once you decide that you should consult a book, copy its call number. The **call number** is the group of letters and numbers usually found in the upper-left-hand corner of the card. It directs you, or the librarian, to the shelf where the book is located. Your library may use either of two numbering systems: the Library of Congress system or the Dewey decimal system. The **Library of Congress system** divides books into categories identified by letters of the alphabet. It then uses additional letters and numerals to subdivide each main category. For instance, the call number of a book on religion would start with a capital *B;* the call number of a book on education starts with a capital *L.* The more widely used **Dewey decimal system** uses numerals to identify the main categories. For instance, 400–499 covers books on language, 800–899 books on literature. The 800 range is then further subdivided into American literature (810–819), English literature (820–829), and so on. Additional numerals and letters distinguish among individual authors and among individual works by the same author.

Along with the call number, you may find a notation directing you to a special section of the library. The book you are looking for may be located in a reference room where encyclopedias, dictionaries, and other reference works are kept. It may be located in a special reading room where books for a particular field of study are on reserve. Although the card catalogue will list magazines and newspapers, most libraries have a separate, compact catalogue for periodicals. It lists, in alphabetical order, all periodicals to which the library subscribes. For each periodical it indicates the location of recent issues (often on the shelves of a separate periodical room) as well as of back issues (usually in bound volumes in the book stacks of the library).

Bibliography Cards. Tracing books in the card catalogue is tiring and time-consuming. It will be even more tiring and time-consuming than usual if you have to return to the catalogue repeatedly for information that you failed to record. You should, therefore, work out an efficient system of recording all bibliographical information that you need for your project.

At an early stage, start your own card catalogue of all materials that seem promising or worthy of investigation. Include a separate note card for each book, pamphlet, or magazine article you intend to use. Be selective, but include enough material so that you can later pick and choose. Your instructor may suggest a minimum number of sources he wants you to consult. Your preliminary bibliography should have more than the minimum.

On each bibliography card, include the library call number or the place in the library where the publication is to be found. This information is for your own personal use, and you should not reproduce it when identifying one of your sources in a footnote or in a list of references in your finished paper. Other entries on your cards, on the other hand, will serve as the basis for references to a source in your paper. Check all entries carefully against the title page of the book or the heading of the magazine article in order to correct discrepancies. Be especially careful to get the *exact spelling* of unfamiliar names.

Usually, the first item you record is the *full name of the author*. Put the last name first to facilitate alphabetizing. If a work has been collected or arranged by a person other than the author (or the authors), you may start with that person's name, followed by "ed." for "editor." Ordinarily, however, the name of an editor or of a translator (followed by "trans.") appears on a separate line below the title. If an article in an encyclopedia is identified only by the author's initials, you may be able to find his full name by checking the initials against a list of contributors.

Start a new line for the *full title of the publication*, including a subtitle, if any. Underline the title of a book, pamphlet, or other work published as a separate entity. Underlining in a typed manuscript corresponds to italics in print. Put the title of an article or short poem in quotation marks and underline the title of the magazine, collection, or encyclopedia of which it forms a part.

Use a separate line for the *facts of publication*. For a book or pamphlet these may include a number of different items:

(1) The *number or description of the edition* (unless a book has not been re-edited since publication).

(2) The *number of volumes* (if a work consists of several, and all are relevant to your investigation).

(3) The *place of publication* (usually the location of the main office of the publishing house, or of the first branch office listed if several are given).

(4) The *name of the publisher*.

(5) The *date of publication* (not always given on the title page, though it can usually be inferred from the copyright date, found on the reverse side of the title page).

(6) The *number of the specific volume used* (if only one of several volumes is relevant to your investigation).

Often, a bibliography card for a book need list no more than the following information:

509   Conant, James Bryant
C743o   *On Understanding Science: An Historical Approach*
         New Haven: Yale University Press, 1947

For a magazine or newspaper article, the facts of publication ordinarily do *not* include the name of the publisher and the place of publication, though the latter is sometimes needed to identify a small-town journal. The pages of most professional or technical magazines are numbered consecutively through the several issues comprising one volume, usually the issues published during one year. For an article in such a magazine, record the *number of the volume* (preferably in Roman numerals), the *date of the issue,* and the *page numbers of the article.* For articles in other magazines and in newspapers, record the date of the issue and the page numbers. If the pages in separate sections of a newspaper are not numbered consecutively, identify the section where the article is to be found.

A bibliography card for an article is likely to contain something like the following:

Periodical   Whyte, Lancelot Law
Room   "Can We Grow Geniuses in Science?"
             Harper's Magazine, CCXIV (June 1957), 46–50

Annotation. You will greatly increase the usefulness of your bibliography cards by annotation. *Write down brief reminders concerning characteristic features of your sources.* Thus, you might want to note that an article on atomic energy is extremely technical; perhaps it requires more knowledge of physics than you command. Another article on the same subject may be a popularized treatment and give none of the specific data which you would need for a paper on, say, the comparative cost of electricity from atom-powered plants and from standard sources. Or you may want to note that one of the books you have found has a helpful glossary of technical terms, or an annotated bibliography, or a convenient summary of historical facts relevant to your investigation. An example of an annotated card appears on page 180.

The sooner you formulate such tentative conclusions about the strong and the weak points of your source materials, the sooner you will be able to concentrate on the sources that are most helpful and profitable. If your project is to provide the basis for further study on the part of your reader, you can help him by annotating the final bibliography which you furnish with your paper.

```
Humanities      Neville, Mark A.
Room            "Who Killed Poetry?"
                The English Journal, XLVII (March 1958),
                                          133-138

     Examines, with examples, conventional methods
of teaching poetry in high schools.  Concludes
that teachers of poetry should stress appreciation
and enjoyment rather than the study of versifica-
tion.
```

4. THE TECHNIQUE OF NOTE-TAKING

While you are investigating possible source materials, your reading will be primarily exploratory. You may read an article in an
encyclopedia or a chapter in a textbook. You may glance through introductory material and selected chapters in a number of promising
books. You may check magazine articles for a summary statement of
purpose and content. Even at this stage you may be jotting down
interesting information, tentative observations, and questions that you
might want to explore. However, it will be some time before you have
a fairly clear idea of the subject matter to which you are going to limit
yourself and of the specific question your paper is going to answer.
Only then will you be ready to start taking notes in a thorough and
systematic manner.

Gathering Material. What to record and how to record it are not
simple questions to answer. Generally, you will *select material for its
relevance to tentative generalizations that you formulate as you go
along.* Ideally, you should become better able to decide what material
is relevant to your purpose with every step in your investigation.

Suppose you are writing a research paper on trends toward increased teaching of foreign languages in the public schools. You are
consulting a number of books published in the late fifties and early

sixties and devoted to the improvement of American public education. By glancing over the table of contents and consulting the index of each book, you locate a number of discussions bearing on your subject. The following passages seem particularly relevant:

> The school board should be ready to offer a third and fourth year of a foreign language, no matter how few students enroll. . . . I have met no teachers of foreign language who felt that anything approaching mastery could be obtained by the study of a foreign language for only two years in high school, nor have the students felt that two years of study had given them any real working knowledge of the language. Four years of study, on the other hand, will yield dividends for those capable of handling foreign languages. This is the recommendation of the foreign language panel of the NEA Conference on the Identification and Education of the Academically Talented held in Washington in February, 1958.
>
> Almost without exception, I found a deplorable state of affairs in regard to foreign languages. . . .—James B. Conant, *The American High School Today*, p. 69.

> . . . In the third field of importance today—foreign languages— the situation is even more serious. One consequence is that we have a diplomatic service where only 50 per cent now have command of a foreign language and where—still worse—a mere 30 per cent of the incoming recruits speak any foreign language; clear evidence of the deterioration of foreign-language teaching in the last generation. . . .
>
> Progressive education must be blamed in large part for our neglect of foreign-language teaching. . . . We are the only major country which neglects the early years when a child can learn foreign languages most easily—from 10 onward.—H. G. Rickover, *Education and Freedom*, p. 109 and App., p. 65.

The American attitude toward the study of foreign languages has changed remarkably in the last decade. Twenty years ago, the future for these subjects seemed bleak indeed. Greek was gone, Latin was going, and enrollments in French and German were steadily declining. . . . In the early fifties, the Modern Language Association of America received from the Rockefeller Foundation a substantial grant for the purpose of setting up a Foreign Language Program. . . . It collected and disseminated information of all sorts and tried with some success to persuade the nation that a revival of foreign languages was in the national interest. The movement called FLES—Foreign Languages in the Elementary Schools—was greatly encouraged by this project.

The shudder that the launching of the Russian satellite sent through the world accelerated the swing back to foreign languages, as to other solid subjects. . . . The most dramatic response was the National Defense Education Act of 1958, which provided funds for the improvement and expansion of instruction in science, mathematics, and modern foreign languages.—Albert R. Kitzhaber e.a., *Education for College*, pp. 113–116.[1]

From these and related passages, a number of tentative areas of agreement emerge. The first is the relatively low state of foreign-language teaching in the past. The second is a growing concern in the last one or two decades with the improvement of foreign-language instruction, reflected in the recommendations of educational authorities like Dr. Conant, in the efforts of professional organizations, and in government support. In further reading, you will look for material that will support or clarify these tentative points. At the same time, these passages suggest avenues for further exploration: You will try to find some of the "information of all sorts" disseminated by the Modern Language Association, some of it likely to be found in its official quarterly, *PMLA*. You will try to find out more about the role of the National Education Association (NEA), again perhaps turning first to an official publication like the *NEA Journal*. You will try to locate authoritative accounts of the original National Defense Education Act, both its original intent and its impact on the schools.

Recording Material. Even while recording information and ideas, you should adapt them for use in your project. You will have to employ a combination of techniques:

(1) Often you will need to *extricate important points from long passages*, to *summarize or condense lengthy quotations*. A formal abridgment, sometimes called a **précis**, preserves all essential generalizations and qualifications while curtailing or omitting altogether such material as explanations, examples, and incidental comments. It uses the most economical kind of wording, substituting one-word equivalents for lengthy phrases wherever possible. (See O 5.)

When you condense material for reproduction in the finished paper, you are likely to be more selective than in preparing a formal précis. You will pick out only those points of a report or of an argument that are directly relevant to your investigation. For instance, you may be investigating Woodrow Wilson's unsuccessful defense of the Treaty of Versailles and the League of Nations in 1919. After reading several pages of a historical study that reviews relevant political facts, you may decide to summarize them for use in an introductory paragraph. Your note, taken from an authoritative political history of the United States, might look something like this:

[1] Albert R. Kitzhaber, Robert M. Gorrell, and Paul Roberts, *Education for College: Improving the High School Curriculum.* Copyright © 1961 The Ronald Press Company.

```
American Politics 1918-1920

     Election of Republican Congress in 1918.
Bitter opposition to President's role in peace
conference from such men as ex-President
Roosevelt and Senator Lodge.  Unprecedented
Republican majority in congressional elections
of 1920.  Final rejection of treaty and of
League of Nations  by U.S. Senate in March
1920.



Commager, History, pp. 411-413
```

(2) Many of the notes you will take for a research project will record information fairly specifically and fully. A flexible method of recording such material is the **paraphrase**. In paraphrasing a passage, you *translate information and ideas into your own words*. This method enables you to select and emphasize points you consider important while at the same time working them smoothly into your text:

```
Wilson's Campaign in Support of League

     Speech at Pueblo, Colorado, shows that
Wilson is very much aware of the activities of
men creating what he considers erroneous im-
pressions concerning the League of Nations.
Speech is designed to dispel mistaken impressions
created in the public's mind.

     The proposed peace treaty is based not on
the desire for territorial acquisition but on the
principle that people should freely choose their
own governments.  The League of Nations is needed
to mobilize the united moral force of the great
nations of the world in support of the principles
of nonaggression and of self-determination for
all nations.



Heffner, Documents, p. 235
```

(3) You should *use well-chosen quotations to pinpoint key ideas or to clinch an argument.* Preserve characteristic phrases that give an insight into the personality of an author, whether by illustrating his aspirations, his sense of humor, or his style. The following note reproduces verbatim an author's position on a debatable point:

Dangers of Conformity

    "The idea that men are created free and equal is both true and misleading: men are created different; they lose their social freedom and their individual autonomy in seeking to become like each other."

Riesman, Lonely Crowd, p. 349

Use **direct quotation** sparingly or not at all in reproducing information, in outlining an author's argument, and in covering minor or noncontroversial points. Unselective recording of verbatim material in your notes is likely to lead to the kind of paper that consists primarily of lengthy excerpts from the original sources, held together by a thin tissue of phrases like "He further says . . ." and "We should also remember that . . ." Frequent use of undigested direct quotations tempts the reader to skip the quoted material and to look in the accompanying text for your main point.

Make sure that your notes differentiate clearly between paraphrase or indirect quotation on the one hand and direct quotation on the other. In other words, *use quotation marks to identify all material quoted verbatim.*

Note Cards. Most composition instructors require that their students take notes for a research project on 3x5 or 4x6 cards. Separate note cards enable you to sort out and reshuffle information, so that the task of organizing the material for your paper can proceed with a minimum of mechanical difficulties. Observing the following suggestions will help you make efficient use of your cards:

(1) Each card should record either *one single item of information or material so closely related that there is no chance of your having to separate it* in order to use it in different parts of your paper. However, generalizations should be accompanied by the specific detail that you will need to illustrate or support them in a paragraph. Include selected examples, statistical figures, definitions of difficult terms.

(2) The *material on each card should be full and clear enough* to make sense to you even after the context in which it originally appeared is no longer fresh in your mind. Of course, you will try to keep your notes free of unnecessary ballast. But excessive use of condensation and of abbreviations may make notes worthless later.

(3) The *material on each card should be representative* of the source from which it was taken. Be careful not to copy, as bare assertion, statements that are modified or qualified by the context in which they originally appeared.

(4) Each card should clearly *identify the source of the material recorded.* Use either a shortened form of the author's name and of the title of the work, or a code number that you have assigned the work in your preliminary bibliography. *Include the exact page reference.* Going back to a 500-page book to find a lost page reference can be like looking for the needle in the proverbial haystack.

(5) If you have arrived at tentative subdivisions for your paper, the *heading to which the material on the card relates* should appear at the top of the card. Use headings that will divide your material into sizable but convenient units. Having too many cards per heading will make your notes unwieldy. Having too few cards per heading will make your notes confusing.

5. WRITING AND REVISING THE FIRST DRAFT

By taking notes on separate cards, you can sort your notes into tentative categories while you are still studying your sources. When you have done most of the necessary reading, you should review your note cards to consider the main divisions they suggest.

Organizing the Research Paper. The principles of organization that apply to the research paper are the same as those applying to the ordinary expository theme. Group together those of your cards that contain related material. Often a group of cards will record details pointing to a common generalization, evidence backing up the same major point. Often a group of cards will record related causes combining to produce a common result. Two related groups of cards may contain parallel sets of data for a detailed comparison of two objects, ideas, or events.

Make sure that such logical relations among individual cards, and then among related groups of cards, are carefully thought through. *The major weakness of many research papers is that the connections between the recorded facts are not clearly worked out.* Make sure your finished paper will not strike the reader as a collection of loosely connected bits of information. One essential step in organizing your note cards is grouping them according to the major conclusions they justify. Another essential step is setting aside cards containing material not relevant to the major points you are trying to establish. The more definite shape your paper assumes in your mind, the more clearly should a unifying purpose or a unifying thesis emerge from your collection of data.

Suppose you are writing a paper on the present state of gambling in the United States. Your main problem will be to keep your paper from becoming a repository of miscellaneous facts about gambling laws, famous gamblers, different games of chance, and tourist life in Las Vegas. To unify your paper, you might concentrate on the legal aspects of gambling. You could then review in some detail the laws of Nevada as exceptions to anti-gambling laws in other states, the legal status of horse and dog races, the question of lotteries and games conducted for charitable purposes. Another way of unifying your paper might be to concentrate on the extent and variety of gambling in this country. You could then examine in some detail some of the most popular kinds of gambling. You could assemble statistics showing that gambling in one form or another plays a role in the lives of perhaps fifty million Americans.

Outlining the Paper. *After arranging your cards in a tentative sequence, write a preliminary outline that reflects their order.* Formulate a tentative thesis sentence summarizing the conclusion that your paper seems to suggest. As your outline and your thesis sentence begin to take definite form, they will enable you to decide which of your note cards contain unnecessary or irrelevant material and should be set aside. They will also help you to decide in which areas your notes need to be supplemented by further reading. A definitive outline preceding the final paper usually shows whether the paper has a unifying purpose, whether the major subdivisions of the paper contribute to that purpose, and whether unrelated odds and ends have been eliminated.[2]

Once you have a preliminary outline, you can start writing a first rough draft of your paper. Keep your eyes on your over-all plan and decide to be temporarily satisfied with less than perfection in details. Where necessary, modify your plan or reorganize your note cards as you proceed. You are bound to encounter unexpected difficulties and unexpected solutions. If you notice unanswered questions or missing evidence, note the inadequacies in the margin and follow them up later.

Using Quoted Material. The most obvious difference between composing a short theme and composing a research paper is the need for working into the text an often considerable amount of quoted material. The following examples illustrate some legitimate, and some illegitimate, ways of incorporating material from a source into the text of a paper:

(1) *Extensive quotation—to be used sparingly.*

such a view. In an article in Fortune that has been fre-

quently reprinted, Adlai Stevenson stated his belief that

American postwar prosperity was due to the cooperation of

business and government:

> It is a curious thing that the two institutional forces in the democratic capitalistic society that contributed most directly to this emergence of the powerful consumer during this quarter-century seemed to snarl at each other every step of their common way. The bounding prosperity of postwar America has been due in large measure to processes in which government and business have in effect played complementary and cooperative roles. The New Deal legislation of the Thirties helped to provide a "built-in" consumer demand that business could then work to satisfy, and the increase of 70 per cent in the scale of the American economy between 1939 and 1944 was achieved by the closest cooperation between government and industry in America's war effort.[7]

---

[7]Adlai E. Stevenson, "My Faith in Democratic Capitalism," Fortune, October 1955, p. 126.

[2] For forms of outlines see O 5.

In this example, a lengthy excerpt from a source is used to buttress an important point. The excerpt is indented and set off from the text as a **block quotation**—*no quotation marks, single-spaced lines.* The sentence introducing the excerpt gives credit to author and publication; the footnote numeral at the end directs the reader to the footnote providing the name of the article and an exact page reference. *The introductory sentence also summarizes the main point or the significance of the quotation.* A reader easily becomes bored and discouraged if he cannot make out why he is asked to give his attention to numerous lengthy quotations.

(2) *Plagiarized version—illegitimate, unacknowledged paraphrase.*

```
has had lasting effects.  But it is surprising that the

two forces in our society that contributed most to the

emergence of the powerful consumer seemed to snarl at each

other every step of the way.  The prosperity of postwar

America has been due to t he fact that government and

business have played complementary and cooperative roles.

The New Deal legislation of the Thirties provided a built-in

consumer demand for business to satisfy.  The increase of

70 per cent in the American economy was achieved by the

cooperation between government and industry in America's

war effort.
```

Much **plagiarism** takes this form: a slightly abridged version of the original source. Even if the source were identified, this way of adapting the material would be unsatisfactory. It preserves far too much of the original author's way of putting things—without using direct quotation. Sentence structure corresponds closely to that of the original. Much of the characteristic phrasing is preserved ("emergence of the powerful consumer," "seemed to snarl," "complementary and cooperative roles"). The only changes are the omission or shortening of incidental phrases. As in much hasty adaptation, qualifications that made the original cautious have been lost ("due to" for "due *in large measure* to"; "provided" for "*helped* to provide").

(3) *Legitimate paraphrase—attributed to the original author.*

Like other observers, Mr. Stevenson points out the
irony in the apparent hostility of the two major institutions
that made the American consumer a powerful force in the
nation's economy. He attributes the rapidly growing prosperity of postwar America at least partly to the cooperation,
intentional or unintentional, of government and business.
Thus, legislation enacted under the Roosevelt administration
helped to increase consumer purchasing power. Similarly,
the extraordinary growth of the American economy between
1939 and 1944 was the result of government and industry
working together in building up the country's military
strength.[7]

This **paraphrase**, documented by a footnote, preserves the essential meaning of the original. At the same time, by translating the
passage into his own words, the adapter shows that he has understood it. He shows how he interprets phrases that are in any way
unusual or metaphorical. For instance, he takes the phrase "a curious
thing" to express irony. For the graphic "seemed to snarl" he substitutes its literal equivalent, "apparent hostility." The metaphorical
"bounding prosperity" becomes "rapidly growing prosperity." He takes
the distinction between "complementary" and "cooperative" roles to
imply a possible difference between unintentional and intentional cooperation. Instead of using percentage points, the adapter describes the
growth of the economy as "extraordinary." Though general, this term
does justice to the intention of the original. Although some of the sentences are roughly parallel to the original in grammatical construction,
others—for instance, the first and second ones—are completely reorganized. This kind of close paraphrase is useful when detailed interpretation and evaluation of a source is desirable.

(4) *Part paraphrase, part direct quotation—worked closely into the text.*

Like economists and sociologists before him, Mr. Stevenson emphasizes that government and business in this country have in effect worked together in assuring postwar prosperity--even though they "seemed to snarl at each other every step of their common way." As he implies but does not directly state, business has never openly acknowledged that "New Deal legislation . . . helped to provide a 'built-in' consumer demand that business could then work to satisfy." He attributes an "increase of 70 per cent in the scale of the American economy between 1939 and 1944" to "the closest cooperation" between government and industry.[7]

This technique is the most flexible and most generally useful one for adapting source material to the adapter's own use. He condenses, restates, and interprets the material he has selected, while at the same time using brief direct quotations for important points and characteristic phrases. Competent use of this technique can effectively break up the deadly "So-and-So says such-and-such" pattern found in many library papers.

(5) *Legitimate summary.*

Mr. Stevenson feels that postwar prosperity in this country was to a large extent the result of cooperation between government and business. Specifically he refers to the role of New Deal legislation in restoring consumer demand and to the joint participation of government and industry in the war effort.[7]

This **summary** gets at the gist of the passage. At the same time it lists briefly arguments or details supporting the main point in the original.

Form of Quotations. *Review carefully the conventions governing the punctuation of quoted material.* Pay special attention to the distinction between direct and indirect quotation, to differences in handling long and short passages, and to ways of indicating omissions and insertions.[3]

(1) There should be no problems of grammar or sentence structure as long as a quotation is a grammatically separate unit. However, if a quotation is only *part of a complete sentence,* you need to work it into the grammatical pattern of the sentence that introduces it, *without* changing the original wording of the material enclosed in quotation marks. Often, you will have to limit direct quotation to those parts of a quotation that fit into the sentence pattern of the introductory sentence, giving the indigestible parts in the form of indirect quotation. Here are some quotations before and after revision:

UNSATISFACTORY: Pope Pius described a just war in this way: "If it has been forced upon one by an evident and extremely grave injustice that in no way can be avoided."

SATISFACTORY: Pope Pius stated that a war is just "if it has been forced upon one by an evident and extremely grave injustice that in no way can be avoided."

UNSATISFACTORY: The writer suggests that Whittaker Chambers, "Having experienced at first hand the evils of communism, he now sees himself clad in shining armor, engaged in deadly combat with that evil."

SATISFACTORY: The writer says of Whittaker Chambers that "having experienced at first hand the evils of communism, he now sees himself clad in shining armor, engaged in deadly combat with that evil."

(2) Quotations must be satisfactory not only grammatically but also logically. *A quotation, to be intelligible, should not require explanations that you do not provide.* Suppose you quote Albert Schweitzer as saying, "I therefore stand and work in the world, as one who aims at making men less shallow and morally better by making them think." To keep the quotation from being logically incomplete, you will have to let your reader know what the "therefore" stands for. If you don't want to include the reasons to which it refers, you will have to shorten or paraphrase the quotation in such a way as

[3] See P 8.

to omit it. A frequent cause of logically unsatisfactory quotations is the orphaned pronoun, whose antecedent was present in the original text but was not included in the passage selected for quotation. If you quote Walter Lippmann as saying, "They must assert a public interest against private inclination," you obviously have to inform the reader who "they" are.

(3) Make sure your text *differentiates clearly between your opinions and the opinions of authors you are investigating.* There is considerable difference between "Capitalism is a moribund system" and "According to Marx, capitalism is a moribund system." If you are citing several authors, make sure that references like "he," "this author," or "the writer" point clearly to the person you have in mind.

Revision. A first draft differs from the finished paper in several important respects. It usually makes jerky reading. The writer is likely to have concentrated on arranging his material in the most logical or the most convenient order without always explaining to his readers how he got from one paragraph to the other. He is likely to have been absorbed in formulating his own observations and conclusions without worrying at every step whether they will make sense to others. He is likely to have concentrated on getting the main body of the paper into shape, providing no more than a routine introduction and allowing the paper to run out without a definite conclusion.

As a result, the writer who merely retypes his first draft and submits it as the finished product of his investigation is cheating himself of a just reward for his efforts. In this form, even the results of a thorough and competent investigation are likely to seem muddled, fragmentary, and opinionated. *Careful revision of the first draft is an essential step, and your timetable should make adequate allowance for it.*

In revising your first draft, you will make changes ranging from the substitution of a semicolon for a comma to the rearrangement of major sections of your paper. However, regardless of the specific improvements needed, your revision should concern itself with several basic requirements for a successful paper:

(1) Check for *adequacy of detail.* See to it that individual points are clearly stated and well illustrated or documented. Make sure that the evidence you present in support of your generalizations is adequate to prevent questions such as "Is this really so?" "Is this merely a superficial impression?" or "Do the experts agree on this point?"

(2) Check for *clarity of explanation.* Many papers suffer from

too much quotation, too much paraphrase, too much summary, and not enough explanation and comparison. Examine key terms to see whether they need to be more explicitly defined. Explain terms like *Hellenistic, psychosomatic,* or *lingua franca.*

(3) Check for *adequate paragraph structure.* Avoid sequences of short paragraphs that give bits of information or quotation from different sources. Instead, work material from different note cards into a coherent paragraph that coordinates, compares, contrasts. Choppy paragraphing makes continuous reading difficult, if not impossible.

(4) Check for *clear attribution.* If you are comparing different sources, keep your reader from getting hopelessly confused about who says what. Constant repetition of phrases like "according to Dewey" or "as his biographer observes" can make a paper seem heavy-handed. However, awkward but exact identification is preferable to elegant but misleading continuity of discussion.

(5) Check for *coherence.* Make your reader see the relationship between different parts of your paper. Anticipate and answer the questions of a reader mired in a mass of details: "How did this get in here?" "Why do I have to study this particular set of statistics?" Make sure there is a clear transition, implied or explicitly stated, from paragraph to paragraph. Inserting a *therefore,* a *nevertheless,* or a *for instance* in a few strategic places can help transform a rambling discussion into a tightly knit argument. Check the organization of the paper against your tentative outline and adjust your outline to reflect any changes you made while writing the first draft and while revising it.

(6) Check for *clarity of over-all intention.* Make sure that the main points or the general conclusions you are trying to bring out are not merely implied but clearly and fully stated. State them preferably at the beginning of the paper following your introduction or, if more appropriate, toward the end of the paper in the form of a summary. Don't take it for granted that your reader will automatically arrive at the same conclusions that you did if you merely present "the facts."

6. PREPARING FOOTNOTES AND BIBLIOGRAPHIES

Documentation enables your readers to identify, trace, and check your sources. Its purpose should not be to impress your readers with a cumbersome scholarly apparatus, but to provide exact and comprehensive information in condensed form.

Footnotes. *In your own paper, the main purpose of footnotes will be to document your sources.* You will use footnotes to indicate the origin of facts, opinions, and illustrative material, whether you quote them directly, paraphrase them, or summarize them. However, footnotes are not used exclusively for the purpose of documentation. **Explanatory footnotes** may define technical terms unfamiliar only to some of the readers. They may provide information not necessary to an understanding of the main trend of the argument. They may contain reservations that would confuse ordinary readers but are needed to satisfy critical ones. Use such incidental material sparingly. Many readers check all footnotes to make sure they miss nothing of importance. They will be annoyed if you make them interrupt their reading for the sake of something trivial or irrelevant.

Current practice favors consecutive numbering of all footnotes for a paper, article, or chapter of a book. In other words, footnotes are not indicated by asterisks or similar symbols. Nor do the footnote numbers start anew on each individual page. The **footnote number** is placed outside whatever punctuation goes with the item to which it refers. The footnote itself is indented like a paragraph and is introduced by a raised numeral; the numeral is *not* followed by a period or other punctuation. The footnote begins with a capital letter and ends with appropriate terminal punctuation, most commonly a period.

In printed publications, the footnotes for each page appear in small print at the bottom of each page. In typed manuscripts, footnotes are usually single-spaced and placed in one of three possible positions. They may be placed between two unbroken lines immediately below the line of typed material to which they belong. This system, when permitted by the instructor, helps the inexperienced researcher to make the right footnote go with the right portion of the text.[4] They

[4] Even when a different system of placing footnotes is required in the final paper, students may find the system of which this footnote is an illustration the most convenient one to follow in the first draft. It prevents errors when footnotes have to be renumbered because of changes in the manuscript.

may be placed at the bottom of the page, separated from the text by an unbroken line or by triple spacing. This system is convenient for the reader, who is used to a similar arrangement in printed material, but it is hard on the amateur typist. It requires him to type his footnotes on a separate sheet of paper so that he can estimate the amount of space needed for each and leave exactly enough space at the bottom of each page for the footnotes that go with it. Finally, footnotes may appear on a separate sheet at the end of the paper.

First References. Of the footnotes used for documentation, the most important type gives full information about a source when the text cites it—that is, quotes it or refers to it—for the first time.

Here are some examples of the standard form for a **first reference** to books and articles:

> [6] Albert C. Baugh, *A History of the English Language* (New York, 1935), p. 450.

> [4] Irving H. Anderson and Walter F. Dearborn, *The Psychology of Teaching Reading* (New York, 1952), pp. 70–72.

> [7] Harold Taylor, "The Aims of Education," *College English*, XVIII (February 1957), 250–251.

> [3] "U.S. Asked to Aid Youth Exchanges," *The New York Times*, June 15, 1957, p. 8, col. 1.

> [2] Jeanne Contini, "The Illiterate Poets of Somalia," *The Reporter*, March 14, 1963, p. 36.

In its standard form, such a footnote starts with the *first name, middle initial, and last name of the author.* Some names of well-known authors usually contain initials for first and middle names: T. S. Eliot, W. H. Auden, I. A. Richards. However, initials used with common names like Brown, Douglas, or Smith may force the reader to hunt through several hundred catalogue entries for publications by Smiths whose first names have the same initial. Note that a footnote, unlike a bibliography or other alphabetical listing, puts the first name first.

The second essential item, or the first if the author's name is unknown, is the *title*, separated from what precedes it by a comma. Titles of books, magazines, and newspapers are underlined (or italicized in print). Titles of articles published in magazines and newspapers or as parts of books are enclosed in quotation marks and separated by a comma from the title of the publication in which they appeared: "How to Deep-Freeze Bait," *The Fisherman's Monthly.*

The third essential item is information about the *circumstances of publication.* The title of a book is usually followed by place and year of publication, separated from each other by a comma and enclosed in parentheses, but not separated from what precedes them by other punctuation: (New York, 1958). The title of a magazine or newspaper may be followed by the date of the issue, separated from what precedes and follows it by commas. The volume number is usually given as a capital Roman numeral, separated from the title by a comma and, if appropriate, followed by the date of the issue in parentheses.

The fourth essential item is the *page reference,* separated from the rest of the footnote by a comma. Page numbers are preceded by the abbreviation "p." for a single page and "pp." for several pages: pp. 163–168. These abbreviations are omitted if the page reference is signaled by a volume number given as a Roman numeral: XV (March 1958), 53.

NOTE: *Pay special attention to the way punctuation marks are used in the sample footnotes in this section.* Use commas, periods, parentheses, and quotation marks as here illustrated unless you are otherwise instructed by the teacher or editor who is to pass judgment on your work.

Variations from Standard Form. At times you will have to omit from a footnote elements usually included or add elements not always applicable. If the *text of your paper gives the author's full name,* or both his full name and the full title of the work, do not repeat them in the footnote. The footnote will then start either with the title or with the facts of publication:

> [6] *A History of the English Language* (New York, 1935), p. 450.
>
> [6] New York, 1935, p. 450.

If the work you cite has a *subtitle,* separate it from the title by a colon unless the original has other punctuation. Underline the subtitle of a book; enclose both the title and the subtitle of an article in the same set of quotation marks:

> [3] Lionel Trilling, *The Liberal Imagination: Essays on Literature and Society* (New York, 1950), p. 47.
>
> [1] John J. Gross, "The Writer in America: A Search for Community," *Queen's Quarterly,* LXIII (Autumn 1956), 387.

If the author's work has been selected, arranged, or translated by someone else, insert the *editor's or translator's name* after the title, separating it from the title by a comma and introducing it with the abbreviation "ed." or "trans." In references to collections of letters, to the work of unknown authors, or to selections from many different authors, the editor's name may take the place of the author's name:

> [2] H. L. Mencken, *The Vintage Mencken,* ed. Alistair Cooke (New York, 1956), p. 49.

⁸ André Siegfried, *America at Mid-Century,* trans. Margaret Ledésert (New York, 1955), p. 227.

⁵ Kenneth Sisam, ed. *Fourteenth Century Verse and Prose* (London, 1948), p. 14.

If a work has been revised or re-edited since its original publication, indicate the *number of the edition* you are using. Place it before the facts of publication, separating it from what proceeds it by a comma:

² Albert C. Baugh, *A History of the English Language,* 2nd ed. (New York, 1957), pp. 7–8.

⁹ M. B. Forman, ed. *The Letters of John Keats,* 3rd ed. (London, 1948), pp. 67–68.

If a work consists of several volumes, insert the *number of the volume* you are citing. Use a capital Roman numeral, insert it after the facts of publication, and separate it from what precedes and follows it by commas. Remember that after a volume number "p." and "pp." are omitted:

³ Vernon Louis Parrington, *Main Currents in American Thought: An Interpretation of American Literature from the Beginnings to 1920* (New York, 1930), III, 355.

Subsequent References. After you have cited a book or article once, subsequent references to it should not repeat the full name of the author, the full title, and the facts of publication. You should aim at saving time and space while at the same time making the **shortened reference** identify the work clearly each time you mention it. When you are using only *one work of an author,* subsequent references may consist of the author's last name, separated from the page reference by a comma:

¹¹ Baugh, p. 9.

When you are using *several works by the same author,* subsequent references may consist of the author's last name, a shortened form of the title, and the page reference, with the different items kept separate by commas:

¹¹ Baugh, *History,* p. 9.

An alternative system for shortened reference, making use of **Latin abbreviations**, is no longer in frequent use. Instead of repeating, in a shortened form, the author's name or the title, the writer may use *ibid.*, an abbreviation of Latin *ibidem,* meaning "in the same place." When used by itself, without a page reference, it means "in the last publication cited, on the same page." When used with a page reference, it means "in the last publication cited, on the page indicated." Like other Latin abbreviations used in footnotes, *ibid.* is no longer commonly italicized. It can refer only to *the last source cited*:

> [1] G. B. Harrison, *Introducing Shakespeare* (New York, 1947), p. 28.
>
> [2] Ibid., p. 37.

A work other than the last one mentioned may be identified by the author's name followed by *op. cit.,* short for *opere citato,* meaning "in the work already cited." This abbreviation is ambiguous and inappropriate if the writer has already cited more than one work by the same author.

> [1] G. B. Harrison, *Introducing Shakespeare* (New York, 1947), p. 28.
>
> [2] B. Ifor Evans, *A Short History of English Drama* (Hammondsworth, Middlesex, 1948), pp. 51–69.
>
> [3] Harrison, op. cit., p. 37.

NOTE: Try to avoid a long string of footnotes giving different page references to the same work. If two or three quotations from the same portion of a work follow one another in one paragraph of your paper, you can sometimes *incorporate the different page references in a single footnote*:

> [11] Harrison, pp. 8–9, 12.

Frequently Cited Sources. A number of well-known and frequently cited sources do not require detailed identification. For instance, *references to standard encyclopedias* usually do not mention the names of the editors or the place of publication. Page numbers are unnecessary for short entries, because articles arranged in alphabetical order can be easily located. However, references to encyclopedias usually include the date or the number of the edition used, since the frequent revisions of major encyclopedias often omit or modify articles contained in earlier editions:

> [2] M. J. Politis, "Greek Music," *Encyclopedia Americana,* 1956.

References to the Bible usually identify only the book, the chapter, and the verse. The edition used is not mentioned unless the differences in wording between different translations are important. Notice that the name of a book of the Bible is not underlined or put in quotation marks:

⁴ Judges 13:5.   or   ⁴ Judges xiii.5.

First *references to literary classics* available in many different editions usually note the edition used. However, they often supplement page references by indicating the location of a passage in other ways for the benefit of readers using a different edition. References to a play usually indicate act, scene, and line; references to an epic poem, such subdivisions as books, cantos, and individual stanzas. After the edition used has been identified upon first reference, a reference to a passage from a Shakespeare play might look like this:

⁷ *Hamlet* II.ii. 311–322.

Such abbreviated identification of passages from the Bible or from literary classics is often inserted in the text immediately following the passage itself. No identification is necessary for *well-known or proverbial lines* like "The quality of mercy is not strained" or "A little learning is a dangerous thing." Burdening the reader with detailed identification of an overworked quotation merely compounds the injury.

Abbreviations. In studying footnotes in scholarly books and articles, you will encounter a number of abbreviations and technical terms in addition to those you will regularly use in your own work. The meaning of many of these will be clear from their context or position; for example, *anon.* for "anonymous," *ch.* and *chs.* for "chapter" and "chapters," *col.* and *cols.* for "column" and "columns," *l.* and *ll.* for "line" and "lines," *n.* and *nn.* for "note" and "notes." Others are not self-explanatory:

c. or ca.   Latin *circa,* "approximately"; used for approximate dates and figures (*c.* 1952)

cf.   Latin *confer,* "compare"; often used loosely instead of *see* in the sense of "consult for further relevant material" (Cf. Ecclesiastes xii.12)

et al.   Latin *et alii,* "and others"; used in references to books by several authors (G. B. Harrison et al.)

f., ff.   "and the following page," "and the following pages" (See pp. 16f.)

loc. cit.   Latin *loco citato,* "in the place cited"; used without page reference (Baugh, loc. cit.)

MS, MSS	manuscript, manuscripts
n.d.	"no date," date of publication unknown
passim	Latin for "throughout"; "in various places in the work under discussion" (See pp. 54–56 et passim)
q.v.	Latin *quod vide;* "which you should consult"

Final Bibliography. Ordinarily you will be required to provide a final bibliography at the end of your finished paper. Its main purpose is to describe in one single alphabetical list all sources you have actually cited. You may include other sources that you have found helpful or enlightening, even though you have not had occasion to quote from them in your paper. However, do *not* list every book or article whose title you have come across during your investigation.

The final bibliography, based on your bibliography cards, includes all the information required to identify a source when first cited. However, entries in the bibliography differ from footnotes both in the arrangement and in the punctuation of the material presented:

(1) The *last name of the author* (or of the first author listed when a book has several authors) is placed first. His full name is separated from what follows by a period.

(2) The *facts of publication* for a book usually include the publisher's name. They are *not* enclosed in parentheses and are separated from what precedes and what follows by periods.

(3) Entries for books do not include page references; entries for parts of books or items in magazines give the *inclusive page numbers* for the whole selection.

In a typed manuscript, single-space each individual item but leave a double space between items. Indent two spaces for the second and for subsequent lines of each item. If you list *several publications by the same author*, substitute a line composed of six consecutive hyphens for his name in second and subsequent entries. If *no name of author or editor is known to you*, list the publication alphabetically by the first letter of the title, not counting "The," "A," or "An."

The following might be the final bibliography for a paper investigating theatrical conventions and stage techniques in the time of Shakespeare:

BIBLIOGRAPHY

Adams, John Cranford. The Globe Playhouse:
    Its Design and Equipment. Cambridge, Mass.:
    Harvard University Press, 1942.

Bailey, Margery. "Shakespeare in Action,"
    College English, XV (March 1954), 307-315.

Brooke, C. F. Tucker. "The Renaissance," in
    A Literary History of England, ed. Albert C.
    Baugh. New York: Appleton-Century-Crofts,
    Inc., 1948.

Chambers, E. K. The Elizabethan Stage. 4 vols.
    Oxford: The Clarendon Press, 1923.

Davies, W. Robertson. Shakespeare's Boy Actors.
    London: J. M. Dent & Sons, Ltd., 1939.

Granville-Barker, Harley, and G. B. Harrison,
    eds. A Companion to Shakespeare Studies.
    New York: The Macmillan Company, 1934.

Greg, W. W., ed. Henslowe's Diary. 2 vols.
    London: A. H. Gullen, 1904-1908.

Harbage, Alfred. Shakespeare's Audience.
    New York: Columbia University Press, 1941.

------. Theatre for Shakespeare. Toronto:
    University of Toronto Press, 1955.

"A New Shakespearean Festival," The Oakland
    Herald, August 12, 1958, p. 7, col. 2.

Rosenberg, Marvin. "Elizabethan Actors: Men
    or Marionettes?" PMLA, LXIX (September
    1954), 915-927.

7. THE STANDARDS OF RESPONSIBLE INVESTIGATION

In preparing a research paper, the student must guard against a
common danger: Preoccupied with procedure and format, he may lose
sight of the purposes the procedures serve. He may come to regard the

research paper as an elaborate ritual rather than as an introduction to the standards of scholarly investigation. In completing your own research project, you should review in your mind some of the lessons to be learned from the experience.

First, *writing a research paper can help you understand the scholar's respect for fact.* Reliable information on important subjects is not as easy to come by as the average newspaper reader thinks. Establishing a fact as fact rather than hearsay often takes considerable time and effort. As a judge must be able to tell relevant evidence from the immaterial, so the biographer, historian, or sociologist must learn to tell fact from fiction.

The careful investigator soon learns to guard against influences that tend to make information unreliable. The most obvious of these is partisan bias: A Democratic reporter may find it hard to give a balanced and objective account of the campaign tour of a Republican candidate. National and ideological bias even more irresistibly colors and distorts accounts of alleged historical fact. A careful investigator is on his guard in reading either a French or a German account of the causes of World War I, in reading about the history of Marxism either in a militantly conservative pamphlet or in the official Soviet encyclopedia. Where historical accounts are not obviously polemical, they may be designed to inspire and edify rather than record. Thus, the historian finds it difficult to verify accounts such as that of Washington's prayer at Valley Forge, which was not reported by witnesses of the incident and seems out of keeping with Washington's well-documented habits and convictions.

Second, *study of competent scholarship shows that facts become instructive only when carefully interpreted.* Facts do not speak for themselves. To make them meaningful, the investigator must sift out the insignificant. He must correlate his data in such a way that they begin to explain a situation or help settle a debated point. When pursued with a single-minded emphasis on accuracy of detail, scholarship becomes pedantry. Competent scholarly work combines accuracy and thoroughness with a grasp of meanings, relationships, and purposes.

Though research should be more than a mere collection of miscellaneous facts, interpretation and evaluation of the facts must be patient, balanced, and systematic. A research paper has even less room for superficial conclusions and hasty judgments than the ordinary expository theme. A historian will call a policy "shortsighted" only after fully exploring the nature of the policy and its relation to views and expectations current at the time. A researcher writing about the disaster that struck the *Titanic* will ascribe it to the negligence of her owners only after a careful study of both their obligations and their failure to fulfill them.

Third, *practice in scholarly investigation trains a writer to make his sources and procedures available for inspection and review.* He learns to identify his sources of information. He enables his readers to consult these sources to see whether the selection of material was judicious and in keeping with the original context. He enables his readers to check whether opinions and judgments attributed to an authority fairly represent the authority's point of view.

Such emphasis on accounting for the sources of his material helps the writer overcome characteristic temptations. The crudest temptation is that of plagiarism: the unacknowledged appropriation of the product of another investigator's labor. Plagiarism is to the scholar what shoplifting is to the businessman. It is true that many facts and ideas are common property and need not be credited to any specific source. Major historical dates and events, key ideas of major scientific or philosophical movements—these are generally accessible in reference books. However, whenever a writer makes use of information recently discovered or compiled, and whenever he adopts someone's characteristic, personal point of view, it is necessary for him to identify his source.

More subtle is another temptation to dishonesty: the reliance on testimony favorable to one's own point of view, the ignoring or playing down of material that would complicate the thread of one's argument. Once the investigator has correlated points *A*, *B*, and *C* to establish a thesis, he is inevitably tempted to play down a point *D* that interferes with his tentative conclusions. Careful consideration of such complications, due attention to authorities who *disagree* with the investigator, reassures his readers that he has not simply solved problems by ignoring adverse evidence.

Detailed documentation helps to convince your reader that you have nothing to hide. It also helps to determine responsibility. Superficial readers (not to mention malicious ones) need to be kept clearly informed that what you quote and explain is not necessarily *your* view. A writer who explains Thoreau's ideas on civil disobedience and the right to revolution may personally be a most obedient and unrevolutionary citizen. An economist explaining Marxist economic theory may be a firm supporter of private property and individual initiative. Careful documentation helps to prevent your reader from mistaking you for an anarchist firebrand or an eighteenth-century philosopher.

To sum up, training in scholarly research can make a writer at once more sceptical and more responsible. It can train him to read patiently and well, and to discount the biased, the sensational, the superficial. Instead of delivering improvised opinions on all possible subjects, he comes to accept, as a matter of course, an often prolonged period of study between question and answer. He habitually takes into account what has been said on a given subject by responsible and qualified observers. He no longer limits the quoting of authorities to "reference to those similarly mistaken." Instead, he quotes other writers to show that he has come to terms with views that merit serious attention.

Obviously, writing a research paper will not make a rash person cautious nor an opinionated person open-minded. However, once a writer acquires a scholarly frame of mind, it will help him produce the kind of writing that represents balanced views and rests on solid foundations.

EXERCISES 8

A. Select one of the three major encyclopedias discussed in this section and one other encyclopedia not mentioned here. Compare their treatment of *one* of the following subjects: atonality, cybernetics, Gestalt psychology, impressionism, semantics, stream-of-consciousness technique, surrealism, transcendentalism.

B. Study the general scheme of the *Book Review Digest* and check it for reviews of books you have read. Describe its treatment of one or two of the books.

C. Study the general scheme and sample entries of *one* of the following reference works: *American Universities and Colleges, Art Index, Cambridge Modern History, Catholic Encyclopedia, Concise Dictionary of American History, Dictionary of World Literature, Education Index, Grove's Dictionary of Music and Musicians, Standard Jewish Encyclopedia, Van Nostrand's Scientific Encyclopedia*. Report your findings, commenting on the scope, usefulness, and possible limitations of the work.

D. Select *one* of the following books and study its preface, table of contents, bibliography (if any), and introductory or concluding sections. Study its treatment of one or two limited topics. Then write a brief report on the intention, scope, level of difficulty, and special features of the book: (1) Ruth Benedict, *Patterns of Culture;* (2) James B. Conant, *On Understanding Science;* (3) Donald J. Lloyd and Harry R. Warfel, *American English in Its Cultural Setting;* (4) Erwin Panofsky, *Meaning in the Visual Arts;* (5) Robert C. Pooley, *Teaching English Grammar;* (6) David Riesman, *The Lonely Crowd;* (7) W. W. Rostov, *The Dynamics of Soviet Society;* (8) René Wellek and Austin Warren, *Theory of Literature.*

E. Study the general scheme of Constance M. Winchell's *Guide to Reference Books* and report on its treatment of a field that is of special interest to you, such as journalism, medicine, business, folklore, or religion.

F. Consult the *Readers' Guide* and find recent articles on *one* of the following: Benjamin Franklin, Alexander Hamilton, Andrew Jackson, Thomas Jefferson, Thomas Paine, George Washington. Compare the intention, tone, and level of difficulty of articles taken from three different periodicals.

G. Consult the *International Index* to find a scholarly article on *one* of the following: (1) the hypothetical parent language of all Indo-European languages; (2) the historical background of Homer's epics; (3) the Roman occupation of ancient Britain; (4) the earliest extant versions of the Old Testament; (5) the origins of medieval drama; (6) Freud's view of imaginative literature. Examine the author's use and identification of the source materials on which he has drawn.

H. Study the arrangement of cards in the central card catalogue of your college library in order to answer the following questions: (1) What are the major subdivisions for subject cards under the heading "Education"? (2) Where would you find a book by an author named John McMillan (under *Mc, Mac, Mi?*), George St. John (under *St., Sa, Jo?*), Antoine de Saint-Exupéry (under *De, Sa, St.?*) (3) Do subject cards for books on the Civil War precede or follow cards for books on the War of Independence? Is the arrangement alphabetical or chronological? (4) Are books about George Washington listed before or after books about the State of Washington, or about Washington, D. C.? (5) Check under *John Keats:* What is the relative order of the author's individual works, his collected works, and books about the author?

I. Transcribe and explain the information that the card catalogue of your college library provides concerning *one* of the following books: Leonard Bloomfield, *Language;* H. W. Fowler, *A Dictionary of Modern English Usage;* Otto Jespersen, *Modern English Grammar;* H. L. Mencken, *The American Language;* Stuart Robertson, *The Development of Modern English.*

J. Interpret the information provided in the following footnotes:

[3] Robert E. Spiller et al., *Literary History of the United States,* rev. ed. (New York, 1953), p. 1343.

[1] James Brown, "Eight Types of Puns," *PMLA,* LXXI (March 1956), 20.

[9] Euripides, *The Trojan Women,* trans. Richmond Lattimore, in *Greek Plays in Modern Translation,* ed. Dudley Fitts (New York, 1947), p. 161.

[2] "America—the Beautiful?" *Life,* June 3, 1957, p. 34.

[8] Kenneth Muir, ed. *Collected Poems of Sir Thomas Wyatt* (Cambridge, Mass., 1950), p. xx.

⁷ I Corinthians iii.18–20.

¹² Cf. *The Complete Works of William Hazlitt*, ed. P. P. Howe (London, 1932), XI, 88ff.

K. Study the style of documentation followed in a scholarly journal in your major field of interest. Determine to what extent its style coincides with that outlined in the preceding discussion and in what respects it differs from it.

L. The following sample paper, adapted from a longer, student-written research paper, illustrates different ways of presenting and documenting evidence. Study the way it reproduces factual information, opinion, and lines of verse. Compare the different kinds of footnotes it employs. Compare the way sources are identified in footnotes and in the final bibliography.

BYRON'S INTEREST IN ANIMALS

by

Richard P. Dean

English 2, Section 8

March 25, 1964

OUTLINE

Thesis: Byron had a continuing interest in animals that helps illuminate his character.

    I.   Byron's menagerie on the road

   II.   Byron's critical reputation

 III.   Byron's animals at Newstead Abbey

      A.   The Boatswain episode

      B.   Wild animals

  IV.   Byron in Italy

      A.   The Italian menageries

      B.   The maddened elephant

      C.   Byron's attitude toward hunting and fishing

   V.   Animals in Byron's poetry

  VI.   Byron's love of freedom

From Ravenna to Venice, in Italy, is a hundred miles through the lush green of the Po valley, and it is a hundred miles again along the road back from Venice to Ravenna. And from Ravenna to Pisa is a long hundred miles, each way, and the road is high and twisted across the backbone of Italy. Here, the tall slim spires of the Lombardy poplars, outlining the roads of the Po valley, give way to the hardy oaks of the Apennines.

In the early nineteenth century, the miles were the same as they are now--some seventeen hundred and sixty yards in length--but they were measured, then, not in the unmufflered roar of sports cars or the squeal of tires on a mountain turn, but by the hooves of horses set patiently down, one after another, again and again and again. And in time, the miles were not measured in minutes, but in long days--days in which there was time enough to absorb the beauty of the plain and of the mountains, time enough, also, to accumulate an intricate film of dust in the ears and nostrils, and to acquire bloodshot eyes and frazzled nerves, and to suffer the carriage-induced curse of constipation.

A stranger, pausing in some small village on the Ravenna road, during that slower time, for a drink of cool water or a glass of warm wine, might have witnessed a most amazing procession. Heralded, perhaps, by the cries of small boys, a splendid team of horses would have first come into view, to be followed by carriage after carriage drawn by equally splendid teams. The carriages were loaded, in large part, with animals and birds, caged and uncaged. [1]

Although the inventory of this menagerie would hardly have re-

---

[1] G. Wilson Knight, Lord Byron: Christian Virtues (New York, 1953), p. 4.

mained constant, we have a good indication of the variety of its probable make-up. One inventory lists eight immense dogs, three monkeys, five cats, an eagle, a crow, a falcon, five peacocks, two guinea hens, and an Egyptian crane. Another account adds a fox and a wolf to this list.[2] This astonishing caravan, with its horses, its attendants, and its master, would have constituted a problem in logistics in any day or time. There had to be meat for the wolf and the fox, for the dogs and the cats, and for the eagle and the falcon. Grain would suffice for the other birds, and fruit and nuts, perhaps, for the monkeys. There had to be nosebags of grain and night grazing for the horses, and there had to be water for all. Added to the feeding problem would have been the care and maintenance of the gear and of the carriages themselves. Obviously, the master of the caravan had to be a man of energy and patience.

Could this procession have been a small circus, or, perhaps, a large group of performing animals? Of course it was neither. It was merely a poet passing by--a poet shifting his household from one city to another. This poet was George Gordon Lord Byron, until his death in 1824 the most flamboyant among the younger generation of English Romantic poets.

Byron was, and continues to be, a controversial figure. His colorful aristocratic ancestry, his reckless and defiant spirit, his scandalous separation from his wife and subsequent exile in Italy, his death after joining the Greek revolutionaries in their fight against Turkey--all these have supplied his biographers and critics with plen-

---

[2]Knight, p. 4. See also Peter Quennell, _Byron in Italy_ (New York, 1941), pp. 185-186.

tiful ammunition for conjecture and recrimination.[3] Some of his critics
go so far as to say that his work survived only on the strength of the
scandal connected with his personal life, that "Byron the poet depended
entirely upon the glamour of Byron the man, who was Byron the rake, the
daredevil, the rebel."[4] His champions, notably G. Wilson Knight, have
tried to demonstrate "Byron's true greatness, his generosity and kind-
liness, his chivalry, courtesy, humility, and courage."[5] They have
found in his poetry a "tough-minded realism and a trenchant satire
often hilarious but always grounded in a basic sanity and a knowledge
of human nature."[6]

It is not my purpose to plunge into the controversies over Byron's
moral and literary qualifications. Rather I propose to explore one
limited facet of his life that indirectly sheds light on both his character and his poetry. I intend to show Byron's constant interest in
the animal world--an interest epitomized in the picture of Byron's
menagerie trekking across the Italian mountains.

Boatswain, the great Newfoundland dog of Byron's youth, is the
best known of all his animals. This is unfortunate, in a way, for the
affair of Boatswain's death and burial, though lauded by dog lovers,
has been derided and picked to pieces by others. When the dog was dying
of rabies, Byron tended him, sponging the foaming jaws with ungloved
hands. Boatswain did not offer to bite his master but buried his fangs

---

[3]The best-known biography of Byron is André Maurois, Byron, trans.
Hamish Miles (New York, 1930). Leslie A. Marchand, Byron: A Biography,
3 vols. (New York, 1957), makes use of recent scholarship and of documents not previously accessible.
[4]Ernest Boyd, Literary Blasphemies (New York, 1927), p. 119.
[5]Lord Byron, p. 29.
[6]Leslie A. Marchand, ed. Selected Poetry of Lord Byron (New York,
1951), p. v.

time and again in his own tormented body.[7]

This display of loyalty and courage did not make Byron more lovable and human in the eyes of many of his critics, for it led to the "excessively misanthropic"[8] inscription that young Byron placed on Boatswain's tomb:

NEAR THIS SPOT
ARE DEPOSITED THE REMAINS OF ONE
WHO POSSESSED BEAUTY WITHOUT VANITY
STRENGTH WITHOUT INSOLENCE
COURAGE WITHOUT FEROCITY
AND ALL THE VIRTUES OF MAN WITHOUT HIS VICES.
THIS PRAISE WHICH WOULD BE UNMEANING FLATTERY
IF INSCRIBED OVER HUMAN ASHES
IS BUT A JUST TRIBUTE TO THE MEMORY OF
BOATSWAIN, A DOG
WHO WAS BORN AT NEWFOUNDLAND, MAY 1803,
AND WHO DIED AT NEWSTEAD ABBEY, NOVEMBER 18, 1808.[9]

More than one critic has accused Byron of theatrical insincerity in this episode. One of them cites as evidence that the inscription for the tomb was composed eighteen days before the dog's death and that Byron wrote a letter on November 18 claiming that the dog had been dead for ten days.[10] So the Boatswain incident must still be regarded as controversial insofar as it pertains to Byron's character.

At Newstead Abbey, the Byrons' grand and gloomy family seat, there were other animals whose presence seems more characteristic of Byron's later interests. During the spring following Boatswain's death, one of Byron's friends wrote from the Abbey describing how one might encounter a bear or a wolf in the halls, roaming freely.[11] One can imagine sleeping in a house where a snuffling in the night did not necessarily

---

[7]Maurois, p. 113.
[8]George E. Brandes, Main Currents in Nineteenth Century Literature (New York, 1906), IV, 263.
[9]Maurois, p. 114.
[10]B. R. McElderry Jr., "Byron's Epitaph to Boatswain," Modern Language Notes, LVIII (November 1943), 553-554.
[11]Knight, p. 4.

mean that someone had a cold! Among other wild, but less fierce, creatures at the Abbey were the hedgehogs and tortoises which Byron had brought back from his early travels in Greece. Byron included information concerning the well-being of these and other animals in his letters to his friends. He mentioned their illnesses and their indispositions in his conversations.[12] To him, the animals were not merely brute creatures but sentient beings worthy of his concern and consideration.

It was in Italy, however, that the full blossoming of Byron's relationship with animals occurred. In Ravenna, Venice, Pisa, and Genoa he maintained his overflowing and ebullient menageries. In Ravenna, all the animals except the horses had free run of the mansion, which virtually exploded now and again under the impact of their unsupervised quarrels.[13] In Venice, the menagerie occupied the ground floor of the Palazzo Mocenigo, along with the stored carriages. As in other pretentious Venetian residences this bottom floor was unfurnished because of its dankness and smell of the sea. Byron, passing to his gondola, would stop to feed the animals and to watch their antics.[14]

On his Italian travels, Byron was always accompanied by his dogs and, according to one of his biographers, usually by his geese. The latter joined Byron's household as a result of his tenacious hold upon the rural English customs of his childhood. These dictated roast goose for Michaelmas. After acquiring a somewhat thin goose a month before the holiday, Byron began to feed it by hand. He soon developed a regard for it that prevented its gracing his table. Instead, the goose became

---

[12]Knight, pp. 7-8.
[13]Quennell, pp. 185-186.
[14]Quennell, p. 118.

his constant companion and the ruler of his courtyard. Later he obtained a companion for it, and the flock eventually grew to four.[15]

Though Byron respected such lesser lights as tortoises and geese, it was at fiercer fires that he warmed his soul. In Venice, for instance, he followed a maddened elephant, which, after breaking loose and killing its keeper, wrecked a fruit shop and finally invaded a church. It was eventually killed by a charge from a cannon. At one spot the elephant showered Byron with flying beams, and the poet gloried in the wild energy expended.[16] Given the space and the opportunity, he would doubtless have welcomed the elephant into his Venetian menagerie.

Although Byron participated in some sports, he condemned many others, including all those that tormented, wounded, or destroyed animals. He castigated the clergy for their fox-hunting vicars.[17] He refused to participate in live target shooting when practicing marksmanship with Italian revolutionaries, although it would have benefited his reputation if he had shown himself to be of sterner stuff. This weakness was the "weakness of a great heart," observed the Countess Guiccioli, Byron's one truly congenial female companion.[18] G. Wilson Knight quotes the passage from Byron's Don Juan that expresses the poet's contempt for the fisherman:

> And angling, too, that solitary vice,
> Whatever Isaac Walton sings or says;
> The quaint, old, cruel coxcomb, in his gullet
> Should have a hook, and a small trout to pull it.[19]
> (XIII, cvi, 845-848)

---

[15]Ernest J. Lovell Jr., ed. His Very Self and Voice: Collected Conversations of Lord Byron (New York, 1954), p. 251.

[16]Knight, pp. 6-7.
[17]For a typical reference see Lovell, p. 474.
[18]Knight, p. 13.
[19]Knight, p. 12. Line references are to The Complete Poetical Works of Lord Byron, ed. Paul Elmer More (Boston, 1905).

All of the many facets of Byron's relationship with animals come to light in his poetry. In his essay on Byron in The Burning Oracle, G. Wilson Knight lists some of the passages from Byron's poetry that show the poet's insight into animal life and energy.[20] They range from the description of the butterfly in The Giaour,

> . . . rising on its purple wing
> The insect queen of eastern Spring
> (388-389)

to the account of the wild horses in Mazeppa, with

> Wide nostrils never stretched with pain,
> Mouths bloodless to the bit and rein.
> (XVII, 680-681)

Byron's sense of animal companionship is implicit in the lines from The Prisoner of Chillon that describe the prisoner's feelings upon his release after years of solitary confinement:

> And half I felt as they were come
> To tear me from my second home.
> With spiders I had friendship made,
> And watched them in their sullen trade;
> Had seen the mice by moonlight play,
> And why should I feel less than they?
> (XIV, 379-384)

Byron liked animals. The word liked is the key to his relationship with them. It is also, to an extent, a key to his character. He was not an "animal lover" in the usual sentimental sense, except perhaps in the case of Boatswain. He had for the others--the representative creatures in his menageries, and their counterparts in the world at large--a vast and genuine liking. Byron must be remembered as a major contributor to the liberation of nineteenth-century Greece from the Turks, and as an advocate and tireless worker in the cause of freedom

---

[20]New York, 1939, pp. 200, 204.

all of his short life. As man, worshipper of light and of the sun, has
imprisoned portions of each in lamps and bulbs and in fire-places and
stoves, so, possibly, Byron surrounded himself with bits of freedom
which shone, for him, through the bars and fretwork of the cages of his
animals, and which blazed forth in sudden spurts of wild energy.
Byron's interest in animals was an inspiriting and inspiring thing,
and without his untimely death it might have emerged as more than just
another eccentricity of the Romantic age.

BIBLIOGRAPHY

Boyd, Ernest. _Literary Blasphemies_. New York: Harper and Brothers, 1927.

Brandes, George E. _Main Currents in Nineteenth Century Literature_. 6 vols. New York: The Macmillan Company, 1906.

Knight, George Wilson. _Lord Byron: Christian Virtues_. New York: Oxford University Press, 1953.

------. _The Burning Oracle: Studies in the Poetry of Action_. New York: Oxford University Press, 1939.

Lovell, Ernest J. Jr., ed. _His Very Self and Voice: Collected Conversations of Lord Byron_. New York: The Macmillan Company, 1954.

Marchand, Leslie A. _Byron: A Biography_. 3 vols. New York: Alfred A. Knopf, 1957.

------, ed. _Selected Poetry of Lord Byron_. "Modern Library College Editions." New York: Random House, Inc., 1951.

Maurois, André. _Byron_, trans. Hamish Miles. New York: D. Appleton and Company, 1930.

McElderry, B. R. Jr. "Byron's Epitaph to Boatswain," _Modern Language Notes_, LVIII (November 1943), 553-554.

More, Paul Elmer, ed. _The Complete Poetical Works of Lord Byron_. "Cambridge Edition." Boston: Houghton Mifflin Company, 1905.

Quennell, Peter. _Byron in Italy_. New York: The Viking Press, 1941.

Boyd, Ernest. _Literary Blasphemies_. New York: Harper and Brothers, 1927.

A CONCISE HANDBOOK

CHAPTER FIVE

ORGANIZATION

9: THE WHOLE THEME

THE NEED FOR PLANNING

The first step in writing an expository paper is to assemble the raw materials. Ideally, the writer will allow time for first-hand observation, for research, for preliminary reading. In practice, the period available for these purposes is almost always too short. As a result, the generally observant and well-informed writer necessarily has an advantage over his less receptive colleague. Your own success as a writer will depend partly on your collecting the material for assignments yet undreamed of—by extensive reading, by careful scrutiny of other people, by looking at the world through open eyes.

Assuming that a writer can draw on adequate material, he faces the problem of organizing it. He has to give it point and coherence; he has to make his readers follow and understand him. If the writer has an established reputation, the reader may go to the trouble of sorting things out for himself. Most other writers have to make their ideas easily accessible and to arrange them to advantage. They have to help the reader proceed step by step without stumbling. They have to give him the feeling that he knows where he is going, and that his effort will have been well spent when he gets there.

The more substantial a project, and the less extensive the writer's previous experience, the greater usually the need for systematic planning. Such planning is not the result of following a pat formula or a set of simple rules. If a writer forces his material into the straight-jacket of a tried-and-true scheme, he may keep himself from doing justice to his subject and from discussing it with conviction. On the other hand, there are general principles of organization that can help a writer find his bearings. There are conventional devices for checking and strengthening the structure of a paper or of a paragraph.

ORGANIZING THE EXPOSITORY THEME

O 1 THE NEED FOR FOCUS

Many papers begin with a vague interest in a general subject area. The instructor assigning a topic does part of the job of narrowing down the general area to something manageable. The writer has to do the rest.

O 1a Limiting the Subject. *The shorter the paper, the greater the danger that an inadequately restricted subject will get only thin, superficial treatment.* Obviously, no one could write a paper on a vast general subject like "Education in America." A writer interested in American education may restrict this field according to kind: academic, social, physical, religious. He may restrict it according to area: a state, a town, the nation's capital, Indian reservations in Arizona. He may limit himself to a particular level: kindergarten, grade school, high school, college. He may limit his discussion to a certain type of student: gifted, retarded, emotionally disturbed. A manageable topic might look like this:

> Science education for gifted students at Washington High
> Home economics for boys at San Lorenzo Junior College
> Released-time religious instruction in local grade schools

Usually, the writer limiting his subject sets out to restrict a less general area. Here are some typical ways in which such a less comprehensive area might be narrowed down:

GENERAL AREA: City Life

TOPICS: Keeping up with the Joneses in Suburbia
"Redeveloped" vs. "grown" neighborhoods
An alternative to teenage gangs
A new trend in city architecture
One major cause of urban blight
Developing a sense of community

O 1b Stating the Thesis. In a short paper, you will do well to *limit yourself to one major point that can be fully ex-*

plained, illustrated, and supported in the space available. Writing gains in clarity and focus when the writer clearly formulates this major point in his own mind. When it appears in the final paper, this statement of the central idea is called the **thesis sentence.**

TOPIC: Urban Redevelopment
THESIS: "Redeveloped" neighborhoods lack the varied life of the "grown" neighborhoods they replace.

TOPIC: Life in Suburbia
THESIS: Living in the suburbs does not prevent people from developing a sense of community.

To be effective in providing a focus for the theme, the thesis should be a true statement, an assertion of a limited point. It cannot be a question, though one excellent way of formulating the thesis is to sum up in one sentence the answer to a question like "What is missing in the typical redeveloped neighborhood?" Nor should the thesis sentence merely map out the general territory:

TOO VAGUE: A modern suburb is an exciting place to live.
MORE CLEARLY FOCUSED: Modern suburbs have kept alive the American tradition of being a good neighbor.

TOO VAGUE: Today's children are spoiled.
MORE CLEARLY FOCUSED: Grade school teachers lack the means of disciplining their students.

O 2   PATTERNS OF ORGANIZATION

Adequate restriction of the subject area sets the outside limits of a theme. In its internal organization, the theme is likely to follow one, or a combination, of a number of common patterns:

O 2a   Space and Time. In much descriptive writing, technical exposition, and autobiographical narrative, the writer follows a **spatial** or **chronological order** inherent in his material. Thus, an account of a vacation trip may derive unity from following the course of a river or from tracing a trail up into mountainous country. An article on radio transmitting may follow the voice of the soprano through microphone and transmitter to the receiving set and the listener's ear. An autobiographical paper may follow a "before-and-after" pattern: family life before and after the loss of a parent; a boy's attitude toward military service before and after induction.

You can often strengthen a paper of this kind by observing the following cautions:

(1) *Make the progression in space or in time clear and consistent.* The professional may attain special effects by flashbacks and by calculated shifts of perspective. The amateur, however, especially when writing a short paper, usually does well to follow a consistent pattern: from the foothills to the wind-swept peak, from childhood to adolescence.

(2) *Break up the whole sequence into major divisions or emphasize the most significant steps.* A monotonous "and-then" sequence becomes confusing, because it gives equal emphasis to many parts, events, or operations. Suppose a paper follows the assembly line in an automobile factory: the basic parts of the body are welded together; the doors are hung; the body shells are dipped into a chemical solution; they are spray-painted; they are dried in ovens; electrical wiring is laid; door locks and other mechanisms are installed; glass is installed; interior lining is installed; and so on. To protect the reader against unnecessary fatigue, the writer will probably break up the body's progress into three major stages:

    I. Building the body shell
    II. Painting the body
    III. Outfitting the painted shell

O 2b   Classification and Analysis. Papers dealing with people, problems, and issues often do not fit into a plausible spatial or chronological scheme. A writer may have to *sort out miscellaneous material into several major categories* (**classification**). He may have to *break up a sprawling, formless subject into three or four plausible parts* (**analysis**). He may merely *arrange several major points of equal importance in the most convenient sequence* (**enumeration**). **Order of division** is the general term sometimes applied to the kind of organization that these methods yield.

Here is a typical preliminary collection of material for a paper about a person:

> SUBJECT: Last semester's psychology teacher
> (1) had a loud, clear voice
> (2) told some interesting stories about students helped by psychology
> (3) came to class late several times
> (4) explained difficult words
> (5) wasn't sarcastic toward students
> (6) wore colorful neckties

(7) walked with a limp
(8) had been an exchange teacher in France
(9) outlined subject clearly
(10) spaced assignments well
(11) talked over test I did poorly on

On studying this list, the writer will conclude that some of his observations are more closely related than others. He might establish three or four major categories:

I. Teaching methods: (2) relevant anecdotes, (4) explanation of terms, (9) clear outline, (10) spacing of assignments, and perhaps (1) effective speech habits

II. Attitude toward students: (5) absence of sarcasm, (11) assistance after class

III. Personal habits: (6) sporty clothes, (7) limp, (3) lack of punctuality

IV. Miscellaneous: (8) teaching experience abroad

If the writer is a student concerned about his academic progress, he may conclude that categories I and II are the most significant. A second look at III may suggest a convenient over-all scheme: an introduction re-creating an unpromising first impression, belied by the teacher's effectiveness. A rough outline of the final paper might look like this:

I. Unpromising external characteristics
II. Effectiveness as a teacher
   A. Presentation of subject
   B. Dealing with students
III. Lesson learned ("Don't judge a teacher by his ties.")

Here are possible major divisions for two other typical papers:

CENTRAL IDEA: President Johnson has several qualifications that a college president needs.

I. Wide and varied experience
II. Selection of a varied and well-qualified faculty
III. Authoritative yet friendly attitude toward students
IV. Firm grasp of administrative and financial problems

CENTRAL IDEA: Joining a fraternity has many advantages.

I. Belonging to a group he is proud of gives the student the incentive to do well.
II. The active social life of the fraternity provides many opportunities for meeting people.

III. The many group projects carried on by the fraternity provide training in cooperation.

In working out the major divisions of such a paper, a writer has to solve various problems of logic, relevance, and proportion.

(1) *The categories should be appropriate to the purpose of the paper.* A paper on campus social life might divide students into Greeks, Co-op dwellers, and Independents. A study of the role of the humanities in a vocational curriculum might divide students into nursing majors, engineering majors, police majors, and so on.

(2) *The major categories should not suffer from illogical overlapping or from a confusing mixture of criteria.* A reader is bound to be bewildered if the writer divides students into graduates of local high schools, children from low-income homes, and Catholics. Suppose a paper investigating student opinion on teen-age marriage sets up the following categories: A. Boys. B. Girls. C. Married Students. This arrangement makes it seem as though the married students were neither boys nor girls. A scheme like this would be more plausible:

    I. Single students
       A. Unmarried boys
       B. Unmarried girls

   II. Married students
       A. Husbands
       B. Wives

If the author's categories are unconventional or somewhat less than obvious, a brief—and preferably unobtrusive—explanation of their relation to each other and of the criteria observed in setting them up may be in order.

(3) *Thoroughness of treatment should not vary unreasonably from one major category to the other.* Some papers seem unbalanced because the writer has tried to analyze the subject exhaustively instead of fully developing perhaps three major categories. A paper on teen-age marriage might proceed like this:

CENTRAL IDEA: Teen-age marriages are not always the result of mature affection.

    I. One possible motive is the desire for independence from parental control. (Several case histories are discussed.)

   II. Another motive may be the sense of satisfaction derived from marrying a popular boy or a popular girl. (No details or examples are given.)

III. A person may marry "on the rebound," marrying one person to spite another. (A sketchy and inconclusive case history is provided.)
IV. A couple may mistake physical attraction for love. (Several cases are discussed; similar cases in fiction and drama are cited.)
V. A boy about to be drafted may marry a girl for fear of losing her. (A case in point is discussed at length.)

The paper is likely to be unconvincing, because the author is stretching himself too thin. In a long paper, he might successfully tackle I, IV, and V. In a short paper, he might do well to limit himself to either I or IV.

(4) *If the major divisions of the paper vary in importance, familiarity, or plausibility, their presentation should follow a consistent pattern.* Many effective papers move from the less important to the more important. This order produces a **climactic effect** and leaves the most important point firmly embedded in the reader's memory. The paper on teen-age marriage, for instance, might start with motives related to external circumstances (I, V) and end with the problem that is probably the most important and the hardest to discuss (IV).

O 2c Comparison and Contrast. Often your strategy of presentation will be determined by your intention to *work out significant similarities between apparently dissimilar things, point out important differences between similar ones, or show why you prefer one of several alternatives.* Why drive a Volkswagen rather than a Ford? Why attend a small private college rather than a state university? Answering such questions calls for systematic **comparison and contrast.**

In many papers of this kind, the writer has collected the necessary material but failed to work out the parallels or the dissimilarities. For instance, a paper might break apart in the middle because it is divided between a discussion of the Volkswagen and a separate discussion of the Ford. One way of unifying the paper would be to set up a *point-by-point comparison*:

I. Economy
  A. Initial cost (data for both cars)
  B. Cost of operation (data for both cars)
  C. Resale value (data for both cars)

II. Comfort and convenience
  A. Space for passengers and luggage (data for both cars)
  B. Maneuverability (data for both cars)

III. Performance
  A. Acceleration and speed (data for both cars)
  B. Durability (data for both cars)

Sometimes, of course, a comparison will be more meaningful or effective if two things are described separately. The writer then has to make a special effort to *keep the two descriptions parallel,* taking up important criteria in the same order and, if necessary, working out similarities or contrasts in a summarizing third section.

O 2d   Logical Argument. Many papers dealing with issues and ideas *follow the order of a logical argument.* Several patterns of such argument are especially worth noting:

(1) The logical coherence of the paper may derive from *cause-and-effect relationships.* The following outline might represent an essay by a teacher concerned about his students' lack of interest in poetry:

I. *First step:* The author states his central concern, bringing out its interesting, startling, or paradoxical aspects:

> Children like poetry; they make up jingles and keep chanting them to each other; they listen avidly to poems about little pigs and clever cats. Most college freshmen, on the other hand, are either indifferent or hostile toward poetry, both traditional and modern.

II. *Second step:* The author asks and answers the obvious question: Why?

> Poetry is often presented to students as something special and solemn; memorizing and reciting make many students regard it as drudgery; prose paraphrase necessarily emphasizes the most prosaic aspect of poetry.

III. *Third step:* The author suggests remedies at least partly implied in the diagnosis:

> Teachers of poetry should emphasize oral reading; they should cater to their students' interest in song and story by including ballads and narrative poetry; they should encourage discussion and writing rather than make poetry the subject of objective tests.

(2) Another logical pattern, particularly effective in setting a paper in motion, leads to the desired conclusion through *qualification of* or *attack upon a familiar idea:*

I. *First step:* A familiar idea is confirmed:

> It is true that many required courses do not help to prepare the student for his professional career (detailed illustrations).

THE WHOLE THEME   229

  II. *Second step:* A qualification or objection is stated:
But a responsible citizen must be able to recognize competence and quackery in fields other than his own (detailed illustrations).

  III. *Third step:* A balanced conclusion is drawn:
Therefore, a student needs required courses that give him a basic understanding of some important disciplines outside his own field.

The same scheme is applicable to more general or more demanding subjects:

  I. *Thesis:* It is true that modern industrial society makes for unprecedented interdependence among its citizens.

  II. *Antithesis:* But such interdependence is an essential condition of mass production and mass consumption.

  III. *Synthesis:* Interdependence is the price modern society pays for a high standard of living.

Students used to simple black-and-white alternatives often accuse a writer of contradicting himself when he proceeds to qualify or to reconsider points he has previously accepted. However, the ability to reach sound conclusions is closely related to the ability to reconcile conflicting points of view.

(3) A third logical pattern is modeled on the **inductive argument**, which *presents examples, case histories, or evidence and then draws a general conclusion:*

  I. *First step:* Data are presented:
Carlotta Brink, heroine of *Vengeance Is Mine,*
    A. is rude to her servants (examples)
    B. insults tradesmen (examples)
    C. attempts to put other people in the wrong (examples)
    D. is unconcerned about her husband's business problems (examples)
    E. scolds her children without provocation (examples)

  II. *Second step:* The conclusion is drawn:
Carlotta is inconsiderate and unkind.

Inductive order is especially effective when a writer has to overcome prejudice or distrust. If, for instance, male readers of *Vengeance Is Mine* are infatuated with Carlotta because of her beauty and wit, the indirect inductive approach may sober them, whereas a blunt initial indictment might merely arouse their chivalric instinct.

(4) If a subject is complicated without being controversial, *initial statement and subsequent support of the central idea* is often the preferable procedure. The inexperienced writer often does well to state a general conclusion first and then present the material that supports it. This way, he can keep out irrelevant material by checking details against the statement of his main idea. At the same time, he escapes the censure of the reader in a hurry, who is likely to be impatient with a paper that "beats around the bush." Here is a tentative outline for a paper putting the central idea first:

I. *First step:* The general conclusion is stated:
    A part-time job can supplement a student's academic training.

II. *Second step:* The reasons for the conclusion are enumerated:
    A. Part-time work can provide a valuable practical education (training for do-it-yourself projects; knowledge useful to future housewife, car owner).
    B. It can provide field work related to the student's major field of study (hospital work for future nurses, tutoring for future teachers, playing in a commercial band for music student).
    C. It can provide valuable psychological training (association with people from different backgrounds, taking orders from superiors).

(5) In many papers an inductive paragraph becomes one link in a logical chain. Sustained logical reasoning makes unusual demands both on writer and reader. It is necessarily rare in popular or informal exposition and most common in scholarly controversy. Here is a rough outline of a **deductive argument**, which *draws conclusions from premises previously established* or *applies generalizations to specific instances:*

I. A college should develop in its students a sense for spiritual values (elaboration and support).

II. Architecture gives tangible expression to such values as dignity and permanence (elaboration and support).

III. The buildings facing the traditional Inner Quad of the college exhibit several of these qualities (elaboration and support).

IV. Of the modern classroom buildings on this campus, few suggest a sense of tradition, a sense of style, a feeling of dignity (elaboration and support).

V. Therefore, the buildings surrounding the Inner Quad should not be torn down to make room for additional "cell block" structures.

O 2e   Imaginative Unity. A writer may *rely on imaginative rather than logical unity.* Writing with a strong imaginative touch often owes its coherence to its consistency of mood or to a unifying symbol. For instance, a foreign visitor may unify his impressions of California by choosing as his central subject a Californian highway, stretching for hundreds of miles with one built-up area merging into another. As he describes the cars, the supermarkets, the jerry-built roadside stores, the highway becomes a unifying symbol for the mobility of the population, the rapid and uncoordinated growth of the state, the lack of focus and tradition in sprawling towns and cities.

The more substantial an essay or an article becomes, the less likely it is to fit into any one simple organizational scheme. A chapter in a book may follow a chronological order in its main outline, with different sections illustrating various kinds of analytic, inductive, and deductive order. In addition, the writer is likely to complicate the thread of his exposition further by repeatedly devoting sections to forecasts of points to come and to summaries or reappraisals of points previously made. Such devices as repeated references to a symbolic incident or repetition of a key quotation can help the writer keep the discussion focused on his basic concerns.

O 3   BEGINNINGS AND ENDINGS

Many writers spend a disproportionate amount of time wondering how to begin and how to conclude. Often, the best advice to such a writer is to begin in the middle and to stop when he has finished what he has to say. Nevertheless, once a writer has worked out the body of his essay, he is justified in thinking seriously about how to approach his readers and how to shape their final impression.

O 3a   Titles. Ideally, the title attracts the reader without promising more than the author is going to deliver. *A good title is specific enough to stake out a limited area, honest enough to prevent later disappointment, and striking enough to compete successfully with other claims on the reader's time.* Conversely, bad titles tend to be vague, colorless, sprawling, or, if colorful, deceptive. Here are some weak titles followed by a choice of suggested alternatives:

BEFORE: BUSINESS SUCCESS
AFTER: SELLING HOME ENCYCLOPEDIAS
             WHERE THE CUSTOMER IS KING

BEFORE: QUALITIES OF A FUTURE HUSBAND
AFTER: WHAT MAKES ELIGIBLE MEN ELIGIBLE
         BREADWINNER OR PRINCE CHARMING?

BEFORE: JUVENILE DELINQUENCY
AFTER: MY STAY AT JUVENILE HALL
         WHAT JUDGE GOODWIN DID ABOUT
         JUVENILE GANGS

BEFORE: THE NEUTRALITY OF POLITICAL SCIENCE
         TEACHERS
AFTER: IMPARTIALITY IN THE CLASSROOM
         TEACHERS, TOO, HAVE OPINIONS

O 3b   Introductions. Like the title, the introduction should help to attract the reader and to put him in a receptive mood. At the same time, it may do important groundwork for the paper. *An effective introduction may sketch out the territory to be covered, establish a common basis for discussion, lead up to a central idea.* Like the title, a good introduction helps to set the tone, whether formal or informal, objective or emotional, serious or facetious. Here are some typical ways of introducing a paper, ranging from the relatively formal to the informal or flippant:

(1) The writer may attract the reader's attention by relating his subject to a *topical event or a current controversy:*

RUSSIAN, ANYONE?

On August 12 . . . the Soviet government announced the launching of Russia's first . . . Though Russian scientific journals had published detailed accounts of . . . , the lack of qualified translators had kept American scientists unaware of the Russians' rapid progress in this field. . . .

(2) The writer may start with a statement that makes the reader take a *new look at a familiar situation:*

THE LIFE OF STRESS

A lot of sympathy is being wasted on executives for leading lives so full of stress and strain that it impairs their health. Actually, their subordinates suffer more from high blood pressure and artery disease. These surprising findings . . .—*Time*

(3) The introduction may limit the subject by *proceeding from a general situation to a specific instance:*

THE WHOLE THEME   233

THE WASTELANDS REVISITED

School people have to put up with a lot, not only from the kids, who must be bad enough, but also from the grown-ups, who probably are worse. Pummeled, pressured, and advised from every side, still bearing the wounds inflicted by super-patriots, super-religionists, super-taxpayers, and super-superintendents, the educators now have to deal with yet another attack from Arthur E. Bestor, Jr.—William Lee Miller, *The Reporter*

(4) An *initial quotation* may serve as the keynote for the rest of the paper:

NO SOCIAL SECURITY FOR COACHES

"Coach Jones Resigns After Second Bad Season." Who has not seen headlines like this one after the annual football or baseball craze has run its course? No matter what his past record, the coach of every prominent team . . .

(5) *Striking facts or statistics* may dramatize the issue to be discussed:

MONOLINGUALISM IS OBSOLETE

Last year, only one out of ten American high school graduates had studied a foreign language. In spite of the publicity recently given to the teaching of foreign languages in primary and secondary schools . . .

(6) A *striking contrast* may heighten the point to be made:

AMERICAN CHILDREN ARE SPOILED

Not too many decades ago, young children were early taught the difference between what they were, and were not, allowed to do. Today, many American parents treat their children as if they could do no wrong. The most obvious manifestation of this change . . .

(7) An *initial definition* may clarify a key term:

WHAT IS AUTOMATION?

Economists do not agree among themselves on what "automation" means. Some writers use the term for any type of large-scale mechanization of industrial or administrative processes. Others, more plausibly, use it in referring to the mechanization of planning, supervision, and control.

(8) Biographical or personal comment worked organically into the introduction may help establish the *writer's qualifications* for dealing with his subject:

VICTORY AND AFTER

When I first came to Germany in November 1945, all the major cities seemed to be curiously alike. . . .

(9) An introduction may gain impetus by *attacking a currently accepted assumption:*

THE NEW ILLITERACY

We hear much about the reawakening interest in the humanities, the new appreciation of the generalness in the liberal arts, the growing dissatisfaction with overspecialization. Maybe so. But these signs are minute, I suggest, [compared with] those coming from the other direction. I offer the proposition that the trends that have been working against the humanities are likely to increase, not decrease, in the decade ahead. . . .—William H. Whyte, Jr., *Saturday Review*

(10) By *anticipating damaging objections,* the writer may disarm would-be critics:

THE HIGH COST OF MISFORTUNE

Nowadays anyone who advocates public health insurance is called a socialist. Thanks to years of skillful and well-financed publicity . . .

(11) A *controversial question,* concisely and provocatively worded, may stir up an apathetic reader:

LOYALTY BEGINS AT HOME

Should a man put loyalty to his country above loyalty to a friend? Does loyalty to the government come before loyalty to one's family? How we answer such a question depends on . . .

(12) An *amusing anecdote* may entertain the reader while at the same time conveying an important idea:

MEDICAL JOURNALISM—
WITH AND WITHOUT UPBEAT

As a veteran writer of medical and psychological articles for the mass-circulation "slicks," I have a fellow feeling for the violinist who rebelled after having been with an orchestra for thirty years. One day, so the story goes, he sat with his hands folded during rehearsal, and when the conductor rapped on the podium with his baton and demanded furiously, "Why aren't you playing?" replied, with a melancholy sigh, "Because I don't like music." Sometimes I feel like sitting at my typewriter with my hands folded. I don't like popularization. It has gone too far. The little learning—with illustrations—which the magazines have been pouring into a thirsty public has become a dangerous thing. . . .—Edith M. Stern, *Saturday Review*

Some common ways of introducing a theme are usually, though not necessarily always, ineffective:

(1) A *repetition, often verbatim, of the assignment.*

(2) A *vague, colorless summarizing statement:* "There are many qualities that the average college graduate looks for in a job. Most of them probably consider the following most important. . . ."

(3) An *unsupported claim to interest:* "Migratory birds are a fascinating subject. Ever since I was a little child I have been interested in the migration of birds. Studying them has proved a wonderful hobby. . . ."

(4) An *unsubstantiated claim that the paper is going to deal with a burning issue:* "There has been much controversy over the question of whether public schools should give their students released time for religious instruction. This question has been debated many times. . . ."

(5) *Complaints about the subject:* "I find it hard to discuss prejudice in a paper of 500 words. Prejudice is a vast subject. . . ."

(6) *Apologies* for the writer's lack of qualifications: "I am really not very well qualified to write about the qualifications that good children's books should have. . . ."

(7) *Evasive or platitudinous remarks:* "Everyone feels differently about the merits of required courses. I think everyone has a right to his own opinion. . . ."

O 3c   Conclusions. *An effective conclusion ties together different parts of a paper and reinforces its central message.* It may simply be an emphatic restatement of an important idea, an explicit assertion of what the writer has been hinting at. At the end of a fairly long and involved paper (but not at the end of a short, simple one) the conclusion may offer a convenient summary of major points. Often an essay concludes with a detail symbolic of the prevailing mood, or with an anecdote reaffirming the central idea in a witty or memorable way.

Here are some examples of effective conclusions:

(1) A *memorable restatement* of the central idea:

> . . . Underneath our shiny fronts of stone, our fascination with gadgets and our new toys that can blow the earth into a million stars, we are still outside the doorway through which the great answers wait. Not all the cameras in Christendom nor all the tricky lights will move us one step closer to a better understanding of ourselves, but only, as it always was, the truly written word, the profoundly felt gesture, the naked and direct contemplation of man which is the enduring glamour of the stage.—Arthur Miller, "The American Theater," *Holiday*

(2) A *final anecdote* that reinforces the central idea without explicit restatement:

> . . . Only once did I ever hear of an official football speech which met with my entire approval. It was made by a Harvard captain. His team had lost to Yale but by a smaller score than was expected. It had been a fast and interesting game. At the dinner when the team broke training the captain said, "We lost to Yale but I think we had a satisfactory season. We have had fun out of football and it seems to me that ought to be the very best reason for playing the game."
>
> A shocked silence followed his remarks. He was never invited to come to Cambridge to assist in the coaching of any future Harvard eleven. His heresy was profound. He had practically intimated that being defeated was less than tragic.—Heywood Broun, "A Study in Sportsmanship," *Harper's*

(3) An apposite *final quotation:*

> . . . Should there be codes of ethics for honesty in government? Must public men declare themselves in writing to be honest men just as some professors have been required to swear solemnly that they do not really intend to overthrow the Government of the United States? Personally, I have no faith in such oaths. A gentleman who much influenced my early life once told me:
>
> "Son, by God, when I invite a man to dinner I do not propose

to count the silver—before or after he leaves the table!"—William S. White, "The American Genius for Hypocrisy," *Harper's*

(4) A sober estimate of the *significance of the conclusions* reached:

> . . . Criticism by outsiders will not miraculously transform the quality of network programs. But as long as criticism finds its way into print, and as long as network presidents take their critics seriously enough to cajole or denounce them, the cause of informative and satisfying television is not lost.

(5) A *forecast or warning* based on facts developed in the paper:

> . . . In education we have not yet acquired that kind of will. But we need to acquire it, and we have no time to lose. We must acquire it in this decade. For if, in the crucial years which are coming, our people remain as unprepared as they are for their responsibilities and their mission, they may not be equal to the challenge, and if they do not succeed, they may never have a second chance to try.— Walter Lippmann, "The Shortage in Education," *Atlantic*

(6) An essential *condition for future progress:*

> . . . When public relations people become as a group more forthright, less designing, more strict in their standards, and more respectful of the public, then—and only then—will the discerning public accept them as real professionals.—Vance Packard, "Public Relations: Good or Bad," *Atlantic*

(7) A suggestion for *remedial action:*

> . . . If the leading citizens in a community would make it a point to visit their state prison, talk with the warden, then return to their communities with a better understanding of actual down-to-earth prison problems, they would have taken one of the most important and most effective steps toward a solution of our crime problem.—Erle Stanley Gardner, "Parole and the Prisons—An Opportunity Wasted," *Atlantic*

(8) A *return from the specific to the general,* relating the findings of the paper to a general trend:

> . . . Inge's family plays constitute a kind of aesthetic isolationism upon which the world of outside—the world of moral choice, decision,

and social pressures—never impinges. Although he has endowed the commonplace with some depth, it is not enough to engage serious attention. William Inge is yet another example of Broadway's reluctance or inability to deal intelligently with the American world at large.— Robert Brustein, "The Men-Taming Women of William Inge," *Harper's*

Here are some examples of lame, ineffective conclusions:

(1) The *noncommittal platitude:* "This problem deserves the serious attention of every right-thinking American."

(2) The *unfounded optimistic prediction:* "When things look their grimmest, a turn for the better is usually not far away."

(3) The *undeveloped panacea:* "The restoration of proper discipline in the nation's schools will make juvenile delinquency a thing of the past."

(4) The *conclusion raising problems* that weaken or distract from the point of the paper: "Of course, a small car has obvious disadvantages for a family with numerous children or for the traveler in need of luggage space."

No separate conclusion is sometimes better than an anticlimatic one—a tacked-on paragraph that raises belated doubts or blurs the reader's understanding of important points.

O 4 CONTINUITY

In a competent piece of writing, sentence follows sentence, and paragraph follows paragraph, in what seems a smooth, natural sequence. Usually, such smooth progression is the result of both habitual skill and conscious effort. When it is lacking, the reader will soon start asking exasperated questions: Where are we going? How does this fit in? What are you leading up to?

O 4a   Key Sentences. *A writer wishing to improve continuity can formulate clear and emphatic key sentences to serve as guideposts to the reader.* Thus, a **topic sentence** becomes a guide to the intention of a paragraph (see O 6a). A more comprehensive programmatic statement may provide the clue to the intention of a major division of a long essay. Here is an outline consisting of key questions and key sentences from an article exceptionally deliberate and clear-cut in its organizational scheme:

What are the students like? They come from all sorts of back-grounds. . . .

Only one thing they are certain to have in common: they are roughly in the same age group. . . .

Why do they come to college? They come because it is assumed that they will come, because almost everyone they know does. . . .

A second and related reason why students come is to make good contacts. . . .

Many come simply to learn to make a living. . . .

To have fun is still another motive. . . .

There are students who actually come because they want to learn. . . .

What happens to students in college? It is the students' first meeting, most likely, with a national and perhaps international group of men and women of their own age. . . .

Furthermore, college is the students' first encounter with live intellectuals. . . .

Students are surprised, too, at their first meeting with really violent political opinion of all possible varieties. . . .

It is in college, too, that the sharp bitter sting of failure is first experienced to any appreciable extent. . . .

What does the student learn? On the simplest level he has acquired a considerable amount of information. . . .

He will also have learned to question. . . .—James K. Feibleman, "What Happens in College," *Saturday Review*

O 4b   Transitional Phrases. *An effective writer uses appropriate transitional phrases to help the reader move smoothly from one paragraph to the next.*

(1) In the kind of systematic, formal exposition characteristic of textbooks and scholarly articles, the reader may be reminded of the relation of each paragraph to the main point by phrases placing it in a numerical sequence. Such **enumeration** is used in the following excerpt from a general discussion of language:

There are *five simple facts* about language in general which we must grasp before we can understand a specific language or pass judgment on a particular usage. . . .

In the first place, language is basically speech. . . .

In the second place, language is personal. . . .

The third fact about language is that it changes. . . .

The fourth great fact about language . . . is that its users are, in one way or another, isolated. . . .

The fifth great fact about language is that it is a historical growth of a specific kind. . . .—Donald J. Lloyd, "Snobs, Slobs, and the English Language," *The American Scholar*

When used in a perfunctory manner, enumeration makes for heavy, plodding reading. The next example, which also proceeds by enumeration, uses less obtrusive, less emphatic transitional expressions:

thesis	An arrangement of shapes is satisfying, or otherwise, to the human eye, because of certain elementary natural
first point	laws. *The most essential of these* is the law of balance. . . .
second point	A picture *also* demands harmony. . . .
summarizing definition	*In speaking* of the harmony, or unity, of a picture, *we mean* that . . .
further development of point 2	The colors, *too,* must be related harmoniously. . . .
summary of points 1 and 2 third point	*Thus* we have balance and harmony as necessities in a picture. We must *also* have variety and subtlety. . . .
definition summarizing points 1 to 3	The design of a picture, which includes *these qualities of* balance, harmony, and variety, is its basis and essential skeleton. . . .—K. W. Maurer, "On the Appreciation of Paintings," *Queen's Quarterly*

(2) In an essay presenting a fairly complex **logical argument**, transitional phrases are likely to be varied. A section of such an essay might proceed like this:

introduces main point	It is plain that . . .
begins to enumerate reasons	Here are some reasons for . . .
elaborates on one of several points	The second of these . . .
summarizes what precedes	In short, . . .
raises a possible objection	Yet . . .
concedes a point	It is true that . . .
returns to original trend of thought	Nevertheless, . . .
draws balanced conclusion	At the very least, . . .

Here are some other common transitional phrases: (**logical conclusion**) *accordingly, consequently, as a result, hence;* (**contrast or objection**) *but, however, on the other hand, conversely, on the contrary;* (**concession**) *granted that, no doubt, to be sure;* (**illustration**) *for example, for instance;* (**paraphrase or summary**) *in other words, to conclude, to sum up.* Often a complete sentence, and in longer papers a complete paragraph, may be needed to establish the transition from one major point to another. Overuse of transitional expressions like *however, therefore,* and *all things considered* can make a paper awkward and mechanical. On the other hand, when used sparingly and when varied to avoid monotony, they help to keep both writer and reader from leaving the tracks.

NOTE: *Avoid transitional expressions that are too vague to give the reader a sense of direction:* "One question that often arises is whether . . ."; "another interesting point is that . . ."; "we should also take a look at . . ."

O 4c   Continuity of Thought. *A well-organized paper shows structural features that reflect continuity of thought.* Notice how the opening sentences of each paragraph in the following excerpt suggest well-planned, systematic forward movement. Notice the frequent use of a *this* or *these* pointing back to a preceding paragraph. Notice the use of a *the one . . . the other* pattern tying two paragraphs together:

thesis	The diversity of higher education in the United States
first major aspect of general topic is taken up; one alternative is considered	is unprecedented. . . . Consider the *question of size.* The small campus offers . . .
second alternative is considered	Others feel hemmed in by these very qualities. They welcome the *comparative anonymity and impersonality* of the big university. . . .
second major aspect of general topic is taken up; first alternative is considered	Another familiar question is whether the student should go to a *college next door, in the next city, or a thousand miles away.* By living at home . . .
second alternative is considered	Balanced against this, there are considerable advantages to a youngster in *seeing and living in an unfamiliar region* of the country. . . .
alternatives are weighed	But this question too must be decided in terms of the individual. . . .
third major aspect of general topic is taken up; first alternative is considered	*Co-education* poses still another problem. Those who favor it argue . . .
second alternative is considered	Others believe that *young men and women* will work better if . . .
alternatives are weighed	There is no pat answer. It might be healthy for one youngster . . .
fourth major aspect of general topic is taken up	The so-called *"prestige"* colleges and universities present a special problem. . . .—John W. Gardner, "How to Choose a College, if Any," *Harper's*

In the following excerpt, notice how the *repetition of key terms* like *work, toil,* or *labor* suggests well-focused discussion:

What elements of the national character are attributable to this long-time agrarian environment? First and foremost is *the habit of work*. For the colonial farmer ceaseless striving constituted the price of survival. . . .

The *tradition of toil* so begun found new sustenance as settlers opened up the boundless stretches of the interior. "In the free States," wrote Harriet Martineau in 1837, *"labour* is more really and heartily honoured. . . ."

One source of Northern antagonism to the system of human bondage was the fear that it was jeopardizing this basic tenet of the American creed. "Wherever *labor* is mainly performed by slaves," Daniel Webster told the United States Senate, "it is regarded as . . ."

Probably no legacy from our farmer forebears has entered more deeply into the national psychology. If an American has no *purposeful work* on hand . . .

This *worship of work* has made it difficult for Americans to learn how to play. As Poor Richard saw it, "Leisure is . . ."

The first mitigations of the daily grind took the form of hunting, fishing, barn-raisings and logrollings—*activities that* had no social stigma because they *contributed to the basic needs of living.* . . .

The importance attached to *useful work* had the further effect of helping to make "this new man" indifferent to aesthetic considerations. . . .—Arthur M. Schlesinger, *Paths to the Present*

Continuity of thought may find its expression in a number of effective unifying devices. Thus, a writer may *ask a central question* in the title or in the introduction, proceed to discuss relevant facts, and then restate and answer the initial question in the conclusion. He may *present a topical anecdote* early in the paper, and then, after examining its implications, return to it at the end. He may *start by stating a series of propositions* and finish by restating them, in parallel form but with important qualifications. Repetition of key phrases, of important metaphors, and of grammatical patterns may help give the reader a sense of purpose.

O 5   OUTLINES AND SUMMARIES

Practice in outlining and in summarizing helps a writer achieve a firm grasp of organization.

O 5a   Working Outlines. *Even in writing a short theme, you will do well to construct a working outline by jotting down major points in a tentative order.* The working outline for a library or research paper is usually a rather carefully developed chart, without which the investigator may lose his way.

Here is a first tentative outline for a short paper on anti-intellectualism in the high schools:

> emphasis in high school on
> > athletics
> > social activities
>
> little recognition for intellectual achievement
> > honor roll
> > debating society
> > drama society ("intellectual"?)
>
> attitude now changing?
> > stress on college entrance

A good outline, reworked and reorganized repeatedly as the paper progresses, resembles an architect's preliminary sketches rather than his finished blueprint. When used effectively, an outline helps the writer visualize and strengthen tentative connections. It helps him work out his general strategy for presenting the material he has collected. It helps him detect weaknesses after he has finished his first draft. Finally, it serves him as a guide in cutting sentences and paragraphs that turn out to be less appropriate, less relevant, or less effective than he had originally thought.

O 5b   Final Outlines. *The final outline, intended as a guide to the reader, usually follows one of several conventional forms.*

(1) The **topic outline** is most useful for quick reference. It presents, in logical order, the topic and subtopics (and often the subsubtopics) that a paper covers. Like other outlines, it is often preceded by a thesis sentence summarizing the central idea of the paper. Here is a representative example:

WHY I WENT TO COLLEGE

THESIS: Going to college offered me both personal satisfactions and practical advantages.

I. Desire for independence
   A. Freedom from direct parental supervision
   B. Absence of demanding brothers and sisters

II. Attraction of changed surroundings
   A. Living in a congenial environment
      1. Quiet and dignity of college town
      2. Natural beauty of its surroundings

B. Meeting people
    1. Classmates and fellow business majors
    2. Social acquaintances
C. Participating in the cultural life of the college community

III. Satisfaction of working for a definite goal
    A. Choice of majors leading to a business career
    B. Opportunities for field work

(2) In a **sentence outline**, the writer sums up, in one complete sentence each, what he has to say on each topic and subtopic. The sentence outline thus forces him to think through his material thoroughly and systematically. It reveals vagueness, indecision, and lack of continuity more reliably than the topic outline, which merely indicates the ground to be covered. A typical sentence outline might look like this:

MAIN STREET ISN'T PENNSYLVANIA AVENUE

THESIS: A successful business career does not automatically qualify an executive for government work.

  I. Prominent businessmen have often occupied high positions in the federal government.

 II. Business executives often lack preparation for important aspects of government work.
    A. They tend to lack the tact and experience necessary for dealing with people from foreign cultures.
      1. They may alienate foreign diplomats.
      2. They tend to ignore public opinion abroad.
    B. They tend to lack the legal training required in interpreting and administering laws.
    C. They tend to be impatient with the delays inherent in democratic processes.

III. Businessmen often have qualifications that government officials tend to lack.
    A. They are in close contact with the wishes and opinions of the general public.
    B. They have thorough training in organizational problems.
      1. They are trained in administrative efficiency.
      2. They are cost-conscious.

IV. The personal qualifications of the individual executive are more important than his business background.

The divisions of an outline do not always correspond exactly to the paragraph divisions in the paper—though in a well-organized paper the two often coincide very closely. Several minor subdivisions may be treated in the same paragraph; one subdivision developed by detailed examples may spread through several paragraphs; short transitional paragraphs may intervene between subdivisions.

(3) Sometimes an instructor asks for a **paragraph outline**, which requires one summarizing statement for each paragraph. Usually these summarizing sentences are simply numbered consecutively, without an attempt to indicate the major divisions of the paper or the relative importance of different paragraphs.

To eliminate common weaknesses, check your finished outlines against the following list of suggestions:

(1) *Be consistent* in the use of symbols, indention, and spacing.

(2) *Avoid using "Introduction," "Conclusion,"* etc., as substitutes for individual headings.

(3) *Avoid single subdivisions.* If there is a subdivision A, there should be a subdivision B. If there is a section numbered 1, there should be a section numbered 2. If a section covers only one major point or one major step, leave it undivided.

(4) *Avoid a long sequence of parallel elements,* such as I X, A F, or 1 8. Unless the subject matter justifies mere undifferentiated enumeration, try to split the sequence into two or three major groups.

(5) *Use parallel grammatical structure* for headings of the same rank in order to emphasize their logical relation. For instance, if A 1 reads "To revive the student's interest," A 2 and A 3 should also be worded as infinitives: "To promote the student's participation"; "To develop the student's independent judgment."

(6) Make sure that *subdivisions are relevant and logically subordinate to the main heading* under which they appear.

(7) Make sure that your thesis is specific rather than vague and that it represents the central idea or the main point of the paper. *Make sure the thesis is a complete statement*—not a question, not a phrase without a predicate, not a dependent clause.

(8) In a topic outline, *make each topic specific and informative.* In a sentence outline, make each subdivision a complete sentence. *Make each sentence sum up an idea* rather than merely indicate a topic.

O 5c Summaries. *Related to skill in outlining is skill in the writing of summaries*—of your own work or, more commonly, of the work of others.[1] To summarize a piece of writing efficiently and fairly, you need to grasp its organization. You can then state essential points and qualifications in the most concise possible form, omitting illustrations, lengthy explanations, and incidental comment. The resulting summary can preserve the gist of an article or a paper for efficient study, for future reference, or for the use of a busy reader.

In writing a summary, you will have to observe several essential requirements:

(1) *Make sure you grasp the main trend of thought.* Isolate key sentences; formulate the major point implied in a paragraph; distinguish between incidental comments and important steps in an argument.

(2) *Reduce explanation and illustration to the essential minimum.* Omit passages that are mere paraphrase. Preserve only the most important details, examples, statistics. Reduce or omit elaboration by metaphor, comparison, anecdote.

(3) *Use the most economical wording possible.* Use the simpler of two alternative terms, the shorter of two synonyms. If you can, substitute a single word for a phrase, a phrase for a clause.

Study the differences between the full text and the summary in the following pairs:

> ORIGINAL: The invention of the process of printing from movable type, which occurred in Germany about the middle of the fifteenth century, was destined to exercise a far-reaching influence on all the vernacular languages of Europe. Introduced into England about 1476 by William Caxton, who had learned the art on the continent, printing made such rapid progress that a scant century later it was observed that manuscript books were seldom to be met with and almost never used. Some idea of the rapidity with which the new process swept forward may be had from the fact that in Europe the number of books printed before the year 1500 reaches the surprising figure of 35,000. The majority of these, it is true, were in Latin, whereas it is in the modern languages that the effect of the printing press was chiefly to be felt. But in England over 20,000 titles in English had appeared by 1640, ranging all the way from mere pamphlets to massive folios.

[1] See Section 8 for detailed discussion of how to summarize and paraphrase quoted material.

The result was to bring books, which had formerly been the expensive luxury of the few, within the reach of all. More important, however, was the fact, so obvious today, that it was possible to reproduce a book in a thousand copies or a hundred thousand, every one exactly like the other. A powerful force thus existed for promoting a standard uniform language, and the means were now available for spreading that language throughout the territory in which it was understood.— Albert C. Baugh, *A History of the English Language*

SUMMARY: Printing from movable type, invented in Germany about 1450 and brought to England about 1476, had a far-reaching influence on all European languages. Within a hundred years, manuscript books had become rare. Though at first most printed books were in Latin, over 20,000 titles in English had appeared by 1640. Books were now within the reach of everyone and could exert a powerful standardizing influence upon language.

ORIGINAL: The tendency to erect "systems"—which are then marketed as a whole—affects particularly the less mature sciences of medicine and psychology. In these subjects we have had a succession of intellectual edifices originally made available only in their entirety. It is as if one cannot rent a room or even a suite in a new building, but must lease the whole or not enter. Starting with a substantial contribution to medicine the authors of such systems expand their theories to include ambitious explanations of matters far beyond the original validated observations. And after the first pioneer, later and usually lesser contributors to the system add further accretions of mingled fact and theory. Consequently systems of this kind—like homeopathy, phrenology, psychoanalysis, and conditioned reflexology (the last dominant for years in Russia)—eventually contain almost inextricable mixtures of sense and nonsense. They capture fervid adherents, and it may take a generation or several for those who preserve some objectivity to succeed in salvaging the best in them while discarding the dross.—Dr. Ian Stevenson, "Scientists with Half-Closed Minds," *Harper's*

SUMMARY: Medicine and psychology have produced a number of intellectual systems that one is asked to accept as a whole or not at all. The ambitious authors and adherents of such systems go beyond original valid findings to produce a mixture of truth and error that attracts enthusiastic supporters. Objective observers may not succeed in separating the valuable from the worthless till much later.

Unless the original version is already severely condensed, a summary of about one third or one fourth the original length can usually preserve the essential points. However, the shorter the summary, the greater the danger of oversimplification or outright misrepresentation. You will have to be careful to preserve essential conditions and dis-

(ex.)

tinctions: *if-* and *unless-* clauses; differences between *is*, *will*, and *might;* qualifiers like *only, almost,* and *on the whole.* You will have to preserve the relative emphasis of the original, giving more prominence to a point treated at great length than to one mentioned in passing. Finally, you will have to preserve something like the original tone. On the one hand, you cannot simply ignore overtones of humor or irony; on the other hand, you should not let facetiousness creep in where it did not exist. Do not allow your own reaction to color the material.

EXERCISES

A. Sort out the suggestions in each of the following lists into major categories. Arrange both your major categories and their subdivisions in the most plausible or the most logical order.

(a) STUDY HINTS

1. Make study time as regular as possible.

2. Work out an understanding with friends and roommates concerning unnecessary interruptions.

3. Avoid dim or glaring light.

4. Get an understanding of the purposes and organization of a course from course outlines, introductory materials in a textbook, or chats with the instructor.

5. If you can, work at an uncluttered desk.

6. Ask yourself practice questions about what you study.

7. Make a point of not protracting lunch hours and coffee breaks indefinitely.

8. If you can, find a congenial corner in a library or study hall.

9. Start studying the first week of each term.

10. Take two or three *short* breaks during each two- or three-hour period of study.

11. In studying a textbook, try to relate what you read to the instructor's lectures or to class discussion.

12. If a subject does not seem immediately practical or interesting, treat it as a challenge to your resourcefulness, agility, and perseverance.

13. Break up the material to be studied into convenient chunks.

14. Reserve the cramming session before final examinations for review and for attention to special difficulties.

15. Summarize, review, and think about one major section before going on to another.

(b) TAKING ESSAY EXAMINATIONS

1. Take up those questions first that you feel best qualified to answer.

2. Check the questions for important qualifying words like *only, always, for the first time, major, most important*.

3. Bolster general points with specific detail.

4. Budget your time carefully.

5. If a question calls for a comparison, trace differences and similarities instead of giving two separate, unrelated accounts.

6. If you gain five points by treating one question at great length, and then lose twenty-five points by slighting the next two questions, you are twenty points behind.

7. Allow time for rereading and revision.

8. Pay attention to the exact wording of the questions.

9. Use preliminary jottings or a scratch outline to organize answers running to more than paragraph length.

10. If you are asked to select "three reasons" or "four qualities," don't list more than are asked for.

11. Think about the questions before you answer them, but don't brood over them.

12. Get a general picture of the examination before you start writing.

13. Be prepared to depart from the order of material in your textbook or in your lecture notes. (Many essay questions call for correlation of material from different parts of a course.)

14. Do not pad weak answers with irrelevant material.

15. Once you have started writing on one of several alternative questions, try to make the best of it rather than shift to an "easier" question in midstream.

16. If a question asks you to "evaluate," a mere recapitulation of facts is not enough.

17. Whenever possible, bolster your answers with specific references to the reading you have done for the course.

(c) WRITING A LETTER OF APPLICATION

1. Be courteous without being elaborately or excessively polite.

2. Stress previous practical experience, especially if relevant to the position for which you apply.

3. Be factual in describing your qualifications, while at the same time presenting them to advantage.

4. Ordinarily, avoid references to such personal reasons for wanting the position as financial need, family pressure, desire for a change of scenery, or lack of more promising prospects.

5. Avoid gimmicks.

6. Proofread your letter carefully for typing errors.

7. Describe your previous training, stressing courses or reading relevant to the employment you seek.

8. Avoid self-praise.

9. Include a list of references.

10. Avoid erasures.

11. Avoid offensive or gross flattery.

12. Make a special effort to secure neat, pleasing appearance of the finished letter.

13. If possible, be specific about the position for which you apply.

14. If possible, obtain prior permission from those whose names you use.

15. Introduce the letter by mentioning the advertisement or the person that informed you of the vacancy (but do not mention leads that smack of the "grapevine").

16. Ask for an interview, suggesting (but not setting) a possible time for it.

17. If the account of your qualifications is extensive, put it on a separate "data sheet."

B. Describe the approach chosen in each of the following introductions and comment on the effectiveness of both introduction and title. Do they make the reader want to go on reading? Do they seem to lead clearly and directly into a specific subject? What kind of paper would you expect in each case?

1.   HYDROPONICS IN THE HOME

Hydroponics is a subject about which many people have little or no knowledge, yet there is nothing really new or mysterious about it. It is merely a system by which plants are grown in water solutions containing the essential minerals for plant growth. The terms *water culture* and *water gardening* refer to this same system. . . .

2.   THE LATEST STYLE

If you picked this paper up expecting a dissertation on frills, frocks, and new brassieres to dream in, you had best put it down again. I am concerned here with a new style in automotive power plants, the free-piston turbine engine. You may ride behind one sooner than you think. . . .

3. THE ESSENCE OF FOOTBALL

To write an account of the essential features of football by giving only a description of its rules and procedures and omitting consideration of its actual practice in American sports would be misleading. A dictionary definition of football does not meaningfully convey to a person totally unfamiliar with the game a genuine understanding. American football is a living thing, not an abstract concept. Thus, American football transcends its mere rules and procedures and must be described accordingly if its essentials are to be validly grasped. . . .

4. THE EDUCATED ANTI-INTELLECTUALS

It is a curious fact that the American people spend more per capita on the schooling of their children than any other people on this globe and yet they persist in proclaiming their anti-intellectualism. Consider the epithets "brain trusters" and "eggheads." Look at the general disdain for the very word "intellectual" . . .

5. BRUTE STRENGTH IS NOT ENOUGH

Football has often been called a game for men who are all muscle and have no brains. This charge may have been justified in the infant years of the game, when it consisted entirely of running plays and when the players used brute strength to crash through the opposing line. Today, a team may use as many as fifty different plays, involving complicated deception and a wide variety of passes. . . .

6. THE ROLE OF GOVERNMENT

The decision between a strong government which governs the people or a weak government is one of importance and one that needs careful thought and consideration. Throughout history, the proper role of government has been a subject of discussion. . . .

7. EXTRA! EXTRA!

Splotch! The sound of the *Ungi Bungi Evening News* careening against my little mud hut stimulates every cultural and educational drive of my little Ungi Bungian mind. Where else can I find such factual and unbiased accounts of history-shaping events? Without further ado I will unfurl the parchment to discover what great accomplishments the world has recorded today. . . .

8. THE BENT AND BLUNTED FREE LANCE

In the chivalry of the thirteenth century, an important figure was the free lance, an independent knight who sold his fighting skill to the highest bidder and, so legend says, tilted his bold weapon in defense of the helpless against all sorts of dragons and outrages. So far in the twentieth century an important adjunct to communication has been the free-lance writer who has made a living, and a considerable social impact, with his pen. . . .—Hartzell Spence, *Saturday Review*

C. Describe the function and estimate the probable effectiveness of the following conclusions:

1. (A paper describing the game of badminton)
   . . . Badminton can be very exciting. If you are ever looking for a good time I suggest that you try this game. I know from experience that it can really be a lot of fun.

2. (A paper discussing a veteran's visit to his former high school)
   . . . As I walked, alone, down the familiar and yet strangely different hall, I began to realize a truth that nostalgic people like myself find hard to learn: Distance gives glamor to the past.

3. (A paper defending women against the charge that they are poor drivers)
   . . . that the woman driver, inexperienced and timid as she may be, is less of a highway menace than the arrogant, inconsiderate male. Of course, this is only one woman's opinion, and yours may be different from mine.

4. (A paper trying to demonstrate the futility of censoring comic books)
   . . . the parents can do most to counteract the comic-book habit. If they read to their children from good books, if they teach their children to treat good books as treasured possessions, if they make it a habit to talk about good books in the home, the positive attraction of good literature may prove more effective than censorship possibly can.

5. (A paper discussing several examples of "tolerance")
   . . . We thus conclude that by "tolerance" we mean allowing beliefs and actions of which we do not wholly approve. Since many of us approve wholeheartedly of only very few things, life without tolerance would be truly intolerable.

6. (A paper examining the proposition that "that government governs best that governs least")
   . . . Government must effectively govern to be a true government, but it must govern with restraint and not to excess. The government that governs least is not necessarily the best one. I would rather say that the government that governs ablest, in the interest of most of its citizens, is the best government.

D. Find three current magazine articles that are clearly or plausibly organized. Choose articles from different magazines and of varying degrees of difficulty. Write a well-developed paragraph on each, describing its organization or the general strategy adopted by the author in presenting his material.

E. Examine the introduction or "lead" in five current articles from different general-interest magazines. Write a well-developed paragraph about each one. Describe the approach followed and evaluate its effectiveness.

F. Select a current magazine article whose organization you find exceptionally clear or effective. Prepare both a topic and a sentence outline. Your instructor may wish to suggest a maximum number of words for each outline.

G. In a page of expository prose selected by your instructor, point out all key sentences, transitional phrases, and words or devices making for continuity.

H. Sort out the following material and arrange it in a topic outline:

EDUCATION WITHOUT REPRESENTATION

THESIS: Students would profit greatly from being given greater influence on curricula and teaching methods than they now have.

1. Training for citizenship through active participation
2. Present lack of student influence
3. Sense of belonging through participation
4. Attitudes toward elective as compared with required courses
5. Success of experimental programs
6. Attitude of night school and business college students toward freely chosen subjects
7. Training for adult responsibilities in business and family through participation
8. Improved motivation through active participation

I. Sort out the following material and arrange it in a sentence outline:

THE VALUE OF GROUP DISCUSSION

THESIS: Training in the techniques of group discussion is an indispensable part of the student's general education.

1. Discussion teaches us to look for evidence that will withstand criticism.
2. Discussion teaches us to control emotional reactions.
3. The primary goal of a discussion is to solve immediate problems.

(ex.)

4. Successful discussion requires ability to focus on the subject at hand.

5. In modern American society, more and more decisions are reached as the result of group discussion.

6. Successful discussion requires willingness to consider the viewpoints of others.

7. Discussion teaches us to estimate the reliability of evidence submitted by others.

8. Comparison of different views enables us to distinguish valid from invalid arguments.

9. The give-and-take of discussion is a humane alternative to one-sided propaganda and the use of force.

10. Discussion teaches us to get along with others.

11. Discussion teaches us to respect people whose knowledge or ability is superior to ours.

12. A successful discussion has educational value.

13. Discussion teaches us to be patient with people whom we assume to be wrong.

14. Discussion teaches us to evaluate evidence.

15. Successful discussion requires careful investigation of the relevant facts.

16. Discussion teaches us how to think.

17. Disagreement forces us to re-examine our views.

J. Outline each of the following student themes. Is there a thesis sentence? How adequate are restriction of subject, organization, and paragraph development? Comment on the effectiveness of title, introduction, and conclusion. Examine each theme for continuity.

1.   CERAMICS—MY HOBBY

Have you ever picked up a piece of free-form earthenware and thought how very satisfying and enjoyable it must have been for the person who worked it up from mere earth and water? By "free form," I mean the potter's own creative idea modeled in clay. Such free-form modeling is rather an involved process—many times, it is true, heartbreaking, but nevertheless an enjoyable and thoroughly gratifying experience.

It is possible to dig one's own clay from the earth. By moistening it with water and adding certain chemicals, one can make the clay mass more elastic, more workable, and stronger. Then follows the mixing of a glaze which, according to a specialized formula, will have an affinity to the original clay body. This in itself can become a long and tedious procedure. So, unless one has a pioneering spirit, it is better to find a standard clay body and glazes which have already been processed according to the manufacturer's own formula.

Cutting, shaping and molding the clay mass into the desired form with one's own hands is one of the biggest thrills imaginable. It is surprising what can be done with moist clay! A creative spirit can really go "wild" and still come up with something both beautiful and practical—say a flower vase or planter in the exaggerated form of some sea shell.

When the piece is thoroughly dry, it is known as "greenware" and is very fragile, but it becomes hardened through firing in a kiln. The firing is done slowly. The heat goes up to about 2000°F. It is measured by a cone-shaped pin set in a clay base and made to melt at the desired temperature. This is known as the pyrometric cone. The entire firing period takes about eight hours. Then the kiln is cooled slowly. It should not be opened or disturbed during the cooling time, which may take twelve hours or more. The greenware is now referred to as "bisque."

Bisque may be painted in a variety of colors, called underglaze, and then dipped in a transparent glaze. It may be sprayed or brushed with or dipped in any of the colored glazes. A second firing to bring out the glaze effect is now necessary. Usually, this firing is slow too, with the temperature not as intense as before—about 1800°F. However, the pyrometric cone must be watched more closely than in the bisque firing, especially with certain glaze formulas.

Glazes are extremely difficult to control, and many unexpected effects are obtained—probably caused by moisture in the air, uneven firing elements, firing time, dirt particles, or some chemical reaction. Many unique and unusual effects can be obtained through experimentation with underglazes, overglazes, colored clay bodies, sifted sands, crushed colored glass and even salt! I remember my first experiment. I used sifted sand which I found in my backyard. I dusted the sand over the glaze coating and, after firing, found there were bright red and black raised granules throughout the glaze.

One can look at this hobby from a practical point of view. Gifts alone, especially at Christmas time, make it worth while. But it is the ideas and experiments that make it a truly fascinating and worthwhile hobby.

2. HAPPINESS IN THE FAMILY

It is a safe venture to say that no one is more familiar with any family than he is with his own, the one he was brought up in. This is certainly the case with me, and it is largely my own family experiences and conditions which have influenced my views of successful family life. I feel that I am fortunate in being part of a successful family and in having been brought up in a happy home environment. When I examine the reasons for our happiness, certain factors stand out, which I will attempt to explain.

(ex.)

Certainly not a prerequisite to family success, but a factor which has considerably influenced my family's happiness, is having many members in the family. I come from a family of eight. Although a large family has disadvantages, I feel that the advantages far outweigh the problems that arise. In a large family, for instance, there is rarely loneliness, and affection usually prevails. I can't exactly pinpoint the reason why there is such a warm atmosphere in large families, but it might partly be that, as in my family, there is always some little sister or brother who needs comforting from a mishap, or someone who needs advice or requires help in a task. The feeling of closeness is promoted so much that it becomes habitual.

Family activities are an integral part of successful family living. The family should take out time now and then to do things together as a group. This strengthens family unity and promotes common interests among the members. I always looked forward eagerly to such family excursions as occasional visits to the museum or outings to a duck pond for a picnic. It has also been a policy of my family to take an annual camping trip to a national park and spend a week "roughing it." We all enjoy such exploits and share a unanimous liking for the outdoors.

I have always been glad that my family lives in a relaxed, informal atmosphere. When strict, formal behavior is enforced in a home, the members sometimes feel constrained and may become reserved in manner. I remember the summer when I was twelve years old, during which I went to live with my aunt's family for four months. It wasn't long before I began to count the days until I was to leave. Not only were my cousins and I made to address my aunt exclusively as "Ma'am," but many other restrictions were imposed upon us. No pace faster than a walk was allowed in the house, no loud talking was permitted, and no discussions were tolerated at the dinner table except between the adults. Even such minor things as eating corn-on-the-cob were regulated. We were instructed to eat two rows of corn at a time and chew each bit twenty-two times. I was so busy regulating bites and counting chews that the distinctive pleasure of eating corn-on-the-cob was lost. I know my cousins were as frustrated by all these restrictions as I was. Spontaneous affection, which I think is a necessary part of family happiness, can hardly be cultivated in an atmosphere like this.

Religion plays an important role in family life. There should be a common religion among the members, and the religious customs should be observed if the religion is to have any meaning for all members. I know of one family in which the mother was of one religion and the father of another. The conflicting religious customs resulted in both parents dropping their own observances, and the children now have no religion at all. Aside from failing to provide each member with religious satisfaction, this family is missing out on the special unity brought about by a common religion.

I think that the conditions essential to a happy family life are those which promote unity among the members, open expression of affection, and the personal contentment of each individual. I hope I can achieve these goals in a family of my own someday, much as they have been achieved in the one in which I grew up.

3.   SOMETHING NEW

Have you ever thought what a joy it would be to be thrilled at the idea of returning to college in the fall, to look forward with anxiety and zeal to your coming classes? If you are the way I am, you probably dread the thought of lugging those old school books down that foggy, cold path to the school buildings in the morning. After that, you fight to stay awake under the heat from the old radiator next to you and the monotonous drone of the econ-professor. Once through with your first hour class, you wander aimlessly through a barrage of other uninteresting subjects. Then, finally, you are through with your last class for the day, and back you plod on the trail home. Not a very exciting day, is it?

That is what college holds for me—or did until recently. You see, I have just finished reading Herman Hundinger's essay, "Education at Beechcroft College." His description of the system that is used by this school has not only greatly aroused and interested me but has affected my entire outlook on college education.

Can you imagine going to school and not having a pre-selected and definite curriculum thrown at you with the command, "Do it or else!" Under the Beechcroft system you will be amazed when you find yourself telling your advisor or counselor just what courses and subjects you wish to pursue. Then too, if you are in doubt, you can test out certain fields of endeavor that you are curious about. In the days ahead, if you find the trial curriculums are not what you wished or expected, you are free to change your major objective. You are allowed two years to "find" yourself; you are given the freedom of every way and means that you need to master and learn your chosen field of study. To aid you in your learning, there will be your counselor, who will meet with you once a week and give you directions and guidance. Your counselor will show you the proper channels and areas that you will need to know; he will also give you encouragement when you are feeling down and praise you when you are accomplishing that next rung on the ladder to the culmination of your life's work.

Let us place you in an example that will be found in a school of the sort described. Suppose you had chosen Industrial Relations for your major (which incidentally is my present major). You would have on your schedule for the day the classes that you yourself had chosen. There is no power or force that compels you to attend these classes, but you do so of your own accord. Some days, instead of going to class, you might visit the library and fall victim to those overpowering stacks. You would probably be so absorbed in your quest for more and more knowledge, contained in those thousands of books, that lunch time would have passed by hours ago. I don't want to convey to you at this point that you will not gain any knowledge or information from attending your classes. On the contrary, during your independent research you will be encountering many difficulties and problems. These obstacles can be overcome with instructions and guidance by your professors; they can be thrashed out and dissected in a group laboratory, or with just the instructor alone. In this way you will acquire more accurate understanding and knowledge.

Then you might spend another day in doing field work. By field work, I mean going out into the world and encountering actual everyday experience. You might decide to visit all the retail department stores in your city and try to determine what harmony, if any, there is in the relations between management and labor. With your instructor's guidance in making charts and plotting curves to find the normal expected behavior, you will be able to make many new and interesting assumptions and conclusions.

This knowledge, that you are studying what you want, and learning facts that you want to learn, will force you (very much I'm afraid) to burn that midnight oil. I am sorry we do not have a system like this in my school today. Picture yourself tearing out of the house before having that second cup of coffee, racing helter-skelter to the college, and roaring with vim and vigor through the day's schedule! Perhaps my children may enjoy these privileges that I have been denied.

10: THE PARAGRAPH

DEVELOPING A PARAGRAPH

In some kinds of writing, paragraph division is arbitrary, in others conventional. In many newspapers, a paragraph break occurs after every long sentence and after every group of two or three short ones. In much informal writing, the writer starts a paragraph as nonchalantly as a speaker pauses momentarily in cultivated conversation. In dialogue, a paragraph break conventionally signals each change from one speaker to another.

In an expository essay, paragraphs are likely to vary considerably in length, in function, and in importance. Some are primarily helps to continuity: programmatic paragraphs stating the author's intention, transitional paragraphs helping the reader see the connection between ideas, summarizing paragraphs recapitulating important points. Some are primarily helps to effectiveness: introductory paragraphs catching the reader's attention, one-sentence paragraphs setting off a statement for emphasis, incidental paragraphs leavening the essay with digressions-that-merely-seem-to-digress.

However, the meat of an essay is likely to be contained in a different kind of unit: the expository paragraph that presents and develops an important idea or an important step in an argument. *In serious expository prose, the paragraph tends to be a logical, rather than a typographical, unit.* It reflects the way the writer has sorted out and organized his material.

O 6 STRUCTURAL DEVICES

In studying paragraphs written by professional writers, and in strengthening paragraphs in your own papers, you should look for devices that reveal structure and guide the reader.

O 6a Topic Sentences. *By formulating topic sentences for key paragraphs, a writer can greatly improve the clarity and continuity of his discussion.* A **topic sentence** contains the central idea of a paragraph. Some paragraphs revolve around a central idea without containing an explicit, concise statement of it. Others range over a number of closely related ideas. In many a typical paragraph, however, a topic sentence promotes clarity because the reader need not infer for himself which of various points touched on is the key to the rest of the paragraph. It promotes unity because stating major points clearly and explicitly helps the writer to weed out irrelevancies and digressions.

Typical topic sentences might look like this:

Many animals are capable of emitting meaningful sounds.

Most of us are less tolerant than we think.

The African students I know are unanimous in demanding complete political independence.

"Impulse buying" plays as much of a role in the buying of a car as in other purchases.

Many campus buildings show the influence of imitation Gothic.

Notice how systematically the material in the following paragraph follows up the key idea stated in the topic sentence:

> *Latin American culture has been and is a dynamic element in the development of our own.* It has, for example, furnished more than 2000 place names to the United States postal directory. Its languages have influenced American English, as such simple examples as "rodeo" and "vamoose" indicate. Its customs are part of our "Westerns" on television. Its housing, its music, its dances, its scenery, its ruins and its romance have been imitated and admired in the United States. One third of the continental area of this republic was for a long period, as modern history goes, under the governance of Spanish viceroys or of Mexico. The largest single Christian church in the United States is identical with the dominant church in Latin America.—Howard Mumford Jones, "Goals for Americans," *Saturday Evening Post*

The topic sentence does not have a fixed place in a paragraph. Often, in fact, it appears at the end of an introductory or transitional paragraph rather than in the paragraph that actually develops it. Usually, however, it is most helpful immediately before or after the material to which it is related.

O 6b   Transitional Phrases. *Transitional phrases help the reader see a paragraph as a well-ordered whole.* In a well-written paragraph, the function of each sentence is more or less self-explanatory, with no need for elaborate directional signals. When used economically and unobtrusively, however, **transitional phrases** help the reader proceed smoothly from sentence to sentence.[1] Notice their use in the following paragraphs:

> Many animals are capable of emitting meaningful sounds. Hens, *for instance,* warn their chicks of impending danger. *Similarly,* dogs growl at strangers to express distrust or hostility. Most of man's pets, *in fact,* have a "vocabulary" of differentiated sounds to express hunger, pain, or satisfaction.

> Most of us are less tolerant than we think. *It is true that* we tend to be tolerant of things sufficiently remote, such as Buddhism or impressionist painting. *But* we lose our tempers quickly when confronted with minor irritations. My friends, *at any rate,* will rage at drivers who block their way, at acquaintances who are late for appointments, or at manufacturers of mechanisms that break down.

Readers tire of constant nudging by superfluous transitional devices. Notice how unobtrusive and yet how effective the transitions are in the following excerpt:

> . . . What must be *even more surprising* is the thinness of coverage right here at home in the center of our national news, Washington. Washington has a very large press corps. The roster of the National Press Club is substantial, *and* the State Department auditorium is easily filled by a glamour press conference. *The trouble is* that most of the Washington press corps runs as a herd, concentrating on the "big" story of the day to the neglect of much else. The news services have large staffs, *and* a few papers priding themselves on their national news maintain bureaus ranging from a half-dozen full-time correspondents to three times that number. *But* most of the so-called bureaus in Washington are one-man affairs. Except for an hour of gossip at the Press Club or at one of the other informal meeting places,

---

[1] On the problem of economical transition, see D 8c.

and for what a lonesome man picks up from his home Congressional delegation, and the steady stream of inspired handouts, the average Washington reporter never gets beneath the surface of the day's one obvious story.—Philip M. Wagner, "What Makes a Really Good Newspaper," *Harper's*

O 6c   Recurrent Terms. *A unified paragraph is often marked by the repetition or paraphrase of important words and phrases.* Such **recurrent terms** reflect continuity of thought and subject matter. Similar in effect is the recurrence of "pointers" like *he, it, they, this, these,* and *those.* Notice in the following excerpt how the idea of change recurs in each successive sentence:

> It is an ominous fact that in the long chain of evolution the latest link, man, has suddenly acquired alchemic powers to *alter* whatever he touches. No other species before has been able to *change* more than a tiny fraction of his habitat. Now there is but a tiny fraction that he has *left unchanged*. A bulldozer *undoes* in an hour the work of a million years.—Paul Brooks, "Canyonlands," *Atlantic*

Notice how the following paragraph on the relation of the "ends" and "means" in politics keeps playing off these two terms, and their synonyms or related terms, against each other:

> The *technical* man isolates one particular field or activity, in order to concentrate upon the *procedure* within it. In order for his work to proceed, he must assume the worth of the *end* to which his work is addressed; in order to get on to his own question, "*How?,*" he must assume that the *end* he is serving has an assured place in a hierarchy of *values* that he does not himself examine. As a cobbler cannot continually be asking himself whether shoes as such are a *good,* so an economist cannot continually ask himself whether "productivity" or "satisfaction" or—now apparently—"economic growth" is a *good;* he must take that for granted and get on with his job. Where the *end* is simple and noncontroversial, such a *technical approach* raises no problems. But in social policy the *ends* to be served admit of no such description: it is of the essence of politics that their meanings shift, that *values* conflict, and that men differ about them. The *ends* of politics, moreover, are not neatly separable from the "*means*" the *technical man* thinks he deals with exclusively; usually he bootlegs in some assumptions about *ends* in his work on the *means.* One might argue that political leadership, which must interpret the situation and fit together these several and conflicting *ends,* is pre-eminently the activity that cannot properly be reduced to sheer *technique.*—William Lee Miller, "Some Academic Questions About a New Yale Man," *The Reporter*

In the sample paragraphs reprinted in the rest of this section, words and phrases that make for unity or continuity are italicized.

O 7   PARAGRAPH DEVELOPMENT

By paying serious attention to paragraph development, you can learn to do justice to one thing at a time. You can make your papers seem like a sequence of solid, well-placed steps. The substantial, well-ordered paragraph is both the basic unit of, and a model for, the substantial, well-ordered theme.

O 7a   **Filling in Detail.** *In descriptive writing, in technical exposition, or in narrative, a paragraph often corresponds to a major unit in the material treated.* Such a paragraph may take up one limited aspect of a scene, outline a step in a process, recount an episode. It will derive its unity from orderly presentation of significant detail. Often the sequence of details is inherent in the subject matter. Thus, a paragraph may trace structural or geographical relationships (**spatial order**), follow the order of events in time (**chronological order**), or proceed from causes to effects (**order of causation**).

Study the selection and the order of details in the following sample paragraphs:

> The jockey *came to the doorway of the dining room, then after a moment stepped to one side* and stood motionless, with *his back to the wall. The room* was crowded, as this was the third day of the season and all the hotels in the town were full. *In the dining room* bouquets of August roses scattered their petals on the white table linen and from the *adjoining bar* came a warm, drunken wash of voices. The jockey *waited with his back to the wall* and *scrutinized the room* with pinched, crêpy eyes. He *examined the room until at last* his eyes reached a table in *a corner diagonally across from him,* at which three men were sitting. *As he watched,* the jockey raised his chin and tilted his head back to one side, his dwarfed body grew rigid, and his hands stiffened so that the fingers curled inward like gray claws. Tense *against the wall of the dining room, he watched* and waited in this way.—Carson McCullers, "The Jockey"

> The *greeting ceremony* when one bird of the pair, after having been away at the feeding grounds, rejoins its mate *is also beautiful. Some little time before* the human watcher notes the other's approach, the waiting bird rises on its branch, arches and spreads its wings, lifts its aigrettes into a fan and its head-plumes into a crown, bristles up the feathers of its neck, and emits again and again a hoarse cry.

The other approaches, settles in the branches near by, puts itself into a similar position, and advances towards its mate; and *after a short excited space* they settle down close together. *This type of greeting is repeated every day until* the young leave the nest; for after the eggs are laid both sexes brood, and there is a nest-relief four times in every twenty-four hours. *Each time* the same attitudes, the same cries, the same excitement; only now at the end of it all, one steps off the nest, the other on. One might suppose that this closed the performance. But no: the bird that has been relieved is still apparently animated by stores of unexpended emotion; it searches about for a twig, breaks it off or picks it up, and returns with it in beak to present to the other. *During the presentation the greeting ceremony* is again gone through; *after each relief* the *whole business of presentation and greeting* may be repeated two, or four, or up even to ten or eleven times before the free bird flies away.—Julian Huxley, *Essays of a Biologist*

Most of New England is glacial country and is, geologically speaking, a *rocky shambles* made by an ice-sheet that ground its massive way eastwards, ripped off the tops of hills and scattered a *hailstorm of stones and boulders* in all the lowlands. It *also* smeared some places with layers of good soil. *But* the only crop you can absolutely depend on anywhere through New England and along the North Atlantic coastal plain is a *crop of stones. So,* although New England is God's garden to a native (unless he happens to be a farmer), to an Englishman it is *pretty rough ground.* I remember one Briton who lived here moodily for years until he found the source of his homesickness: "There isn't a *field you can lie down in,*" he said. *This* may sound very fussy but when you consider that the *grass-pack* of the pasture regions of Iowa and Minnesota is the pride of the United States, and that it is still only about one third as tight and luscious as the grass-pack of southern England, it is easy to see why southern Englishmen can seem so snooty when real-estate men confront them with a *"rural paradise"* in Connecticut.—Alistair Cooke, *One Man's America*

Comparing these sample paragraphs with similar paragraphs from typical student papers will reveal one immediate contrast: the amount of **specific detail** that the professional writer uses to give substance to one limited point. Quite apart from fluency and effectiveness of expression, a superior command of detail is often the most noticeable qualification of the successful writer.

O 7b Explanation and Illustration. *In many expository paragraphs, developing a key idea is a matter of explanation and illustration.* A topic sentence is often intentionally terse and emphatic. It may be developed by material that amplifies it, spells out its implications, clarifies a key term (**definition**). It may be developed by two or three representative examples, or by one exceptionally detailed example, which, though it may seem less representative of a general trend, is more likely to seem authentic (**illustration**).

Notice how the following sample paragraphs vary the basic pattern of *statement—explanation—illustration:*

key idea

detailed
restatement

first example

second example

third example

The deep sea has its *stars*, and perhaps here and there an eerie and transient equivalent of *moonlight*, for the mysterious *phenomenon of luminescence* is displayed by perhaps half of all the fishes that live in dimly lit or darkened waters, and by many of the lower forms as well. Many fishes carry *luminous torches* that can be turned on or off at will, presumably helping them find or pursue their prey. Others have *rows of lights* over their bodies, in patterns that vary from species to species and may be a sort of recognition mark or badge by which the bearer can be known as friend or enemy. The deep-sea squid ejects a spurt of fluid that becomes a *luminous cloud*, the counterpart of the 'ink' of his shallow-water relative.—Rachel Carson, *The Sea around Us*

key question

key idea

first set of examples

second set of
examples

restatement of key
idea

Where do the terms of businesese come from? Most, *of course,* are hand-me-downs from former generations of businessmen, *but* many are the fruit of cross-fertilization with other jargons. A businessman who castigates government bureaucrats, *for example,* is at the same time apt to be activating, expediting, implementing, effectuating, optimizing, minimizing, and maximizing—and at all levels and echelons within the framework of broad policy areas. *Similarly,* though he is amused by the long-hairs and the social scientists, he is beginning to speak knowingly of projective techniques, social dynamics, depth interviewing, *and* sometime soon, if he keeps up at this rate, he will probably appropriate that hallmark of the sound sociological paper, "insightful." Businesese, *in fact,* has very nearly become the great common meeting ground of the jargons.—William H. Whyte, "The Language of Business," *Fortune*

introductory
anecdote

When Paul Garrett arrived in Detroit twenty-five years ago to begin General Motors' public relations program, the first question fired at him was: "How do you make a billion dollars look small?" Garrett said damned if he knew, and furthermore damned if he thought that was his job. Public relations, he argued, was not an "act," but a continuing effort on the part of management to win the confidence of the people with whom it came into contact. *Hence* you will find General Motors engaged in a host of activities in which altruism and self-interest come together in a creamy blend. Plant City and Field Relations, *for example,* stimulates local GM participation in the community affairs of the sixty-eight cities where it has factories, thereby helping both the community and itself. Educational Relations works with the schools, providing them with such useful educational material as films on safe driving, and providing itself with a flow of applicants for jobs. The Speakers Bureau is glad to send a company-sponsored lecturer to your club or association to edify it with an inspirational talk—or to educate it with a "sound" economic one. Institutional Advertising tells the story of GM's role in supporting some twenty thousand suppliers, and leaves you with the pleasant impression that what's good for General Motors is good for small business, too. The billion dollars may not look any smaller as a *result of these efforts. But* it looks much, much nicer. —Robert L. Heilbroner, "Public Relations—The Invisible Sell," *Harper's*

Not the least remarkable thing about Huck's feeling for people is that his tenderness goes along with the *assumption that his fellow men are likely to be dangerous and wicked.* He travels incognito, never telling the truth about himself and never twice telling the same lie, for he *trusts no one* and the lie comforts him even when it is not necessary. He *instinctively knows* that the best way to keep a party of men away from Jim on the raft is to beg them to come aboard to help his family stricken with smallpox. And if he had not already had the *knowledge of human weakness and stupidity* and cowardice, he would soon have acquired it, for all his encounters forcibly teach it to him—the insensate feud of the Graingerfords and Shepherdsons, the invasion of the raft by the Duke and the King, the murder of Boggs, the lynching party, and the speech of Colonel Sherburn. Yet his *profound and bitter knowledge of human depravity* never prevents him from being a friend to man.—Lionel Trilling, *The Liberal Imagination*

Perhaps the most wearing thing about television is that most of the time it talks in a language so bare, so elementary, and so lacking in overtones that it can only be called baby talk. *Certainly* the commercials are baby talk, complete with coo and wheedle; and some of them

Margin notes:
key idea
first example
second example
third example
fourth example
restatement of key idea, alluding to initial anecdote
key idea
first example
second example
further support for key idea
restatement of key idea
key idea
narrowed to limited area

specific examples

even press the toddlers into service to do the selling for them. *I am thinking of* the little girls who wash their dolls' clothes in Ivory and of the one little girl who, holding up a roll of paper, says "Hudson tissues tear so stwaight!"— Marya Mannes, "Channels," *The Reporter*

One point about these paragraphs deserves special attention: the satisfying and self-evident **relevance** of explanations and examples to the central idea. Not only is the illustrative material ample, but its appropriateness is immediately clear.

O 7c   Logical Patterns. *Many expository paragraphs, instead of presenting one key idea, weigh several closely related points or work out a conclusion in a series of closely related steps.* Such a paragraph may follow a number of different logical patterns. The following are among the most common:

(1) *Comparison and contrast.*

key idea (linked to preceding step in discussion)

first subtopic (situation in Alger's books)

second subtopic (contrasting situation today)

Just as Alger's view of money as something to be made and kept no longer generally operates, [neither] does his view of how it should be given away. There is a great deal of "charity" in Alger, but *it is always man-to-man, even palm-to-palm.* It is a gesture in the tradition of the New Testament, a retail transaction between two individuals, spiritual in essence, monetary in form. The adjective that comes first to mind when we think of it is "Christian." *The adjective that comes first to mind when we think of charity today is "organized."* Via drives, community chests, red feathers, we can give more away more quickly. At the same time the primitive-Christian heart of the process, man-to-man giving, is weakened. Warm-heartedness is communized.—Clifton Fadiman, "Party of One," *Holiday*

(2) *Examination of causes and effects.*

key idea

cause (with specific examples)

Europeans with time-honored experience in the technique of painlessly extracting cash from foreigners' pockets have correctly gauged that Americans like to travel abroad provided they don't really have to leave home. *They've seen* the U.S. armed forces and U.S. oil companies spend millions to give their personnel the illusion of living in a European or African suburbia filled with shopping centers, post exchanges, movie houses, ice-cream parlors, juke effect (with specific examples) — boxes, and American-style parking lots. *Smart promoters now give* the American abroad exactly what he wants. Hotel rooms are furnished to please him, meal hours drastically advanced to suit the American habit of eating dinner at 6 p.m., arrangements made to satisfy the Americans' affection for crowds, action, and noise.—Joseph Wechsberg, "The American Abroad," *Atlantic*

(3) *Drawing logical conclusions from evidence* (**inductive order**).

detailed report of experiment — Psychologists studying race prejudice have many times made an interesting experiment. They seat a few people in a row, show a picture to the first in line, and ask him to whisper a description of it in a few words to a second who will whisper the information to the third, and so on. The picture is of a policeman and a badly dressed, uncouth Negro. The policeman is holding a knife in his hand; the Negro is unarmed. Almost never is the description transmitted to more than two or three individuals in succession, before the knife has passed from the hand of the policeman and is now being held in a threatening manner, by the Negro! *In other words,* the picture is transformed until it fits the preexisting concept in the mind, which is that an open knife is far more likely to be held by a Negro than a policeman. *This sort of unconscious alteration* of what is perceived, to make it accord with what is already believed, is universal and is one of the most important of all the facts with which communication has to deal.—Bruce Bliven, *Preview for Tomorrow*

interpretation of experiment

general application of findings

(4) *Drawing logical conclusions from accepted premises* (**deductive order**).

first observation — In the history books of the future this age of ours may come to be known as the Age of Statistics. In the biological and physical as well as the sociological sciences, statistics have become, as they never were before, the most important tool of investigation. *But* as every philosophical scientist knows, the conclusions drawn by a science depend to a considerable extent upon the tools used. *And* it is in the nature of statistics not only that they deal with quantity but that they emphasize the significance of averages and medians. What usually exists or usually happens establishes The Law, and The Law is soon thought of as identical with The Truth. In all the arts, *nevertheless,* it is the exceptional and the unpredictable which really count. It is the excellent, not the average, which is really important. And there is, *therefore,* one aspect of the cul-

second observation

third observation (specific application of point 2)

fourth (contrasting) observation

logical conclusion

tural condition of a civilization to which statistical study is curiously inappropriate.—Joseph Wood Krutch, *Is the Common Man Too Common?*

(5) *Choosing among alternatives.*

first alternative examined and rejected

second alternative presented and supported

History shows that wars between cities, states, and geographic regions cease once the originally independent units have amalgamated under the leadership of a single government with the power of making and enforcing laws that are binding upon individuals. *One might reason on this basis that* if all of the industrialized and semi-industrialized regions of the world were to federate under a common government, the probability of another war would be greatly decreased. It seems likely that this conclusion would be valid if the resultant federation were as complete as was the federation formed by the original thirteen colonies in America. *On the other hand,* it is extremely unlikely that such a highly centralized federation could come into existence at the present time; nationalistic feelings of individual men and groups of men, and conflicts of economic interests, are too strong to permit rapid transition. *Also,* those nations which have high per capita reserves of resources and high per capita production would be most reluctant to delegate their sovereignties to higher authority and to abandon the economic barriers that now exist.—Harrison Brown, *The Challenge of Man's Future*

What matters about such a paragraph is not whether it fits into a familiar logical scheme but whether it is written with a sense of purpose and direction. The writer needs to focus clearly on the point that he wants his readers to reach. He can then proceed to help them bridge the gap from thought to thought instead of merely calling to them from across the water.

O 8 PARAGRAPH REVISION

In revising the first draft of a paper, you will do well to look for common sources of weak paragraph development.

O 8a Lack of Focus. Some paragraphs show that the writer has not proceeded beyond the first jotting down of possibly significant details and observations.

(1) *Give focus to a blurred paragraph by eliminating material not bearing on the central point.* A paragraph in a paper describing

a magazine might contain a comment on a striking cover, information about the price, and a brief summary of an interesting article. However, once the eye-catching qualities of the magazine are mentioned, describing and illustrating them adequately will take at least one full paragraph. Observations and comments not **relevant** to eye appeal will have to make room for more unified material.

(2) *Give unity to a rambling paragraph by selecting and rearranging details in order to bring out a logical connection previously missed or ignored.* Study the revision of the following paragraph for greater **coherence**:

POOR: San Francisco is a city of beautiful parks and public buildings. Golden Gate Park, with its spacious lawns and graceful ponds, enjoys international fame. The city's Bohemian section has become the national headquarters for jazz-age poetry and philosophy. Every tourist must visit Fisherman's Wharf and Coit Tower. The city is famed for its cultural events and conventions.

REVISED: It is not surprising that tourists and convention managers are attracted to San Francisco. Miles of varied waterfront, spacious parks, and impressive public buildings contribute to the city's unique appearance and cosmopolitan atmosphere. Fisherman's Wharf, with its seafood smells and colorful shops, attracts sightseeing crowds. Coit Tower affords a spectacular view of bay and city. Golden Gate Park, with its spacious lawns and graceful ponds, enjoys international fame.

O 8b   **Undeveloped Generalizations.** Some paragraphs consist of nothing more than a statement of a general point, often in a single sentence. Such one-sentence paragraphs can effectively emphasize an idea elaborated in what precedes or what follows. They make for stringy writing if the author expects them to serve as a substitute for detailed discussion.

(1) *Avoid paragraphs that merely reiterate a single point already sufficiently clear.* Strengthen your paragraphs by removing weak repetition and providing **specific detail**:

POOR: My roommate is very considerate. I have always found him helpful and eager to be of service. He has really taught me something about the role of kindness in everyday living.

REVISED: My roommate is very considerate. He makes a point of not disturbing me when I study. He is always glad to let me use his typewriter or lend me a small sum. When I have visitors, he helps to make them feel at home. His example is teaching me something about the role of kindness in everyday living.

(2) *Avoid paragraphs that are merely a series of undeveloped general observations,* each a possible topic sentence for a separate paragraph:

POOR: The poems I liked best were those by A. E. Housman. *His poems were easy to comprehend without being overly simple.* With most other poems I need the assistance of an expert who can "translate" them for me. *The thoughts and attitudes expressed in Housman's poems represent the wisdom of an experienced, educated man. His poems are short and to the point,* a great help to enjoyment. *They are written in such a manner that the reader does not feel the author is preaching to him.*

Unless intended for forecast or summary, such a paragraph suggests inadequate **restriction of the subject** or excessive confidence in the reader's willingness to accept the writer's mere say-so.

(3) *Avoid weakening otherwise well-developed paragraphs by undeveloped afterthoughts.* Suppose a paragraph illustrates in some detail the thoughtful, critical attitude a voter should have toward political leaders. The last sentence adds: "Of course, a respectful attitude is also deserved." Obviously, the question of respect needs separate explanation and illustration.

Generally, both a sequence of one- or two-sentence paragraphs and a typed page without any paragraph break at all are signals of inadequate paragraphing. Revising such defects of paragraph structure usually requires attention to the organization of the whole theme.

EXERCISES

A. Describe in detail the methods of development used in each of the following student-written paragraphs. Point out topic sentences, transitional phrases, and other clues to continuity and relevance. Comment on the general effectiveness or adequacy of each paragraph.

1. My own pet feature of the magazine are the advertisements. Well I know that their sole purpose is to induce the reader, including me, to spend as many dollars as possible for the product pictured. Knowing this in no way detracts from my enjoyment of the color and pictorial values of what I see. Fully aware as I am of the appeals being made to my baser instincts ·(snobbishness and greed, to name just two) by the artful devices of the advertising fraternity, I still enjoy looking at the pictures. The allure of an ordinary metal cooking utensil pictured in a setting more fit for a precious gem can spur me, a representative reader, on to the kitchen with grim de-

termination to substitute for my own quite adequate pots just *such* pots, with or without daisies. Utilized more sensibly, the power of such an imaginative appeal can bring about many small changes in the average home simply by giving a new slant on an old topic.

2. Although I never attended a class there, the abandoned main building that crowned the top of the hill was a favorite monument of mine. It was weathered by salt air, wind, and fog; its surface was scarred by dozens of holes where engineers and inspectors had bored into the plaster for samples; many of the windows were broken or missing, and they stared out at the rest of the campus like the huge, vacant eye-sockets of a skull. In spite of these mutilations, the old building radiated an atmosphere of dignity and benevolence. Its massive stone steps extended outward from the barricaded door like the arms of the Lincoln monument, inviting students to gather there.

3. When I attended my first class meeting in World History, I was disappointed to learn that during the year we were not to study and discuss the reasons why an event occurred; we were apparently expected to spend most of our time memorizing dates and names. At least, I thought, when a test came up I would have to think back to remember what happened in 1492, for instance. But when the students sat down for the final examination, the question was not "What important event occurred in 1492, and how did it affect world history?" No! It was as follows: "In 1492, Columbus sailed to the New World—true or false?" or "What year did Columbus sail to the New World? (a) 1942; (b) 1812; (c) 1912; (d) 1492." What kind of thought is provoked by tests such as these?

4. Detective stories tend to glorify crime. Murderers, gangsters, and crooks of all kinds are described as tough, cunning, and courageous individuals who know how to take care of themselves and who know how to get what they want. In James M. Cain's *The Postman Always Rings Twice*, for instance, the villain is a much more impressive character than his victim. He is casual, brave, smart, and successful with women. It is true that he finally gets caught. But he is punished for a crime that he did not commit, so that his conviction is hardly a triumph of justice. Besides, looking back over the exciting life of the criminal, the reader might conclude that it was worth the risk.

5. One obvious result of modern technology has been the increasing dependence of one workman upon another. We have "geared the machines and locked all together into interdependence." In Detroit's factories, thousands of workers are specialized; each performs a specific task. On the assembly line, an automobile is mass produced in a matter of hours. One worker installs wires, a second fastens lining

in the interior, a third installs the windshield. Further down the line, groups of specialized personnel have assembled the dashboard and the seats. The finished body is lowered onto a chassis that has come down a similar line, operating on the same principle of each man doing a particular job. In a short time, the test driver drives the finished car through the factory gates. This is division of labor. This is specialization.

B. Discuss in detail the principles of paragraph development illustrated in the following examples. Pay special attention to the features that give each paragraph focus and direction.

Just under three hundred years ago, the Lucasian Professor of Mathematics at Cambridge did a distinctly unusual thing. He decided that one of his pupils was a much better mathematician than he was, and in all respects more fitted for his job. He wasn't content with this exercise in self-criticism. He promptly resigned his Chair, on condition that his pupil be immediately appointed. In the light of history, no one can say that his judgment was wrong. For the Professor's name was Barrow, and he was a very good mathematician by seventeenth-century standards; but his pupil was Isaac Newton.— C. P. Snow, "On Magnanimity," *Harper's*

Nobody has succeeded in explaining the connection between the private sources and the public functions of art. But art does have its public functions, though we often lose sight of them. In primitive agricultural societies, and even in Western Europe until the Renaissance, the functions were more clearly defined. It was the duty of the artist to celebrate the community in its present oneness, in its divine past, and in its glorious future. Thus he invented dances and rituals for the group, he retold the stories of its gods and heroes, he fashioned their images, and he persuaded the "people"—his own tribe that is, the only genuine persons—that they were reenacting the lives of the gods, who would some day return and reinstitute the golden age. Thus the artist played a recognized part in the daily life of the people.—Malcolm Cowley, "Artists, Conscience, and Censors," *Saturday Review*

Primarily, the brain is an organ of survival. It was built by nature to search for food, shelter, and the like, to gain advantage—before addressing itself to the pursuit of truth. Hence most human brains are unable to distinguish between truth and advantage, and accept as truth that which is only advantage. We use our brain mainly for finding ways to reach what we want. Simultaneously, we produce the thoughts and arguments which justify our feelings and dealings. I suspect that if I were in the business of selling shelters, my brain would tend to dwell rather steadily on the probability of nuclear war.

If I were in politics, I might find my brain devoting itself less to the next generation than to the next election.—Albert Szent-Gyorgyi, "The Persistence of the Caveman," *Saturday Review*

The real Baltimorean is convinced that the real Baltimore vanished long ago. That damnable contraption, the horseless carriage, put it on the skids, and Kaiser Wilhelm II finished it. It was during the incivilities exchanged with the Kaiser that Baltimore, a drowsy but delectable city of half a million people, was dragooned into becoming a great port by reason of the Allies' insatiable demand for steel, coal, and foodstuffs, especially grain. The wharves of Baltimore lie ninety miles nearer the wheat fields of the Middle West than those of any other saltwater port. Speed was of the essence in the task of feeding J. J. Pershing's personally conducted party then touring Europe, so Baltimore was hustled into the twentieth century willy-nilly, and in the process lost its identity.—Gerald W. Johnson, "Baltimore: The City Nobody Knows," *Atlantic*

Reading is a habit. Once you've got the habit you never lose it. But you must somehow be exposed to reading early enough in life to have it become a part of your daily routine, like washing your face or breathing. Many an unfortunate grade-school child in our highly seasoned, electronic, picture-conscious age has never been exposed to the reading habit and cannot, therefore, read without effort. Some modern children seldom if ever read for fun. Like muscles that are almost never used, their concentration and interest give way quickly. They long for the automatic, pictorial sensation of TV (which can be highly instructive and entertaining at times) rather than the tedium of moving the eyes from left to right, from left to right, from left to right, on line after line after line of unillustrated print. There's a certain sadness in realizing that a whopping segment of the exploding new teen-age generation never *really* reads anything, unless forced to do so.—Richard L. Tobin, "Reading Is a Habit," *Saturday Review*

When films first broke on the world, let's say with the full-length, full-scale achievement of D. W. Griffith, *The Birth of a Nation,* one of its most persuasive and hitherto unexperienced powers lay in the absolute reality of the moving image. The camera is a scientific instrument, not a paintbrush: its special virtues are accuracy and actuality. Thus, when Griffith organized a pan-shot which began with a mother and child huddled in terror on a mountain and then moved slowly to a raging battle on the plain beneath, we were left breathless by a juxtaposition in scale—from the individual to the group, from the passive to the active—that was, quite literally, taking place before our eyes. Our belief in the medium had begun with actual railroad trains roaring down actual tracks right at us, with actual ocean waves breaking somewhere near our feet. Griffith moved from simple documentation to high imagination, from fact to fiction, from present to past; and he took us with him because he used his camera as a faithful recorder of something that was really and truly going on: he did not abandon his camera's ability to state visual facts.— Walter Kerr, "What Good Is Television?" *Horizon*

C. Examine the material in the following paragraphs for relevance and continuity. Write a topic sentence summing up the general idea that the paragraph implies.

1. I am sure that the Romans, whose lives were lived under stately porticoes and amid the pomp of great temples, found in that background an ever present dignity which must have followed them even into the poverty and confusions of the crowded, many-storied *insulae.* The wide forums and the glittering *thermae* did not arise merely from the vanity of emperors and the corruption of the people. These were the songs in which the Roman soul made itself known above the cries of the circus and the clash of civil swords. The Gothic cathedrals were, in part at least, prayers of thanksgiving for a joy discovered in the revival of cities, and the *piazze* into which Venice poured her compressed splendor are jubilant with that new enfranchisement. These are not each an ornament added to a city but summations of a city's spirit to which houses and streets, walls, canals, and the domes of public buildings are the harmonious counterparts. Florence, Padua, Cordoba; the Paris of Richelieu, the Philadelphia of Franklin: each of these might have been the work of a single architect so consistent is the ordinance and expression of their streets and structures.—Joseph Hudnut, *Architecture and the Spirit of Man*

2. During my month of vigil and research, I heard an able physiologist who has a radio program say, quite simply, "We do not use up all the food we take in." He wasn't allowed to get away with that piece of clarity, however. "Ah," cut in his announcer, for the benefit of those no longer able to understand simplicity, "the utilization factor!" I turned from this station to a droning psychologist, just in time to hear him say, "The female is sometimes the sexual aggressor." Here a familiar noun of mental illness and military invasion was clumsily at work beating in the skull of love with a verbal bungstarter. The sweetheart now often wears the fustian of the sick man and the Caesar. In the evening, I tuned in on one of the space-patrol programs that gleefully exude the great big blockyisms. "Your astrogation bank will tell you!" cried the captain of a space ship to another interplanetary pilot, meaning his navigational instruments. In a fairy tale, an astrogation bank would be a "star panel," but the quality of a fairy tale is nowhere to be found in these dime novels of the constellations.—James Thurber, "The Psychosemanticist Will See You Now, Mr. Thurber," *The New Yorker*

(ex.)

D. Write a one-paragraph theme describing a face, a dress, the façade of a building, an abstract painting, or a tree. Work out a plausible sequence of details and try to achieve a unified general impression.

E. Write a one-paragraph theme describing a memorable moment. Avoid anticlimactic or confusing sequence of details.

F. Write a one-paragraph theme describing and illustrating a character trait of someone you know fairly well.

G. Select a key sentence from your current writing or reading. Use it as a topic sentence in three different paragraphs. Follow a different pattern of development each time, using different material as far as possible.

H. Study paragraph division and sequence of material in half a dozen news reports selected from a local newspaper. What is the relation between paragraphing and over-all organization? What effect does the paper's system of paragraphing have on its presentation of news? Report your findings.

I. Study paragraph division and paragraph development in an essay by a nineteenth-century writer like Thomas Babington Macaulay, Robert Louis Stevenson, or John Henry Newman. Report distinctive features.

CHAPTER SIX

GRAMMAR, DICTION, AND USAGE

11: GRAMMAR

REVIEWING GRAMMAR

When a child begins to talk, he must learn not only to name things but also to work the names of things into complicated patterns. Soon he is able to say "Suzie won't give me my ball back" or "Johnny says there isn't any Santa Claus." He has evidently mastered the major principles of **grammar**; that is, *the system by which words combine into larger units to convey ideas and information.*

G 1 GRAMMAR AND USAGE

The grammatical proficiency of small children unfortunately does not protect them against difficulties when they grow up. Schools are full of students trying to "learn" grammar, while at the same time considering it a difficult or unpleasant subject. Actually, they are not trying to learn grammar but to adapt grammatical patterns already learned to changing needs. The language employed by the average educated adult in serious conversation and in writing differs to some extent from the language he uses when not on his best behavior. The child must learn that often he should say "is not" rather than "ain't," "can hardly wait" rather than "can't hardly wait," and "this kind of car" rather than "these kind of cars." Such differences are often discussed under the heading of **usage** rather than of grammar. While grammar concerns itself with generally applicable principles, the study of usage investigates our *choices among alternative words, word forms, and constructions.* A writer needs to realize that usage varies, at least to some extent, from period to period, from area to area, from social group to social group, and from one kind of writing to another.

G 1a   Standard and Nonstandard. **Standard** usage is the language of educated speech and writing. It is the *variety of English that enjoys social and cultural prestige.* You will use it in your written work except when you record or deliberately imitate illiterate or **nonstandard** speech. Nonstandard speakers have usually had relatively little formal education. Their jobs often require little reading of instructions and little writing of reports. They may have few dealings with teachers, lawyers, newspapermen, and other presumably highly literate persons.

Here are some of the distinctive forms and constructions of nonstandard English: [1]

VERB FORMS:	he *don't,* you *was,* I *says; knowed, growed;* I *seen* him
PRONOUN FORMS:	*hisself, theirself; this here* book, *that there* car; *them* boys
CONNECTIVES:	*without* you pay the rent; *on account of* he was sick; *being as* she couldn't come
DOUBLE NEGATIVES:	we *don't* have *no* time; a little rain *never* hurt *no* one

G 1b   Formal and Informal. Most college students have learned to employ standard English in speech and writing. Their main problem is usually their failure to distinguish between *different kinds of standard English appropriate to different occasions.* On the one hand, there are relatively **informal** usages, found primarily in casual conversation, but also in writing that is designed to sound chatty or familiar. On the other hand, there are relatively **formal** usages, characteristic of the language of scholarly studies, books on serious subjects, articles in serious magazines. Though more characteristic of written than of spoken English, these usages are also found in formal lectures, speeches, and discussions.

Here are some characteristic features of informal English:

CONTRACTIONS:	*don't, doesn't, isn't, won't, can't; I'm, you've, they're*
CONVERSATIONAL TAGS:	*well, . . .; why, . . .; now, . . .*
PRONOUN FORMS:	it's *me,* that's *him; who* did you invite
PRONOUN REFERENCE:	everybody took *theirs;* somebody left *their* gloves
INTENSIFIERS:	*so* glad, *such a* surprise; *real* miserable, *awful* fast

[1] See the Glossary of Usage (Section 16) for further examples of nonstandard usage.

The line between informal and formal English is not easy to draw. It is a matter not only of forms and constructions but also of word choice, sentence style, and organization.[2] The difference is often a matter of degree, with some expressions sounding more easygoing than others. At one extreme, the term **colloquial**, used in this book mainly in reference to word choice, describes the *usages most clearly suggestive of informal, improvised speech.* At the other extreme is usage so punctiliously formal as to be stilted or affected. As used in this book, the term *formal* describes usage generally appropriate to the discussion of serious issues.

Most college writing requires a knowledge of formal usage. Even if you are content to have your writing sound casual and relaxed, you have to be able to use a more formal style when the situation clearly demands it. Fortunately, the forms and constructions generally accepted as touchstones of formal written English are not very numerous. Later parts of this section review the most important of these.

G 1c **Sentence Construction.** Learning to choose between alternative usages is not all there is to grammar—let alone to effective writing. As a college student, you are exploring new areas of knowledge and learning to digest complicated and unfamiliar ideas. To meet new and varied demands, your language patterns need to grow in accuracy, scope, and flexibility.

For one thing, you have to learn how new words or phrases fit into sentences. A child, when first introduced to the idea of freezing, learns to say "it froze" rather than "it freezed." Similarly, the high school student who is introduced to the word *criteria* learns to write "*These* criteria *are* unreliable" rather than "*This* criteria *is* a phony." More important, however, you have to *improve your skill in making relationships between words reflect relationships between ideas.* The more complicated and the more ambitious your ideas become, the more you will try to state them in compact form, giving proper emphasis to the points you want to stand out.

In a first draft, you may put down disjointed odds and ends: "My father bought a store in Oakland. Soon afterward property values went up. He sold the store at a handsome profit." In the finished paper, you may want the information about his making a profit to stand out as the main point. You will then arrange the material accordingly:

---

[2] For a discussion of formal and informal diction, see D 3. For a more general discussion of formal and informal style, see Section 7, Tone and Style.

My father, who had bought a store in Oakland, sold it at a handsome profit when property values went up soon afterward.

Notice how the more complex version of the following passage emphasizes the point that the word discussed has many different meanings:

SIMPLE: The term *democracy* originated in ancient Greece. Different people have used it to describe quite different political systems. Usually the person who uses the word thinks it has only one meaning.

COMPLEX: *Democracy,* a term that originated in ancient Greece, has been used to describe quite different political systems, though the person who uses it usually thinks it has only one meaning.

It is obviously easier to get lost in a long, complex sentence than in a short, simple one. If you have had little training in stating complicated ideas, you may produce sentences that are in various ways garbled or confused. They may suffer from scrambled word order, with major elements arranged upside-down. They may have a chopped-off effect because they start a pattern and leave it incomplete. They may be shaky because of inconsistent construction, combining patterns that do not go together. Through grammatical analysis you can sort out such sentences, identifying the various familiar speech patterns they contain. You can then combine these patterns in such a way that they are grammatically complete in themselves and at the same time convey the intended meaning as accurately and as efficiently as possible.

G 2   GRAMMATICAL ANALYSIS

Words convey only vague and tentative meanings as long as they are loosely strung together. G.I.'s and tourists traveling in foreign countries can carry on a rudimentary conversation with foreigners after picking up a number of isolated words. Similarly, a foreign visitor coming to the United States can make at least a dent in the language barrier by taking individual words from a dictionary. "Father—alcohol—baby—crying—beating—doctor—courtroom—jail" tells some kind of a story. However, what makes it broken English rather than standard English is the absence of definite relationships among words.

G 2a   Grammatical Devices. English employs several kinds of grammatical devices to give precise meaning to a sequence of words. One of them is its system of **inflections**. Inflections are *changes in the form of a word that correspond to differences in grammatical relationships.* Inflections signal the differences in meaning between the sentences in each of the following pairs:

Stop*s* annoy*ed* our passenger.
Stop annoy*ing* our passenger.

The physician studi*ed* burn*s*.
The physician*'s* study burn*ed*.

The endings spelled *s, ed,* and *ing* are the inflections most frequently used in English.

Some languages, such as Latin and German, rely heavily on inflections. Originally, English was close to German in number and importance of inflected forms. Through the centuries, however, English has shed many of these. Modern English relies primarily on other grammatical devices. One of these is **word order**. In English, *different arrangements of words in a sentence produce different meanings.* Compare the sentences in the following pairs:

Gentlemen prefer *blondes.*
Blondes prefer *gentlemen.*

A *tramp* called *the mayor a liar.*
A *liar* called *the mayor a tramp.*
The mayor called *a tramp a liar.*

He ate *only* the steak.
He ate the *only* steak.

Another major grammatical device is the use of *words whose main function consists in clarifying relationships among other words.* Many modern grammarians group these words together as **function words**. Function words account for the differences in meaning in the following pairs:

George set *a* poor example.
George set *the* poor *an* example.

He left the lady his estate.
He left *with* the lady *for* his estate.

The nurse neglected the patient.
The nurse *was* neglected *by* the patient.

In the typical written sentence, inflections, word order, and function words combine to help the reader select among the possible meanings of individual words and work those words into a meaningful sequence.

G 2b   Basic Sentence Elements. In analyzing sentences, grammarians assign words to basic categories, or **parts of speech**, according to the functions they perform. Identical words often serve different functions, and belong to different grammatical categories, in different sentences. The word *light,* for instance, performs a different function in each of the following:

> Turn off the *light.*
> Let's *light* a candle.
> She had *light* hair.
> The water was *light* blue.

The most important of the basic categories are those required to make up the various typical sentence patterns. Of these sentence types most actual sentences are variations or elaborations.

(1) *The basic model of the English sentence consists of only two major elements.* A complete sentence normally has at least a **subject** and a **predicate**:

SUBJECT	PREDICATE
The boy	reads.
A car	stopped.
Dogs	bark.

The most important part of the subject is usually a **noun**: *car, student, bulldog, college, education.* Traditionally, grammarians have defined the noun on the basis of meaning. Characteristically, nouns name or classify things, places, people, animals, concepts. The housewife looking up entries in the Sears Roebuck catalogue, the chemist giving names to new plastics, the businessman naming new products —all rely on the naming function of the noun. Modern grammarians have preferred to base their definitions on more concrete criteria, such as position and form. Nouns occur in such typical noun positions as "*Dogs* bark," "I like *dogs,*" and "for my *dogs.*" Their appearance is often signaled by such noun markers as *a, an,* and *the* (**articles**); *this, these, that,* and *those* (**demonstrative pronouns**); or *my, our,* and *your* (**possessive pronouns**). Most nouns add the inflectional *s* to refer to more than one of a kind (plural): boy*s*, dog*s*, car*s*, idea*s*. Many nouns show noun-forming endings (**suffixes**) like *-acy, -age, -ance, -dom, -hood:* liter*acy,* bond*age,* import*ance,* king*dom,* nation*hood.*

The place of nouns may be taken by **noun equivalents** or noun substitutes, such as the **personal pronouns**:

> *He* reads.
> *It* stopped.
> *They* bark.

The predicate, the second major part of a simple sentence, normally makes some kind of assertion concerning the subject. (Sometimes the predicate asks a question about the subject.) The most important word, or group of words, in the predicate is the **verb**: *reads, stopped, has left, will return, is reprimanded, has been elected.* Traditional definitions of the verb are based on meaning. The verb signals the performance of an action, the occurrence of an event, or the presence of a condition. A noun may *name* an action: *theft, movement, investigation.* A verb refers to present, future, past, possible, or hypothetical performance: *steals, has moved, may investigate.* A noun may *name* a condition: *existence.* A verb refers to its occurrence: *exists, has existed, will exist.*

Modern grammarians base their definitions on structure and form. Verbs occur in typical verb positions: "Let's *eat,*" "*Eat* your cereal," and "Big fishes *eat* little fishes." Most verbs change from the plain form to the plain form plus *s* after *he* or *she* (third person singular): "He eat*s,*" "She write*s,*" "He investigate*s.*" In verb forms consisting of several words, a limited number of **auxiliaries** recur: "I *am* eating," "he *has* eaten," "she *had* eaten," "they *will* eat," "you *should* eat," "we *may* eat," "he *has been* eating," "it *must be* eaten." Typical verb-forming suffixes are *-ize* and *-en:* organ*ize,* sharp*en,* redd*en.*

(2) *Several typical sentence patterns are expansions of the basic subject-predicate group.* In many sentences, the verb is an action verb, indicating what the subject does or what happens to the subject. Such an action verb may be followed by one or two **objects**. An object is a noun or a noun equivalent. It may indicate a possible target of an action; it may indicate something that is in some other way affected by or involved in what the subject does.

SUBJECT	ACTION VERB	OBJECT	OBJECT
The student	reads	a book.	
My friend	sent	me	a letter.
Fred	called	his roommate	a liar.

In other sentences, the verb is a **linking verb**, which introduces a description of the subject. A linking verb links the subject to a description that identifies the subject or points out some of its characteristics.

SUBJECT	LINKING VERB	DESCRIPTION
Schnoogle	is	a mailman.
He	may be	your brother.
The price	seemed	reasonable.
The food	tasted	good.

The description following the linking verb is often a noun (*mailman, brother*). It may also be an **adjective**, a word that can point out a quality of a noun (see G 2c). A noun or an adjective used to complete the predicate is called a **complement**.

(3) *Several other typical sentence patterns are important because of the way they modify the usual subject-predicate relationship.* One of them uses the **passive** construction. It reverses the more common actor-action sequence by making the receiver, the target, or the result of the action the subject of the sentence. The passive construction can be recognized by characteristic forms of the verb, using the auxiliary *to be* and the **past participle**. (See G 4a.)

SUBJECT	PASSIVE VERB
A letter	was sent.
Prices	have been raised.
The series	will be discontinued.

The second pattern employs the verb form used in requests and commands (**imperative**) and omits the subject.

VERB	COMPLEMENT
Shut	the door.
Be	a man.
Keep	quiet.

A third pattern, beginning with *there is* or *there are*, postpones the subject:

	VERB	SUBJECT
There	is	hope.
There	was	no time.
There	were	few survivors.

NOTE: In identifying basic sentence elements, you will have to distinguish between verbs and **verbals**. *Verbals are derived from verbs but do not by themselves function as predicates.* The most distinctive and the most important of the verbals are the *to* forms (**infinitives**) and the *ing* forms (**gerunds** and **present participles**). Infinitives and gerunds often serve as subjects or as complements, taking the place of nouns.

Speeding	causes	accidents.
He	refused	*to pay.*
Teachers	discourage	*cheating.*

These verbals do have some important similarities to verbs. For instance, they are often followed by objects.

Studying *grammar*	inspires	me.
Fred	refused	to pay *his dues.*
Courtesy	forbids	calling *a policeman a cop.*

The *ing* forms are called present participles when they function as adjectives. (See G 2c.)

G 2c Modifiers. Modifiers are *words, or groups of words, that in various ways develop, restrict, or otherwise modify the meaning of the basic sentence elements.* Modifiers can be roughly divided into two main groups: those that modify nouns or noun equivalents and those that modify other parts of a sentence or the sentence as a whole. All of the modifiers italicized in the following examples modify the noun *dog* and thus belong in the first group:

A *shaggy* dog barred my way.
A *big, yellow* dog was chewing the rug.
A dog *wearing a muzzle* emerged from the door.
A *police* dog tracked me down.
A dog *with droopy eyes* dozed in the sun.

Of these modifiers, the first three (*shaggy, big, yellow*) have the structural and formal characteristics of adjectives. An **adjective** can be identified as occurring in typical adjective positions: "a *reasonable* price," "The price is *reasonable*," "a very *reasonable* price." Most adjectives have distinctive forms for use in comparisons: *small—smaller —smallest; good—better—best; reasonable—more reasonable—most reasonable.* Typical suffixes serving to derive adjectives from other words are *-ic, -ish, -ive,* and *-ous: basic, foolish, expensive, courage*ous.* In traditional grammar, however, any modifier that modifies a noun or noun equivalent is said to *function* as an adjective.

The second group of modifiers is illustrated in the following sentences:

> The bell rang *twice.*
> *Suddenly* the bell rang.
> The bell rang *loudly.*
> The bell rang *at intervals.*

Twice, suddenly, and *loudly* belong to a class of words known as **adverbs.** Many of these show the distinctive *ly* ending. *At intervals* is not formally an adverb, but in traditional grammar it is said to serve an adverbial function.

NOTE: Combinations introduced by *with, at, on,* and similar words may modify either nouns or other parts of a sentence:

> The man *with the ax* opened the door.   (adjective function)
> The man opened the door *with the ax.*   (adverbial function)
>
> The girl *from Chicago* disappeared.   (adjective function)
> The girl disappeared *from Chicago.*   (adverbial function)

With, at, on, and *from* are **prepositions.** Their most characteristic function is to relate a noun or noun equivalent to the rest of the sentence. Other common prepositions are *about, by, during, in, of, through, to, under, until,* and *without.* A preposition plus the noun it introduces is called a **prepositional phrase.**

G 2d   **Joining Clauses.** *When several subject-predicate groups combine, the individual subject-predicate groups need to be distinguished from the sentence as a whole.* They are traditionally referred to as **clauses.**

The following sentences illustrate different ways of joining one clause to another:

My brother proposed to Elvira;	*however,*	she dislikes him.
My brother proposed to Elvira,	*but*	she dislikes him.
My brother proposed to Elvira,	*though*	she dislikes him.
My brother proposed to Elvira,	*who*	dislikes him.

(1) Clauses are called **independent** when they are self-sufficient enough to stand by themselves, to be punctuated as complete sentences. They are still considered independent when they are joined to another independent clause by an adverbial connective or by a

coordinating connective.[3] **Adverbial connectives** (often called conjunctive adverbs) are such words as *however, therefore, moreover, nevertheless, besides*. **Coordinating connectives** (often called coordinating conjunctions) are such words as *and, but,* and *for*. A grammatically complete sentence ordinarily contains at least one independent clause. A sentence combining two or more independent clauses is called a **compound sentence**.

(2) Clauses become **dependent** on the clause to which they are joined if they are introduced by a subordinating connective or by a relative pronoun. **Subordinating connectives** (often called subordinating conjunctions) are words like *if, when, because, though,* and *whereas*. **Relative pronouns** are *who, which,* and *that*. A sentence combining an independent clause with one or more dependent clauses is called a **complex sentence**.

Dependent clauses can be considered as modifiers. Those introduced by subordinating connectives usually, though not always, serve adverbial functions: "The bell rang *when I started to answer*." Those introduced by relative pronouns usually serve adjective functions: "The bell *that had startled me* had ceased to ring."

(3) A special type of dependent clause, rather than being joined to the main clause, replaces one of its nouns. Such a clause-within-a-clause is called a **noun clause**.

NOUN:	*The thief*	returned my documents.
NOUN CLAUSE:	*Whoever stole my wallet*	returned my documents.
NOUN:	He was excited by *the news*.	
NOUN CLAUSE:	He was excited by *what he had heard*.	

That, frequently used as a relative pronoun, is also used to introduce a noun clause:

> Osbert denied *that he had forged the check*.
> *That Osbert forged the check* has not been proved.

NOTE: Dependent clauses are often hard to recognize, because one or more elements of the clause may be missing. Especially in informal writing, *whom, which,* and *that* are often omitted. Supplying the missing element in such constructions often facilitates grammatical analysis:

[3] For a full discussion of connectives and their bearing on punctuation, see P 3–4.

(ex.)

The speaker [*whom*] *we had invited* failed to appear.
The support [*that*] *we received* was inadequate.

After a subordinating connective, the subject and all or part of the verb are often omitted, provided they can be inferred from the context. The resulting clause is sometimes called an **elliptical clause**:

When [*you are*] *in doubt,* consult your dictionary.
When [*he was*] *questioned,* the suspect readily admitted the theft.

EXERCISES

A. How successful are the following attempts to reproduce in writing the characteristic forms and constructions of nonstandard speech? Which features of nonstandard usage do you recognize?

1. I be dog iffen there wadden more folks there. Coming by wagon and foot and car, they was. Brother Slynum, he was standing at the entrance in his preaching suit just a-waving and helloing to everybody. The women was in their print dresses and sunbonnets. The men folks, too, was in their Sunday-go-to-meeting clothes. That ere tent with the sign painted over the door, "Welcome! All Day Singing and Dinner on the Ground," it was sagging in the wind. Outen front was the tables where everybody was putting the victuals: salads, cakes, cornbread, preserves, puddins, and Lord knows what all. At the far end of the table over a stone-built stove they was frying the catfish.

It was a jump-rope day. The spring was all stretched out on the pastures beyond, pretty and a little shy maybe, like a lazy gal waiting for her feller. With buttercups for freckles. But that ere spring didn't have nothing on me, I had more freckles than ere was buttercups. Yep. Mama said I swollered a dollar and it broke out in pennies. But she was just spoofing. I hadden never seen a dollar.—Clancy Carlile, "The Animal Fair," *New Campus Writing*

2. Well, anyway, they come over to help us celebrate the Golden Wedding and it was pretty crimpy weather and the furnace don't seem to heat up no more like it used to and Mother made the remark that she hoped this winter wouldn't be as cold as the last, referring to the winter previous. So Edie said if she was us, and nothing to keep us home, she certainly wouldn't spend no more winters up here and why didn't we just shut off the water and close up the house and go down to Tampa, Florida? You know we was there four winters ago and staid five weeks, but it cost us over three hundred and fifty dollars for hotel bill alone. So Mother said we wasn't going no place to be robbed. So my son-in-law spoke up and said that

Tampa wasn't the only place in the South, and besides we didn't have to stop at no high price hotel but could rent us a couple rooms and board out somewheres, and he had heard that St. Petersburg, Florida, was *the* spot and if we said the word he would write down there and make inquiries.—Ring W. Lardner, "The Golden Honeymoon," *How to Write Short Stories*

B. Take five groups of three or four words each (for example, *boy—follow—dog*). Arrange each group in five different patterns, using the grammatical devices described in G 2a. Example: *The boy follows the dog. Dogs followed the boy. Follow the boy's dogs. Follow the dog, boys. Dog the following boys.*

C. Collect five groups of words that show the same root taking different suffixes for different parts of speech.

EXAMPLES: *red*   red*ness*   redd*ish*   redd*en*
           organ   organ*ism*   organ*ic*   organ*ize*

D. Choose three simple subject-predicate sentences that can be expanded and modified so as to illustrate several of the sentence types described in G 2b.

EXAMPLE: John called.
            John called me.
            John called me rude.
            I was called by John.
            Call a taxi!
            There is John calling.

E. Compose ten simplified sentences illustrating the variations in sentence pattern described in G 2b.

F. From your current reading, select ten short sentences (one clause each) in which typical sentence patterns are complicated by modifiers. Underline all basic sentence elements: subjects, verbs, complements.

G. From your current reading, select ten sentences that illustrate different ways of joining clauses. Underline the basic elements of each clause.

H. In the following sentences, identify the basic elements in each clause. Describe the function and grammatical category of as many other elements as you can. Point out distinctive grammatical features.

1. The water in the bowl was purple, and the goldfish were gulping for air.   2. Throughout the length of the valley, the river's course widens and narrows by turns.   3. In recent years, sport parachuting has enjoyed a small boom.   4. The only means of access was to hack

one's way through hundreds of miles of jungle.   5. He painted with the suppleness of an artist who wanted a deep union with nature. 6. Many customs were common to both sides of the Rio Grande when the river became a frontier.   7. Recipes for happiness cannot be exported without being modified.   8. Uncle Alfred complained that outboard motors had driven off the fish.   9. Avoiding traffic policemen is easy if they ride in specially marked cars.   10. Fritz annoyed the neighbors by blowing the bugle his father had brought back from France.

I. Analyze the following passage, using the terminology provided in G 2. Identify all basic sentence elements. Describe the function and grammatical category of as many other elements as you can. Point out unusual or difficult grammatical features.

The rain began with gusty showers, pauses and downpours; and then gradually it settled to a single tempo, small drops and a steady beat, rain that was gray to see through, rain that cut midday light to evening. And at first the dry earth sucked the moisture down and blackened. For two days the earth drank the rain, until the earth was full. Then puddles formed, and in the low places little lakes formed in the fields. The muddy lakes rose higher, and the steady rain whipped the shining water. At last the mountains were full, and the hillsides spilled into the streams, built them to freshets, and sent them roaring down the canyons into the valleys. The rain beat on steadily. And the streams and the little rivers edged up to the bank sides and worked at willows and tree roots, bent the willows deep in the current, cut out the roots of cottonwoods and brought down the trees. The muddy water whirled along the bank sides and crept up the banks until at last it spilled over, into the fields, into the orchards, into the cotton patches where the black stems stood. Level fields became lakes, broad and gray, and the rain whipped up the surfaces. Then the water poured over the highways, and cars moved slowly, cutting the water ahead, and leaving a boiling muddy wake behind.
—John Steinbeck, *The Grapes of Wrath*

OBSERVING BASIC RELATIONSHIPS

To get at the basic elements of a long and involved sentence, you will have to find the subject and the verb of each independent clause it contains. The subject and the verb are not necessarily the most striking or the most significant parts of a sentence, but they are its most important parts grammatically.

G 3 AGREEMENT

The subject and the predicate of a sentence are connected by a close reciprocal relationship. The nouns and pronouns that can make up the main part of the subject usually have two forms, one referring to a single item (**singular**), the other referring to more than one item of the same kind (**plural**). The verbs that make up the main part of the predicate may also have two forms, one to be used when the subject is singular, the other to be used when the subject is plural. When subject and verb are both either singular or plural, they are said to agree in **number**:

SINGULAR	PLURAL
The boy *goes* home.	The boys *go* home.
Love *makes* fools.	Fools *make* love.
My girl friend *was* pleased.	My girl friends *were* pleased.

G 3a Irregular Plurals. Sentences in which the subject and the verb fail to agree are usually caused by a limited number of tricky words and constructions. For instance, although most English nouns use the familiar *s* plural (car*s*, building*s*, tree*s*, book*s*, petition*s*), a number of words have difficult, irregular alternative forms.

(1) *Many Greek and Latin words require you to learn irregular plurals:*

SINGULAR	PLURAL	SINGULAR	PLURAL
crisis	crises	criterion	criteria
thesis	theses	phenomenon	phenomena
analysis	analyses	medium	media
hypothesis	hypotheses		

NOTE: "Dat*a*" *are* items of information, and "bacteri*a*" *are* very small organisms that may cause disease. The singular forms of these two words (*datum* and *bacterium*) are rarely used, with the result that *data* now often occurs as a singular. A boy who graduates from college becomes an "alumn*us*," a girl an "alumn*a*." Several male graduates would call themselves "alumn*i*," several female graduates "alumn*ae*." On the other hand, an "alumn*i* organization" may include both men and women. For a mixed group, use the form that goes with the male rather than the female members of the group.

(2) *Many other Greek and Latin words are shedding their original plurals.* According to recent dictionaries and handbooks of gram-

mar, it is becoming both common and acceptable to say "curricul*ums*" rather than "curricul*a*," "memorand*ums*" rather than "memorand*a*," and "formul*as*" rather than "formul*ae*." However, many scientists, physicians, and teachers who use Greek and Latin terminology as a matter of daily routine prefer the older forms.

G 3b **Confusing Singulars and Plurals.** *Agreement problems are caused by a number of everyday expressions that are not clearly either singular or plural.*

(1) *Each, neither, either,* and *everyone* (**indefinite pronouns**) may seem to refer to more than one person or thing, but they are treated as singulars in formal written English:

> Each of the students *is* going to receive a diploma.
> Either of the plans *sounds* all right.

A *number of* is treated as a plural if it means "several" or "many":

> A number of people *were* standing in the hallway.

(2) *Expressions indicating quantity* may be treated as singulars even when they seem plural in form, provided the sentence is concerned with the whole amount rather than with the individual units:

> In those days two dollars *was* much money.

> It is the most imperative social truth of our age that about one-third of the world is rich and two-thirds of the world *is* poor.—C. P. Snow, "On Magnanimity," *Harper's*

(3) Words like *audience, committee, family, group, jury, police,* and *team* may be singular in one sentence and plural in another. We use these **collective nouns** as singulars when we are thinking of the group as a whole; we use them as plurals when we are thinking of the individual members of the group:

SINGULAR: The family *is* a crucial social unit.
PLURAL: The family *were* seated around the dinner table.

SINGULAR: The police *has* many responsibilities.
PLURAL: The police *are* not always helpful.

(4) Words ending in *ics* look like plurals but are often singular. Singulars are *aeronautics, mathematics, physics,* and similar words that identify a branch of knowledge or field of study:

> Mathematics *is* an indispensable tool of modern science.

Athletics is used most often as a plural but may also occur as a singular: "Athletics *are* said"—could be "*is* said"—"to be good for a boy." Other words ending in *ics* are singular in some senses and plural in others. We say "Statistics *doesn't* appeal to me" when speaking of the science of statistics; we say "Statistics *don't* convince me" when speaking of statistical data.

Consult a college dictionary when you are not sure of the different forms of a noun or when you are not sure whether a given form is to be treated as a singular or as a plural.

G 3c   Compound Subjects. *Agreement problems occur in sentences that contain a* **compound subject**—that is, more than one subject per clause. In such sentences, the verb may appear in the plural form even if each of the subjects is singular when taken by itself:

> Tom and Sue *don't* smoke.
> Hiking and canoeing *are* fun.

Whereas *and* actually adds one possible subject to another, *or* merely gives us a choice between two possible subjects, each of which may be just one single item. Thus, we say "Both his father and his mother *are* to blame" but "Either his father or his mother *is* to blame."

Some special difficulties should be noted:

(1) *As well as, together with,* and *in addition to* often seem to establish the same relationship between two possible subjects as *and.* In formal English, however, they usually do not add one subject to another. They merely show that what is said about the subject applies also to other things or persons, or that the subject is accompanied by other things or persons:

> Aunt Martha, together with her six children, *is* leaving town.

Some writers use the plural form when the singular seems to fight with the over-all meaning of such a sentence—as it often does. However, you will be safer from criticism if you revise the sentence, using *and:*

> The president, as well as the deans and department heads, *was* sitting on the platform.
> The president, the deans, and the department heads *were* sitting on the platform.

(2) Sometimes even two nouns joined by *and* do not add up to a plural. They may be merely different parts of the *description of a single thing or person:*

Pork and beans *is* not one of my favorite dishes.
My closest friend and associate *was* a cocker spaniel.

(3) In some sentences, an *or,* an *either . . . or,* or a *neither . . . nor* gives the reader a *choice between a singular subject and a plural one.* The least confusing and the most generally acceptable practice makes the verb of such a sentence agree with the subject closer to it:

> Either laziness or excessive social obligations *have kept* him from his work.
>
> Either excessive social obligations or just plain laziness *has kept* him from his work.

However, the sentence often sounds more natural if the subjects can be changed so that they are both singular or both plural:

> Too much social life or just plain laziness *has kept* him from his work.

G 3d   Blind Agreement. *Complicated or unusual word order may lead you to make the verb agree with a word that stands in front of it but that is not its subject.* The result is sometimes called **blind agreement.** Look for agreement errors when modifying material intervenes between the subject and the verb, or when you reverse the usual order and make the subject follow the verb rather than precede it.

(1) Agreement errors are common when *a plural noun intervenes between a singular subject and its verb.* If most of your friends *were* late and only one of them *was* on time, you should say: "Only one of my friends *was* ready in time"—not *"were* ready in time." The subject is not your friends in general but only one of them, whom you have singled out. Beware of faulty agreement whenever the subject of a sentence is one thing singled out among several, one quality shared by several members of a group, or one action affecting different things or persons:

> The usefulness of his remedies *has been* questioned—not *"have been* questioned."
>
> Understanding the opponent's motives *is* important—not *"are* important."

(2) In most sentences we determine the number of the subject first and then adjust the form of the verb accordingly. When for some reason *the subject follows the verb,* we have to make sure that we do not make the verb agree with a stray noun that stands in front of it:

> Sleeping in the cradle *were* two rosy-cheeked infants.
> (Who was sleeping? The infants *were* sleeping.)

In the very first chapter *occur* several incredible incidents.
(What occurs? Incidents *occur*.)

G 3e   Agreement after *There* and *It*. *Special problems occur in
sentences starting with "there is," "there are," and their
possible variations. There* is neither a noun nor a pronoun and cannot
be the subject of a sentence. After *there,* the verb agrees with the
postponed subject—that is, with whatever is "there":

SINGULAR: There *was* much work to be done.
PLURAL: There *were* scattered rumblings of dissent.

In formal usage, the plural verb is required even when followed
by a compound subject of which each part is singular:

> On the crown of the hill, there *are* a miniature plaza, miniature ca-
> thedral, and miniature governor's palace.—Arnold J. Toynbee, "The
> Mayan Mystery," *Atlantic*

It, on the other hand, is a pronoun and can occur as a subject.
After *it,* the verb is always singular:

> It*'s* your last chance.
> It *was* the Joneses.

G 3f   Agreement after *Who, Which,* and *That*. *A number of agreement problems are caused by relationships between several
clauses.* For instance, *who, which,* and *that* often serve as subjects in
adjective clauses—that is, dependent clauses that modify a noun or
pronoun. The verb following the *who, which,* or *that* agrees with the
word being modified:

SINGULAR: I hate a man who *stares* at me.
PLURAL: I hate men who *stare* at me.

Formal English requires agreement in combinations like "one of
those who does" and "one of those who do." "Jean is the only one of
those girls who *goes* to college for an education" means that one girl
goes to college for an education but that the others don't. "Jean is
one of those girls who *go* to college for an education" means that a
number of girls *go* to college for an education and that Jean is one of
them.

G 4   DIFFICULT VERB FORMS

The **tenses** of a verb are the various *forms that indicate primarily,
though not exclusively, different relationships of events in time:*

ACTIVE

		Progressive
Present	I ask	(I am asking)
Past	I asked	(I was asking)
Future	I shall (will) ask	(I shall be asking)
Perfect	I have asked	(I have been asking)
Past Perfect	I had asked	(I had been asking)
Future Perfect	I shall (will) have asked	(I shall have been asking)

PASSIVE

Present	I am asked	(I am being asked)
Past	I was asked	(I was being asked)
Future	I shall (will) be asked	—
Perfect	I have been asked	—
Past Perfect	I had been asked	—
Future Perfect	I shall (will) have been asked	—

Most English verbs, the regular verbs, have two basic forms (**principal parts**). One form is the plain form of the verb (*consent, smoke, depart, investigate, organize*). Standing by itself, it can form the **present tense**. This "simple" present may indicate that something is actually happening now, but it often indicates that something is done regularly or habitually or that it will take place in the immediate future: "We *consent*." "I *smoke* a pack a day." "They *depart* tonight."

The plain form can combine with *will* or *shall* in the **future tense**: "He *will talk* to you later." [4] The plain form plus *ing* makes up the present participle, used in the various tenses of the **progressive construction**. The progressive construction normally indicates that at a given time an action or event is actually in progress: "We *are considering* your request." "Her husband *was painting* the house."

The second basic form of a verb can stand by itself as the **past tense**, which indicates that an action took place in the past and came to an end in the past. To form this "simple" past, regular verbs add *ed* or *d* to the plain form: "He *consented*." "We *asked* him." "They *investigated* him thoroughly."

Regular verbs make the *ed* form do double duty as a verbal (past participle) combining with the various forms of *have* to make up the **perfect tenses**. These consider an action as "perfected," in the sense of completed, prior to a given point in time. "I *have considered* your request" describes something that has happened in the fairly

---

[4] See the Glossary of Usage for discussion of *shall—will, should—would.*

recent past and that has a bearing on the present. "I *had considered* his request very carefully" describes something that had already happened when other events in the past took place.[5]

> **G 4a   Irregular Basic Forms.** *Irregular verbs often have not two but three basic forms.* These may be either confusingly different or confusingly similar. First, the difference between the simple present and the simple past is not merely a matter of adding a characteristic ending. Instead, there are changes difficult to schematize: *run—ran; know—knew; go—went.* Furthermore, the simple past is often different from the past participle: *run—ran—run; know—knew—known; go—went—gone.*

(1) Pay special attention to verbs whose basic forms are *confusing in spelling or in sound.* Here is a brief list:

PRESENT	PAST	PERFECT
begin	began	have begun
blow	blew	have blown
break	broke	have broken
bring	brought	have brought
choose	chose	have chosen
come	came	have come
deal	dealt	have dealt
do	did	have done
draw	drew	have drawn
drink	drank	have drunk
drive	drove	have driven
eat	ate	have eaten
fall	fell	have fallen
flee	fled	have fled
fly	flew	have flown
freeze	froze	have frozen
go	went	have gone
grow	grew	have grown
know	knew	have known
lead	led	have led
run	ran	have run
see	saw	have seen
send	sent	have sent
sing	sang	have sung
speak	spoke	have spoken
swim	swam	have swum
take	took	have taken
throw	threw	have thrown
wear	wore	have worn

[5] See G 12a for sequence of tenses and shifts in tense.

(2) Sometimes you have a *choice of two acceptable forms:*

They gracefully *dived* (or *dove*) into the pool.
She *dreamed* (or *dreamt*) of a sloe-eyed Arab prince.
He *lighted* (or *lit*) his cigarette.
Your prediction *has proved* (or *has proven*) wrong.
The ship *sank* (or *sunk*) within minutes.
Business *thrived* (or *throve*) as never before.
The sleepers *waked* (or *woke*) refreshed.

(3) In a few cases different forms for the same tense correspond
to *differences in context or in meaning.* For instance, it is "The picture
was *hung*" but "The prisoners were *hanged*"; "The sun *shone*" but
"The boy *shined* my shoes."

When you are in doubt about the basic forms of a verb, guessing
will do no good. Your dictionary lists the basic forms of all irregular
verbs in the *choose—chose—chosen, run—ran—run* order.

G 4b   Verbs with Confusing Doubles. *Some verbs have doubles just different enough to be confusing.*

(1) *Lie—lay—lain* indicates that somebody or something is situ-
ated somewhere. The same basic forms are used in the combination
lie down:

On hot days the animals *lie* in the shade.
A letter *lay* on the floor.
He *should have lain down.*

Lay—laid—laid indicates that somebody is placing something somewhere. Use it when you can substitute *place* or *put:*

I wish I *could lay* my hands on him.
The weary travelers *laid down* their burdens.
You *should have laid aside* some money for emergencies.

(2) *Sit—sat—sat* indicates that someone is seated. *Sit down*
follows the same scheme:

Though he told me that he seldom *sat* while at work, he *has sat* for
an hour exactly where he *sat down* when he looked for a place to *sit.*

Set—set—set, one of the few verbs with only one basic form, belongs
with *lay* as a possible substitute for *place* or *put.* You, yourself, *sit,* or
sit down; you *set,* or *set down,* something else:

When you *have set* the alarm, *set* it down by the cot I *set* up.

(3) *Rise—rose—risen* means "get up" or "go up." *Raise—raised
—raised* refers to lifting something or *making* it go up:

Since you *rose* this morning, the tax rate *has risen* ten cents.

Though he *is* always *raising* his prices, he *has* not *raised* the salaries of his employees.

G 4c   Subjunctive Forms. *One special set of verb forms is disappearing from informal speech and writing but is still often required in formal usage:* "She would call us if she *were*"—not "if she *was*"—"ill." "We demand that he *answer*"—not "that he *answers*"—"the question." *Were* and *answer* here represent special forms that make no distinction between singular and plural. These **subjunctive** forms occur in certain types of clauses that are concerned with possibilities rather than with facts.

(1) After *if, as if,* and *as though,* use *were* instead of *was* if the possibility you have in mind is *contrary to fact or highly improbable:*

The bird looked as if it *were* a plane.
If I *were* you, I would try to improve my language habits.
He acts as if his name *were* John D. Rockefeller.

However, *is* or *was* is required if you are considering a genuine possibility:

If your brother *was* ill, he should have notified you.
It looks as if the plane *is* going to be late.

In borderline cases, make sure that the *if*-clause uses a verb form that corresponds to the point of view adopted in the main clause. Use the ordinary or factual form after *if* when the main clause uses a matter-of-fact form like *will, shall, can,* or *may.* Use the subjunctive form when the main clause uses a form suggesting improbability:

FACTUAL: If she *is* wise, he *will* propose.
SUBJUNCTIVE: If she *were* wise, he *would* propose.

NOTE: Do not use *would* in the *if*-clause as a kind of poor man's subjunctive: "If he *were* elected"—not "*would be* elected"—"he would eliminate corruption and graft."

(2) Use subjunctive forms in noun clauses *after verbs indicating that something is desirable or necessary* but has not yet come about. *Were,* for instance, occurs in sentences like the following: "I wish I *were*"—not "I *was*"—"a wise old man." Forms like *answer* instead of *answers, go* instead of *goes* or *went,* and *be* instead of *is* or *was* occur after verbs signaling a suggestion, a request, a command, or a resolution:

(ex.)

His wife insists that he *spend* more time at home.
We demand that he *repay* all his debts.
I move that this question *be* referred to one of our innumerable committees.

Often an alternative form using *should* is possible:

I suggested that he *should apply* in the fall.

(3) In some set phrases (*be* that as it may) and *in writing that is distinctly formal or literary in tone*, the subjunctive expresses ordinary conditions or alternatives:

He was determined to go on, *come* what may.

The artist must have faith in the all-importance of art, and particularly in his own form of art, *be* it painting, sculpture, poetry, drama, fiction, or music.—Malcolm Cowley, "Artists, Conscience, and Censors," *Saturday Review*

EXERCISES

A. In a college dictionary, look up the plural forms of the following nouns: *antenna, appendix, beau, bureau, cactus, cello, cherub, focus, hippopotamus, index, nucleus, oasis, stadium, stigma, stimulus, vertebra, virus.* Check whether the following forms are singular or plural or both: *addenda, agenda, apparatus, candelabra, deer, dice, Saturnalia, series, species, strata.*

B. Select appropriate forms, paying special attention to irregular plurals.

1. Constant crises *(1)has/(2)have* undermined the confidence of the people in their government. 2. For many of us, prestige is one of the most important *(3)criterion/(4)criteria* of success. 3. Jean and Margaret were the only *(5)alumna/(6)alumnae/(7)alumni* present at the ceremony. 4. The college offers more than twenty *(8)curriculum/(9)curricula.* 5. The mass media of communication *(10)has/(11)have* rapidly increased their influence in recent decades. 6. The *(12)analysis/(13)analyses* of such material takes time. 7. The memoranda he sent out *(14)was/(15)were* often unintelligible. 8. These data *(16)invalidates/(17)invalidate* all previous *(18)hypothesis/(19)hypotheses* concerning the origin of life.

C. Select appropriate forms, paying special attention to common sources of faulty agreement.

1. In many of my classes the attitude of the students *(1)was/(2)were* very poor. 2. The benefits that the city has derived from its new industries *(3)is/(4)are* negligible. 3. Cooking, as well as sewing or

cleaning, *(5)has/(6)have* always bored me.   4. I was raised in a home where smoking and excessive drinking *(7)was/(8)were* not permitted. 5. Getting along with one's neighbors *(9)is/(10)are* not always easy. 6. The qualities that a girl looks for in a future husband *(11)is/(12)are* determined in part by her family background.   7. The World Fair dazzled everyone who *(13)was/(14)were* there.   8. The ability to talk about something other than money and children *(15)is/(16)are* important if a marriage is to last.   9. Colleges have to make provision for students who are below average academically but who nevertheless *(17)wants/(18)want* a college education.   10. Using words like *dichotomy* and *schizophrenia (19)is/(20)are* no sign of superior intelligence.   11. She was one of those hostesses who *(21)makes/(22)make* no attempt to entertain the guests.   12. His father felt that five dollars *(23)was/(24)were* more than sufficient as a monthly allowance. 13. According to the judge, neither of the witnesses *(25)was/(26)were* guilty of perjury.   14. We soon realized that our supply of food and fuel *(27)was/(28)were* dangerously low.   15. Weapons like the bow and arrow, the spear, or the knife *(29)was/(30)were* among the first major inventions of man.

D. Select verb forms appropriate to formal written English.

1. If a teacher *(1)lays/(2)lies* a hand on an unruly student, he is likely to be sued by the student's parents.   2. In discussions touching on religious issues, many perplexing questions can be *(3)raised/(4)risen*. 3. After the class *(5)sat/(6)set* down, Mrs. Pidnack wanted to know who had *(7)wrote/(8)written* "baloney" on the blackboard.   4. The picture showed two elderly gentlemen *(9)setting/(10)sitting* at a table and playing chess.   5. While the boys *(11)swam/(12)swum* in the clear, cold water, I *(13)sat/(14)set* in the canoe watching them.   6. While *(15)setting/(16)sitting* up a new filing system, we must have *(17)mislaid/(18)mislain* your letter.   7. The report has been *(19)laying/(20)lying* on his desk all summer; at least I saw it *(21)lay/(22)lie* there last week.   8. When I *(23)saw/(24)seen* the deserted entrance, I *(25)knew/(26)knowed* that the performance had already *(27)began/(28)begun*.   9. The Park Department finally *(29)sat up/(30)set up* benches for visitors who might want to *(31)set down/(32)sit down*. 10. Satisfied with the conditions *(33)sat/(34)set* by the negotiators, the rebels last week *(35)laid down/(36)lay down* their arms.

E. Select subjunctive forms where appropriate.

1. If there *(1)is/(2)was/(3)were* another war, untold millions would lose their homes or their lives.   2. I wish grammar *(4)was/(5)were* less complicated than it is.   3. If the Obunga *(6)are/(7)were/(8)would be* vegetarians, why do they have sharply filed teeth?   4. It looks as if there *(9)is/(10)were* just enough gasoline to get us back into town. 5. The ordinance requires that subdivision signs *(11)are/(12)be* kept

smaller than the houses they advertise.   6. If the vocationally minded student *(13)was/(14)were/(15)would be* sent to a trade school, high schools could put more emphasis on academic subjects than they do now.   7. If your record *(16)is/(17)were/(18)would be* as clean as you claim, the commission will gladly grant your request.   8. Mariners used to drink rum as if it *(19)is/(20)was/(21)were* water.   9. No one suggested to Raymond that he *(22)read/(23)reads The Brothers Kara-mazov* rather than *Treasure Island*.   10. These practices would not be tolerated if the founder *(24)is/(25)was/(26)were/(27)would be* still alive.

F. From the current issue of a magazine, select five sentences that illustrate different uses of the subjunctive.

G. (**Review**) Check all verb forms for agreement and for conformity to the conventions of formal usage. Identify each sentence that needs revision.

1.   (1) At one time I thought of college as a place where everyone studies hard during the week and then relax during the weekend. (2) Since I came to college I have found my theory to be quite wrong.   (3) Sometimes I think I am the only one of the girls in our house who does any homework.   (4) A number of them go out almost every night.

2.   (5) There are different ways of teaching American history.   (6) In grade school and high school, Washington or Jefferson is often presented as if he were a god-like figure.   (7) The political-science courses one takes in college often shows that the nation's great men were men with human feelings.   (8) Such an approach requires that the student reconsider many familiar notions.

3.   (9) In college, maturity and a sense of responsibility begin to make themselves felt.   (10) The college girl's ideals and outlook on life broadens.   (11) She soon becomes one of those who look for more in a boy than physical appearance.   (12) She demands that her future husband be ambitious and reliable.

4.   (13) Advertisers are often unfairly accused of insincerity or outright fraud.   (14) It is true that there are misleading advertisements and commercials.   (15) But the number of advertisers who practice deliberate deception are relatively small.   (16) Many well-established business firms value their reputations too highly to join the ranks of those who mislead their customers.

5.   (17) The significance of many of the words used by Shakespeare are hard to understand.   (18) The language and especially its vocabulary have changed since he wrote his plays.   (19) *Rede* is used for "advice," *husbandry* means "economy," and a porcupine is called

a "porpentine." (20) These examples are taken from just a few pages of *Hamlet*.

DEALING WITH PRONOUN PROBLEMS

To make a pronoun stand for the right noun, you have to place the right pronoun in the right position. Furthermore, you may have to choose between several different pronoun forms, depending on how the pronoun is related to the other elements of the sentence.

G 5 REFERENCE OF PRONOUNS

When you use *he, it,* or *this,* it should be clear to your reader who or what *he, it,* or *this* is. A pronoun has to refer clearly to its **antecedent**, the thing or person for which the pronoun is a substitute.

G 5a Ambiguous Reference. *A pronoun should not point to more than one possible antecedent.* Look at the use of *she* and *her* in the following example: "Mary was friendly to my sister because *she* wanted *her* to be *her* bridesmaid." Reading this sentence, we have no way of knowing which of the two girls was getting married and which was going to be a bridesmaid. The sentence is **ambiguous**; it confuses the reader because of an unintended double meaning.

(1) If the substitute could refer to more than one antecedent, you may have to repeat the noun itself: "When Tom was talking to Jim's brother, *Jim's* girl friend smiled at *Jim's brother* from across the street." Using *his* and *him* in this sentence would cause much confusion. However, you will often do better to shuffle the different parts of the sentence until the pronoun is preceded by only one possible antecedent:

AMBIGUOUS: After *Father* brought *Junior* back from the game, we took pictures of *him.*

CLEAR: We took pictures of *Father* after *he* brought *Junior* back from the game.

CLEAR: We took pictures of *Junior* after *Father* brought *him* back from the game.

(2) The pronouns that most often cause ambiguity have distinctive forms for singular and plural antecedents: the singular *he, she,* or *it,* as against the plural *they.* If a *they* is preceded by two plural

nouns, you can sometimes avoid ambiguity by making one of them singular:

AMBIGUOUS: *Students* like *science teachers* because *they* are realistic and practical.

CLEAR: A *student* usually likes his *science teachers* because *they* are realistic and practical.
(*They* can no longer be mistakenly referred to *students.*)

Similarly, one of two possible singular antecedents might be changed into a plural:

> A *writer* must necessarily talk to his *readers*—better than "to his *reader*"—in simple language if *his* vocabulary is limited.
> (The singular *reader* would leave it doubtful whose vocabulary is assumed to be limited.)

G 5b Reference to Modifiers. *Pronouns are usually taken to refer to one of the basic elements of a sentence rather than to a modifier.* The following sentence would sound absurd: "During the summer, Grandfather worked on a river boat, but in the winter *it* usually froze over." The *it* seems to refer to the boat, but, needless to say, boats do not freeze over. Similarly absurd sentences may result when a pronoun is expected to refer to a **possessive**:

AMBIGUOUS: I reached for the horse's bridle, but *it* ran away. (The bridle seems to be running away.)

CLEAR: The horse ran away after I reached for *its* bridle. (The possessive has been made into a pronoun and the noun put where it is needed to prevent confusion.)

NOTE: Reference to a possessive accounts for the awkwardness of sentences like the following: "In *John Steinbeck's* novel *The Grapes of Wrath*, he describes the plight of the marginal farmer"—better "In *his* novel . . . *John Steinbeck* describes . . ."

G 5c Vague *This* and *Which*. Making *this* or *which* refer to the over-all idea expressed in the preceding statement is known as **idea reference**. *Idea reference frequently causes ambiguous sentences.* Students often write sentences like the following: "I knew that Bob was cheating, but the other students were not aware of *this.*" The *this* may refer either to Bob's cheating or to the writer's knowing it. Or they will say something like this: "She spent her time getting special help for her English course, *which* her roommates considered unfair." What did her roommates consider unfair? There are several possibilities: the English course, her getting special help, her getting special help for this particular course, her spending her time that way.

A vague *this* can be easily supplemented by a noun indicating the idea referred to: "this fact," "this assumption," "this outrage." A vague *which* is more difficult to improve. Often you will find it easier to do without it. Suppose you say: "I have received only one letter, *which* frightens me." If you mean that you were frightened not by the letter itself but by receiving only one, it would be clearer to say:

> Receiving only one letter frightened me.

G 5d   **Implied Antecedents.** *To make a sentence acceptable in formal English, we may have to eliminate indirect reference.*

(1) In informal conversation, we often make a pronoun refer to an antecedent that we have not actually mentioned, though we expect its identity to be understood. We say, "In London, *they* have a great deal of fog" without explaining that the *they* means "Londoners" or "the people living in London." We say, "I like *Life* magazine, because *they* print many interesting articles." The implied antecedent of *they* is not the magazine itself but its editors or its publishers.

REVISED: London has much fog.
REVISED: *Life* magazine prints many interesting articles.

(2) A special problem in student writing is the orphaned *it*, the use of *it* to refer to an implied idea in a sentence like the following: "My mother was a teacher; therefore, I have also chosen *it* as my profession." The *it* stands not for "teacher" but apparently for "teaching":

REVISED: My mother was a teacher; therefore, I have also chosen *teaching* as my profession.

Equally objectionable is the orphaned *they*: "The prisoner's hands were manacled to a chain around his waist, but *they* were removed at the courtroom door." What was removed? The prisoner's hands? Apparently "the manacles":

REVISED: The prisoner's hands were manacled to a chain around his waist, but *the manacles* were removed at the courtroom door.

G 5e   **Indefinite Antecedents.** Formal English avoids an inconsistency that occurs in the everyday use of **indefinite pronouns** like *everybody, somebody, anybody,* or *nobody.* Everyday language uses a singular verb after these words but then sometimes switches to a plural pronoun. *In formal usage, indefinite pronouns are treated as singular antecedents:*

> Someone left *his* gloves—not *"their* gloves."
> After hours everybody does as *he* pleases—not "as *they* please."
> Nobody should meddle in affairs that are none of *his* business—not "none of *their* business."

One and *a person* belong in the same category:

> One must honor *his* (or *one's*) obligations—not *"their* obligations."
> One can never be too careful about *his* language—not *"their* language."

None started as the equivalent of "no one," but today either singular or plural forms after it are acceptable:

> None of the students *has his* books ready—or *"have their* books ready."

NOTE: When we use *everybody, a person,* or *none,* we are often thinking of both men and women. However, "Everybody ate *his or her* lunch" would sound clumsy. Since grammatically it is a man's world, *his* can do double duty in such cases.

G 6   PRONOUN FORMS

Pronouns have alternative forms, used depending on the function of the pronoun in the sentence. *I* and *he* are **subject-forms,** identifying the person that the predicate says something about. *Me* and *him* are **object-forms,** identifying the object of a verb. Only half a dozen pronouns have a distinct object-form: *I—me; we—us; he—him; she—her; they—them; who—whom.* Other pronouns use the same form both in subject and in object positions: *you, it,* the impersonal *one,* the relative pronouns *which* and *that.* The subject- and object-forms of pronouns are grouped with the possessive of nouns as forms indicating grammatical **case.**

A third possible form indicates that the object is the same as the subject: "He cut *himself.*" "They asked *themselves* what had gone wrong." *Himself, themselves, myself, ourselves,* and similar forms are called **reflexive forms;** they point back to the subject. They are also used as **intensives** reidentifying something for emphasis: "The dean told me so *himself*." "We should also weigh the testimony of the accused men *themselves*."

NOTE: Formal English avoids the use of the reflexive forms as indiscriminate substitutes for the plain subject- or object-forms:

My friend and I—not "and *myself*"—were the last ones to leave.
I asked both his wife and *him*—not "and *himself*"—to come over after dinner.

G 6a Inappropriate Subject- and Object-Forms. *The conventions governing the use of subject- and object-forms in written English differ from those of informal and nonstandard speech.*

(1) Take care to choose the standard form when a pronoun is *one of several subjects or objects in a clause:*

My brother and *I*—not "*me* and my brother"—were reading comic books.
(Who was reading? *I* was reading.)

She asked my brother and *me*—not "my brother and *I*"—to dry the dishes.
(Whom did she ask? She asked *me*.)

Since nouns make no distinction between subject- and object-forms, be careful with pronoun-noun combinations like *we Americans—us Americans* or *we girls—us girls:*

We boy scouts are always eager to help.
He told *us boy scouts* to keep up the good work.

(2) In formal usage, subject-forms are required *after linking verbs,* which introduce not an object of an action but a description of the subject:

The only ones not invited were *she* and a girl with measles.

The need for this use of the subject-form seldom arises except after "it is," "it was," "it must be," and so on. (See the Glossary of Usage for *it's me/it is I*.)

(3) Object-forms are required *after prepositions* (with *her;* because of *him;* for *me*). Make sure to use object-forms for pronouns that are not the first but the second or third object in a prepositional phrase:

This kind of thing can happen to you and *me*—not "to you and *I*."
I knew there was something between you and *her*—not "between you and *she*."

(4) *As* and *than* are often treated as connectives even when most of the clause they presumably introduce is missing. To decide whether they should be followed by the subject- or the object-form of a pronoun, you may have to reconstruct the missing clause:

> He is as tall as *I* (am).
> I owe you as much as (I owe) *them.*
> Her sister was smarter than *she* (was).
> I like her better than (I like) *him.*

G 6b   **Who and Whom.** Who *and* whom *are easily confused because their function in a sentence is not always obvious.* Furthermore, *who* is increasingly replacing *whom* in speech:

SPOKEN: Tell me *who you are thinking of.*

WRITTEN: It is good for the sanity of all of us to have *someone whom we continue to think of* as Mister even though we address him by his given name.—Philip M. Wagner, "Mencken Remembered," *The American Scholar*

A writer with imperfect knowledge of the distinction may sprinkle his sentences with an occasional *whom.* However, while an inappropriate *who* may sound too informal for its context, an inappropriate *whom* may sound ignorant and forced.

(1) When *who* or *whom* occurs *at the beginning of a question,* it is fairly simple to select the form appropriate to formal usage. *Who,* the subject-form, asks a question about the subject. *He, she, we,* and *they* would be possible answers: *Who* did it? *He* did. *Whom,* the object-form, asks a question about an object. *Him, her, us,* and *them* would be possible answers: *Whom* did you meet? I met *him. Whom* also serves as the object of a preposition: To *whom* should I write? To *him.* The pronoun remains in the object-form even if the preposition does not precede the pronoun but follows the verb: *Whom* are you looking *for?* I am looking for *him.*

In more complicated questions it may not be obvious whether a *who* inquires about a subject or about an object. However, the *he-* or-*him* test will always work:

> *Who* do you think will win? (I think *he* will win.)
> *Whom* did you expect to come? (I expected *him* to come.)

(2) *Who* and *whom* are often confusing when they *introduce dependent clauses.* They may introduce an indirect question; that is,

a question presented not as a request for information but as part of another sentence (**noun clause**). They may link a modifier to the noun or pronoun being modified (**adjective clause**). In order to apply the *he*-or-*him* test to a dependent clause, separate it from the rest of the sentence:

SUBJECT: Ask her / *who* wrote the letter. (*He* wrote the letter.)
SUBJECT: We approached the man / *who* was waiting. (*He* was waiting.)
SUBJECT: Here is a nickel for / *whoever* gets there first. (*He* gets there first.)

OBJECT: *Whom* we should invite / is a difficult question. (*We* should invite *him*.)
OBJECT: She knew my brother, / *whom* I rarely see. (I rarely see *him*.)
OBJECT: He knew few people / on *whom* he could rely. (He could rely on *them*.)

G 6c   ***Who, Which, and That.*** *Who* and *whom* refer to persons (the man *whom* I asked), whereas *which* refers to ideas and things (the car *which* I bought). A *who, whom,* or *which* introducing a **restrictive modifier** may be replaced by *that* (see P 5):

The man *that* I asked liked the car *that* I bought.

A *whom* or a *which* that is the object in a restrictive modifier is often left out:

The man [whom] I asked liked the car [which] I bought.

G 6d   **Possessives with Verbal Nouns.** *Formal usage prefers a possessive pronoun before a verbal used as a verbal noun.* A combination of a pronoun and a verbal with the *ing* ending may express two different relationships. In the sentence "I saw *him returning* from the library," you actually saw *him*. In the sentence "I object to *his using* my toothbrush," you are not objecting to *him* as a person but merely to one of *his* actions. In the first sentence, the object of the verb is *him*, while *returning* is a **present participle** modifying the object. In the second sentence, the object of the verb is *using*, while *his* is a **possessive pronoun** indicating *whose* action the speaker has in mind. The verbal here is a **gerund**, or **verbal noun**.

Use *my, our, his, their* instead of *me, us, him, them* when the object of a verb or of a preposition is not the person himself but one of his actions, traits, or experiences: [6]

[6] In formal usage, nouns observe a similar distinction, provided they have a distinctive possessive form. See Glossary of Usage under "possessives."

(ex.)

We investigated the chances of *his* being elected.
There is no excuse for *their* not writing sooner.
I do not like *your* associating with the neighborhood children.

EXERCISES

A. Of the numbered pronouns in each passage, identify the one that is vague, ambiguous, or misleading.

1. No one (1)who has ever been at a horse race can forget (2)his excitement at seeing (3)them come down the home stretch. 2. On the far side of the town, (4)they are clearing land for a housing project, (5)which is to be completed before next July. 3. When leading newspapers have (6)their top correspondents write stories accusing (7)our government of being corrupt, steps should be taken to correct (8)this. 4. We finally bought Uncle Peter a power lawnmower, but (9)he rarely cuts (10)it more than once every three or four weeks. 5. Gophers have been eating our geraniums. (11) This annoys my father, (12)who has been trying to get rid of (13) them for a long time. 6. A good secretary does not discuss business matters with (14)her friends unless (15)they are generally known or unless (16)she has the permission of (17)her employer. 7. While the little boy's father read (18)his newspaper, (19)he kept reaching for (20)it and crying "Daddy!" 8. The public often discovers that (21)it has been deprived of important information, (22)which goes counter to the traditional policy of (23)our government. 9. When Elizabeth came home, (24)she told (25)her grandmother that the cost of (26)her new permanent alone was enough to curl a woman's hair. 10. (27)My history instructor announced to the students in (28)his class that (29)they would write a paper on the fall of Constantinople. (30)This was a major catastrophe.

B. Select pronoun forms appropriate to formal written English.

1. Belonging to too many organizations keeps a person away from (1)*his*/(2)*his or her*/(3)*their* studies. 2. A child that has real problems is often too embarrassed to discuss them with (4)*his*/(5)*their* parents. 3. Teen-agers often adopt a new fad as a way of expressing (6)*his*/(7)*their* rebellion against authority. 4. A newspaper can never satisfy all (8)*its*/(9)*their* subscribers. 5. The American public enjoys Westerns because they give (10)*it*/(11)*them* a chance to escape from humdrum reality. 6. Participation in student government is good for the students because it develops an understanding of the institution of which (12)*he is*/(13)*they are* a part. 7. Sometimes it seems as if nowadays no one has the time to enjoy (14)*himself*/(15) *themselves*. 8. A number of my friends take more interest in playing golf in a gym class than (16)*he does*/(17)*they do* in solving mathematical problems. 9. Love stories are popular because love is some-

thing that everyone knows or will experience in *(18)his/(19)his or her/ (20)their* lifetime.   10. Much confusion would have been avoided if each one of them had waited for *(21)his/(22)their* turn.

C. Select pronoun forms appropriate to formal written English.

1. When my mother punished my sister and *(1)I/(2)me/(3)myself*, she always seemed to suffer more than *(4)we/(5)us*.   2. I stopped at Jane's house because I had some letters for her mother and *(6)she/ (7)her/(8)herself*.   3. My parents did not mind *(9)me/(10)my* associating with artists as long as I did not imitate their habits.   4. Most of *(11)we girls/(12)us girls* were looking for the tall, handsome athletic star with the winning personality.   5. I recognize the man's face; it was *(13)he/(14)him* who started the riot.   6. My sister is much better than *(15)I/(16)me/(17)myself* at learning foreign languages.   7. In discussing contemporary authors, the lecturer objected to *(18)their/ (19)them* painting too gloomy a picture of the American scene.   8. Every year, my father takes my brother and *(20)I/(21)me* camping. 9. Between you and *(22)I/(23)me*, I would rather have a husband in a Ford than a friend in a Jaguar.   10. Space navigators need to protect *(24)them/(25)themselves* against the powerful radiation of the sun to prevent *(26)their/(27)them* dying from acute sunburn.

D. Select *whom* where required by formal usage.

1. No matter *(1)who/(2)whom* I meet, I always in the end have to listen to his problems.   2. I felt more at ease talking to boys *(3)who/ (4)whom* had definite ambitions in life than to those *(5)who/(6)whom* lived from football game to football game.   3. As a principal, he knew many parents *(7)who/(8)whom/(9)which* took only a casual interest in their children's education.   4. The man *(10)who/(11)whom* knocked at the door was not the one *(12)who/(13)whom* we expected. 5. After the abortive revolt, the prince surrounded himself with subordinates on *(14)who/(15)whom/(16)which* he could rely.   6. *(17) Who/(18)whom* she corresponds with and *(19)who/(20)whom* is allowed to visit her are jealously guarded mysteries.   7. *(21)Who/(22) whom* do you think was the girl with *(23)who/(24)whom* I saw him? 8. I wonder *(25)who/(26)whom* you expect to believe these fantastic stories.

E. From a local newspaper, select ten sentences using *who* or *whom*. Which of them conform to the conventions of formal usage?

F. (**Review**) Check all pronouns for clarity of reference and for conformity to the conventions of formal usage. Identify each sentence that needs revision.

1. (1) The hedgehog is the English version of its cousin, the porcupine.   (2) English gypsies used to prepare hedgehogs by baking

them whole in a thick coat of clay. (3) The spines and the outer skin would come off together with the clay, which had become brick-hard. (4) They are said to make good eating.

2. (5) Dr. Bain has made a name for himself by a column devoted to popularized psychology. (6) Occasionally my friends and I agree with him. (7) Last week, for instance, he said that a person should not be unrealistic in what they expect of their future mate. (8) On the whole, however, I object to his treating all psychological problems as if they could be solved with a stamped, self-addressed envelope.

3. (9) As a long-time admirer of Walt Sidney, I liked his treating cartoon animals as if they were people, but I object to his making people as simple as cartoon animals. (10) One of his motion pictures tells the story of a white boy whom Indians take from his parents and who grows up as the adopted son of an Indian chief. (11) Later the boy is returned to his true parents as the result of a peace treaty, which raises the problem of how he will adjust to civilized surroundings. (12) As you no doubt suspect, blood and the pure love of a white girl finally triumph over the savage ways of his childhood.

CHOOSING AND PLACING MODIFIERS

The nouns, pronouns, and verbs that make up the basic sentence patterns often do not by themselves adequately describe people, objects, and events. A noun like *man,* for instance, is usually accompanied by modifiers telling us which particular man the sentence refers to or what kind of man he is. A verb like *shoots* is usually accompanied by modifiers telling us when, where, how, or why the shooting takes place.

G 7 FORMS OF MODIFIERS

Modifiers may be single words. Such single-word modifiers fall into two main categories. *Beautiful, strange,* and *happy* are **adjectives,** whose most characteristic position is that adjacent to a noun. An adjective modifies a noun by identifying it as one of a kind or by pointing out one of its characteristics. *Beautifully, strangely,* and *happily* are **adverbs.** Characteristically an adverb comments on the manner or the circumstances of the action or condition indicated by the verb. (See G 2c.)

G 7a   Adverb Forms. Most adverbs are distinguished from the corresponding adjectives by the characteristic *ly* ending: *bright—brightly, cheerful—cheerfully, considerable—considerably, frequent—frequently, happy—happily, rapid—rapidly, rare—rarely, single—singly.* However, some adverbs, such as *fast, much, thus,* and *well,* have no distinctive ending. Some words ending in *ly* are not adverbs but adjectives: "A *friendly* talk," "a *leisurely* drive," "a *lonely* life," "a *manly* reply."

Formal English requires a more frequent use of distinctive adverb forms than everyday conversation:

(1) Formal usage prefers "talks *loudly*" to "talks loud," "go *slowly*" to "go slow," or "come *quickly*" to "come quick," though both the long form and the short form of these adverbs have long been standard English.

(2) *Good* and *bad* used as adverbs are nonstandard. In standard English, "I don't hear so good" would be "I don't hear *well.*" "I write pretty bad" would be "I write *badly.*" The adverb *well* may, however, do double duty as an adjective, especially in the sense of "healthy," "not ill."

G 7b   Adjectives with Linking Verbs. *Not every modifier appearing next to a verb is necessarily an adverb.*

(1) Linking verbs link the subject to a description of it, which may be a noun but is often an adjective:

> His habits are *expensive.*
> Most of the bottles were *empty.*
> The speaker seemed *nervous.*

A **predicate adjective**, even though it becomes part of the predicate, points back to the subject. Here are some other verbs that may function as linking verbs:

Genevieve *turned* pale.	Honeysuckle *smells* sweet.
The heat *grew* oppressive.	The soup *tasted* flat.
He *became* rich overnight.	His hands *felt* moist.
Your fears *will prove* silly.	Sirens *sound* frightening.
The accused *remained* silent.	Your friend *looks* ill.

Some verbs may function either as ordinary verbs or as linking verbs. In "The waiter appeared hurriedly," *hurriedly* tells us how the man acted. In "The waiter appeared hurried," *hurried* describes the man himself. In "John slowly looked at me," *slowly* describes John's action. In "John looked slow," *slow* describes John.

(2) In some sentences, a verb and its object are followed by a description of the object. The description, called the **objective complement**, may be either a noun (He called me *a genius*) or an adjective (He called me *lazy*). Notice the difference between adjective and adverb in the following pairs:

> He called the meeting accidental.
> He called the meeting accidentally.
>
> George called his girl friend eager.
> George called his girl friend eagerly.

G 7c   Adverbs to Modify Modifiers. *In formal usage, use the distinctive adverb form to modify either an adjective or another adverb.* In "a *poorly* informed American," *poorly* is an adverb modifying the adjective *informed*. The man's supply of information is poor, though he himself may be wealthy.

ADVERB + ADJECTIVE: a surprising*ly* beautiful bird
a hopeless*ly* retarded student
an impressive*ly* versatile actor

ADVERB + ADVERB: You sang admirab*ly* well.
He answered surprising*ly* fast.
She worked incredib*ly* hard.

Many everyday expressions use adjective forms as **intensifiers**: "He speaks *awful* fast." "Dean Howard is *real* popular." "I am *dreadful* sorry." Since formal English tends to be more restrained than informal conversation, you can often omit such informal intensifiers altogether. If you are really sorrier than usual, a formal intensifier is *very*. Use *fairly* or *rather* to replace the informal *pretty* in "pretty old."

G 8   POSITION OF MODIFIERS

A modifier may modify different things depending on where it is placed in a sentence. You therefore need to place your modifiers in such a way as to prevent misunderstanding or unintended double meanings.[7]

G 8a   Only and Almost. *Certain adverbs need to be placed with special care.* A word like *only*, which serves both as an adjective and as an adverb, may appear almost anywhere in a sen-

---

[7] See the Glossary of Usage for discussion of the split infinitive.

tence. "*Only* I asked the man for his pen" means that only you did and nobody else. "I asked *only* the man for his pen" means that you asked only the man and nobody else. In addition, you might have asked "the *only* man" (he was the only man there); you might have asked for "his *only* pen" (he had only one) or for "his pen *only*" (not for anything else).

Almost is another word that needs to be carefully placed. Compare:

> The car *almost* broke down on every trip we took. (It never quite did.)
>
> The car broke down on *almost* every trip we took. (It did quite frequently.)

G 8b Misplaced Prepositional Phrases. *Modifiers may make the reader stumble when they do not occur in the most logical place in the sentence.* One type of easily misplaced modifier is the **prepositional phrase** (*in good faith, with due caution, after the dinner, on all fours, for the good of the country*). Here is an example of a misplaced prepositional phrase: "This picture was described as the best ever painted *by my art teacher*." Did your art teacher paint the picture, or did he describe it as the best ever painted?

(1) Though it is easy to misplace a prepositional phrase, it is usually equally easy to *shift it into a more appropriate position:*

MISPLACED: He looked at the tree he had felled *with his hands in his pocket.*

REVISED: *With his hands in his pocket,* he looked at the tree he had felled.
(It is hard to fell trees with one's hands in his pocket.)

MISPLACED: I hate crooks *like the district attorney.*
REVISED: *Like the district attorney,* I hate crooks.
(This revision presupposes that you have no reason to doubt the district attorney's honesty.)

(2) Like pronouns, modifiers point to nouns or pronouns used as major sentence elements in preference to possessives. "*At the age of ten,* my grandfather died" seems to mean that your grandfather died when he was ten years old. To improve such a sentence, you often need to *spell out the meaning intended by the modifier:*

> *When I was ten,* my grandfather died.

G 8c   Misplaced and Dangling Verbals. *Verbals used as modifiers have to be clearly related to what they modify.* In
the sentence "*Singing,* the mother cared for the baby," the verbal is
placed next to the person who does the singing. In the sentence "*Singing,* the baby was cared for by the mother," the verbal is **misplaced**,
unless the baby has learned to sing unusually early. In the sentence
"*Singing,* the baby was cared for," the verbal is left **dangling**, because
the person who does the singing has disappeared from the sentence.

What applies to verbals applies equally to **verbal phrases**—that
is, verbals plus other material which they introduce:

MISPLACED: *Being a naughty little boy,* my father often whipped me.
REVISED: *Being a naughty little boy,* I was often whipped by my father.

DANGLING: *To do well in college,* good grades are essential.
REVISED: *To do well in college,* a student needs good grades.

Misplaced and dangling verbals can create absurd images in
the reader's mind: "*Racing across the ocean,* land was sighted" (the
land was racing across the ocean); "*Walking down the aisle,* the
wedding march began to play" (the wedding march was walking
down the aisle); "*While shaving,* the telephone rang" (the telephone
was shaving). To make such a sentence less extravagant, you may
have to replace the verbal with a clause stating explicitly whose activity or condition you had in mind:

As *the ship* was racing across the ocean, one of the crew sighted land.
While *the bride and groom* were walking down the aisle, the organist
started to play the wedding march.
While *I was shaving,* the telephone rang.

G 8d   Absolute Constructions. *Some verbal phrases are not intended to modify any one part of the main sentence.* These
are called **absolute constructions**. The most common ones are the many
generally acceptable expressions that *clarify the attitude or intention
of the speaker:*

Generally speaking, traffic is getting worse rather than better.
He had numerous children—seven, *to be exact.*
Considering the location, the house is not a bad bargain.

Formal English, more frequently than informal English, uses verbals
that *carry their own subjects along with them:*

The air being warm, we left our coats in the car.
Escape being impossible, he prepared for the worst.
Most of his colleagues having left the room, Senator Hoakum decided
to omit the last twenty pages of his speech.

EXERCISES

A. In simplified sample sentences, use each of the following words
once as an adjective and once as an adverb: *better, early, fast, hard, just,
only, well.*

B. Select the modifier appropriate to formal written English.

1. In the few weeks Judy spent in France, her French improved *(1)
considerable/(2)considerably.*   2. Selling Christmas cards, I had to
talk fast and *(3)furious/(4)furiously* before the householder could slam
the door in my face.   3. Many students who have the ability to do
(5)good/(6)well in their studies nevertheless lack the incentive.   4.
We found that our visitor had an *(7)amazing/(8)amazingly* knowledge
of American literature.   5. No matter what dish Carolyn prepared,
it tasted *(9)flat/(10)flatly.*   6. I read the questions as *(11)careful/(12)
carefully* as the time allowed.   7. The book contained biographies of
people who behaved *(13)noble/(14)nobly* in the face of adversity.
8. The characters in many current motion pictures speak and dress
fairly *(15)realistic/(16)realistically* for Hollywood standards.   9. An
experienced cryptographer can decipher a simple code very *(17)easy/
(18)easily.*   10. As the questions continued, the lecturer sounded
more and more *(19)impatient/(20)impatiently.*   11. Most drivers drive
too fast and too *(21)careless/(22)carelessly* most of the time.   12. The
cabin looked *(23)solid/(24)solidly* and well built.   13. A girl should
not plan to become a secretary if she does not spell *(25)good/(26)well.*
14. Falling from the slippery roof, he hurt himself *(27)bad/(28)badly.*
15. The man we had been following turned the corner *(29)hurried/
(30)hurriedly.*

C. Check the following sentences for confusing or misleading modifiers.
Label each sentence S (satisfactory), *DM* (unsatisfactory because of a
dangling modifier), or *MM* (unsatisfactory because of a misplaced modifier). If your instructor desires, rewrite unsatisfactory sentences.

1. Stopped by a policeman in a 30-mile zone, George Van Meter was
given a ticket for doing 42 mph on his bicycle.   2. While riding in
pursuit of the bandits, the hero's horse was shot from under him.   3.
Being a high school sophomore, Shakespeare meant very little to me.
4. Having lived in India for many years, he knew many of the country's problems from first-hand experience.   5. By assigning question-
and-answer problems, students fail to develop the ability to think a

problem through by themselves. 6. The weather being unusually mild, we decided to have supper on the terrace. 7. As a child, my mother used to tell me stories of handsome princes on white chargers and of lovely princesses asleep in charmed castles. 8. Its siren wailing frantically, the ambulance skidded into the stalled sedan. 9. Sharks are a danger when vacationing in tropical waters. 10. Considering his lack of training, his performance has been truly remarkable. 11. The author's critics conducted a running argument in a literary magazine, which lasted for several months. 12. Listening to a live concert, music has a spontaneous quality that no mechanical equipment can reproduce. 13. To speak a language well, one has to know the overtones as well as the dictionary meanings of words. 14. The searching party returned to the camp, all efforts to find the missing girl having been unsuccessful. 15. Sir Malcolm heard the news that an heir had been born with great pleasure.

IMPROVING SENTENCE STRUCTURE

To develop adequate sentence control, you will have to read and grasp complicated sentences as one unit of meaning, learning to see each element as part of the whole. In the long run, the most important requirement will be that you become sentence-conscious. Get into the habit of looking at each one of your sentences as something that is man-made, subject to revision, and likely to be in need of improvement. In the meantime, you can make headway by studying the most predictable causes of faulty construction.

G 9 CONFUSED SENTENCES

Many garbled sentences are the result of hasty writing, inaccurate copying, or careless typing. Even when the reader can make out the intended meaning, he will be annoyed at being temporarily tripped up by a defect that the writer should have caught in revision.

G 9a Omission and Duplication. *In rereading and revising your themes, check for carelessly omitted or duplicated elements.* Make sure you have transcribed each sentence in full, without omitting minor sentence elements like *a, the, has, be,* or *am.* Make sure you have not awkwardly repeated minor elements, especially connectives like *that* or *when:*

> I think *that* because he is ill (*that*) he will not come.
> When school starts in the fall (*that is when*) most parents sigh with relief.

Many hastily written sentences appear on paper before the writer has quite formulated what he was going to say. Look at the following example: "After my sister moved to Ohio, her little girl contracted polio, but did not cause paralysis." After stumbling over this sentence in a theme, you would probably realize that it was not the girl that didn't cause paralysis, but the disease. *Polio,* which is the object of *contracted,* was supposed to become the subject of *did not cause,* but it never did. Revised, the sentence might read:

> After my sister moved to Ohio, her little girl contracted polio, but fortunately *the disease* did not cause paralysis.

G 9b Mixed Construction. *The inexperienced writer may confuse different ways of expressing the same idea.* The experienced writer will try out various possible constructions and select the one that seems to fit best. The inexperienced writer may plunge ahead, confusing the various possibilities. The result is known as **mixed construction**:

CONSISTENT:	*Whenever he saw a pretty girl,* he ran after her.
CONSISTENT:	Any pretty girl *caused him* to run after her.
MIXED:	*Any pretty girl* he ran after her.

CONSISTENT:	The department manager *rejected his application.*
CONSISTENT:	The department manager *did not want him to be* one of his assistants.
MIXED:	The department manager *rejected him to be* one of his assistants.

To unscramble such sentences, you have to consider the alternatives and limit yourself to one of them. Thus, "In case of emergency should be reported to the head office" yields "*In case of emergency, report* to the head office" and "*Emergencies should be reported* to the head office."

NOTE: Confusion of *because* and *because of* is an especially frequent cause of mixed construction. *Because* introduces a clause: "The course was canceled *because not enough students registered.*" *Because of* introduces a prepositional phrase: "The course was canceled *because of insufficient enrollment.*" Disregard of this distinction produces sentences like this one: "The course was canceled *because of not enough students registered.*"

G 9c Faulty Predication. The subject-predicate relationship is the skeleton that holds a sentence together. *Many sentences are structurally unsound because the predicate says something about the subject that does not logically apply to the subject.* For instance, a writer may anticipate in the subject all or part of the assertion contained in the predicate. Suppose you say, "*The choice* of our new home *was selected* by my mother." What was actually selected? Not a choice, but a home:

LOGICAL: The choice *was made* by my mother.
LOGICAL: *The home* was selected by my mother.

The idea anticipated in the subject may only partly overlap with that expressed in the predicate. *Price* is the subject in the following sentence: "*The price* of our new cabin cruiser *was* rather *expensive.*" What was actually expensive? The cabin cruiser, not the price. A price can be high, and the expense can be great, but a price cannot be said to be expensive. Here is another example:

FAULTY: At the beginning of the year, *the participation* in club activities is always *overcrowded.* (The meetings—not the participation—are overcrowded, though the fact that many people participate is of course the reason for the overcrowding.)

LOGICAL: At the beginning of the year, *our club meetings* are always overcrowded.

G 9d Faulty Equation. *Linking verbs account for a special type of faulty predication.* An *is, was,* or *becomes* should not equate two things that are not equal. Nor should it introduce a description inapplicable to the subject. In informal English, such equations are often loose and illogical. "His job *is* a mailman" is illogical because a mailman is a person, not a job. Formal English would require "*He* is a mailman" or "His job is *that of* a mailman."

(1) The most common type of faulty equation makes a linking verb introduce not a description of the subject, but an **adverbial clause.** Children, for instance, will say, "A zoo is *when you go to look at animals.*" "When you go to look at animals" is not logically a description of a zoo; normally it would indicate *when* an action takes place or a condition occurs.

FAULTY:	Punishment is *when you are told to stand in the corner.*
SATISFACTORY:	When you are told to stand in the corner, you are being punished.
SATISFACTORY:	One form of punishment is to make the child stand in a corner.
SATISFACTORY:	Punishment is a means of keeping children out of mischief.

Only rarely does an *is-when* or an *is-where* sentence actually describe a time or a place:

Tuesday *was* [the day] *when* I saw him last.
Poughkeepsie *is* [the place] *where* I was born.

(2) Linking verbs often cause faulty equation when they introduce **prepositional phrases** that would normally indicate the circumstances of an action:

Our only hope *is to convince* your parents—not "*is by convincing* your parents."
Their method of selection *was to question* the candidates carefully—not "*was by questioning* the candidates."

G 9e Faulty Appositives. An **appositive** is a noun placed next to another noun to explain or describe it: "John, *a sophomore,* came to see me." We know that John and the sophomore are identical from the way they have been placed next to each other. *Make sure that your appositives can be equated with the nouns they modify.* It does not make sense to say, "There was only *one telephone call, a friend* of yours." A friend can *make* a telephone call, but we would not say that he *is* one.

FAULTY:	We have only one *vacancy, a mathematics teacher.* (A teacher is not a vacancy, and a vacancy is not a teacher.)
REVISED:	We have only one *vacancy,* a *position* for a mathematics teacher. (What is actually vacant is a *position* for a teacher.)

G 10 INCOMPLETE CONSTRUCTIONS

Formal written English requires accuracy in a number of relationships that, though common, are less central to the basic structure of a sentence than predication and apposition.

G 10a Informal So and Such. *One type of relationship that needs to be accurately worked out in formal English* occurs in statements of degree. *So* and *such* often indicate that something has reached a definite point, producing certain characteristic results:

> She was so frightened *that she was unable to speak.*
> There was such an uproar *that the chairman banged his gavel in vain.*

Informal English often omits the characteristic result. *So* and *such* then function as **intensifiers**: "I am *so* glad." "He is *such* a lovely boy." You can make such sentences generally acceptable in two different ways. You can substitute an intensifier like *very* or *extremely:* "I am *very* glad." You can add a characteristic result: "He is such a lovely boy *that all the kindergarten girls are running after him.*"

G 10b   Incomplete Comparison. *Formal English frowns on incomplete comparisons.* Normally, *more, better,* and *whiter,* the **comparative forms**, establish a comparison between at least two elements:

> *Carpenters* make more money than *teachers.*
> *Half a loaf* is better than *a slice.*

Most, best, and *whitest,* the **superlative forms**, establish a comparison within a group of at least three elements: [8]

> The annual classic at Le Mans is the most dangerous *automobile race in Europe.*
> Peep-o-matic is the best *television set made in this country.*

(1) Formal English gives a writer less leeway than informal English in letting the reader find out for himself what is being compared with what. Most obviously informal are incomplete comparisons resulting from the use of *more* and *the most* as intensifiers: "That girl has *more* luck" (than who or than what?). "I had *the most* wonderful experience" (of the day? of the year? of a lifetime?). "I saw *the most* exciting play" (the most exciting play of the season? the most exciting play by this author? the most exciting play ever produced?). In formal English, only *most,* when not preceded by *the,* is used as an intensifier: "a *most dangerous* precedent," "a *most skillful* maneuver."

(2) To satisfy demanding readers, state explicitly what is being compared even when the terms of a comparison can be inferred from the context:

---

[8] See the Glossary of Usage for discussion of the double comparative and of the superlative in reference to two.

After I took a course in Remedial Reading, I read twice as fast (*as I had before*).

When we saw the revised estimate, we realized we would have to spend more money (*than we had planned*).

G 10c   Illogical and Ambiguous Comparison. Hasty writing often causes comparisons that are absurd or ambiguous.

(1) *Some sentences compare things that are not really comparable:* "The skin of her cheeks was as soft as a child." Actually, her skin was as soft as a *child's* (skin), or as soft as *that* of a child. Check for logical balance in sentences like the following:

LOGICAL: The *teachings of* Horatio Alger reached a wider audience *than those of* Whitman.—Saul Bellow, "The Writer as Moralist," *Atlantic*

Sometimes the absurdity of an illogical comparison is not immediately obvious: "Their fullback was heavier than any man on their team." Their fullback is part of their team, and he cannot be heavier than *any man* on the team, including himself. He can be heavier than *other* men on the team:

LOGICAL: Their fullback was heavier than *any other man* on their team.

(2) *Some comparisons mention three comparable items without making it clear which two are being compared.* "Tom liked Dick better than Harry" may mean two different things:

CLEAR: Tom liked Dick better than Harry *did*.
CLEAR: Tom liked Dick better than *he liked* Harry.

G 10d   Contraction of Coordinate Elements. When several items of the same kind are coordinated by a connective like *and* or *but,* we often omit forms that would cause unnecessary duplication. However, *telescoping of coordinate elements does not work in formal written English if the forms concerned are merely similar rather than identical.*

(1) Unsatisfactory telescoping occurs most frequently in *sentences with several predicates*. In "It *can* be done and *will* be done," the *be done* after *can* is identical with that after *will*. We can therefore omit it and say: "It *can and will* be done." However, formal writing would avoid "It *can and has* been done." The complete forms are *can*

be done and *has been done. Been* would have to serve as a substitute for an omitted *be.*

If one of several verbs in a sentence appears in a shortened form, fill in the complete forms first to make sure that only identical items are omitted:

INCOMPLETE: Some men never have and never will master the funda-
              mentals of punctuation.
COMPLETE: Some men never have *mastered* and never will *master* the
              fundamentals of punctuation.

INCOMPLETE: The patient was given an injection and the instruments made
              ready.
COMPLETE: The patient *was* given an injection, and the instruments *were*
              made ready.

(2) A special kind of unsatisfactory telescoping occurs in *double-barreled comparisons.* Most common is the *as-good-if-not-better* type: "My theme is as good if not better than yours." "English is as important if not more important than courses in how to raise petunias." The complete forms would be *as good as* and *better than,* and *than* cannot substitute for an omitted *as.* Formal English would require "My theme is as good *as,* if not better *than,* yours." Less awkward and equally acceptable is the practice of shifting the second part of the comparison to the end of the sentence:

> My theme is as good as yours, *if not better.*
> English is as important as courses in how to raise petunias, *if not more so.*

(3) When you coordinate *several prepositional phrases,* guard against omitting prepositions that are not identical but merely express a similar relationship. For instance, you can say "I have great *admiration and respect* for him." Taken up separately, the two prepositional phrases would prove identical: "admiration *for him*" and "respect *for him.*" However, you should not say "I have great *respect and faith* in him." Taken up separately, the two prepositional phrases would require different prepositions: "respect *for him*" and "faith *in him.*" If you draw the two phrases together, you have to preserve both prepositions: "I have great respect *for* him and faith *in* him."

NOTE: Telescoped prepositional phrases usually sound awkward, and many writers avoid them. However, working them out accurately will serve a useful purpose if it makes you realize that a preposition is often definitely tied to a given expression:

> She was jealous *of* but fascinated *by* her rival.
> His behavior during the trial adds *to* rather than detracts *from* my admiration for him.

G 11 PARALLEL STRUCTURE

Many sentences that work out grammatical relationships fully and accurately nevertheless suffer from inefficient construction. Like a road full of unexpected twists and turns, such sentences slow down and confuse the reader. To help the reader find his way, a sentence should be laid out with some regard for consistency.

G 11a Faulty Parallelism. *Formal English requires consistency in the coordination of elements serving a similar function in a sentence.* Sentence elements joined by *and, or,* and *but* have to be **parallel**; they have to fit into the same grammatical category. If you put an *and* after *chicken,* the reader expects another noun: "a chicken and *a duck,*" "a chicken and *mashed potatoes.*" If you put an *and* after *swore,* he expects another verb: "swore and *affirmed,*" "swore and *raved.*" The same principle applies to other elements, including whole clauses:

INFINITIVES: Two things that a successful advertisement must accomplish are *to be noticed* and *to be remembered.*

PARTICIPLES: I can still see my aunt *striding* into the corral, *cornering* a cow against a fencepost, *balancing* herself on a one-legged milking stool, and *butting* her head into the cow's belly.

CLAUSES: The young people *who brood* in their rooms, *who forget* to come down to the dining hall, and *who burst out* in fits of irrationality are not worrying about who will win the great game.—Oscar Handlin, "Are the Colleges Killing Education?" *Atlantic*

Observe the following points in revising sentences for parallel structure:

(1) If you use *and, or,* and *but* to connect elements belonging to different grammatical categories, your sentences will seem off balance. For instance, "*ignorant* and *a miser*" is off balance because it joins an adjective and a noun. You can often make such elements parallel by

shifting one of them to a different grammatical category. For instance, you could make *ignorant* into a noun (He was an *ignoramus* and a miser) or *miser* into an adjective (He was ignorant and *miserly*).

Many ideas, however, are not easily shifted from one grammatical category to another. You may have to consider several different ways of shortening, expanding, or rewording a sentence until you hit upon a satisfactory revision:

FAULTY: High school students want to be *popular* and *leaders*.
PARALLEL: High school students want to *be* popular and *become* leaders.

FAULTY: My grandfather liked *the country* and *to walk* in the fields.
PARALLEL: My grandfather liked *to live* in the country and *to walk* in the fields.

FAULTY: He told me *of his plans* and *that he was leaving*.
PARALLEL: He *informed* me of his plans and *told* me that he was leaving.

(2) Lack of parallelism is especially obvious after **correlatives**: *either . . . or, neither . . . nor, not only . . . but also, whether . . . or.*

FAULTY: I used to find him either *on the porch* or *dozing* in the living room.
PARALLEL: I used to find him either *sitting* on the porch or *dozing* in the living room.

FAULTY: We wondered whether *to believe* him or *should we try* to verify his story.
PARALLEL: We wondered whether we should *believe* him or *try* to verify his story.

(3) Formal English often reinforces parallel structure by retaining prepositions or connectives that might be omitted in informal situations:

The high school teacher usually has little time *for helping* badly prepared students and *(for) performing* the many clerical tasks required of him.

G 11b   **Faulty Series.** *Faulty parallelism frequently occurs in a series of three or more elements.* Often a writer will lead his reader into what looks like a conventional series only to trip him up by making the last element snap out of the expected pattern: "Her new friend was polite, studious, and *an only child*." "He liked to swim, relax, and *everything peaceful.*" In a revision, each element of the series would have to fit into the same grammatical category.

Sometimes the elements in a faulty series are parallel neither in form nor in meaning. A revision might then clarify meaning by breaking up the series altogether:

PARALLEL: Her new friend was *a gentleman, a scholar,* and *an only child.*
BROKEN UP: Her new friend, *an only child,* was a gentleman and a scholar.

PARALLEL: He liked *swimming, relaxation,* and *peaceful surroundings.*
BROKEN UP: He liked to swim and to relax and *preferred peaceful surroundings.*

G 12   CONSISTENT POINT OF VIEW

The need for consistency makes a serious writer guard against confusing shifts in the perspective he adopts toward people and events.

G 12a   Shifts in Tense.
A writer should be consistent in his use of verb forms that indicate the relationship of events in time.

(1) *Avoid the shift from the past tense to the present tense when something remembered becomes so real that it seems to be happening in front of you.* Note the shift in time in the following sentences:

> We *disembarked* at noon and fought our way through the jungle in the sultry afternoon heat. Suddenly, there *is* a tiger! I *aim* my rifle and *pull* the trigger! Nothing *happens*—the gun *wasn't* loaded. Luckily, one of my bearers *saved* me from the consequences of my carelessness.

If the writer wants the description to be especially vivid, he should tell the whole story as though it were happening now: "We *disembark . . . fight* our way . . . one of them *saves* me." Otherwise, he should describe everything in the past, since he could hardly be saved in the past from a tiger attacking him in the present.

(2) *Avoid shifts in perspective when two events happen not at the same time or in simple chronological order but at different times or during different periods:* "When I *saw* the F on my report card, I *was* terribly disappointed, because I *studied* very hard." If studying hard was a matter of past history by the time the student received his grade, the **sequence of tenses** would be more accurate like this:

> I was terribly disappointed, because I *had studied* very hard.

Hasty writing tends to confuse the *distinction between the different perfect tenses,* of which *had studied* is an example. (See G 4.) Formed with *have* or *has,* the **present perfect** indicates that something has happened recently, prior to events taking place now: "He *has finished* his supper and *is getting* up." Formed with *had,* the **past perfect** indicates that something happened in the relatively distant past, so that it had been concluded by the time other events in the past took place: "He *had finished* his supper and *was getting* up." A confusing shift often results when a writer makes the present perfect go with the simple past or the past perfect with the simple present:

SHIFT:　　　Last March, the Secretary of the Air Force told the committee what *has happened* to air transport in this country.

CONSISTENT:　Last March, the Secretary of the Air Force told the committee what *had happened* to air transport in this country.
　　　　　　(The secretary could not have told the committee what *has happened* since he testified and up to the present time.)

(3) *Avoid shifts resulting from failure to observe the distinction between direct and indirect quotation.* What the speaker felt or observed at the time he spoke would occur in the present tense in direct quotation: He said, "I *feel* fine." It would occur in the past tense in indirect quotation: He said that he *felt* fine. What the speaker had felt or observed before he spoke would occur in the past, or perhaps in the present perfect, when quoted directly: He said, "I *felt* fine." It would occur in the past perfect when quoted indirectly: He said that he *had felt* fine. Failure to adjust the tenses in indirect quotations can lead to sentences like the following:

Her husband admitted that he *was*—should be *"had been"*—a confirmed bachelor.
Mr. Chamberlain said that there *will be*—should be *"would be"*—peace in our time.

When *a statement made in the past formulates a general truth,* many writers find the present tense plausible:

Galileo said that the earth *moves* and that the sun *is* fixed; the Inquisition said that the earth *is* fixed and the sun *moves;* and Newtonian astronomers, adopting an absolute theory of space, said that both the sun and the earth *move.*—A. N. Whitehead, *Science and the Modern World*

(4) *Avoid inconsistent combinations between forms that indicate differences in attitude toward possible events* (called differences in **mood**). In the following sentences, note the differences between factual reference to a possibility and the **conditional**, which makes the same possibility seem less probable, or contrary to fact. (See also G 4c.)

INCONSISTENT: If he *comes* to this country, the army *would* draft him.
FACTUAL: If he *comes* to this country, the army *will* draft him.
CONDITIONAL: If he *came* to this country, the army *would* draft him.

G 12b   Shifts in Reference. A writer has to decide what pronouns he is going to use to refer to himself, to his reader, and to people in general. The least ambiguous pronoun he can use to refer to himself is of course *I, me,* or *my* (**first person singular**). When he does not want to focus attention on his personal preferences and experiences, he may use *we, us,* or *our* instead (**first person plural**). However, this "editorial" *we* sounds artificial in most student writing, especially in short themes. In reports, surveys, or formal arguments the author often keeps out all personal elements by using the **passive** to indicate things done or believed by himself ("it *has been found,*" "three experiments *were conducted,*" "it *must be concluded*").

No matter how a writer chooses to refer to himself and others, he should stick to his choice all through the paper, report, or book he is writing. The meaning of *we,* for instance, should not shift from "I, the author" to "I and my readers" to "I and my fellow Rotarians."

(1) When a writer wants to speak directly to his reader, he can of course call him *you* (**second person singular** and **plural**) and use *we* to refer both to the reader and himself:

You will agree that *we* must do everything in our power.
As *you* no doubt remember, *we* have witnessed several similar incidents during the past year.

On the other hand, *you* often appears as an informal equivalent of *one* or *a person,* referring not so much to the reader as to people in general:

FORMAL: *One* cannot be too careful.
INFORMAL: *You* can't be too careful.

Confusion results when a writer shifts to the indefinite, generalized *you* after he has already identified the person he has in mind in some other way: "I don't want to be a famous actress. *I* would rather lead my own life without people always knowing what *you* are doing." The easiest way to avoid this kind of shift is to use *you* only to mean "you, the reader."

(2) Similar in effect to shifts to *you* are shifts to the **imperative**, the request form of verbs: "*Come* in." "*Put* it down." "*Leave* him alone." Imperatives are most appropriate in directions and exhortations; they startle the reader when they suddenly break into ordinary expository prose:

SHIFT: High schools *should stop* educating all students at the same rate. *Give* aptitude tests for placement and then *separate* the students accordingly.

CONSISTENT: High schools *should stop* educating all students at the same rate. They *should give* aptitude tests for placement and then *separate* the students accordingly.

G 12c   Shifts to the Passive. Some sentences confuse the reader by shifting from an **active** construction ("*He built* the house") to a **passive** one ("*The house was built* by him").[9] *Avoid shifting to the passive when the person in question is actually still the active element in the sentence.* Suppose you say, "He returned to the office as soon as *his lunch had been eaten*." This sentence makes it sound as though his lunch might have been eaten by someone else. To keep the reader straight on who ate what, stick to the active construction:

CONSISTENT: He *returned* to the office as soon as he *had eaten* his lunch.

Unsatisfactory shifts to the passive are especially frequent after an impersonal *one* or *you*: "As *you scan* the area of your backyard, a small patch of uninhabited earth *is located*." Once you start using *one* or *you* to identify a hypothetical person whose experiences you describe, stick to the same method of identification:

CONSISTENT: As *you scan* your backyard, *you locate* a small patch of earth.

EXERCISES

A. In the following sentences, point out all instances of hasty writing, mixed construction, faulty predication, and faulty apposition. Label each

[9] For a fuller discussion of the passive see S 2a.

sentence S (satisfactory) or U (unsatisfactory). If your instructor desires, revise unsatisfactory sentences.

1. In modern industrial society, the sponsorship of the fine arts is no longer supported by wealthy aristocratic patrons.   2. Amnesia is when a character in a second-rate novel temporarily loses his memory.   3. According to recent statistics, the divorce rate for couples from different racial backgrounds compared with couples of different religion had more success in marriage.   4. The purpose of the reception was to acquaint old-timers with some of the newcomers to the area.   5. A prizefighter is not the kind of profession that offers its devotees economic security.   6. Shirley's husband was unable to support her in the style to which she had become accustomed to.   7. At night, a thousand neon signs hide the shabbiness of the jerry-built stores and offices from the traveler's view.   8. Surrealism was a movement dedicated to artistic expression of the irrational and the subconscious.   9. It is certainly very difficult for a teacher in the social sciences to avoid becoming personally involved than a teacher of chemistry or of physics.   10. I believe that if the government allowed everyone to do as he pleased that our country would not long survive.   11. A flash flood is when a river suddenly rises over its banks.   12. Sandra was offered her first acting role by the Civic Theater, an amateur group that picked up Broadway plays after everyone else was done with them.   13. Just because a person has a college degree does not mean that he is exceptionally intelligent.   14. Jargon is a kind of language composed mainly of words like *homologous, processual,* and *socializee.*   15. In case of new outbreaks of the disease should be reported to the health authorities immediately.   16. A jurisdictional dispute is where two different agencies claim jurisdiction in a given case.   17. Don's sales technique was to flash a big smile and to call all customers by their first names.   18. Cornelia had always wanted to meet one of the artists of whom she had heard a great deal about.   19. Joe had hardly batted the ball over the fence than we heard a splintering of glass and an anguished yell.   20. I suddenly realized that we were no longer on level ground and that the road was tilting upward on great concrete stilts.

B. Check the following sentences for incomplete and ambiguous constructions. Point out unsatisfactory comparisons and unsatisfactory contraction. Label each sentence S (satisfactory) or U (unsatisfactory). If your instructor desires, revise unsatisfactory sentences.

1. Women on the whole understand children better than men.   2. Roger's stews and sauces were as good as the best restaurant in Paris, if not better.   3. Religion today is receiving a better press and more general attention than it has had for many years.   4. In this district, teachers have always been and will always be hired on the basis of their professional competence alone.   5. In much of Europe, American films are more popular than any other country.   6. The discus-

sion grew so heated that David decided to keep his views to himself. 7. Children seem to like the so-called "adult" Westerns as much as adults do. 8. Year after year, American colleges produce more physical education teachers than mathematics. 9. The Secretary of State usually attracts more criticism than any member of the President's cabinet. 10. Critics of our schools must realize that they can and are doing great harm by indiscriminate attacks. 11. Unlike a track coach, a history teacher seldom has a newspaper article written about him when his students do exceptional work. 12. The impact of American books, magazines, and comics in Great Britain is much greater than British publications in the United States. 13. We spend about one and one-half times as much on tobacco products each year as we spend on higher education. 14. A good background in the liberal arts is excellent preparation for such practical professions as engineers and lawyers. 15. The United States has more television sets to the square mile than any other country in the world. 16. The ingredients used in the most expensive cosmetics often cost no more than those used in cheap products. 17. Mike never has and never will succeed in making his restaurant something more than a place to eat food. 18. Many of the legislators lacked the taste—and the capacity—for brilliant political debate. 19. Unlike America, traveling abroad is a rare luxury in many foreign countries. 20. Few of my friends were preoccupied or even interested in making a living.

C. Check the following sentences for parallel structure. Label each sentence S (satisfactory), FS (unsatisfactory because of a faulty series), or FP (unsatisfactory because of other instances of faulty parallelism). If your instructor desires, rewrite unsatisfactory sentences.

1. The editorial called the governor's speech vague, insincere, and repetitious. 2. He seemed like the type of person who would brag about his income and be extravagant with his money. 3. What the children lacked was the feeling of really belonging and that someone really cared. 4. Barbara was waiting for a talent scout to discover her and who would take her to Hollywood. 5. Newspapers do not always provide a reliable record of what ordinary people are thinking, saying, and doing. 6. A girl learns a lot about children when she cares for younger brothers and sisters or as a baby sitter during high school days. 7. This country needs a President skilled in diplomacy and who knows foreign countries well. 8. A physician has to be good not only at diagnosing diseases but also at understanding his patients. 9. Advertisers should admit that a deodorant cannot make a woman beautiful and that a healthy complexion alone cannot make a person happy. 10. A successful businessman usually has a pleasant personality, poise, and is a good speaker. 11. We should not judge a candidate's qualifications by whether he is a lawyer, farmer, or from some other occupation. 12. Maurice claimed to be Napoleon's great-grandson and that he was the rightful heir to the throne of

France. 13. Apparently my friend's work consisted of sitting at a desk for eight hours a day and give orders. 14. Our Christmas dinner would consist of roast turkey with cranberry sauce, whipped potatoes, vegetables, and followed by mincemeat pie. 15. The mass media shy away from frank discussion of love but permitting the detailed treatment of crude violence. 16. Foreign exchange students often expect to see rugged, tanned cowboys roaming the prairies and pug-faced gangsters shooting people down in the streets. 17. My father thought that young girls should not go to dances, see young men only in the company of a chaperone, and many other old-fashioned prejudices. 18. In many gangster movies, the hero deceives the police, moves in the best society, and comes to a bad end only because his mother-in-law shoots him for having slapped her daughter. 19. To most readers, the word *home* suggests security and comfort as well as a place to live. 20. The success of a television program depends on how well the program has been advertised, the actors taking part, and is it comedy or serious drama.

D. Write or collect ten sentences illustrating parallel structure. Devote each sentence to a different type of word or construction.

E. Check the following passages for unnecessary or confusing shifts in perspective. Label each sentence S (satisfactory) or U (unsatisfactory). If your instructor desires, revise unsatisfactory sentences.

1. If one insists on telling the truth at all times, he is not likely to be very popular. 2. After I finished my pie, a cup of coffee was ordered and a cigarette lighted to top off a perfect meal. 3. In the next scene, Antonio, who has just arrived in Venice, tells his friends that he is going to elope with the beautiful Elvira. 4. If a war comes, many small nations would be at the mercy of those countries that have nuclear weapons. 5. Though Nietzsche is often mentioned, his books are infrequently read and seldom understood. 6. If you came early, you could join us for a walk along the shore. 7. Several witnesses testified that the crossing signal had failed to operate. 8. During the spring rains, the valley would have been flooded if it were not for the dams recently completed. 9. One doesn't gain anything by exercising to lose weight if afterward you are allowed to eat all you want. 10. The college catalogue says that all students would take a year of science and a year of mathematics. 11. Often when you have an unemployed father there may be friction in the home and the child may feel unwanted. 12. Our newspapers should stop wasting their time on trivialities. Leave the love life of the stars to the fan magazines and put the news back on the front page. 13. If we refuse poorly qualified students admission to college, we would solve the problem of overcrowding. 14. Having a friend that really cares for you is one of the best things that one can get out of life. 15. As the lights go out and the curtain rises, the principal was re-

vealed trying to abate the clouds of smoke pouring from the witches' cauldron.   16. College should mean a place where one learns things to fit him for his chosen place in life.   17. If the club limited its membership, it would have to raise its dues.   18. Perhaps Marcia would have enjoyed the concert if her escort had stopped keeping time with his foot.   19. Suddenly the sky darkens, a breeze springs up, and a premonitory rumble rolls across the lake.   20. The boat moved quietly down the river, the girls sang, and mandolins were played by some of the older boys.

F. (**Review**) Check the following passages for adequate sentence structure, including position of modifiers, parallelism, and consistency in point of view. Identify each sentence that needs revision.

1.   (1) Marilyn was the only one of my classmates whom I thoroughly disliked.   (2) She was one of those girls who talk to a person when they want something from him but completely ignore him at other times.   (3) When she walked down the hall, she often pretends not to notice a fellow student getting ready to greet her.   (4) She often walked into the classroom late, so that the boys could see her make a grand entrance.

2.   (5) I recall an election in which two boys were running for student body president.   (6) To outdo his fellow candidate, one of the boys invited the students to a steak dinner.   (7) The second boy, unable to afford such an expensive meal, gave a hot-dog barbecue.   (8) Unswayed by the bribe, the second boy was elected by a landslide.

3.   (9) In a true gentleman, courtesy toward women would not be second but first nature.   (10) He would always open doors, walk on the side toward the curb, and helping whenever needed.   (11) Even when the lady did not actually need his assistance, he would, by his attentions, make her feel like a lady.   (12) He would make her feel like something precious and fragile, something to be cared for and protected.

4.   (13) My parents realized that each child has its own individuality and is different from any other child.   (14) I was grateful to them because they were not always comparing my own achievements with my sister.   (15) My sister had straight A's in most of her high school subjects.   (16) My parents, however, never asked me, "Why aren't your grades as good as hers?"

5.   (17) The Mercedes is one of the finest and most expensive cars sold in the United States.   (18) The prices for the various models range from $4,000 to $14,000.   (19) Considering the superior workmanship, these prices are not extravagant.   (20) Being conservatively styled, many executives prefer it to other cars.

6.　(21) In high school I had a friend who used to say, "I am too smart to have to study."　(22) Even then I suspected that he studied more than he admitted.　(23) But now that he is in college he definitely found that he must meet competition.　(24) He no longer believes that knowledge is something with which a person is born.

12: DICTION

USING THE DICTIONARY

Your first few weeks in college will demonstrate to you the need for paying close attention to vocabulary and **diction**; that is, word resources and word choice. The need for developing a comprehensive and flexible vocabulary accounts for a large part of the intellectual growing pains experienced by the college student. In each major field he enters, he is confronted with terms for the objects and ideas discussed, the standards applied, and the procedures followed. In a literature class, he is confused by words like *monograph, didactic, elegiac,* and *allegory.* In a philosophy or humanities course, he has to learn the meaning of *metaphysics, asceticism, dogmatism,* or *anthropology.* In addition to new and unfamiliar words, he encounters familiar words used in unfamiliar ways. He registers for a course devoted to the teaching of exceptional children because he takes *exceptional* to mean "outstanding" or "gifted"; he finds that much of the course is devoted to children who are exceptional because they are retarded or maladjusted. He is asked to write a critical paper and discovers too late that *critical* did not mean "fault-finding" but "objective," "thoughtful," or "analytical."

Still other words contain familiar elements which encourage the student to guess at their meanings. Often such guessing turns out to be misleading. *Apologist,* for instance, does not mean a person who apologizes for what he realizes is wrong. It means a person who defends what he claims is right. *Determinist* does not mean a person who believes that people determine their own actions by free choice. It

Vocabulary Entry — **beau·ty** (bū′tĭ), *n., pl.* **-ties. 1.** that quality of any object of sense or thought whereby it excites an admiring pleasure; qualification of a high order for delighting the eye or the aesthetic, intellectual, or moral sense. **2.** something beautiful, esp. a woman. **3.** a grace, charm, or pleasing excellence. [ME *beute*, t. OF: m. *beaute*, der. *beau*. See BEAU] **—Syn. 1.** loveliness, pulchritude.

Syllabication Dots —

Pronunciation — **be·di·zen** (bĭ dī′zən, -dĭz′ən) *v.t.* to dress or adorn gaudily. [f. BE- + DIZEN] **—be·di′zen·ment,** *n.*

Part of Speech and Inflected Forms — **be·gin** (bĭ gĭn′), *v.,* **began, begun, beginning.** **—***v.i.* **1.** to enter upon an action; take the first step; commence; start. **2.** to come into existence; arise; originate. **—***v.t.* **3.** to take the first step in; set about; start; commence. **4.** to originate; be the originator of. [ME *beginne(n),* OE *beginnan*] **—be·gin′ner,** *n.*

Synonym Study — **—Syn. 3.** BEGIN, COMMENCE, INITIATE, START (when followed by noun or gerund) refer to setting into motion or progress something which continues for some time. BEGIN is the common term: *to begin knitting a sweater.* COMMENCE is a more formal word, often suggesting a more prolonged or elaborate beginning: *to commence proceedings in court.* INITIATE implies an active and often ingenious first act in a new field: *to initiate a new procedure.* START means to make a first move or to set out on a course of action: *to start paving a street.* **4.** institute, inaugurate, initiate. **—Ant. 1.** end.

Variant Principal Parts — **be·jew·el** (bĭ jōō′əl), *v.t.,* **-eled, -eling** *(esp. Brit.)* **-elled, -elling.** to adorn with or as with jewels.

Variant Spelling — **be·la·bor** (bĭ lā′bər), *v.t.* **1.** to beat vigorously; ply with heavy blows. **2.** to assail persistently, as with ridicule. **3.** *Obs.* to labor at. Also, *Brit.,* **be·la′bour.**

Hyphenated Entry — **belles-let·tres** (bĕl lĕt′r) *n.pl.* the finer or more elegant forms of literature; literature regarded as a fine art. [F] **—bel·let·rist** (bĕl lĕt′rĭst), *n.* **—bel·le·tris·tic** (bĕl′lĕ trĭs′tĭk), *adj.* **—Syn.** See **literature.**

Word Element — **bene-,** a word element meaning "well", as in *benediction.* [t. L, comb. form of *bene,* adv.]

Consecutive Definition Numbers — **be·neath** (bĭ nēth′, -nĕth′), *adv.* (1) below; in a lower place, position, state, etc. (2) underneath: *the heaven above and the earth beneath.* **—***prep.* (3) below; under; *beneath the same roof.* (4) further down than; underneath; lower in place than. (5) lower down on a slope than: *beneath the crest of a hill.* (6) inferior in position, power, etc., to: *a captain is beneath a major.* (7) unworthy of; below the level or dignity of: *beneath contempt.* [ME *nethe,* OE *beneothan,* f. *be* by + *neothan* below] **—Syn. 3.** See below. **—Ant. 1.** above.

Etymology —

Usage Note — **bent**[1] (bĕnt), *adj.* **1.** curved; crooked: *a bent stick, bow, etc.* **2.** determined; set; resolved (fol. by *on*) **—***n.* **3.** bent state or form. **4.** direction taken (usually figurative); inclination; leaning; bias: *a bent for painting.* **5.** capacity of endurance. **6.** *Civ. Eng.* a transverse frame of a bridge or a building, designed to support either vertical or horizontal loads. [pp. of BEND[1]]

Synonym List — **—Syn. 4.** tendency, propensity, proclivity, predilection.

bent[2] (bĕnt), *n.* **1.** bent grass. **2.** a stalk of such grass. **3.** (formerly) any stiff grass or sedge. **4.** *Scot. and N. Eng.* a grassy tract, a moor, or a hillside. [ME; OE *beonet,* c. G *binse* rush]

Example Contexts — **bet·ter** (bĕt′ər), *adj. (comparative of* **good**). **1.** of superior quality or excellence: *a better position.* **2.** of superior value, use, fitness, acceptableness, etc.: *a better time for action.* **3.** larger; greater: *the better part of a lifetime.* **4.** improved in health; healthier. **—***adv. (comparative of* **well**). **5.** in a more excellent way or manner: *to behave better.* **6.** in a superior degree: *to know a man better.* **7.** more: *better than a mile to town.* **8. had better,** would be wiser, safer, etc., to. **9. better off,** in better circumstances. **10. think better of,** to reconsider and decide more favorably or wisely. **—***v.t.*

Idiomatic Phrases — **11.** to make better; improve; increase the good qualities of. **12. better oneself,** to improve one's social standing, education, etc. **13.** to improve upon; surpass; exceed: *they bettered working conditions.* **—***n.* **14.** that which has superior excellence, etc.: *the better of two choices.* **15.** *(usually pl.)* one's superior in wisdom, wealth, etc. **16.** superiority; mastery: *to get the better of someone.* [ME *bettre,* OE *betera,* c. Goth. *batiza*] **—Syn. 11.** See

Antonyms — improve. **—Ant. 1.** worse. **11.** worsen.

Explanation of Dictionary Entries, from *American College Dictionary.*

means a person who believes that people's actions are determined by causes beyond their control.

D 1 COLLEGE DICTIONARIES

A good dictionary is a comprehensive inventory of words, giving information on their history, meanings, and limitations. It is not based on the limited experience of one author but is the result of scholarly teamwork. It records the way words have been used in the past and are being used at present, and tells how certain words are *not* used.

Webster's New World Dictionary (NWD) is the most recent of three widely used college dictionaries. It makes a special effort to explain the meanings of a word in simple and clear language. It gives exceptionally full information on the history of a word and its current uses, including slang.

The American College Dictionary (ACD), like the NWD, strives for intelligibility, though it uses a greater number of technical and not-so-common words in its definitions. It thus offers an incentive to the user who likes to browse through an entry for related words. Unlike its two major competitors, the ACD usually places the most common meaning of a word first.

Webster's New Collegiate Dictionary (NCD), in its current seventh edition, is an abridgment of *Webster's Third New International Dictionary*. The latter, like the *Collegiate* published by the G. & C. Merriam Company, is the most authoritative and comprehensive unabridged dictionary of current American English. Like the parent work on which it is based, the NCD arranges different meanings in historical order. Thus the reader can easily survey the historical development of a word. Unlike the NWD and the ACD, the *New Collegiate* lists names of people and places in indexes at the end of the book.

Like its more familiar competitors, the Funk & Wagnalls *Standard College Dictionary* (SCD), first published in 1963, was compiled with the cooperation of eminent linguistic authorities. The SCD presents the most common, rather than the earliest, meaning of a word first. Like the NWD, the *Standard College Dictionary* contains valuable introductory materials on the history of English and on modern approaches to the study of language.

In the wording of definitions, the major college dictionaries range from the everyday language of the NWD to the more technical and scholarly style of the NCD. Compare the first two meanings of *peach* in each of the three books:

1. a small tree with lance-shaped leaves, pink flowers, and round, juicy, orange-yellow fruit, with a fuzzy skin and a single, rough pit. **2.** its fruit.

From *Webster's New World Dictionary*

1. the subacid, juicy drupaceous fruit of a tree, *Prunus Pérsica*, of many varieties, widely cultivated in temperate climates. **2.** the tree itself.

From *The American College Dictionary*

¹**peach** \'pēch\ *n* [ME *peche,* fr. MF, fr. LL *persica,* fr. L, pl. of *persicum,* fr. neut. of *persicus* Persian, fr. *Persia*] **1 a :** a low spreading freely branching Chinese tree (*Prunus persica*) of the rose family that is cosmopolitan in cultivation in temperate areas and has lanceolate leaves, sessile usu. pink flowers borne on the naked twigs in early spring, and a fruit which is a single-seeded drupe with a hard endocarp, a pulpy white or yellow mesocarp, and a thin downy epicarp **b :** the edible fruit of the peach

From *Webster's Seventh New Collegiate Dictionary* [1]

D 1a **Synonyms and Antonyms.** Frequently, your dictionary indicates the meaning of a word by a formal definition. For instance, it may define *ambiguity* as an expression with more than one possible meaning, or *allegory* as a story whose characters and events have a symbolic significance. Often, however, it indicates meaning by a **synonym**, a word that has nearly the same meaning as the word you are looking up. Thus, your dictionary may give "sad" or "mournful" as a synonym for *elegiac,* or "instructive" as a synonym for *didactic.* Often, your dictionary will explain a word by giving an **antonym**, a word of approximately opposite meaning. *Desultory,* for instance, is the opposite of "methodical"; *hackneyed* is the opposite of "fresh" or "original."

A good dictionary discriminates between the exact meanings of closely related terms. Synonyms are seldom simply interchangeable. Usually, they are only partially synonymous; their areas of meaning overlap, but at the same time there are subtle differences. *Burn, char, scorch, sear,* and *singe* all refer to the results of exposure to extreme heat, but whether a piece of meat is charred or merely seared makes a difference to the person who has it for dinner. Here is how a dictionary discriminates between the synonyms of *pay:*

[1] By permission. Copyright, 1963 by G. & C. Merriam Co., Publishers of the Merriam-Webster Dictionaries.

syn PAY, COMPENSATE, REMUNERATE, SATISFY, REIMBURSE, IN-
DEMNIFY, REPAY, RECOMPENSE, REQUITE mean to give money or its
equivalent in return for something. PAY implies the discharge of
an obligation incurred; COMPENSATE implies a making up for
services rendered or help given; REMUNERATE more clearly suggests
paying for services rendered and may extend to payment that is
generous or not contracted for; SATISFY implies paying a person
what is demanded or required by law; REIMBURSE implies a return of
money that has been expended for another's benefit; INDEMNIFY
implies making good a loss suffered through accident, disaster, warfare; REPAY stresses paying back an equivalent in kind or amount;
RECOMPENSE suggests due return in amends, friendly repayment,
or reward

From *Webster's Seventh New Collegiate Dictionary* 2

With less concrete terms, such shades of meaning are often less obvious but equally important. For instance, *loyalty* is a synonym of *allegiance*. However, *allegiance* is primarily a political term describing the relationship between a citizen and his country; *loyalty* describes a devotion that is not necessarily a legal obligation and whose object is not necessarily political. *Dogmatic* and *doctrinaire* are synonyms of *arbitrary*. However, we call a man "arbitrary" if he follows his personal whims or desires without the restraint of tradition, logic, or consideration for others; we call him "dogmatic" if he is stubbornly convinced of the truth of his position and unwilling to reconsider it; we call him "doctrinaire" if he adheres to a theory or doctrine without due regard for its practical application or consequences.

D 1b Denotation and Connotation. *A good dictionary pays attention to the associations of words and to the attitudes they imply.* Many words **denote**—that is, point out or refer to—very nearly the same objects or qualities. At the same time, they **connote** —that is, suggest or imply—different attitudes toward the objects or qualities they point out. Differences in connotation are most obvious in the different ways of addressing one and the same person. Applied to John Smith, "Sir" expresses respect, "Mr. Smith" routine politeness, "John" familiarity, "hey, you" contempt, and "honey" affection.

Equally significant variations are possible when we give names to objects, ideas, or relationships. *Cheap* and *inexpensive* both mean relatively low in price or cost. However, we may call an article "cheap" to suggest that we consider it shoddy or inferior; we may call it "inexpensive" to suggest that we consider it a good bargain, valuable in

2 By permission. Copyright, 1963 by G. & C. Merriam Co., Publishers of the Merriam-Webster Dictionaries.

spite of its low price. *Unwise* and *foolish* both indicate a lack of wisdom. However, calling a proposal "unwise" suggests a certain amount of consideration or respect for the person who made it; "foolish" suggests ridicule and contempt. Similarly, it makes a difference whether we call a boy of low intelligence a "slow learner" or a "dunce," a new history of the United States "ambitious" or "pretentious."

Here is how a dictionary discriminates between the connotations of synonyms of *plan:*

> *SYN.*—**plan** refers to any detailed method, formulated beforehand, for doing or making something (vacation *plans*); **design** stresses the final outcome of a plan and implies the use of skill or craft, sometimes in an unfavorable sense, in executing or arranging this (it was his *design* to separate us); **project** implies the use of enterprise or imagination in formulating an ambitious or extensive plan (they've begun work on the housing *project*); **scheme,** a less definite term than the preceding, often connotes either an impractical, visionary plan or an underhand intrigue (a *scheme* to embezzle the funds).

From *Webster's New World Dictionary*

D 1c **Context.** To determine which of the meanings listed in your dictionary is appropriate, you have to examine the **context** in which the word occurs. The context may be another word ("square meal"), a whole sentence or paragraph ("Square your precepts with your practice"), a whole article or book (a treatment of squares in a book on plane geometry), or a situation (a policeman directing a pedestrian to a square). *Often a dictionary supplies phrases suggesting the kind of context where a given meaning is appropriate:*

> **bot·tle**[1] (bŏt′əl), *n., v.,* **-tled, -tling.** —*n.* **1.** a portable vessel with a neck or mouth, now commonly made of glass, used for holding liquids. **2.** the contents of a bottle; as much as a bottle contains: *a bottle of wine.* **3. the bottle,** intoxicating liquor. **4.** bottled milk for babies: *raised on the bottle.*

From *The American College Dictionary*

Even when the denotation of a word remains fairly stable, its connotations may vary in different contexts. *Academic,* for instance, basically means "associated with higher learning." "Academic standards," then, may mean standards of responsible and competent scholarship. An "academic argument," on the other hand, may mean an argument that is unrealistic or impractical because, like higher learning, it is removed from the hustle and bustle of economic and political reality.

Most of the time, context regulates your interpretation of words with several possible meanings more or less automatically. You automatically interpret *open* as "outstretched" in "open arms," as "undefended" in "open city," as "undecided" in "open question." You are likely to take *free* to mean "illegitimate" in "free love," "gratuitous" in "free beer," and "unregulated" in "free enterprise."

Context becomes especially important when your reading leads you onto unfamiliar ground. You will find familiar words used in puzzling ways because in an unfamiliar context they have a different meaning. For instance, an author praising modesty and thrift may describe them as "homely virtues." Looking up the word, you will find that its original meaning, as you might expect, is "associated with the home." Favorable associations of domestic life account for such meanings as "simple," "unpretentious," "intimate"; unfavorable associations account for such meanings as "crude," "unpolished," "ugly."

When your reading takes you into a period of history, a country, or a technical field unfamiliar to you, make sure to look up words that seem to have been wrenched out of their usual contexts. For instance, an eighteenth-century writer may talk about the "wit" of a person who does not seem at all "witty" in the sense of cleverly humorous or ironic. *Wit* in this context means general intellectual and imaginative capacity, as in phrases like "half-wit" and "at one's wit's end." The same writer may use the word *humor* in talking about a person noted for his melancholy disposition. *Humor* in this context probably has the general meaning of "temperament," which is related to the expression "to humor a person," meaning to go along with his moods or whims.

D 1d Grammatical Labels. Learning a new word involves learning not only its meaning but also its grammatical status. *A good dictionary gives reliable information about the functions a word can serve in a sentence.* For instance, *human* is usually labeled both as an **adjective** (adj.) and as a **noun** (n.), with some indication that the latter use ("a human" rather than "a human being") is not generally accepted as appropriate to written English. *Annoy* is labeled a **transitive verb** (v.t.); it is incomplete without an object. In other words, we usually annoy somebody or something; we don't just annoy. *Set* also is usually transitive ("*set* the bowl on the table"), but it is labeled **intransitive** (v.i.) when applied to one of the celestial bodies. In other words, the sun doesn't set anybody or anything; it just sets.

D 1e   Idiom. A word often combines with other words in an expression that is not modeled on common grammatical patterns but that nevertheless becomes the habitual way of conveying a certain idea. Such expressions are called **idioms.** *A good dictionary lists idiomatic phrases whose meanings may be more than the sum of their parts.* Here is an exceptionally full list of idiomatic phrases using the word *mind:*

bear in mind, to remember.
be in one's right mind, to be mentally well; be sane.
be of one mind, to have the same opinion; agree.
be of two minds, to be undecided or irresolute.
be out of one's mind,   1. to be mentally ill; be insane.   2. to be frantic (*with* worry, grief, etc.).
call to mind,   1. to remember.   2. to be a reminder of.
change one's mind,   1. to change one's opinion.   2. to change one's intention, purpose, or wish.
give a person a piece of one's mind, to tell a person plainly one's disapproval of him; rebuke; scold.
have a (good or great) mind to, to feel (strongly) inclined or disposed to.
have half a mind to, to be somewhat inclined or disposed to.
have in mind,   1. to remember.   2. to think of.   3. to intend; purpose.
keep in mind, to remember.
keep one's mind on, to pay attention to.
know one's mind, to know one's real thoughts, feelings, desires, or intentions.
make up one's mind, to form a definite opinion or decision; resolve.
meeting of minds, an agreement.
never mind, don't concern yourself; it doesn't matter.
on one's mind,   1. occupying one's thoughts.   2. worrying one.
pass out of mind, to be forgotten.
put in mind, to remind.
set one's mind on, to be determined on or determinedly desirous of.
speak one's mind, to say plainly what one thinks.
take one's mind off, to stop one from thinking about; turn one's attention from.
to one's mind, in one's opinion.

From *Webster's New World Dictionary*

To write idiomatic English, you have to develop an ear for individual phrases and ways of saying things. For instance, we *do* a certain type of work, *hold* a job or position, *follow* a trade, *pursue* an occupation, and *engage* in a line of business. We *replace* an original *with* a copy, but we *substitute* a copy *for* the original.

A special problem for inexperienced writers is the idiomatic use of **prepositions.** For instance, we fail *in* an attempt or fail *to* attempt it; we entrust something *to* a person or entrust him *with* it. The following list reviews idiomatic uses of some common prepositions:

abide *by* (a decision)

abstain *from* (voting)

accuse *of* (a crime)

acquiesce *in* (an injustice)

adhere *to* (a promise)

admit *of* (conflicting interpretations)

agree *with* (a person), *to* (a proposal), *on* (a course of action)

alarmed *at* (the news)

apologize *for* (a mistake)

aspire *to* (distinction)

assent *to* (a proposal)

attend *to* (one's business)

avail oneself *of* (an opportunity)

capable *of* (an action)

charge *with* (an offense)

collide *with* (a car)

compatible *with* (recognized standards)

comply *with* (a request)

concur *with* (someone), *in* (an opinion)

confide *in* or *to* (someone)

conform *to* (specifications)

deficient *in* (strength)

delight *in* (mischief)

deprive *of* (a privilege)

derived *from* (a source)

die *of* or *from* (a disease)

disappointed *in* (someone's performance)

dissent *from* (a majority opinion)

dissuade *from* (doing something foolish)

divest *of* (responsibility)

find fault *with* (a course)

identical *with* (something looked for)

ignorant *of* (a fact)

inconsistent *with* (sound procedure)

independent *of* (outside help)

indifferent *to* (praise or blame)

infer *from* (evidence)

inferior *to* (a rival product)

insist *on* (accuracy)

interfere *with* (a performance), *in* (someone else's affairs)

jealous *of* (others)

long *for* (recognition)

object *to* (a proposal)

oblivious *of* (warnings)

part *with* (possessions)

partial *to* (flattery)

participate *in* (activities)

persevere *in* (a task)

pertain *to* (a subject)

preferable *to* (an alternative)

prevail *on* (someone to do something)

prevent someone *from* (an action)

refrain *from* (wrongdoing)

rejoice *at* (good news)

required *of* (all members)

resolve *on* (a course of action)

rich *in* (resources)

short *of* (cash)

secede *from* (the Union)

succeed *in* (an attempt)

superior *to* (an alternative)

threaten *with* (legal action)

wait *for* (developments), *on* (a guest)

College dictionaries vary in their coverage of idioms. Only an unabridged dictionary giving one or more sample quotations for each possible use of a word can come close to being a complete guide to idiomatic usage.

EXERCISES

A. Look up the following entries in your dictionary: *denouement, epigram, farce, flying buttress, hauberk, limerick, machete, solecism, symbiosis, syncopation.* What special fields of interest do they represent? How clear or adequate are the definitions?

B. Explain to what extent the synonyms in each of the following groups overlap and how they differ: *agreement—contract—covenant; amateur—dilettante—tyro; apology—excuse—pretext; bearing—behavior—conduct; betray—divulge—reveal; common—ordinary—familiar; correct—discipline—punish; decline—reject—spurn; democracy—representative government—republic; destiny—doom—lot; enterprise—project—venture; fad—fashion—vogue; fantastic—imaginary—visionary; flippant—glib—impertinent; mumble—murmur—mutter.*

C. Explain the differences in connotation between the words in each of the following pairs: *childish—childlike; clever—intelligent; famous—notorious; gaze—ogle; godsend—windfall; juvenile—youngster; lucre—wealth; obedient—obsequious; obstinate—persistent; petty—punctilious; populace—population; regret—remorse; revenge—retribution; revolt—revolution; slender—thin.*

D. How does your dictionary distinguish among the changing meanings of each of the following words? Show how context determines your choice of the meaning appropriate in each phrase.

Bay leaves, at *bay, bayed* at the moon, *bay* window, bomb *bay,* a breeze from the *bay; head* of lettuce, *head* the procession, a *head* of steam, *heads* or tails, over the listeners' *heads,* went to his *head, heads* of government, *head* off complaints, not have a *head* for figures; *let* blood, without *let* or hindrance, *let* him be, *let* go, *let* me see it, *let* us ignore him, rooms to *let;* car of recent *make, make* the beds, *make* money, *make* excuses, *makes* my blood boil, *make* a speech, *makes* easy reading, *made* him a sergeant; *repair* a car, *repaired* to the meeting, in good *repair, repair* the damage; *straight* to the point, *straight* alcohol, *straight* party line, the comedian's *straight* man, *straight* hair, thinking *straight.*

E. Each of the italicized words in the following expressions is a familiar word used in an unfamiliar sense. Find the meaning that fits the context.

To write an *abstract* of a speech; to write an *apostrophe* to the gods; a monster of fearful *aspect;* to give someone a *civil* answer; an anti*clerical* political party; to give *countenance* to a crime; to wear a

(ex.)

characteristic *habit;* to receive *intelligence;* to *justify* a line of type; to cultivate *polite* learning; a *process* server; to make a character stand out in full *relief;* to lie in *state;* to be *transported* with gratitude; the *virtue* of a medicine.

F. Check your answers to the following questions by consulting your dictionary: (1) Is *incompetent* used as a noun? (2) Which of the following words are used as verbs: *admonition, loan, lord, magistrate, minister, sacrilege, spirit, war?* (3) Is "superior than" idiomatic English? (4) Is *smooth* used as an adverb? (5) Is *entertain* used as an intransitive verb? (6) Is *very* used as an adjective? (7) What idiomatic preposition goes with *glory* used as a verb? (8) Do we always censure somebody or something, or can we just censure, period? (9) How many different grammatical categories can *ill* belong to? (10) Are "angry with," "angry at," and "angry about" interchangeable? (11) Is *animate* used as an adjective? (12) Is *predominate* used as an adjective?

G. Point out and correct unidiomatic use of prepositions.

1. To seek a good grade at someone else's expense would be a violation to our standards of conduct. 2. During the past fifty years, deaths caused by highway accidents have been more numerous than those incurred from two world wars and the war in Korea. 3. Plans for cost reduction have been put to action by different agencies of the federal government. 4. Several families volunteered to take care for the children of flood victims. 5. Only the prompt help of the neighbors prevented the fire of becoming a major disaster. 6. During the first years of marriage we had to deprive ourselves from many things that other people take for granted. 7. The arrival of the ship to its destination caused general rejoicing. 8. Though I support Mr. Finchley's candidacy, I take exception with some of his statements. 9. We Americans do not hesitate in waving our flag if the occasion arises. 10. The people of this country naturally shun at the thought of having any kind of censorship imposed upon their newspapers. 11. As an instrument of the popular will, the senate suffers from defects inherent to its constitution. 12. A businessman cannot succeed unless he takes heed to the preferences of his customers.

H. Study the general scheme, the introductory material, and several sample entries of *one* of the following specialized dictionaries. Report your findings.

Bartlett's Familiar Quotations; Lester V. Berrey and Melvin Van den Bark, *American Thesaurus of Slang;* Sir William A. Craigie and James R. Hulbert, *A Dictionary of American English on Historical Principles;* H. W. Fowler, *A Dictionary of Modern English Usage;* H. W. Horwill, *A Dictionary of Modern American Usage;* John S. Kenyon and Thomas A. Knott, *A Pronouncing Dictionary of American*

English; Mitford M. Mathews, *A Dictionary of Americanisms;* Eric Partridge, *A Dictionary of Slang and Unconventional English;* Roget's *Thesaurus of English Words and Phrases.*

INVESTIGATING WORD HISTORY

After giving the spelling, pronunciation, and grammatical category of a word, college dictionaries often summarize its **etymology;** that is, they briefly trace its origin and history. The following sample entry relates the word *lock* to corresponding words in earlier English (ME. = Middle English; AS. = Anglo-Saxon or Old English), in other Germanic languages (G. = German; ON. = Old Norse or Early Scandinavian), and in the hypothetical common parent language of most European languages (IE. = Indo-European):

> **lock** (lok), *n.* [ME. *lokke;* AS. *loc,* a bolt, bar, enclosure, prison; akin to G. *loch,* a hole, ON. *lok,* a lid; prob. IE. base **leug-,* to bend, seen also in AS. *lucan,* to close (cf. LEEK)],

From *Webster's New World Dictionary*

Etymological information helps in several ways to make difficult words meaningful and familiar. For instance, you are likely to remember that *recalcitrant* means "uncooperative" or "defiant" after you find out that the Latin word contained in it refers to the kicking of a stubborn mule or unruly bronco. *Egregious* will make sense after you find out that it originally meant "standing out from the common herd," even though today it always refers to things that stand out because of undesirable qualities. Many people find it easier to remember a word after they recognize elements in it which they have already encountered in other combinations. For instance, in order to remember that *bibliophile* means "lover of books" you might note that its basic elements occur in *Bible* (Scriptures, writings) and in *philosophy* (love of wisdom) or *philanthropy* (love of man).

In addition to tracing words to other languages, the etymologist is concerned with **semantic change**—that is, gradual changes in meaning. The most complete record of such changes is the unabridged *New English Dictionary on Historical Principles,* reissued in 1933 as the *Oxford English Dictionary* (OED). This monumental reference work gives the earliest date a word occurs and then provides quotations tracing its development down through the centuries.

D 2 WORD HISTORY

The most extensive changes in vocabulary come about not through gradual change but through contacts between different cultures. Armed conquest, colonial expansion, international trade, and cultural influences all make possible the absorption of words from other languages. The early American settlers, for instance, assimilated Indian names for features of native life, such as *caucus, mackinaw,* and *tobaggan,* as well as Indian names for native animals and plants, such as *chipmunk, hominy, moose, raccoon,* and *succotash.* From the Spanish colonists of the Southwest and the West Indies they absorbed *adobe, canyon,* and *rodeo;* from the French colonists and traders of Canada and Louisiana *bayou, portage, prairie,* and *shanty;* from the Dutch settlers of the Hudson valley *coleslaw, cookie,* and *waffle.*

Compared with earlier borrowings, the words absorbed into English as a result of the colonization of the North American continent were not very numerous. Roughly three fourths of the words in your dictionary were absorbed into English from foreign sources. When the Anglo-Saxon tribes came to England from continental Europe during the period between 450 and 600 A.D., they spoke Germanic dialects, closely related in both grammar and vocabulary to the dialects from which modern Dutch and German are derived. The American tourist coming to Germany can still easily recognize the German equivalents of *arm, drink, father, fish, hand,* or *house.* However, the basic Germanic vocabulary of **Anglo-Saxon** or **Old English** was enriched and modified by an almost continuous absorption of words from other languages throughout early English history.

D 2a Latin and Greek Borrowings. *The most persistent influences on the English vocabulary were Latin and Greek, the languages of classical antiquity.* Latin had been the language of the Roman empire. It became the official language of the Roman Catholic Church, which established itself in England in the seventh century and remained the supreme spiritual authority until the sixteenth century. English early absorbed many Latin words related to the Scriptures and to the doctrines and ritual of the church, such as *altar, candle, chalice, mass, palm, pope, shrine, relic,* and *rule.* Other early

borrowings were related to church administration, to the everyday life of monks and clergymen, and to the exclusively church-controlled and church-conducted medieval system of education. Many have long since lost all suggestion of foreignness: *beet, cap, circle, cook, fever, lobster, mat, pear, school, silk, sock,* or *turn.*

Greek was the language of the literature, philosophy, and scientific knowledge of ancient Hellenic culture, flourishing both in Greece proper and in other parts of the Mediterranean world. Either in the original Greek or in Latin translation, this body of knowledge exercised a continuous influence on Christianity and Western civilization during the Middle Ages. Its influence became even stronger during the Renaissance, the "rebirth" of ancient Greek and Roman culture in the sixteenth and seventeenth centuries.

Latin was used as an international language by scholars and scientists as late as the eighteenth century, and the study of Latin and Greek was compulsory in high schools or colleges till the early decades of the twentieth century. Modern philosophical, scientific, and technological terminology draws heavily on Latin and Greek roots. More generally, the language of educated people is saturated with words that are in one way or another derived from one of the classical languages. Examples of words absorbed either directly from Greek or from Greek through Latin are *anonymous, atmosphere, catastrophe, chaos, climax, crisis, enthusiasm,* and *skeleton.* Examples of words absorbed from Latin are *contempt, gesture, history, incredible, index, individual, intellect, legal, mechanical, picture,* and *rational.*

(1) *Latin and Greek Roots.* Because of the central role of Latin and Greek in the educated man's vocabulary, knowledge of a common Latin or Greek root often provides the key to a puzzling word. For instance, the Greek root *phys-* usually refers to the body or to material things, whereas the Greek root *psych-* usually refers to the mind or the soul. This distinction explains *physician* (heals the body) and *psychiatrist* (heals the mind), *physiology* (study of bodily functions) and *psychology* (study of mental functions), *physical* (characteristic of material reality) and *psychic* (going beyond material reality). However, even a knowledge of less common roots can be helpful. For instance, *bell-,* the Latin root for "war," explains *bellicose* (inclined toward war), *belligerent* (engaged in warfare), and *ante-bellum* (prewar, specifically pre-Civil War).

Here is a very brief list of common Latin and Greek roots. See

whether you can explain how each root is used in the sample words
given for it:

auto-	*self*	autocratic, automatic, automobile, autonomy
capit-	*head*	capital, decapitate, per capita
carn-	*flesh*	carnal, carnivorous, incarnation, carnival
chron-	*time*	anachronistic, chronometer, synchronize
culp-	*fault*	culpable, culprit, exculpate
doc-	*teach*	docile, doctor, doctrine, indoctrinate
graph-	*write*	autograph, graphic, geography, orthography
hydr-	*water*	dehydrate, hydrant, hydraulic, hydrogen
jur-	*swear*	conjure, juror, perjury
man-	*hand*	manacle, manicure, manual, manufacture
phon-	*sound*	euphony, phonetics, phonograph, symphony
terr-	*land*	inter, terrestrial, subterranean
urb-	*city*	suburb, urban, urbane
verb-	*word*	proverb, verbal, verbiage, verbose
vit-	*life*	vitality, vitamin
vol-	*wish*	volition, voluntary, volunteer

(2) *Common Prefixes and Suffixes.* Especially useful is a knowledge of the most common Latin and Greek **prefixes** and **suffixes**—that
is, syllables attached at the beginning or at the end of a word to modify
its meaning. A common prefix like *sub-*, meaning "below" or "beneath,"
helps to explain not only *substandard* and *subconscious* but *submarine*
(below the sea), *sublunar* (below the moon—that is, on earth; characteristic of existence on this earth), *subterranean* (beneath the surface, underground). *Mon-*, meaning "one" or "single," helps to explain
monarch (sole ruler; emperor or king), *monocle* (eyeglass for one eye),
monologue (discourse by a single speaker, speaking by or to himself),
monogamy (practice of being married to one person at a time). The
suffix *-cide* means "killer" or "killing" in *homicide* (of a human being),
suicide (of oneself), *fratricide* (of a brother), *parricide* (of a parent),
and *insecticide* (of insects).

Here is a brief list of Latin and Greek prefixes:

bene-	*good*	benediction, benefactor, benefit, benevolent
bi-	*two*	bicycle, bilateral, bisect
contra-	*against*	contraband, contradict, contravene
ex-	*out, out of*	exclude, exhale, expel
extra-	*outside*	extraordinary, extravagant, extrovert
omni-	*all*	omnipotent, omnipresent, omniscient
per-	*through*	percolate, perforate, permeate
pre-	*before*	preamble, precedent, prefix

poly-	*many*	polygamy, polysyllabic, polytheistic
re-	*back*	recall, recede, revoke, retract
tele-	*distant*	telegraph, telepathy, telephone, television
trans-	*across, beyond*	transatlantic, transcend, transmit

Although the percentage of words derived from Latin and Greek is greatest in the vocabulary of scholars and scientists, many such words have become thoroughly domesticated. Some will seem difficult when you first encounter them but will prove their value by making possible precise and economical communication of complicated ideas. For example, *substantiate* conveniently sums up the idea of backing up an assertion or claim by evidence. *Premise* clearly identifies a statement that is not merely a random assertion but a step in a logical argument. However, some words of Greek or Latin origin are merely awkward polysyllabic synonyms of short familiar words. They can make your writing become artificial and excessively formal.

D 2b   French Borrowings. In addition to the influence of Latin and Greek there were other major changes in the English vocabulary, most of them closely associated with the history of medieval England. The historical event that most drastically influenced the development of the language was the conquest of England by the French-speaking Normans in the years following 1066. *Over the centuries, thousands of words were absorbed into English from French.*

At the beginning of the so-called **Middle English** period, about 1150, the Norman conquerors owned most of the land and controlled the most important offices in state and church. The language of law, administration, and literature was French. When the native English of the conquered people gradually re-established itself as the language of political and social life, thousands of French words were retained. Many of these words were associated with the political and military role of the aristocratic Norman overlords: *castle, court, glory, mansion, noble, prince, prison, privilege, servant, treason, treasure, war.* But hundreds of other words absorbed into Middle English were everyday words like *avoid, branch, chair, demand, desire, disease, envy, praise, table, uncle.*

Many French words passed into English through the hands of English poets who found them in medieval French poetry and romance, both Norman and continental. Some of these words are still used primarily in imaginative literature and preserve a poetic and often old-fashioned flavor. Such words are *chevalier* for "knight," *damsel* for "girl," *fealty* for "loyalty," *paramour* for "sweetheart," *prowess* for "valor," *puissance* for "power" or "strength," *travail* for "toil."

D 2c   Recently Borrowed Words. Since the consolidation of **Modern English** (about 1500), a number of *foreign languages have influenced the vocabulary of special fields of interest.* For instance, the leadership of seventeenth- and eighteenth-century France in elegant living, artistic style, and military organization is reflected in words like *apartment, ballet, battalion, cadet, caress, corps, façade, infantry, negligee, patrol.* Italy, which saw the origin of modern opera and symphonic music, provided terms like *cantata, concert, falsetto, sonata, solo, soprano, violin.* From Spain, which pioneered in the discovery and exploitation of new continents, came words like *alligator, banana, cannibal, cocoa, mosquito, negro, potato, tobacco, tomato,* some of them absorbed into Spanish from New World sources.

Modern English has a number of foreign words in different stages of assimilation. If they are still felt to be foreign rather than English, your dictionary puts a special symbol in front of them or labels them "French," "Italian," or whatever is appropriate. A writer may use an occasional foreign word because it sums up the particular flavor of a thing or of an idea more aptly than any possible native equivalent. For instance, the French word *esprit* describes a kind of irreverent and brilliant wit for which it is hard to find an English name. Do not use such foreign phrases merely in order to impress your reader.

EXERCISES

A. Investigate the history of the following words: *bedlam, bowdlerize, bowie knife, carnival, credit, curfew, dollar, emperor, fellow, gerrymander, glamour, gossip, hallmark, Halloween, jeep, kerchief, lynch, picayune, propaganda, thug.*

B. Select one of the following words. Report fully on the contrast in nature and extent of its treatment in your own dictionary and in the *Oxford English Dictionary: boor, cattle, fee, husband, hussy, knave, lewd, meat, villain, virtue.*

C. Explain the meaning of the common element in each of the following groups of words: *anarchy—monarchy—oligarchy; anthropology —misanthrope—philanthropy; antibiotic—biography—biology; audio-visual —audition—inaudible; biennial—centennial—perennial; centipede—cen-*

tury—per cent; cosmic—cosmopolitan—microcosm; credence—incredulous; describe—prescribe—proscribe; eugenics—eulogy—euphonious; heterogeneous—homogeneous; insect—intersection—section; magnify—magnificent—magnitude; portable—portage—transport; precedent—procedure—secede.

D. Indicate the basic meaning of the Latin and Greek prefixes used in the following words: *anesthetic, ambivalent, antedate, antipathy, circumvent, concord, disunity, hypersensitive, international, introvert, malpractice, multimillionaire, neofascist, postgraduate, prelude, pseudo-scientific, retroactive, semitropical, synchronize, ultramodern, unilateral.*

E. Find out from which languages the following words were derived: *bandana, boomerang, brunette, caviar, chocolate, crescendo, cynic, focus, hurricane, Mumbo Jumbo, pretzel, pundit, skin, snoop, vaudeville.*

F. What is the meaning of the following expressions? How many of them does your dictionary consider foreign rather than English? *Ad hoc, ad nauseam, aficionado, à la carte, auto-da-fé, alma mater, blitz, corpus delicti, coup de grâce, cum laude, de jure, enfant terrible, ersatz, eureka, fait accompli, femme fatale, hara-kiri, hoi polloi, laissez faire, non sequitur, pax Romana, quod erat demonstrandum, touché, tour de force, Zeitgeist.*

RECOGNIZING VARIATIONS IN USAGE

No matter what dictionary you buy, you should study the introductory notes and find out the significance of the various symbols and abbreviations used. The most important abbreviations are the so-called **restrictive labels.** They indicate that a word is used only under certain circumstances and that it can be out of place when used without attention to its limitations. In the following dictionary entry, six of the nine principal meanings of *brass* are preceded by restrictive labels:

brass (brăs, bräs), *n.* **1.** a durable, malleable, and ductile yellow alloy, consisting essentially of copper and zinc. **2.** a utensil, ornament, or other article made of brass. **3.** *Mach.* a bearing, bush, or the like. **4.** [*Music.*] — Subject Label
a. a musical instrument of the trumpet or horn families.
b. such instruments collectively in a band or orchestra.
5. [*Brit.*] a memorial tablet incised with an effigy, coat of — Geographic Label
arms or the like. **6.** metallic yellow; lemon, amber, or reddish yellow. **7.** *U.S. Slang.* **a.** high-ranking military officers. **b.** any important officials. **8.** [*Colloq.*] exces- — Usage Label
sive assurance; impudence; effrontery. **9.** *Brit. Slang.* money. —*adj.* **10.** of brass. **11.** using musical instruments made of brass. [ME *bras*, OE *bræs*] —**brass'**-**like'**, *adj.*

From *The American College Dictionary*

D 3   USAGE LABELS

Many words are appropriate to almost any occasion. A hand can be appropriately called a "hand" at any time and at any place. Other words are limited in their usefulness because of the company they keep or because of the situations in which they are usually found. For instance, words like *anywheres, nohow,* and *irregardless* are either not listed in your dictionary at all or labeled illiterate, **nonstandard,** or vulgate. Like nonstandard grammatical patterns, they are often associated with low social standing or a lack of formal education. (See G 1a.)

D 3a   Colloquial Words. *Some words suggest relaxed conversation rather than systematic exposition or argument.* Many dictionaries label such words **colloquial.** The word does *not* mean "local." It is related to *eloquent* ("talking well") and *loquacious* ("talking too much") and means "characteristic of informal speech."

Since people tend to be stiff and formal with strangers or in public and at ease when with their friends, colloquial language often sounds folksy and friendly. However, the man who is most comfortable in a robe and slippers puts on a tie and a business suit when going to the office on Monday morning. Similarly, the writer who feels at ease with colloquial language has to be able to use more formal language in formal situations. In particular, he has to guard against sudden shifts from the tone of the lecture hall to the tone of the snack bar around the corner.

COLLOQUIAL	FORMAL	COLLOQUIAL	FORMAL
boss	superior	kid	child
brainy	intelligent	knock off	stop working
buddy	friend	mean	ill-natured
faze	disconcert	skimpy	meager
flunk	fail	sloppy	untidy
folks	relatives	snoop	pry
hunch	premonition	snooze	nap
job	position	stump	baffle

Other familiar words are generally acceptable in one sense but colloquial in another. Colloquial are *alibi* in the sense of "excuse," *aggravate* in the sense of "annoy," *funny* in the sense of "queer," and *mad* in the sense of "angry." Colloquial language uses qualifiers like *kind of, sort of, a lot, lots;* abbreviated forms like *ad, bike, exam, gym, phone.* It uses many **phrasal verbs**, verbs that combine a short basic verb with one or more prepositions: *check up on, chip in, come up with, cut out* (noise), *get across* (a point), *take in* (a show), *take up with* (a person). Colloquial English usually contains a liberal sprinkling of catch-all words like *nice, cute, awful, wonderful,* or *terrible.* It is fond of **figurative expressions** like *play ball, polish the apple, have a brainstorm.*

Apt and discriminating use of colloquial expressions sets the casual, leisurely tone in much informal writing. When used with discretion, they can give just the right touch of humor and just the right personal note to an article or an essay:

> There was a broad streak of mischief in Mencken. He was forever *cooking up* imaginary organizations, having *fake* handbills printed, inventing exercises in pure nonsense. I remember a fake business card that he *got* some job printer to execute for him and that gave him great joy.—Philip M. Wagner, "Mencken Remembered," *The American Scholar*

On the other hand, colloquialisms can easily alienate the critical reader. At their worst, they suggest the put-on folksiness of the person who tries too hard to convince his public that he is one of the crowd. They suggest the public-relations heartiness of some advertisers and some political candidates (Uncle Sam from a billboard: "My folks mostly drive Ford V-8's"). Because of the pitfalls of colloquial language, many college teachers require the student to keep expository writing free from a colloquial tinge.

D 3b **Slang.** Many dictionaries make a distinction between colloquial diction and a special subdivision of it called **slang.** *Slang is appropriate only in the most informal kinds of writing or when deliberately used for special effects.* It is especially popular with adolescents, and it has some characteristically adolescent qualities: a disregard for convention, a lack of restraint, a tendency to regard people and accepted social attitudes with condescension or contempt. In slang, these qualities combine to give free rein to the impulse to play with the language. One unmistakable characteristic of slang is its faddishness. New slang expressions are born overnight, repeated over and over, and then forgotten. Different high schools, colleges, and professions develop their own special varieties of slang, which change from year to year. As a result, much slang is unintelligible to outsiders.

Because of its free-wheeling, experimental attitude toward language, slang often has a vigor missing in more cautious and pedestrian diction. The figurative expressions it substitutes for less imaginative formal terms are often apt: *highbrow* for "sophisticated" or "intellectual," *rubberneck* for "tourist," *sawbones* for "surgeon" or "physician," and *whirlybird* for "helicopter." Often a striking slang expression has no very satisfactory formal equivalent: *eager beaver, eyewash, run-around, stuffed shirt.* Many slang terms appeal to our sense of the incongruous: *blow one's top, chew the fat, fly off the handle, hit the ceiling, kick the bucket, lay an egg.*

Slang is the major resource of many a humorous writer:

> Despite that great wellspring of love and pity I have for the afflicted and the misbegotten, and those who have been *just plain took,* I find it hard to get worked up over the plight of those *gaffers* who play golf on the city's links. Little boys lurk in the brush, and when one of the superbly conditioned athletes knocks a *nifty* their way, they keep the ball. Then, if things haven't changed since my day, they sell the balls to other superbly conditioned athletes, who then *scream like banshees* when the golf-ball connoisseurs *steal'em* again. Since grabbing the little thieves by the scruff of their necks and *beating the bejabbers out of them* would obviously be in violation of their civil rights, we must look elsewhere for a solution.

On the other hand, the humor in slang tends to be crude. Calling a person "fatso" or "skinny" or "bonehead" may be funny, but it also suggests a lack of tact or respect. The extravagant and contemptuous elements in slang make many readers interpret all slang expressions as signs of bad taste and bad manners. Whether a given slang expression is acceptable depends not only on the situation and the skill of the writer but also on the standards of the reader.

D 3c   Fancy Words. Students whose writing has been criticized as slangy or excessively colloquial sometimes have difficulty finding middle ground. Trying to avoid excessive informality, they may go to the opposite extreme. *When writing formal English, avoid words that are pompous, affected, or stilted.* Do not imitate writers who habitually prefer the fancy word to the plain word, the elegant flourish to the blunt phrase.

Dictionaries do not usually distinguish between plain and fancy words. Some of the latter may carry the label *poetic* or *literary,* indicating that they are most appropriate in poetry, in fiction, in imaginative description. Here is a brief list of words that can make your writing seem affected, especially if you habitually prefer them to a simpler or more natural equivalent:

FANCY	PLAIN	FANCY	PLAIN
adumbrate	hint	nuptials	wedding
ameliorate	improve	obsequies	funeral
asseverate	assert	pachyderm	elephant
astound	amaze	potentate	ruler
betrothal	engagement	presage	predict
commence	begin	pulchritude	beauty
concomitant	result	purchase	buy
demise	death	quaff	drink
diurnal	daily	residence	home
emolument	pay, reward	tome	volume
eschew	avoid	vernal	springlike
gelid	cold	vista	view

Whether a word sounds natural or affected depends not only on the word but also on its use. A word appropriate in a stylized social note may sound artificial in a personal letter. A phrase befitting a solemn speech may seem pretentious in a paper on an everyday subject. Contemporary expository prose, on the whole, avoids both "fine writing" and the forced conviviality of a self-consciously colloquial style in favor of simple, unpretentious language.

D 4   GEOGRAPHIC LABELS

Some words have only regional or local currency. Dictionaries indicate their status by geographic labels.

D 4a   American and British English. In the different English-speaking countries variations in vocabulary have developed. As a result, the British reader of an American magazine may occasionally stumble over **Americanisms**. The Canadian reader of an Australian newspaper will be puzzled by words that only a dictionary specializing in the regional variations of English could explain.

The regional variants that you are most likely to encounter in your own reading are words common in **British English**. Reading a novel about life in Liverpool or Manchester, you will discover that a "tram" is a streetcar, a "lorry" a truck, a "lift" an elevator, a "torch" a flashlight, a "wireless" a radio, or a "fortnight" two weeks. Most college dictionaries indicate words occurring primarily either in Britain or in the United States by restrictive labels.

D 4b Dialects. The American tourist exploring Europe soon finds that there are language differences not only from country to country but also from province to province, from county to county, and sometimes from village to village. Through the centuries, most European languages, including British English, have developed a great number of local varieties called **dialects**. These often differ greatly in pronunciation, grammar, and vocabulary from the standard language used in the schools, on stage and radio, or in books, magazines, and newspapers. Students of English literature usually encounter some dialect writing. For instance, a poet to whom a pretty girl is a "bonny lass," a church a "kirk," and a landowner a "laird" is using one of the dialects of Scotland and Northern England rather than standard British English.

In the United States, various circumstances have prevented the development of dialect differences comparable to those of British English, German, or French. The migrations of large numbers of people have led to a continual intermingling of settlers from various parts of the country, with a resulting leveling of language differences. Today, the mass media of communication promote national norms of taste, fashion, and language.

Such dialect differences as have developed in the United States are primarily a matter of pronunciation rather than of grammar and vocabulary. Linguists are now in the process of tracing a number of **American dialects**. The results of their work are being recorded in linguistic atlases mapping out differences in speech from region to region. However, few areas have a regional identity distinct enough to make possible the preservation of differences easily caught by the untrained ear of the layman. A Yankee may recognize a Southerner by his use of *you all* instead of "both of you" or "all of you," *reckon* instead of "guess" or "suppose," *poke* instead of "bag," or *tote* instead of "carry." He may recognize certain features of a "Southern drawl." A student from the Middle West may recognize something like an Eastern or New England accent that in some ways comes close to standard British English.

Dialect differences are exploited by comedians and comic-strip writers for comic effects. On the other hand, many serious dramatists and novelists reproduce dialectal differences to give a realistic, down-to-earth quality to the conversation of their characters. You yourself may at times experiment with dialect expressions when striving for local color or a quaint, folksy touch.

D 5   TEMPORAL LABELS

Some words are no longer in general use or not yet generally established. When you read an eighteenth-century philosopher, see a play by a contemporary of Shakespeare, or read a sermon preached to the Pilgrim Fathers, you will find words that have since gone out of use or changed in meaning. A complete record of such words can be found in the *Oxford English Dictionary*. Your own dictionary is necessarily much less complete. It nevertheless records most of the words you are likely to find in the works of early English and American historians, philosophers, playwrights, and novelists.

D 5a   Obsolete Words. Some words, or meanings of words, that were commonly known two or three centuries ago have gone out of use altogether. Such words and meanings are called **obsolete**. Examples of obsolete meanings are the use of *coy* in the sense of "quiet," *curious* in the sense of "careful," *nice* in the sense of "foolish." Explanations of obsolete words and meanings account for most of the bulky footnotes in student editions of early English classics.

D 5b   Archaic Words. Words or meanings that are no longer in common use but still occur in special situations are called **archaic**. The King James version of the Bible and the vocabulary of religious devotion preserve many archaisms that were in common use in seventeenth-century England. *Thou* and *thee* for "you," *brethren* for "brothers," and *kine* for "cattle" are familiar examples. Poets often use archaisms, either because of their associations with the colorful days of yore, or because of their ability to startle the reader into paying attention: *brand* (sword), *childe* (aristocratic youth), *fere* (companion), *rood* (cross), *sprite* (ghost). Historical novels may contain various archaic tags: *anon* (at once), *eftsoons* (again), *erst* (formerly), *fain* (glad or gladly), *forsooth* (truly), *methinks* (it seems), *ywis* (certainly), *yon* (over there).

Some words have an old-fashioned flavor even though they may not be labeled archaic in your dictionary. *Albeit* (though), *lief* (gladly), and *threescore* (sixty) would sound quaint in a paper written by a college student.

D 5c   Neologisms. Some writers supplement current usage by creations of their own. Such newly coined words are called **neologisms.** Occasionally a writer coins an apt and useful word that finds general acceptance. Technological and scientific advances create a constant need for new words, from *typewriter* and *refrigerator* to *cybernetics* and *semantics.* Sometimes there is considerable groping before a new term definitely establishes itself, as for instance with *horseless carriage, automobile,* and *motor car; phonograph, gramophone,* and *victrola;* or *video* and *television.*

Inexperienced writers sometimes coin new words inadvertently by extending common words analogously to other familiar forms: *vanishment* (analogous to "banishment"), *neglectfulness* (analogous to "bashfulness"), *outdoorsman* (analogous to "woodsman"). Much wordy, awkward, inexact prose suffers from improvisations like *cowardness* (cowardice) and *unpainful* (painless).

Intentional word-coiners present a different kind of problem. Journalists, advertisers, and propagandists are constantly inventing terms designed to dazzle their customers. The most popular type is the combination of two familiar words, as in *beautility* (beautiful utility) or *modelovely* (lovely model). Some of these are entertaining, like *Time's phenomoppet* (phenomenal moppet). Many others are painfully facetious, like the book on how to attain happiness that concluded with a "Happilogue." However, many intentional neologisms are neither humorous nor ingenious. Many readers squirm when confronted with words like *escapee, finalize, jumboize, moisturize, paperamics, personalize,* and *usership.*

D 6   SUBJECT LABELS

Labels like *Law, Naut.* (nautical), or *Mach.* (machinery) are called subject labels. *A term, or one of its several meanings, may be used mainly by specialists and may not be familiar to laymen.* The **technical terminology** or, on a less formal level, the **shoptalk** of a trade or profession makes possible precise and rapid communication among its members but requires careful definition or explanation in writing addressed to the general reader.

Some words associated with a specific field have acquired unfavorable associations, which are often too subjective and variable to be registered by a dictionary. *Contact* for "get in touch with," *deal* for "transaction," *feature* for "exhibit" or "offer for sale," and *proposition* for "proposal" are words used primarily by salesmen. Even when used in a noncommercial context, they may carry overtones of the hard sell. *Personnel* in the sense of "people," *domicile* in the sense of "address," and *dependents* in the sense of "family" are used primarily by public officials and administrators. Even when used in a nonofficial situation, such words suggest impersonality and red tape.

Since dictionaries can give only limited coverage to the overtones and associations of words, you will have to get into the habit of watching for such overtones when listening and reading. Dictionary labels are guidance that needs to be tested and made meaningful by experience.

EXERCISES

A. Which of the following expressions would you expect to carry restrictive labels? Check your answers with the help of your dictionary. *Bookworm, bower, Chinaman, complected, costermonger, dogie, go Dutch, goodman, grease monkey, guttersnipe, guzzle, hubbub, highfalutin, jalopy, mob, moniker, mooch, moonshiner, perpend* (verb), *petrol, ritzy, schoolmarm, shyster, thorpe, victuals, walkie-talkie, windbag, wallop, Yankee, yestreen.*

B. Check the standing of the following abbreviations. Which does your dictionary list without a restrictive label? *Ad-lib, auto, bus* (for "omnibus"), *doc, econ, IQ, lab, math, photo, plane* (for "airplane"), *prof, snafu, TV, ump* (for "umpire"), *VIP.*

C. Observe the language used by your fellow students, friends, or acquaintances to find ten current slang expressions not listed in your dictionary. Define them, explain their use, and indicate what, if anything, they reveal about the speaker's attitude.

D. Study the writing of a columnist who makes frequent use of colloquialisms or of slang. Examine and describe his attitude toward his material and toward his readers.

E. Point out colloquialisms and slang expressions and comment on their appropriateness. If your instructor desires, rewrite the sentences, avoiding all expressions that are not appropriate to formal written English.

1. Uncle Amos was a spendthrift in his youth, but he changed after he married a penny-wise wife. 2. My family was on the move all through my early childhood, but we finally located in the state of

New York.   3. Psychologists have discovered that many young people get a kick out of cutting up in front of a group.   4. Our unlimited material resources will avail us nothing unless we keep alive the gumption that comes down to us from colonial farmers.   5. When the refugees were told that the train was going to leave in ten minutes, there was a mad rush to the station.   6. Parents only confuse a child by bawling him out every time he commits a minor mistake.   7. I prefer being blown to pieces by an atomic bomb to being brained with a club.   8. Sent to size up our new allies, he found most of them in good shape.   9. The concert was scheduled to start at eight o'clock, but unfortunately the soloist did not show up.   10. Guests who crash a party must not be surprised if the host gives them a cold shoulder.   11. In view of the late hour, we decided we better shove off and get some shuteye.   12. My education was rather lopsided; it never came to grips with the problems that really interested me.   13. It is too bad that we should run out of gas only a couple of miles from home.   14. When Lovelace fails to suggest a definite date for the wedding, Clarissa begins to suspect that he is only pulling her leg.   15. Modern medicine has found ways of licking many dread diseases.

F. Read a scene from a play by Shakespeare or by one of his contemporaries. Compile a list of ten words or meanings that have become obsolete, archaic, or old-fashioned. Check in an unabridged dictionary words not listed in your own.

G. Compile a list of ten current advertising terms that you consider neologisms. Indicate those that you think may eventually become standard English and explain why.

CULTIVATING EFFECTIVE DICTION

D 7   ACCURATE WORDS

Effective diction is a matter not only of learning new words but also of making discriminating use of old ones. An effective writer uses accurate words, employs exact shades of meaning.

D 7a   Hit-or-Miss Diction. *Inaccuracy in the use of words often results from lack of time.* The journalist writing to meet a deadline often has to be content with words that express the intended meaning almost but not quite. Thus, an editorial may start like this: "Only by widespread voting will the desires of the nation be executed on the administrative and legislative levels of our government." If the writer had had the time to revise this editorial, he would have noticed several inexact expressions. Orders are "executed," but desires are "realized," "fulfilled," or "complied with." They would be fulfilled not *by* voting but perhaps as a result of it. Finally, the main divisions of the United States government are not really "levels," of which one could be more elevated than another, but collateral branches, each with more or less clearly defined and independent authority.

Similar instances of hit-or-miss diction are common in student papers that are merely a hasty first draft rather than a carefully revised final version:

HASTY: The news about widespread corruption was first *exposed* by the local press.

REVISED: The news about widespread corruption first *appeared* in the local press. (Evildoers or shortcomings are "exposed," but news about evildoers is "printed," "presented," or "reported.")

Often, inaccurate diction results from a writer's being insensitive to overtones and associations:

HASTY: Life in the suburbs *subjects* a family to the beauties of nature.

REVISED: Life in the suburbs *brings* a family *closer* to the beauties of nature. (The connotations of *subject* are unfavorable; it implies that we are exposed to something unwillingly.)

D 7b   **Imprecise Connectives.** *The relationship between ideas may be obscured by vague all-purpose connectives.* Avoid overusing *and, as,* and *so:*

As—better "because"—we had no money, we gave him a check.
He was growing sideburns *so*—better "so that"—he would look like Valentino.

While is less precise than *whereas* in sentences that point out a contrast:

The administration occupies an ultra-modern building, *while*—better "whereas"—the faculty offices are located in temporary wooden structures.

D 8   ECONOMY

Effective writing is clear and concise. An effective writer gets to the point without being weighed down by unnecessary verbiage.

D 8a   Redundancy. The most easily spotted kind of wordiness is **redundancy**, or unnecessary duplication. *Many sentences become redundant through mere careless repetition.* The phrase *basic fundamentals* is redundant because *basis* and *foundation* mean very nearly the same thing. *Important essentials* is redundant because something could not be essential and unimportant at the same time. Colloquial English uses many phrases that show a weakening of etymological meanings. For instance, *continue* means "go on," *refer* means "point back," *eliminate* means "take out." *Continue on, refer back,* and *eliminate out* would be considered redundant in formal situations.

In the following sentences one or the other way of expressing the same idea should be omitted:

> We left *in the morning* at about six o'clock *a.m.*
> *As a rule,* the weather was *usually* warm.
> There is more to it than *seems apparent.*
> I was given the *choice* of *choosing* whether I wanted to go.
> *Physically,* he has not grown much in *height.*
> *In my opinion, I think* you are right.

D 8b   Padding. Wordiness is often caused by **all-purpose nouns.** *Some words come easily because they say nothing specific.* Look at the word *situation* in the following sentence: "When I first came to Smith College, *there was a situation where* some students lived in better houses than others." This sentence would say exactly the same thing if shortened to read: "When I first came to Smith College, some students lived in better houses than others." Words like *situation, angle, factor, aspect, line,* or *element* are often mere senseless padding: *INVOLVE*

PADDED: Another *aspect* of the *situation* that needs to be considered is the consumer relations *angle.*
CONCISE: We should also consider consumer relations.

D 8c   Economical Transition. *A common cause of wordiness is lack of simple and direct transition from one sentence or one paragraph to another.* Suppose you have said: "Many students feel that liberal-arts courses are impractical." Perhaps you want to continue with an example. Don't say: "*An example of this is the fact that* only five per cent of our freshmen take English literature." Say: "*For example,* only five per cent of our freshmen take English literature." Perhaps you want to add an alternative or a possible objection.

Don't start: "*In considering this situation we must also take into account the fact that* other students do not feel this way." Say: "Others, *however*, do not feel this way." Perhaps you want to draw a general conclusion. Don't start a sentence beginning with "*Taking this factor into consideration we must conclude that . . .*" Use a simple "*Therefore . . .*" instead.

D 9 DIRECTNESS

An effective writer must know how to be blunt and direct. Indirect expression slows down the reader and occasionally makes him lose his way.

D 9a Euphemisms. *Much roundabout diction results from the desire to be elegant.*

(1) Pleasant or impressive names for unpleasant or trivial things are known as **euphemisms**. The most common motive of such verbal upgrading is the speaker's or writer's desire to seem dignified or refined. The most familiar euphemisms are those for elementary facts of human existence:

birth	*blessed event; new arrival*
pregnancy	*to be expecting; to be in a family way*
spinsterhood	*bachelor girl; career woman*
age	*senior citizens; the elderly*
death	*pass on, expire; the deceased; mortal remains*

Often euphemisms are required by politeness or tact. When referring to people you respect, you will prefer *stout* to *fat, intoxicated* to *drunk, indolent* to *lazy,* and *remains* to *corpse.* More often, however, euphemisms mislead, or even deliberately deceive. In advertising, and in business generally, euphemisms are used to upgrade services or products. Waitresses become "hostesses," plumbers "sanitary engineers," file clerks "research consultants," undertakers "funeral directors," door-to-door salesmen "customer-contact personnel," and fortune tellers "clairvoyant readers." A tailor, referred to as a "stylist," does not design but "creates" a blouse or a dress.

In much public-relations prose and political propaganda, euphemisms cover up facts that the reader is entitled to know. *Straitened financial circumstances* for "bankruptcy," *planned withdrawal* for "disorganized retreat," and *resettlement* for "forcible expatriation" are devices for fooling the unsuspecting and confusing the suspicious.

(2) The practice of using euphemisms to avoid the repetition of more unpretentious words is often called **elegant variation**. A writer describing the habits of the swordfish will rightly feel that repeating the name of the fish in every second sentence would be monotonous. However, his writing will sound strained if he starts using circumlocutions like "scaled creature," "aquatic marauder," "denizen of the deep," and "knight of the brine."

D 9b   Jargon. Jargon, like the use of euphemisms, reflects the desire to make the trivial seem important. *Much inflated diction results from a writer's using two highbrow words where one lowbrow word would do.* Jargon cultivates an impressive pseudo-scientific air by using indirect, impersonal constructions; by blowing up simple ideas through abstract or roundabout diction; and by seeking out heavy, technical-sounding Latin and Greek terms.

The jargon addict says "Reference was made" rather than "I mentioned"; "the hypothesis suggests itself" rather than "I think." He prefers the technical jawbreaker to the familiar everyday word: *effectuate* for "bring about," *hypothesize* for "assume," *magnitude* for "size," *methodology* for "methods," *interrelationship* for "relation." His writing suffers from chronic overemphasis because of his routine use of words like *actual, definite, real,* and *virtual.* He uses terms like *essential, primary,* and *individual* where no distinction between "essential" and "nonessential," "primary" and "secondary," or "individual" and "society" is implied or important. He discusses simple everyday happenings in terms of "factors," "phases," "aspects," "situations," "criteria," "data," "problems," "facets," "phenomena," "structures," "levels," and "strata."

JARGON: Procedures were instituted with a view toward the implementation of the conclusions reached.
PLAIN ENGLISH: We started to put our ideas into practice.

JARGON: Careful consideration of relevant data is imperative before the procedure most conducive toward a realization of the desired outcomes can be determined.
PLAIN ENGLISH: Look before you leap.

Obviously, many occasions call for language that is impersonal, technical, and antiseptic. Scientific and philosophical terminology makes for clear and efficient communication because it minimizes irrelevant emotions and associations. Pseudo-scientific jargon, on the other hand, borrows the prestige of science or scholarship, building up the dignity of the author and his material at the expense of clarity and economy. As one critic said, jargon is "saying what everybody knows in language nobody can understand."

D 9c   Flowery and Extravagant Diction. *Flowery and extravagant diction interferes with a writer's doing justice to his subject.* Some writers cannot resist the temptation to call a policeman a "minion of the law," an Irishman a "native of the Emerald Isle," a colonist who served in the War of Independence a "gallant warrior defending our infant republic." A stay with one's grandparents becomes "a sojourn at the ancestral mansion"; a person bringing good news, "a harbinger of glad tidings." Such flowery expressions distract attention from the subject being discussed.

In the more showy, flamboyant kinds of journalism, the flowery phrase is supplemented by the journalist's tendency toward **hyperbole**, exaggeration for dramatic effect. "Crises" are constantly "racing toward a climax," "tragedies" are "stunning" peaceful communities, "daring" new detergents are overjoying housewives by bleaching clothes to a "dazzling" white. Basketball teams "clobber," "bludgeon," and "exterminate" each other; a 250-pound fullback "gambols," "capers," or "romps" to a touchdown; a boxer "slaughters" his opponent. Not surprisingly, the style of the sports writer caters to his public's appetite for color and excitement rather than to the scholar's preference for clarity, accuracy, and objectivity. However, the same qualities that make **journalese** successful in newspapers and advertisements intended for mass consumption make it sound breathless or juvenile in serious discussion.

D 10   EXPRESSIVE LANGUAGE

Careful word choice can make the difference between vague or colorless language and language that is fresh, graphic, and concrete.

D 10a   Specific Words. *A conscientious writer searches for specific and informative words.* Instead of using the colorless, generally applicable term *building*, he will use a more specific word like *barn, mansion, warehouse, bungalow, shack, workshop,* or *cabin.* (For more detailed discussion, see Section 1 under "Finding the Right Word.")

D 10b   Figurative Language. *Figurative expressions make writing graphic and colorful by exploiting similarities between different things.* A compressed but explicit comparison, introduced by *as* or *like,* is called a **simile.** An implied comparison that uses one thing or quality as the equivalent of another is called a **metaphor.** Literally—that is, in its original or in its ordinary sense—*monkey* refers to a small, long-tailed animal. Metaphorically, it may mean a person who, like a monkey, is agile, mischievous, imitative, or playful. (See also Section 1.)

To be effective, a metaphor must be apt and unforced. Avoid figurative expressions that are labored or extravagant:

EXTRAVAGANT: When the average overmothered college student is removed from parental control, the severance of the umbilical cord causes him to bleed to death, psychologically speaking.

When you use more than one figurative expression at a time, the pictures they evoke should blend in a more or less harmonious whole. Too often, a writer jumps from picture to picture so rapidly that the reader has trouble keeping up with him:

MIXED: America's colleges are the key to national survival, and the future of the country lies in their hands.
(The second part of the statement is illogical, because keys do not have hands.)

MIXED: Enriched programs give the good student a chance to dig deeper into the large sea of knowledge.
(Most people do their digging on solid ground rather than at sea.)

D 10c   Triteness. *Many phrases that may originally have been vigorous or striking have become trite through overuse.* Such trite phrases, called **clichés,** can infiltrate a writer's vocabulary till his writing begins to sound like a phonograph record of a popular song which has been played so often that nobody can bear to hear it even one more time.

To the cliché expert, ignorance is always "abysmal," fortitude always "intestinal," necessity always "dire." Daylight is always "broad," silence always "ominous," and old age always "ripe." People make a "clean break" and engage in "honest toil" till the "bitter end." When they make something clear, they make it "crystal clear"; when they wait, they wait "with bated breath"; when they work, they work "by the sweat of their brow"; when they marry, they marry a "blushing bride." "Last but not least," "sadder but wiser" and "a little the worse for wear," they retire to the "sidelines" to let a new generation make its appearance "upon the busy stage of life."

Here are some of the clichés that tend to appear in student writing:

believe it or not	the last straw
better late than never	let's face it
beyond the shadow of a doubt	malice aforethought
bolt out of the blue	nature's glory
burn the midnight oil	off the beaten track
crying shame	pride and joy
easier said than done	proud owner (father, mother)
the facts of life	rear its ugly head
few and far between	rude awakening
the finer things	a shot in the arm
first and foremost	sink or swim
free and easy	sneaking suspicion
get in there and fight	something tells me
good time was had by all	straight and narrow
green with envy	strike while the iron is hot
in one fell swoop	to all intents and purposes
in the last analysis	truer words were never spoken
it goes without saying	truth is stranger than fiction
it stands to reason	

The basic objection to clichés is that "echo talk" easily leads to "echo thinking." A writer who has something fresh to say should try to express it in fresh and expressive language.

EXERCISES

A. Make sure you can distinguish between the confusing words in the following pairs: *antic—antique; biography—bibliography; clique—cliché; connive—conspire; difference—deference; ethical—ethnic; feudalism—fatalism; gentle—genteel; literal—literary—literate; manners—mannerisms; sensible—sensitive; specie—species; unfaithful—infidel; venal—venial.*

B. Select the appropriate word.

1. Soldiers and government workers lined the streets; the former in colorful uniforms, the *(1)later/(2)latter* in drab civilian clothes. 2. An important problem facing all of us is the *(3)amount/(4)number* of

traffic accidents that occur each day of the week.   3. The March of Dimes was organized to help those *(5)afflicted/(6)inflicted* with infantile paralysis.   4. The chairman *(7)attributed/(8)contributed* the low attendance figures to inadequate publicity.   5. Although he has not yet resigned, his remarks *(9)implied/(10)inferred* that he would shortly do so.   6. One of the things my teachers never *(11)learned/ (12)taught* me was how to improve my diction.   7. His fiancée used to tell him that she was too *(13)impracticable/(14)impractical* to make a good housewife.   8. According to one of the students, the *(15) moral/(16)morale* of Ibsen's play was that a girl should not marry a college professor.   9. The voters can hardly be *(17)credible/(18)credulous* enough to believe some of the things they are told.   10. Arvin had accumulated a small fortune through *(19)judicial/(20)judicious* buying and selling of stocks.

C. Point out and correct examples of inaccurate or unidiomatic diction.

1. He felt that a hands-off policy was the best one for the government to play.   2. A teacher has to be able to handle emotionally disturbed children without bias or ill-favored feelings.   3. Few people accomplish the asset of ignoring gossip circulated about them by thoughtless persons.   4. The United States lost much of the prestige that other countries used to have for her.   5. The support we received from our parent organization has aided greatly to our success.   6. The situation has become drastic and requires immediate action.   7. Nations armed with nuclear weapons will be a constant fear to their less powerful neighbors.   8. In his speech, the mayor suggested several ways of helping the traffic problem.   9. The administration, in exposing the apathy of Congress, has done a great deed to the country.   10. If we accept your theory, our whole concept of democracy will have to make a drastic change.   11. If the new city hall is to serve the whole community, it should be centralized in the city.   12. In an emergency, some drivers become a panic and freeze to the wheel.   13. Most of our objections to the behavior of other people fall under the generalization of prejudice.   14. Competence alone should be the judge whether a teacher should be allowed to teach or not.   15. In high school many of us never realized the importance that grammar would portray in later life.

D. Point out and correct examples of wordiness.

1. The reason that married students have high grades academically is that they have a definite goal in the future to come.

2. At the present time, some of today's popular music seems to revert back to music popular thirty years ago. However, in due time a new fad will eventually replace this current craze.

3. The fact that the college forces one to pay for membership in a student organization seems to me a coercion of the student's funds.

4. As far as weather conditions are concerned, the climate of the country is very much like that of my native state.

5. Though many steps toward equal opportunities were taken in the early days of our government's reign, for various reasons the reaching of this goal has been impeded.

6. In the modern world of this day and age, economical operation has become an indispensable condition for business success. The modern businessman knows that he cannot cut expenses by continually adding on new employees to the pay roll.

7. As a traveler who has made several trips to Europe of varying lengths of stay, I venture to say that I have reasonable background to discuss the merits of the various different types of transportation now available for travel to Europe.

8. To be right at home in this modern age of today, one should choose a hobby like flying, which is right up to date with the times.

9. The majority of the time the literature of the nineteenth century was didactic in nature.

E. From your themes, select a paragraph that is wordy or indirect. Rewrite it, using more economical and precise diction. Hand in both versions.

F. Collect five expressions that you consider euphemisms. Explain how they are used and discuss their effect and appropriateness.

G. Translate the following specimens of jargon into plain English.

1. To answer this question without clarification of my rationalizing would be senseless, since there are a great number of determinants that can be expressed pro and con.

2. Being in a profession marks a tangible asset usable as a means of support throughout life, including advancing years.

3. The individual's mental attitude is the factor that seems to make time spent in one geographical location more enjoyable than time spent in another.

4. Finding genuine leadership is a deciding factor in the possibility of the existence of good government.

5. As far as the status of women is concerned, I feel the strong tendency toward domestication in our society will never change, only modify. The physical aspect plays an important part, it being the role of a woman to reproduce the offspring.

6. If an observation of the streets in various cities were to be made,

it would reveal a considerable number of situations where traffic is delayed because of congested conditions.

7. Aid along the lines of scholastic achievement and integration into the social group is accorded the younger members of a fraternity by their older brothers.

8. The student commencing matriculation in the institution of his choice should not be subjugated to general education requirements above and beyond the prerequisites stipulated in his major field.

9. The existence or nonexistence of sufficient socio-economic incentives can be presumed to be a major factor in determining the availability of instructional personnel requisite to the successful functioning of the nation's educational establishment.

H. From one of your past or present textbooks, select a passage that you consider jargon. Explain which features of jargon it illustrates.

I. Comment on the use of figurative language in the following sentences:

1. The student council elections were a fascinating spectacle from the first kick-off to the final curtain.

2. The television audience is becoming more aware of the pitfalls used by advertisers.

3. In this poem, the poet seems to be coming out of a dream-world and stepping into the face of reality.

4. Many American writers now famous made their way in part by feeding the grist of the weekly magazines.

5. The railroads, once a powerful force in the nation's economy, have been rapidly losing headway in recent decades.

6. Americans revere their constitution, because the birth of their country was founded from its pages.

7. Coming at a point when our country faces a serious reappraisal of our policy toward Latin America, this timely book fills a much-needed void.

8. Neither of the major characters in the play turned out to be a pillar of moral fiber.

J. Study the language used by your favorite sports writer, fashion analyst, or society editor. Write a brief report, providing samples of characteristic diction.

K. Compile a list of ten clichés widely used in news reporting, in campaign oratory, or in advertising. What explains their popularity?

L. (**Review**) Examine and evaluate the diction of each of the following passages. Point out features that limit their effectiveness or appropriateness.

1. For some people the cartoons shown at the theaters are the high spot of the program. The majority of these people is the children. The slapstick comedy affords loads of laughs to the younger folks. However, the cartoons have more than a little effect on the older people too. Sometimes this effect is negative, and sometimes it is positive. The main criticism against the cartoons is that they are so completely abstract and ridiculous. For those people who enjoy the cartoons, the abstractness is the backbone of their favoritism.

2. Alpha Tau Omega's hopes for the local basketball championship were put to what the chemistry kids call the acid test last night. A tall gang of Pi Alpha Kappa cagers staged a tremendous second half point-scoring spree to wallop the ATO underlings and win the intramural basketball crown. ATO's glaring lack of rebounding strength told the tale in the second half, as the champs made a farce of it by canning 43 points while holding the small hustling ATO's to but 18 counters. After ATO held a razor-thin halftime lead, PAK's Glen Abel, who until recently was in drydock with a pulled leg muscle, led the offensive surge and the PAK's were off to the races.

3. Tax money is just a great big beautiful hunk of coin toward which few persons in government feel the slightest moral responsibility. It means a bigger and faster gravy train, a better pork barrel, and more pie in the sky, and not by-and-by. It means further funds to be whacked up among the ever more powerful blocs that scratch each other's respective backs and operate in and around government. Everyone is in there getting his, and never mind that poor faceless slob, the taxpayer, with the achin' back.

4. We think of our audio-visual program as a method or medium, not as an end in itself. For example, a curriculum committee at its inception does not necessarily include a visual-aids representative. However, following the formulation of general philosophy and basic content, visual aids become an active and integral part of curriculum organization. The materials available then serve in many ways to orient and implement the program. The individual teacher is responsible for enriching the individual learning situation through the preplanned utilization of visual materials that vitalize interest. The principal must provide for physical and monetary aspects. But perhaps the greatest contributing factor to the success of the program is provision for continuous growth. Our concentration of effort is on individual evaluations of materials immediately following their use.

(ex.)

This is further implemented by periodic evaluations by groups, on the vertical and horizontal grade-level basis.

5. Whistling Dick waited as long as his judgment advised, and then slid swiftly to the ground. Assuming as far as possible the air of an honest laborer who seeks his daily toil, he moved across the network of railway lines, with the intention of making his way by quiet Girod Street to a certain bench in Lafayette Square, where, according to appointment, he hoped to rejoin a pal known as "Slick," this adventurous pilgrim having preceded him by one day in a cattle-car into which a loose slat had enticed him.—O. Henry, "Whistling Dick's Christmas Stocking"

13: SENTENCE STYLE

WRITING EFFECTIVE SENTENCES

The ability to write grammatically acceptable sentences is not the only, nor the central, goal of college writing courses. Competent use of standard English is a prerequisite, not a guarantee, of good writing. Once you achieve adequate control of basic patterns and relationships, you can concentrate on what makes one grammatically acceptable sentence better than another.

A paper may be tiring to read even if it contains no obvious deviations from standard usage. It may suffer from awkwardness, indirectness, misplaced emphasis, and monotony. To cure these defects, the writer has to be able to recognize grammatical patterns. The defects themselves, however, are not so much a matter of grammar as of **style**. Attention to style makes the difference between writing that is easy to grasp and easy to remember, and writing that is easy on the writer but hard on the reader.

Generalizations about effective style are necessarily tentative and inconclusive. You will have to rely primarily on a kind of sixth sense that comes from careful reading. You will have to become aware of variations in sentence length, of different ways in which clauses combine to form sentences, of the ways in which sentence patterns vary and repeat themselves.

S 1   WORD ORDER

Word order can become monotonous when repeated in sentence after sentence without change; it can become awkward when changed without good reason.

S 1a Varied Word Order. *Variations from normal word order can keep sentences from being tiresomely alike.* English sentences characteristically proceed from the subject to the verb and from there to other possible sentence elements. Though the great majority of your sentences will follow the subject-verb sequence, there will usually be enough variety in the remaining sentence elements to prevent tiresome repetition. Monotony is most likely to result when a number of sentences start with the same subject, especially a pronoun like *I* or *he:*

MONOTONOUS: He reversed the direction of the canoe. . . . He stopped paddling. . . . He made the canoe drift close to the bank. . . . He grabbed one of the overhanging branches. . . . He tied a piece of rope around one of the trunks. . . . He picked up his jacket. . . . He leaped ashore.

(1) One way to break up a monotonous sequence is to make a modifier that usually occurs later in the sentence precede the subject:

VARIED: He reversed the direction of the canoe. *After a few seconds* he stopped paddling. *Slowly* he made the canoe drift close to the bank. *When within a yard of the shore,* he grabbed one of the overhanging branches.

VARIED: The Trans World Terminal stems from the work of contemporary architects like Corbusier of France and Nervi of Italy, masters of the curve in concrete. *Like a true eagle,* this building is all curves and muscle, no right angles. *Built of reinforced concrete,* the whole structure swoops and turns and rises.—Ken Macrorie, "Arriving and Departing," *The Reporter*

Like all stylistic effects, the **introductory modifier** can become an annoying mannerism if overused. Used sparingly, it becomes a reliable way of introducing variety into a group of plodding sentences. Sometimes merely shifting a *perhaps,* a *recently,* or a *nowadays* from the middle to the beginning of a sentence has a bracing effect on a tired paragraph.

(2) A less frequent variation from normal word order is **inversion.** The subject-verb sequence is usually reversed only in questions, where all or part of the verb characteristically precedes the subject: "*Are* you ready?" "*Will* he *be* back?" "Why *did* your wife *leave* the car?" Writers aiming at poetic or dramatic effects occasionally make a verb precede its subject even in ordinary declarative sentences:

Slowly *climbs* the summer moon.
Everywhere *was* silence.

S 1b   Emphatic Word Order. *Variations from normal word order can direct attention to the word or phrase occurring in an unusual position.*

(1) Complements are sometimes shifted from their usual position as third element of the basic pattern to a more emphatic initial position. The **introductory complement** is normal in exclamations beginning with *what* or *how:* "*What stories* that man told!" "*What a liar* you are!" "*How true* that is!" In other situations, the introductory complement is effective especially when it takes up something mentioned earlier:

EFFECTIVE: The committee has asked me to resign. *That* I will never do.

EFFECTIVE: Mr. Schlumpf fried two small pieces of fish. *One of these* he fed to his cat. *The other* he ate himself.

EFFECTIVE: We really should not resent being called paupers. *Paupers* we are, and *paupers* we shall remain.

Like other attention-getting devices, the introductory complement sometimes attracts attention to the speaker rather than to what he is saying. Sometimes the construction smacks of old-fashioned oratory:

More patient wife a husband never had.
Gone are the days of my youth.
Such deeds of glory we shall see no more.

(2) A word or phrase placed in an initial position catches the reader's attention as he approaches a sentence. A word or phrase placed at the end is most likely to stay with him as he goes on reading. In sentences with much modifying material, the main point has to stand out clearly. Often a sentence becomes clearer after you *shift the predicate of the main clause toward the end* and work some of the modifiers into the sentence as interrupters. Such treatment may strengthen a sentence especially if a **final modifier** is a belated qualification or concession:

WEAK: We shall never dismiss a teacher because of the political beliefs of his associates without careful investigation. (*Without careful investigation* is a lame reversal of what starts out as a strong statement in support of teachers with controversial associations.)

IMPROVED: We shall never, *without careful investigation,* dismiss a teacher because of the political beliefs of his associates.

WEAK: Richard Wagner became one of the most successful composers of all time in spite of the jeers of his contemporaries. (This version may make your readers remember the jeers rather than the man's success.)

IMPROVED: Richard Wagner, *though jeered at by his contemporaries,* became one of the most successful composers of all time.

NOTE: Sentences that make the ending of the sentence coincide with the ending of the main clause are known as **periodic** sentences. Sentences that complete the main statement first and then add various secondary elements are known as **loose** sentences:

PERIODIC: Having lost the position he had held for twenty-five years, *Harry became unbearably depressed.*

LOOSE: *Harry became unbearably depressed* after he lost the position he had held for twenty-five years.

Long periodic sentences often seem formal and deliberate; they look as though they were carefully planned. Long loose sentences often seem natural and relaxed; they look as if they just grew:

LOOSE: Bird-watchers were once figures of fun and they are still good for a laugh in *New Yorker* cartoons but they are so numerous and often so highly placed that they might protest against "offensive stereotypes" as effectively as the other large minorities—racial, national, and religious—so vociferously do.—Joseph Wood Krutch, "If You Don't Mind My Saying So . . .," *The American Scholar*

S 1c   Awkward Word Order. *Unintentional variations from normal word order may result in awkward sentences.* Many students compose their sentences a phrase at a time. The result often sounds awkward and synthetic:

AWKWARD: The committee was to meet him *in the morning* at the station.
IMPROVED: The committee was to meet him at the station *in the morning.*

Here awkwardness resulted from a violation of the general tendency in English sentences to make place modifiers precede time modifiers. Usually, however, the reasons for awkward word order are difficult to schematize. You will often have to rely on the kind of sentence sense that a competent writer develops through careful listening and reading.

S 2 AWKWARD CONSTRUCTION

A special problem in student writing is the overuse of constructions that change the relationships existing within the normal subject-verb-complement pattern.

S 2a Awkward Passive. Students often make their writing awkward and indirect by overusing the **passive**, which looks at an action from the point of view not of the actor or agent but of the target or recipient.

(1) *The passive can serve to pull an object into an emphatic initial position.* Compare the changes in emphasis in the following sentences:

ACTIVE: The general gave many an actress a sports car.
PASSIVE: *Many an actress* was given a sports car by the general.
PASSIVE: *Many a sports car* was given to actresses by the general.

As a result, the passive is often the most appropriate construction when the *recipient or target of an action seems more important than the performer:*

> *The unpretentious monarchs* of Scandinavia and the Low Countries are respectfully accepted by their sober subjects.—Kingsley Martin, "Strange Interlude," *Atlantic*

When no special emphasis is intended, the passive is most appropriate when the *originator or the performer of an action is unimportant, irrelevant,* or *hard to identify:*

> Some of John's brain cells *were damaged* when he was a small child. In World War II, millions of people *were driven* from their homes.

(2) *Reversing the actor-action-target perspective when the actor is important may create an upside-down effect.* The reader is used to the who-does-what sequence; he can follow an account easily if he focuses first on the persons or forces at work and then on the work they do. Unnecessary use of the passive can make it hard for the reader to visualize actions or events. It often makes necessary a kind of mental translation:

AWKWARD: Preparations *are being made* by the freshman class for a picnic at Wallflower Lake.
IMPROVED: The freshman class *is planning* a picnic at Wallflower Lake.

(3) *Since it shifts attention away from the agent or performer, the passive tends to be indirect.* The reader may find it hard to determine the person responsible for a statement or an idea:

EVASIVE: A plan for popular election of Supreme Court justices *is* now *being advanced.*

Advanced by whom? The passive spreads a protective cloak of anonymity around the authors of the proposal. Students sometimes use the chopped-off passive from false modesty. "Here *are presented* some of the underlying fundamentals of football" usually means "I am going to explain football."

S 2b   Impersonal Constructions. The impersonal *one,* the *it* without antecedent, and *there-is* or *there-are* constructions are most appropriate when the identity of persons or forces initiating an action is of secondary importance. We naturally say "it rains" or "it snows" when we are interested in the process and its results rather than in its causes.

(1) *Impersonal constructions are annoying when they unnecessarily obscure the identity of the forces at work.* The **impersonal one,** for instance, is often a tiresome substitute for fuller identification of the persons concerned, especially if their identity is indirectly revealed by modifiers:

TIRESOME: *When teaching, one* should be patient.
IMPROVED: *Teachers* should be patient.

TIRESOME: *As a father, one* should not spoil his children.
IMPROVED: *Fathers* should not spoil their children.

TIRESOME: *If one is a citizen of a democracy, he* should exercise his voting rights.
IMPROVED: *A citizen of a democracy* should vote.

(2) *In "it-is" and "there-is" sentences, the first two words are mere structural props, which can make the sentence sound lame and indecisive.* Sometimes the subject of a sentence receives needed emphasis if it is introduced by *it is* or *there is* and has its predicate changed into a modifying clause:

EMPHATIC: It is *his competence* that we question—not his honesty.

However, more often the rearrangement of sentence elements made necessary by *it is* or *there is* causes awkwardness:

AWKWARD: In 1958, *there was* a strike participated in by five thousand union members.
IMPROVED: In 1958, five thousand union members went on strike.

S 2c   Excessive Use of Nouns. *A characteristic feature of much contemporary jargon is overuse of nouns.*

(1) If *actions, events, and activities frequently appear as nouns* rather than verbs, writing becomes static and opaque:

STATIC: *Violent argument* frequently took place.
IMPROVED: We often *argued violently.*

STATIC: A certain *element of confusion* was present.
IMPROVED: He *confused* me.

STATIC: A *criticism* which is prevalent against modern poetry is that its *appeal* is to the super-sophisticated.
IMPROVED: Many critics *charge* that modern poetry *appeals* only to the super-sophisticated.

STATIC: The *solution* to the problem was the result of a careful *examination* of available records.
IMPROVED: We *solved* the problem by carefully *examining* available records.

Remember that an arguing couple, a confusing speaker, or an exasperated critic is easier to visualize than argument, confusion, or criticism in the abstract.

(2) Much bureaucratic writing owes its lumpy quality to its frequent use of *nouns as modifiers preceding another noun.* Often an adjective or a prepositional phrase would make for more natural or more fluent English:

AWKWARD: The report cards record the child's *school* and *activities* achievement.
IMPROVED: The report cards record the child's *academic* and *social* performance.

AWKWARD: At Kilby College the *student-teacher* relationship was exceptionally cordial.

IMPROVED: At Kilby College the relationship *between students and teachers* was exceptionally cordial.

S 3   SENTENCE BUILDING

Word order and grammatical perspective have a bearing on the effectiveness even of simple sentences consisting of only one clause. Other problems of style become important when several clauses combine to form more complicated sentences.

S 3a   Sentence Length. *A skillful writer maintains at least some variety in the length of his sentences.*

(1) Excessive use of *short, isolated clauses* can make your writing sound immature. The more you develop your capacity for sustained thinking, the more you will get away from clauses like the following:

CHOPPY: Many teachers can give students information. Very few can inspire students to learn. Information is of little use to the student. Soon he will leave college. Then he will forget what he has memorized. He must be inspired to learn on his own.

IMPROVED: Many teachers can give students information, but few can inspire them to learn. When a student leaves college, the information he has memorized will be of little use and will soon be forgotten. What he needs most is the ability to learn on his own.

(2) Sentence length in itself does not guarantee maturity of thought. If a steady succession of short sentences can seem breathless and childish, a steady succession of long sentences can seem rambling and undisciplined. A complex, elaborate sentence is often appropriate for detailed explanation or argument. A short, incisive sentence is often appropriate for a *summary of key ideas:*

ELABORATE: Though the tobacco industry has been understandably reluctant to admit it, all the evidence now available points to the conclusion that smoking may be a major threat to the health of our people.

INCISIVE: Smoking is a threat to health.

Your writing will gain in clarity and emphasis if you occasionally make your reader stop short at a *concise, memorable statement of an important point.* Notice the emphatic short sentences in the following passages:

With the great growth in leisure-time activities, millions of Americans are turning to water sports: fishing, swimming, water skiing, and skin diving. *Clean water exhilarates and relaxes.*—Vance Packard, "America the Beautiful—and Its Desecraters," *Atlantic*

Bennett was always facing the wonder of the actualities of living. It was wonderful to him that we live as we do, that time will pass and change us, that we will die and perhaps die painfully, that life is what it is. *He never decorates or embroiders. He is wholly materialistic. Common sense is the salt of his plate.* We are never swept away, but we are curiously won over, and we, too, are filled with wonder at the slow unspinning of life.—John Van Druten, "My Debt to Arnold Bennett," *Saturday Review*

A short sentence can be especially effective if it sets off an important conclusion or a *key observation at the end of a passage composed of longer sentences:*

They have a constitutional right, of course, to tell us what we must do to be saved; as they have always done. Twenty years ago they were telling us the direct opposite of what they tell us now; but they were just as sure then as now that they had the sole and sufficient key to salvation, and that those who did not accept it were forever damned. *One becomes bored.*—Elmer Davis, "History in Doublethink, *Saturday Review*

S 3b   Effective Coordination. Coordination and subordination, the two most characteristic methods of working individual clauses into more complicated sentences, differ in effect. *Coordination is most appropriate when related ideas are about equally important.* In sentences like the following, both clauses are about equally relevant to the general trend of the report, narrative, or argument:

We tried to locate the files, *but* we were unsuccessful.

We shall have to build several new classrooms, *for* we expect a large increase in the school-age population.

Our press is essentially provincial in this country, *and* except for a few syndicated columnists the reputation of our newspapermen is mainly local.

Excessive use of coordination suggests a failure to examine the relative importance of ideas. Overuse of *and*, for instance, results from the indiscriminate tacking on of one unevaluated idea to the other. *And* merely adds without indicating any specific relationship; it does not prepare the reader for what is coming:

RAMBLING: A member of the Reserve has to participate in weekly drills, *and* it may be called up in emergencies, which came as an unpleasant surprise to me during the Korean war, *and* so you would do better to stay away from it.

If you are in doubt about the appropriateness of a coordinating connective like *and* or *but*, test the sentence by inserting a parenthetical "equally important":

EFFECTIVE: Each member of the group received a monthly living allowance, *and* (equally important) his four-year college course was paid for in full by the Navy.

EFFECTIVE: Under one of the plans, a reservist spends only six months on active duty, *but* (equally important) he remains in the Ready Reserve for seven and one-half years.

S 3c Effective Subordination. *Subordination is most appropriate when details, reasons, or qualifications accompany a main point.*

(1) Effective subordination *clarifies relationships in a sentence.* Merely placed next to each other, the following two statements may seem disjointed: "Kroger organized a counterfeiting ring. He had studied printing in Germany." When one is subordinated to the other, the connection between them becomes clearer:

> Kroger, *who had studied printing in Germany*, organized a counterfeiting ring.

Coordinated by *but*, the following *two* statements leave the relationship between fishing and strong wind vague: "We spent the days fishing, but sometimes there was a strong wind." The subordinating connective *unless* leaves no doubt about the relationship:

> We spent the days fishing *unless there was a strong wind*.

(2) Subordinating connectives (*when, while, since, because, if, though*) and relative pronouns (*who, which*, and *that*) can make the material they subordinate seem of secondary importance. "*I was ten* when we moved to Alaska" focuses the reader's attention on you and your age. "When I was ten, *we moved to Alaska*" focuses the reader's attention on Alaska. **Upside-down subordination** results when the wrong item seems to stand out. In the following sentence, an essential point is placed in a deceptively unemphatic position: "*I wouldn't pet that dog*, because it is rabid."

When tucked away in a subordinate part of a sentence, important information may catch the reader unawares and, as a result, have an ironic effect. *Avoid upside-down subordination when no irony is intended:*

UPSIDE-DOWN: The salary was considered good by local standards, *though it was not enough to feed and clothe my family.*

IMPROVED: *Though* considered good by local standards, my salary was not enough to feed and clothe my family.

UPSIDE-DOWN: He had a completely accident-free record up to the last day of his employment, *when* he stepped on a power line and almost lost his life.

IMPROVED: On the last day of his employment, *after* ten years without a single accident, he stepped on a power line and almost lost his life.

Dependent clauses are harder to focus on, to remember, and to quote than independent ones. Your reader may lose the trend of your argument if too many essential points appear in unobtrusive dependent clauses.

S 3d   Effective Modifiers. *Part of the secret of effective prose is skillful use of modifying words and phrases where an inexperienced writer might use coordinated and subordinated clauses.* Observe the tightening of relationships and the gain in continuity in the following pairs:

ROUTINE: She had shiny eyes, an upturned nose, and a lively mouth, and her face never seemed to be at rest.

EFFECTIVE: Her face, *with its ever-shining eyes, its up-turned nose, and mobile mouth,* was never in repose.—John Mason Brown, "Blithe Spirit," *Saturday Review*

ROUTINE: We caught two bass. We hauled them in briskly, as though they were mackerel. After we pulled them over the side of the boat, we stunned them with a blow on the back of the head.

EFFECTIVE: We caught two bass, *hauling them in briskly* as though they were mackerel, *pulling them over the side of the boat* in a businesslike manner without any landing net, and *stunning them with a blow on the back of the head.*—E. B. White, *One Man's Meat*

S 4 SENTENCE OVERLOADS

Sentence overloads result when a writer becomes entangled in cumbersome grammatical machinery. Effective sentences may be long and complicated, as long as the words and structural relationships convey meaning clearly and directly. On the other hand, the grammatical equipment even in relatively short sentences may become so heavy that it interferes with effective communication.

S 4a   Deadwood. *Often a sentence proceeds more smoothly after it has been pruned of deadwood.* Avoid unnecessary *there are*'s and *who were*'s:

AWKWARD: *There are* many farmers in the area *who* are planning to attend the meeting *which is* scheduled for next Friday.

IMPROVED: Many farmers in the area are planning to attend the meeting scheduled for next Friday.

Other sentences can be cleared of deadwood by effective use of pronouns:

AWKWARD: A child of pre-school age often shows a desire to read, but *the child's* parents often ignore this *desire.*

IMPROVED: Often a child of pre-school age shows a desire to read—*which his* parents ignore.

Some connectives, prepositions, and pronouns are unnecessary or unnecessarily heavy:

AWKWARD: I wrote little, *because of the fact that* my childhood had been *an* uneventful *one.*

IMPROVED: I wrote little, because my childhood had been uneventful.

S 4b   Excessive Subordination. *Excessive subordination causes various types of overburdened sentences.*

(1) One common type dovetails several dependent clauses into each other, thus making a subordinating connective follow another subordinating connective or a relative pronoun. The resulting ***that-if, if-because, which-when* constructions** need not be awkward, but they almost always are when used by inexperienced writers:

AWKWARD: I think *that if* there were less emphasis on conformity in high school, college students would be better prepared for independent thinking.

IMPROVED: In my opinion, college students would be better prepared for independent thinking *if* there were less emphasis on conformity in high school.

AWKWARD: I am against football scholarships *because if* football players are given preferential treatment, who will want to participate in other college sports?

IMPROVED: I am against football scholarships. *If* football players are given preferential treatment, who will want to participate in other college sports?

(2) Another type of excessive subordination results in **"house-that-Jack-built" sentences**. Several dependent clauses of the same type follow each other, making the sentence trail off into a confusing succession of modifiers:

AWKWARD: When I was in Mexico City, I visited Jean, *who* was living with a Mexican girl *who* posed for the local artists, *who* are usually too poor to pay their rent, let alone the model's fee.

IMPROVED: When I was in Mexico City, I visited Jean. She was living with a Mexican girl *who* posed for the local artists but seldom received any money for her work. Most Mexican artists are too poor to pay their rent, let alone the model's fee.

AWKWARD: We had to rely on home-brewed beverages *because* the well had run dry *because* it was a very hot summer.

IMPROVED: We had to rely on home-brewed beverages *because* it was a very hot summer and the well had run dry.

Sometimes too many dependent clauses of the same type delay the main clause:

AWKWARD: *When* a child is constantly watched *when* he is born and *while* he is a baby, the reason is that his mother wants to see whether he is developing as her books say he should.

IMPROVED: Some mothers constantly watch young children to see whether they are developing as the books say they should.

(3) Unskillful subordination sometimes causes sentences with a teeter-totter effect. Such **seesaw sentences** start with a dependent clause, proceed to the main clause, and then add a second dependent clause that in an unexpected or confusing way qualifies the meaning of the first one:

CONFUSING:	*If you are a good boy,* I'll buy you an ice-cream cone *if I can spare the money.*
CLEARER:	*If you are a good boy,* I might buy you an ice-cream cone. *However,* I'm not sure I can spare the money.
CONFUSING:	*Because many teen-agers marry hastily,* their marriages end in divorce, *because they are too immature to face adult responsibilities.*
CLEARER:	Many teen-agers are too immature to face adult responsibilities. They marry hastily, and often their marriages end in divorce.

S 4c   Awkward Modifiers. *Awkwardness results when disproportionately heavy modifiers break up the pattern of a clause.* Lengthy appositives, complicated verbal phrases, or clumsy dependent clauses sometimes separate elements that belong together:

AWKWARD:	The pilot told his friends that he had flown Clinton Morris, *a resident of New York City sought by the government for income tax evasion,* out of the United States.
AWKWARD:	The club treasurer, *being* the son of a father constantly *stressing* the importance *of maintaining* a proper sense of the value of money, refused to pay our expenses.
AWKWARD:	In 1943, Independence Hall, *which had been the first building built on the campus and which had housed the administration of the college for many decades,* was torn down.

In such sentences, the exact line between just enough and too much is hard to draw. Successful authors sometimes use sentences that would trip up a writer with less sure a touch:

> The boys in his books got ahead by outwitting thieves and sharpers—yet he himself, a mild and generous little man who gave freely of his earnings to newsboys and bootblacks on the New York streets (the sort of boys who were his favorite heroes), was an easy mark for impostors.—Frederick Lewis Allen, "Horatio Alger, Jr.," *Saturday Review*

> Finding the course of history littered with the *débris* of exploded philosophies, the historians of the last century, unwilling to be forever duped, turned away (as they fondly hoped) from "interpretation" to the rigorous examination of the factual event, just as it occurred.—Carl L. Becker, "Everyman His Own Historian," *The American Historical Review*

A writer with whom such sentences become a habit is obviously in for trouble. Nevertheless, the proof of an awkward sentence is in the reading. Mere bulk does not in itself make the difference between sentences that proceed smoothly and those that wearily drag themselves from line to line.

S 5   REPETITION

Unintentional, haphazard repetition can make a passage sound clumsy. Deliberate repetition, on the other hand, can emphasize important points and give continuity to a sentence or a paragraph.

S 5a   Awkward Repetition. Unintentional repetition of sounds, syllables, words, or phrases violates the requirements of **euphony.** A passage should sound pleasing, or at least inoffensive, when read aloud. *Carelessly repeated sounds grate on the reader's ears:*

AWKWARD: Congress *strengthened* the laws re*stricting* the right to *strike.*
IMPROVED: Congress bolstered the laws qualifying the right to strike.

AWKWARD: Commercials seldom make for entertaining and relaxing listening.
IMPROVED: Commercials seldom entertain and relax the listener.

AWKWARD: Close examin*ation* of the results of the investig*ation* led to a reorganiz*ation* of the department.
IMPROVED: Close study of the results of the inquiry led to a reorganization of the department.

AWKWARD: We listened to an account *of* the customs *of* the inhabitants *of* the village.
IMPROVED: We listened to an account of the villagers' customs.

Unintentional repetition is especially annoying when the similarity in sound covers up a *shift in meaning or relationship:*

My father lost his savings during the depression because he had *banked* on—better "relied on"—the well-established reputation of our hometown *bank.*

S 5b   Emphatic Repetition. *Intentional repetition makes for clarity and continuity.* A writer may repeat important words and phrases for emphasis:

EMPHATIC: When I returned to State, *I studied* as I have never studied since. *I studied* before classes. *I studied* after classes. *I studied* till English, history, and zoology merged into one blurry mass of incoherent erudition.

EMPHATIC: In my mother's world, *no one ever* shrugged his shoulders; *no one* was *ever* bored and lazy; *no one* was *ever* cynical; *no one ever* laughed.—Alfred Kazin, "The Bitter 30's," *Atlantic*

More often, a writer will make use of parallel structure, *drawing together related elements by repeating characteristic grammatical patterns*. The following passage makes effective use of **parallelism**:

The air *must be* pure *if we are to* breathe; the soil *must be* arable *if we are to* eat; the water *must be* clean *if we are to* drink.

In prose of exposition and argument, repetition and parallel structure are used for some of the following purposes:

(1) When a writer's ideas become complicated, parallelism can do much to help the reader find his way. The following two passages are from a discussion of the relationship between public opinion and democratic government. The first passage shows how parallel structure helps to *line up related ideas in a sentence;* the second, how parallel structure *draws together related ideas in a paragraph:*

When the world wars came, the people of the liberal democracies could not be aroused to the exertions and the sacrifices of the struggle until they *had been frightened by* the opening disasters, *had been incited to* passionate hatred, and *had become intoxicated with* unlimited hope.

The people wanted to be told that when this particular enemy had been forced to unconditional surrender, they would re-enter the golden age. *This* unique *war would end* all wars. *This* last *war would make* the world safe for democracy. *This crusade would make* the whole world a democracy.—Walter Lippmann, *The Public Philosophy*

(2) Often, parallel structure helps to *line up dissimilar ideas for comparison or contrast:*

His remarks provoked much comment, *self-righteous from his enemies, apologetic from his friends.*

Whereas *it is desirable that* the old *should treat with respect* the wishes of the young, *it is not desirable that* the young *should treat with respect* the wishes of the old.

> The European democracies *chose to rely on* unarmed appease-
> ment, and the American democracy *chose to rely on* unarmed isola-
> tion.

(3) A writer may state his central point first and then use grammatically parallel patterns while he keeps pounding away at it. By
reversing the process, a writer can *make a series of parallel sentences
build up to a* **climax**. Notice how the author of the following passage
starts with fairly innocuous generalities and leads up to a specific point
dear to his heart:

> The future *is not for* little men with little minds. It *is not for*
> men without vision who fear progress. It *is not for* timid men who
> early were frightened by the story of 'Frankenstein. And it *is not for*
> those arch reactionaries who seek to shatter big enterprise and to
> force American industry back into the puny production patterns of
> its nineteenth-century infancy.

S 5c   Rhythm and Balance. *Frequent use of parallel constructions
           makes for regularity and balance, especially when the
parallel elements are of approximately equal length.* Parallelism produces rhythmical patterns that are more distinctly felt than the highly
variable rhythms of ordinary speech. At the same time, a writer with
an ear for rhythm makes use of the variations in sentence structure that
prevent such regularity from becoming predictable. Notice how in the
following sentence the *which*-clause separating the subject and verb
of the main clause makes for variety, while the prepositional phrases
(*with remarkable vistas . . . , with weeping birches . . .*) make for
balance:

> Seattle, *which sits like Rome on seven hills,* was endowed by na-
> ture *with remarkable vistas* of water and mountains, *with weeping
> birches and monkey trees and dogwoods* big as maples.—Russell
> Lynes, "Seattle Will Never Be the Same," *Harper's*

Notice the role of variety and balance in the following passage:

> India *is a poetic nation, yet it demands* new electrical plants. It
> *is a mystical nation, yet it wants* new roads. It *is* traditionally *a peace-
> ful nation, yet it could,* if misled, *inflame* Asia.—James A. Michener,
> "Portraits for the Future," *Saturday Review*

There is just enough variation to keep the repetition of the pattern from becoming monotonous: "poetic—mystical—traditionally peaceful"; "demands—wants—could, if misled, inflame."

The prose of a writer with a strong sense of rhythm often has a musical quality. Here is a passage whose rhythm is exceptionally stately and elaborate:

> *That* Man is the product of causes which had no prevision of the end they were achieving; *that* his *origin,* his *growth,* his *hopes and fears,* his *loves and* his *beliefs,* are but the outcome of accidental collocations of atoms; *that* no *fire,* no *heroism,* no *intensity of thought and feeling,* can preserve an individual life beyond the grave; *that* all *the labours* of the ages, all *the devotion,* all *the inspiration,* all *the noonday brightness* of human genius, are destined to extinction in the vast death of the solar system, and *that* the whole temple of Man's achievement must inevitably be buried beneath the débris of a universe in ruins—all these things, if *not quite beyond dispute,* are *yet so nearly certain,* that no philosophy which rejects them can hope to stand. *Only within the scaffolding of* these truths, *only on the firm foundation of* unyielding despair, can the soul's habitation henceforth be safely built.—Bertrand Russell, *Mysticism and Logic*

The long series of noun clauses making up most of the first sentence, and the multiple subjects in most of them, are the most obvious instances of parallelism. Toward the end of the passage there are several pairs of neatly balanced phrases (*if not quite beyond dispute —yet so nearly certain; only within the scaffolding of these truths— only on the firm foundation of unyielding despair*). As writing that employs parallelism often does, the passage illustrates other features that can complicate and enrich language. It uses words and phrases with a poetic tinge, whether merely unusual (*prevision, collocation, habitation*) or metaphorical (*noonday brightness of human genius, vast death of the solar system, temple of Man's achievement*). Both in structure and in vocabulary, its sentences represent the opposite extreme from the "I-did-so-and-so,-and-then-I-did-such-and-such" of the first-grader.

Like other stylistic devices, patterns that make for euphony and balance are most effective when the reader responds to them without becoming consciously aware of them. The grand style of the passage just quoted seems a natural reflection of the grandeur of its subject. Its solemn rhythms seem appropriate to the writer's somber view of man's origin and destiny. When applied to less solemn subject matter a grand style can easily seem artificial. Today, workaday expository prose avoids elaborate parallelism and obtrusive rhythm.

EXERCISES

A. Which of the following sentences suffer from obvious stylistic defects? If your instructor desires, rewrite weak sentences to make them clearer, more coherent, more direct, or more emphatic.

1. My father came from a wealthy family, and my mother came from a very poor home, and it was strange that she held the purse strings in the family.   2. The magazine that is chosen by the reader is one that contains articles that the reader enjoys.   3. The contribution of the alumni to the growth of the college will be in proportion to their information about its educational situation.   4. The natural environment of the college, atop beautiful rolling hills, is the kind that a benevolent Providence must have created to induce men to quiet reflection.   5. A child's first impressions of people and places shape the course of his future life, frequently.   6. One incident which I remember vividly is the time when all three of us children had committed the same offense but my younger sister, who was very sensitive to disapproval, criticism, and pain suffered by others, was spared a spanking because after watching my brother and me being punished besides being scolded first was crying so hard and had learned her lesson so well that it wasn't necessary.   7. Knowing the right answers is sometimes less important than asking the right questions.   8. As we left the city, we approached a range of hills which seemed like giant waves which were about to break.   9. Having brothers and sisters to argue with and to adjust to was a useful experience because it helped me understand other people, because I don't always meet people sharing all my opinions.   10. John Milton was the first English writer who clearly and convincingly stated the idea that incompatibility is grounds for divorce, if I am not mistaken.   11. His grandfather had left Haiti because of the constant threat of revolution, the abnormally high disease rate, and the mosquitoes.   12. If a student wants a gay social life and a sense of belonging, he should try to join a Greek organization if he feels confident that he will be accepted.   13. There are many ways in which a student who is interested in meeting a foreign student may come to know one.   14. Is the child who after he has spent the afternoon at the movies spends the evening watching television and goes to bed late at night (this is the daily routine of many children I know) leading a healthier life than the boy who would climb up into a tree to read *Robinson Crusoe?*   15. Warren believed in applauding politely to reward effort, generously to reward competence, and frenetically to reward genius.

(ex.)

B. Revise the following sentences to eliminate excessive or awkward use of nouns.

1. A conscientious teacher's satisfaction is incomplete unless he reaches a full realization of his goals. 2. The public schools must serve personal and society needs as they evolve. 3. My high school teachers never analyzed my essays from the structural and content point of view. 4. A plan for safe driving is of no use if the cooperation of the individual driver is not present. 5. The accumulation of pressures to conform is so great that the student is in constant awareness of their presence. 6. The new dean will need a few days to acquaint himself with the school's administration procedures. 7. The conclusion is inevitable that there has been a considerable impairment of our country's military strength. 8. There were repeated interruptions of the deliberations of the committee.

C. Write three sentences showing normal word order. Then rewrite each sentence showing several possible variations in emphasis or perspective.

EXAMPLE: An old man taught the boy chess on a hot afternoon.

(introd. modifier)	*On a hot afternoon,* an old man taught the boy chess.
(introd. complement)	*Chess* an old man taught the boy on a hot afternoon.
(*there-is*)	*There was* an old man *teaching* the boy chess on a hot afternoon.
(first passive)	*The boy was taught* chess by an old man on a hot afternoon.
(second passive)	*Chess was taught* to the boy by an old man on a hot afternoon.

D. Write three pairs of related clauses. Then combine each pair in different ways, illustrating different possibilities of coordination and subordination.

EXAMPLE: The spring rains were heavy. The weeds grew at a furious rate.

The spring rains were heavy, *and* the weeds grew at a furious rate.

The weeds grew at a furious rate, *for* the spring rains were heavy.

Because the spring rains were heavy, the weeds grew at a furious rate.

The springs rains being heavy, the weeds grew at a furious rate.

The weeds, *with the spring rains heavy,* grew at a furious rate.

E. Examine the following paragraphs for sentence style. Point out weaknesses or strengths. Suggest improvements where necessary.

1. The monkey family is large. It includes monkeys, baboons, lemurs, and apes. The animals in the monkey family are closely related to man. They are imitative. They can be trained to perform simple tasks. However, their intelligence is low.

2. We go to our libraries in order to read and take advantage of the experiences of others. I think we all realize that not every written word in a library is entirely true. Many different authors have here written what they think, what they have experienced, what they believe is true, and sometimes what they wish were true. Some are wrong, a few are right, and many are neither entirely wrong nor entirely right.

3. Many high school teachers follow a textbook word for word, and they go over each page until everyone understands it. In college, many teachers just tell the student to read the textbook, and then they start giving lectures on the material covered in the text, but they don't follow it word for word.

4. A good example of a topic drawn from personal experience is a bus accident I once had. I wrote a paper about this experience of mine. I remembered the events which took place during the accident. I could describe them well. After all, I had experienced them. It was a shocking experience. I will never forget it. The facts stand out in my memory because it was so shocking.

5. In high school, the student finds that his teachers act like parents toward him—always nagging. One moment it's "You're growing up now; you should know better." The next moment it's "I'm sorry, but you know perfectly well you aren't old enough." What is the teenager supposed to do?

F. Examine the following passages for sentence style. Comment on such features as length, complexity, variety, emphasis, and parallelism. Point out any special or unusual effects.

1. This is not a Utopian tract. Some of those who complain about the quality of our national life seem to be dreaming of a world in which everyone without exception has talent, taste, judgment and an unswerving allegiance to excellence. Such dreams are pleasant but unprofitable. The problem is to achieve some measure of excellence *in this society,* with all its beloved and exasperating clutter, with all its exciting and debilitating confusion of standards, with all the stubborn problems that won't be solved and the equally stubborn ones that might be.—John W. Gardner, *Excellence*

(ex.)

2. If liberal education is not concerned with vocational skills, it is profoundly concerned with other skills and abilities. There are many things which the student, as a human being, should be able to do. He should be able to care for his body, his physical welfare. He should be able to speak, to read, to write, on a plane suited to his college years and later life. He should know how to think: how to think in the concrete terms of science, how to think in the abstract manner of mathematics and philosophy, and how to think (and feel and will) in the humanistic realm of value-judgments. He should be able to relate his growing abilities and knowledge in the gradual development of a philosophy of life to which he is willing provisionally to commit himself. He should be able to relate his developing philosophy to active experience in living, to complete the revolving circle of thought and action. Through the discipline of his entire nature he will come into ever fuller possession of himself as a human being and as a particular person.—Norman Foerster, *The Humanities and the Common Man*

3. If canned baby-food were free no doubt some people would eat nothing but canned baby-food day in and day out. But not many. Not for long. The most miserly person, after working his way through a certain number of cans, would break down and buy something more tempting to the adult palate. No doubt baby-food is nourishing, aseptic, reinforced with abundant vitamins; no doubt it would sustain life indefinitely if there were nothing else obtainable, but you don't want it and I don't. You don't want the first bland bite probably, to say nothing of long, increasingly boring years on the stuff.

Yet the case for baby-food, if it were free, would be the same as the case for the television and radio fare provided for humans throughout the United States. That fare is made up out of the cheapest available nutrients, put together with the intent of offending no taste, of remaining so innocent and innocuous that no sect, no religion, no race, no school of thought, no philosophy, no frame of mind, no possible audience can find it objectionable. This severely limits the flavors and contents of the cans. The networks have been searching for years for the lowest common denominator. Sometimes they think they have found it. Sometimes I think they have found it. However, writers, actors, directors and producers are human and unpredictable. They sometimes give a little meaning to a program. When this happens there is a rush of feet and a strangled cry.—Maxwell Anderson, "It Comes with the Set," *New York Herald Tribune*

4. Twenty-five years ago, when Calvin Coolidge and George V reigned over the English-speaking peoples, when H. L. Mencken was tearing the booboisie to shreds, when Lytton Strachey was demolishing one reputation after another, and when the monthly discovery of

a radical new masterpiece by each of several book clubs still carried conviction, one department of literature was being thoroughly purged, revolutionized, and set in its place. This was biography. It had been attacked by various columns of shock-troopers. Groups who had read "Eminent Victorians" with savage glee; groups who had gone like a cyclone through Freud (or a manual on Freud); groups intoxicated with the satiric mockery of Shaw and the mordant irony of Henry Adams; groups of second-sight psychologists who at a moment's notice could describe the ideas which surged through Cromwell's mind the night before Naseby, and report the precise words of an unrecorded conversation of Emerson and Thoreau—all these were lustily creating a "new biography."—Allan Nevins, "How Shall One Write of a Man's Life?" *New York Times Book Review*

5. For the production of a work of art is not the result of a miracle. It requires preparation. The soil, be it ever so rich, must be fed. By taking thought, by deliberate effort, the artist must enlarge, deepen and diversify his personality. Then the soil must lie fallow. Like the bride of Christ, the artist waits for the illumination that shall bring forth a new spiritual life. He goes about his ordinary avocations with patience; the subconscious does its mysterious business; and then, suddenly springing, you might think from nowhere, the idea is produced. But like the corn that was sown on stony ground it may easily wither away; it must be tended with anxious care. All the power of the artist's mind must be set to work on it, all his technical skill, all his experience, and whatever he has in him of character and individuality, so that with infinite pains he may present it with the completeness that is fitting to it.—W. Somerset Maugham, *The Summing Up*

CHAPTER SEVEN

THE MECHANICS OF WRITING

14: MECHANICS AND SPELLING

PREPARING THE MANUSCRIPT

M 1 MANUSCRIPT MECHANICS

Whenever you hand in a theme or a report, you should remember that the outward appearance of your manuscript is the first thing to strike your reader. A good first impression is likely to put him in a tolerant and receptive mood. A bad first impression is likely to linger even after he discovers compensating virtues in the text.

M 1a Penmanship and Typing. *All copy, whether handwritten or typed, should be neat and legible.* To produce legible handwritten copy, you will need composition paper of standard size, preferably ruled in *wide lines,* and a reliable pen. You may find that you don't write fast enough, especially when you are asked to write in class. Don't try to develop speed by substituting a smudge for letters like *a, e,* or *i;* by running together combinations like *mm* or *mn;* or by substituting a vague scrawl for endings like *ing* and *tion.* Instead, practice speed writing while at the same time forcing yourself to make every *a* and *e* as distinct as your grade school penmanship book required. Dot all your *i's* and cross all your *t's.* Distinguish clearly between capitals and lower-case letters.

Try to prune your writing of all flourishes that interfere with the immediate perception of the standard letters and symbols. Avoid excessive slanting or excessive crowding. Unconventional handwriting is much more likely to annoy and distract than it is to impress the reader.

To prepare typewritten copy, you will need unlined paper of standard size. Onion-skin paper or semi-transparent sheets are for carbon copies; use solid, nontransparent paper of good quality for the copy you turn in. Change your typewriter ribbon at reasonable intervals.

Double-space all material except block quotations and footnotes. Leave two spaces after a period or other end punctuation; use two hyphens—with no space on either side—to make a dash. Proofread all typewritten copy carefully for typographical errors and for errors in transcription.

M 1b **Corrections.** On papers written outside class all major revisions are of course made on the rough draft. *Last-minute corrections are permissible on the final copy, provided they are few in number, look neat, and conform to standard practice:*

(1) Draw a line through words and phrases that you want to omit; *do not use parentheses or square brackets for this purpose.*

(2) To correct a word, draw a line through it and insert the corrected word in the space immediately above; avoid crossing out or inserting individual letters.

(3) To add a missing word, insert a caret ($\wedge$) and write the word immediately above.

M 1c **Titles of Themes.** *Titles of themes follow the general rules for the capitalization of words in titles of publications* (see SP 7b). Do *not* underline or put in quotation marks the title that you assign to one of your own themes. Use a question mark or exclamation mark after it where appropriate, but do *not* use a period even if your title is a complete sentence:

> Chivalry Is Dead
> Is Chivalry Dead?
> Chivalry Is Dead!

M 1d **Spacing and Syllabication.** *Observe conventional spacing and syllabication.* Whether your papers are handwritten or typed, leave adequate margins. An inch and a half on the left and at the top, and an inch on the right and at the bottom are about standard. Indent the first lines of paragraphs, about an inch in longhand or five spaces in typed copy. To make a last-minute change in the paragraphing of a paper, insert the symbol ¶ to indicate an additional paragraph break. Insert *no* ¶ in the margin to indicate that an existing paragraph break should be ignored.

On the whole, a somewhat uneven right margin is preferable to the practice of dividing words at the end of every second or third line. Dictionaries generally use centered dots to indicate where a word may conventionally be divided (*com·pli·ment*). A few generally observed practices are worth remembering:

(1) The setting off of single letters saves little or no space and tends to confuse the reader. Do not divide words like *about, alone,* and *enough* or like *many* and *via.* Similarly, do not set off the ending *ed* in words like *complained* or *renewed.*

(2) Hyphenated words become confusing when divided at any other point than at the original hyphen. Do not break up the *American* in "un-American" or the *sister* in "sister-in-law."

(3) Do not divide the last word on a page.

M 1e Italics. Italics (or slanted type) are indicated in the handwritten or typed manuscript by underlining.

(1) Italics identify *technical terms* and *words borrowed from foreign languages.* (See P 8e.)

(2) Italics serve to emphasize or *call special attention to part of a sentence:*

> The judge told me to apologize *in person* to everyone who had sat down in the freshly painted pews.

> The company is not liable for accidents caused by the negligence of employees or *by mechanical defects.*

Like other means of procuring emphasis, such italics lose their value if overused.

(3) Italics serve to set off the *title of a publication* from the text in which it is cited. Italicize titles of periodicals and of works published as separate units. Use **quotation marks** to set off titles of articles, chapters, or poems that are merely a part of a complete publication:

> Kipling's "Recessional" can be found in *A Treasury of Verse.*

> For many years, Chicago has had one of the best book-review sections in the country in the *Tribune's* "Sunday Magazine of Books."

USING ABBREVIATIONS AND NUMERALS

M 2 ABBREVIATIONS

Abbreviations save much time and space. Here as in other matters, however, formal written English discourages excessive short cuts. The short cuts are obviously excessive in a sentence like the following: "Chas. told his prof. that during the past 3 yrs. he had been working for the govt. in L.A." To avoid the impression of excessive hurry, observe the conventions governing the use of abbreviations and numerals in ordinary expository prose.

M 2a   **Acceptable Abbreviations.** *Some abbreviations are generally appropriate in expository writing:*

(1) Before or after names, the titles *Mr., Mrs., Dr., St.* (*Saint*); the abbreviations *Jr.* and *Sr.;* degrees like *M.D.* and *Ph.D.* (Mr. John J. Smith, Jr.; Dr. Alfred Joyce or Alfred Joyce, M.D.).

(2) Before or after numerals, the abbreviations No., A.D. and B.C., A.M. and P.M.; and the symbol $ (in 1066 B.C.; at 5:30 A.M.; $275).

(3) Initials standing for the names of agencies, organizations, business firms, technical processes, chemical compounds, and the like, when the full name is awkward or unfamiliar: *AFL-CIO, FBI, PTA, TVA, UNESCO, DDT, FM radio.*

(4) Some common Latin abbreviations: *e.g.* (for example), *etc.* (and so on), *i.e.* (that is), *viz.* (namely). However, the modern tendency is to prefer the corresponding English expressions.

M 2b   **Restricted Abbreviations.** *Some abbreviations are appropriate in addresses, newspaper reports, technical reports, and other special contexts.* Most of these have to be written in full in ordinary expository prose:

(1) With a few exceptions, names of countries, states, streets, and the like, are spelled out in ordinary writing: *United States; Schenectady, New York; Union Street* (Exceptions: *USSR; Washington, D.C.*).

(2) The ampersand ("&") and abbreviations like *Inc.* and *Bros.* occur in ordinary writing only in references to organizations that employ those abbreviations in their official titles: *Smith & Company, Inc.*

(3) In ordinary expository prose, *lb.* (pound), *oz.* (ounce), *ft.* (foot), and *in.* (inch) are usually spelled out. Some units of measurement are more unwieldy and are abbreviated, provided they are used with figures: *45 mph, 1500 rpm.*

Check your dictionary whenever you are not sure of the use of capitals and periods with an abbreviation. Some dictionaries include common abbreviations in the main listing; others list them in a special appendix.

M 3 NUMBERS

In ordinary expository prose, the use of figures is to some extent restricted. They are generally appropriate in references to the date of the month (*May 13*), the year (*1917*), street numbers (*1014 Union Avenue*), and page numbers (*Chapter 7, page 18*). For other uses of numbers, the following conventions are widely observed:

(1) Numbers from one to ten, and round numbers requiring no more than two words, are usually spelled out (*three dollars a seat; five hundred years later; ten thousand copies*).

(2) Figures are used for exact sums, technical measurements, decimals, and percentages, as well as for references to time using A.M. or P.M. (*$7.22; 500,673 inhabitants; 57 per cent; 2:30 P.M.*).

(3) Figures are avoided at the beginning of a sentence: "Fifteen out of 28 replied . . ." or "When questioned, 15 out of 28 replied . . ." Except in special situations like this one, changes from figures to words (and vice versa) in a series of numbers are generally avoided.

(4) When spelled out, compound numbers from 21 to 99 are hyphenated: *twenty-five; one hundred and forty-six.*

EXERCISE

Rewrite the following passage, using abbreviations and numerals in accordance with standard practice:

> Mister Geo. Brown had resided at Eighteen N. Washington St. since Feb. nineteen-hundred and forty-four. Though he weighed only one hundred and twenty-six lbs. and measured little more than 5 ft., he was an ardent devotee of the rugged life. He did his exercises every a. m. and refused to send for the Dr. when he had a cold. 3 yrs. after he moved here from Chicago, Ill., the Boy Scouts of America made him an honorary member, & he soon became known in scout circles for the many $ he contributed to the Boy Scout movement. One Sat. afternoon B. forgot to spell out the amount on a check for one-hundred and twenty-five dollars intended for a bldg. drive and payable to the B. S. of A. The treasurer, Bernard Simpson of Arlington, Va., wrote in 2 additional figures, spelled out the changed amount, and left the U. S. after withdrawing B.'s life savings of twelve-thousand five-hundred and fifty dollars from the local bank. "Ah," said Geo. when he found 2 $ and 36 cts. left in his account, "if I had only spelled out the No.'s and abbrev.!"

REVIEWING SPELLING DIFFICULTIES

English spelling is irregular and confusing. It developed haphazardly and became fixed before a reasonably consistent system had established itself. Many words, like *enough, knight,* or *should,* are spelled the way they were pronounced in fifteenth-century England. Some words, like *chase, journey,* and *question,* reflect in their spelling the pronunciation of various stages of medieval French; others, like *psychology, rhythm,* or *telephone,* the pronunciation and the writing system of Greek as used around 400 B.C.; still others, like *ghost* and *ghastly* or *debt* and *doubt,* the arbitrary innovations of printers, editors, and reformers.

Attempts to simplify English spelling, and to bring it closer to the actual sounds of modern English, have been unsuccessful. It is true that American, as contrasted with British, spelling now generally prefers *labor* to *labour, medieval* to *mediaeval, plow* to *plough, theater* to *theatre,* and *traveled* to *travelled.* In addition, dictionaries now list such alternative forms as *tho* for *though, thru* for *through,* and *catalog* for *catalogue.* Even these innovations, however, raise the eyebrows of many a reader. A writer who goes beyond them to use *nite* for *night* or *publisht* for *published* risks general disapproval.

SP 1 SPELLING HABITS

The average high school graduate spells correctly most of the words he uses. According to recent studies, most of the trouble that college students have with spelling is caused by perhaps fewer than 250 words out of the 5,000 or 10,000 that they are likely to use. The most common troublemakers are everyday words like *believe* or *definite,* which we see in print many times. Since they are familiar, we grasp them at a glance, without focusing on the individual letters and on the way they are put together. When we use such a word in our own writing, two or three different spellings may seem possible. We usually choose the one that looks right. However, it may look right not because we have seen it in this particular word but because we have seen it in another word that is confusingly similar. Thus, we spell the main syllable in *believe* like the main syllable in *receive.* We spell the ending in *definite* like the ending in *ultimate.* To spell such a word correctly, we have to memorize it letter by letter, while at the same time seeing each letter as a part of the whole.

SP 1a   Corrective Drill. Most students find that improvement in their spelling habits is possible—if they persist long enough to see it come about. Merely looking up misspelled words has little long-range effect. The following procedure has a good chance of producing favorable results:

(1) *Find out which words you tend to misspell.* Make a list of all spelling errors pointed out to you in your themes, quizzes, and exams. Supplement your list by working your way through a list of common spelling demons, such as the one printed under SP 4. Copy out those that you have found troublesome in your own writing.

(2) *Put in twenty minutes three times a week over a fairly long period of time.* Unless you work on your spelling regularly, you will make little progress. You cannot unlearn in two or three hours the spelling habits that you developed over many years.

(3) *Work out a definite routine and stick to it.* At each sitting, take up a group of perhaps ten or twenty spelling words. Some people learn primarily by memorizing visual images. If you are a "visualizer," place your spelling words before you in clear, legible handwriting. Try putting them on a set of small note cards that you can carry around with you. Run your eyes over each word until you can see both the individual letters and the whole word at the same time. Circle the letters that cause the most trouble.

You may find that you learn primarily by ear. If so, read each word aloud. Then spell each letter individually: *Receive*—R-E-C-E-I-V-E. You may find that you learn best when you can bring your nerves and muscles into play. If so, try writing each word in large letters. Trace it over several times. Combine or alternate the three methods in the manner that seems to yield the best results. Once the correct form has a chance to make itself at home in your subconscious, recall will be painless and easy. The word will come to you with the ease of a successfully established habit.

(4) *Make use of memory devices like the following:*

> MAC got ACquainted.
> ALL RIGHT means ALL is RIGHT.
> There's an INNING in begINNING.
> Don't beLIEve LIEs.
> There's a CRITIC in CRITICism.
> There's IRON in the envIRONment.

Men who GOVERN are a GOVERNment.
There's a COG in reCOGnition.
There's a VILLA in VILLAin.

SP 1b New Words. You will need an efficient system for dealing with potential troublemakers as you first encounter
them. *Copy out difficult new terms and names that you encounter in
your reading for various courses.* Study and memorize them. If you
are a science major, master words like *enzyme, anesthesia, protein,* or
arteriosclerosis. If you are taking a literature course, focus on the exact
spelling of names like *Oedipus, Xanthippe,* or *Omar Khayyam.* Your
misspelling such a term in a theme or on a test will inevitably reflect
on your knowledge of the subject matter.

SP 2 SPELLING PROBLEMS

Some words can be conveniently grouped together because they
share common characteristics. Others are best studied together because they need to be carefully distinguished from each other.

SP 2a Spelling and Pronunciation. *Some words become spelling
problems because the gap between spelling and pronunciation is unusually wide.*

(1) Frequent causes of confusion are *vowels occurring in unstressed positions.* For instance, *a, e,* and *i* become indistinguishable
in the endings *ate* and *ite, able* and *ible, ance* and *ence, ant* and *ent.*
You can sometimes learn to choose the right ending by associating the
word with a closely related one: *definite* (finish, definition); *separate*
(separation); *ultimate* (ultimatum); *indispensable* (dispensary). For
many other words no such crutches are available. Watch out for the
following:

a: accept*able,* accept*ance,* attend*ance,* attend*ant,* brilli*ant,* perform*ance*

e: consist*ent,* excell*ence,* excell*ent,* exist*ence,* experi*ence,* independ*ent,* persist*ent,* tend*ency*

i: irresist*ible,* plaus*ible,* poss*ible,* suscept*ible*

(2) A number of words are difficult to spell because of *silent or
slurred consonants.* Be sure to insert the silent consonants in "con-
dem*n*," "de*b*t," "dou*b*t," "forei*g*n," "mor*t*gage," and "sovere*i*gn." Some
consonants are silent only in hasty or in nonstandard speech: "can-
di*d*ate," "Feb*r*uary," "gove*r*nment," "lib*r*ary," "quan*t*ity."

sp

(3) In unstressed positions, words like *have, can,* or *will* tend to appear in shortened forms. Do not substitute *of* for *have* in combinations like *could have been, might have come, should have seen.*

SP 2b Variant Forms. *Some words are confusing because they appear in a variety of forms.*

(1) Especially confusing are different spellings in variant forms of the same root word: "til*l*" but "unti*l*," "*four*" and "*four*teen" but "*forty*," "*for*ward" but "*fore*most," "*nine*" and "*nine*ty" but "*nin*th." Watch out for spelling differences in pairs of words representing different grammatical categories:

absor*b*—absor*p*tion, advi*se* (v.)—advi*ce* (n.), conscien*ce*—conscien*tious*, court*eous*—court*esy*, curi*ous*—curi*osity*, dissen*t*—dissen*sion*, gener*ous*—gener*osity*, geni*us*—ingeni*ous*, proc*eed*—proc*edure*, pron*ounce*—pron*uncia*tion, ren*ounce*—ren*unciation*

Notice the *ed* in "He *used* to come" and "He was prejudic*ed*."

(2) Sometimes a confusing change in spelling accompanies a change in the grammatical form of the same word. For instance, you "ch*oo*se" and "l*ea*d" in the present, but you "ch*o*se" and "l*e*d" in the past. Most nouns have distinctive forms for one of a kind (**singular**) and several of a kind (**plural**). These sometimes cause spelling difficulties: one *man* but several *men,* one *woman* but several *women.* Remember these especially:

SINGULAR:	hero	Negro	potato	tomato	wife
PLURAL:	hero*es*	Negro*es*	potato*es*	tomato*es*	wi*ves*
SINGULAR:	freshman	postman	life	veto	calf
PLURAL:	fresh*men*	post*men*	li*ves*	veto*es*	cal*ves*

Your dictionary lists the correct spelling of plural forms that are difficult or unusual. Sometimes it lists two acceptable forms: *buffalos* or *buffaloes, scarfs* or *scarves.*

SP 2c Confusing Words. *Some words need attention because they sound similar but differ in spelling or in meaning.* Here is a partial list of these:

| ACCEPT: | to *acc*ept a bribe; to find something *acc*eptable; to make an *acc*eptance speech |
| EXCEPT: | everyone *exc*ept Judy; to make an *exc*eption; to *exc*ept (exempt, exclude) present company |

ADOPT: to ad*o*pt a proposal (in its present form); the ad*o*ption racket

ADAPT: to ad*a*pt it to our needs (to make it more suitable); an ad*a*ptable worker; an ad*a*ptation from a novel

CAPITAL: unused capit*a*l; modern capit*a*lism; the capit*a*l of France; capit*a*l letters

CAPITOL: the cupola of the Capit*o*l; remodeling the façade of the Capit*o*l

CENSOR: to cens*or* a reporter's dispatch; to object to cens*or*ship

CENSURE: to cens*ure* (blame, condemn) someone for his behavior; a vote of cens*ure*

CITE: *c*ited for bravery; to *c*ite many different authorities; a *c*itation for reckless driving

SITE: the *s*ite of the new high school (where it is *sit*uated or located)

CONSUL: the American c*o*nsul in Berlin; the French c*o*nsulate in New York

COUNCIL: the members of the city coun*ci*l; Coun*ci*lor Brown

COUNSEL: the coun*se*ling staff of the college; camp coun*se*lors

DESERT: he lost his way in the de*s*ert; he de*s*erted his family; he got his just de*s*erts

DESSERT: the dinner did not include a de*ss*ert

EFFECT: to *e*ffect (produce, bring about) a change; immediate *e*ffects; an *e*ffective speech

AFFECT: it *a*ffected (had an influence on) his grade; he spoke with an *a*ffected (artificial) British accent

LOOSE: *loose* and fast; *loose*n your grip

LOSE: win or *lose*; a bad *lose*r

PERSONAL: a person*al* appeal; speak to him person*al*ly

PERSONNEL: a perso*nnel* bureau; hire additional perso*nnel*

PRESENTS: visitors bearing presen*ts*

PRESENCE: your presen*ce* is requested; presen*ce* of mind

PRINCIPAL: his princip*al* (main) argument; the princip*al* of the school

PRINCIPLE: princip*les* (rules, standards) of conduct; the princip*les* of economics

QUIET: be qui*et*; a qui*et* neighborhood

QUITE: qui*te* so; not qui*te*

RIGHT: *right* and wrong; *right* and left; all *right*

RITE: savage *rites* (ceremonies); the *rites* of spring

-WRIGHT: a play*wright;* a wheel*wright* (a man who wrought, or made, wheels and carriages)

sp

THAN: bigger th*a*n life; more trouble th*a*n it is worth
THEN: now and th*e*n; until th*e*n

THERE: here and th*ere;* th*ere* you are; no one was th*ere*
THEIR: they lost th*eir* appetite; mental ills and th*eir* cure

TO: go *to* bed, cut *to* pieces; easy *to* do, hard *to* deny
TOO: *too* good to be true; bring your children, *too*
TWO: *two* and *two* makes four

WHETHER: *whe*ther good or bad
WEATHER: bad *wea*ther; to *wea*ther the storm

SP 3   SPELLING RULES

The purpose of spelling rules is *not* to make English spelling appear more regular than it is but to help you memorize words that follow a common pattern. *Spelling rules provide a key to a group of words that you would otherwise have to study individually.*

SP 3a   *I* **before** *E.* Identical sounds are often spelled differently in different words. For instance, *ie* and *ei* often stand for the same sound. If you sort out the words in question, you get the following:

ie: achieve, believe, chief, grief, niece, piece (of pie), relieve
cei: ceiling, conceited, conceive, perceive, receive, receipt

In the second group of words, the *ei* is regularly preceded by *c.* In other words, it is *i* before *e* except after *c.* About half a dozen words do not fit into this pattern:

ei: either, leisure, neither, seize, weird
cie: financier, species

SP 3b   **Doubled Consonant.** In many words a single final consonant is doubled before an ending, or suffix, that begins with a vowel: *ed, er, est, ing.* Doubling occurs under the following conditions:

(1) *The vowel preceding the final consonant must be a single vowel,* not a double vowel (**diphthong**) indicated in writing by combinations like *oa, ea, ee,* and *ou* or by a silent final *e* (*k*ite, h*o*pe, h*a*te). Note the differences in pronunciation and in spelling in the following pairs:

bar—barred	bare—bared
bat—batted	boat—boating
hop—hopping	hope—hoping
plan—planned	plane—planed
red—redder	read—reading
scrap—scrapped	scrape—scraped
slip—slipped	sleep—sleeping
stop—stopped	stoop—stooped

(2) In words of more than one syllable, the syllable immediately preceding the ending and containing the single vowel *must be the one stressed in pronunciation.* Sometimes a shift in stress will be reflected in a difference in the spelling of different forms of the same word. Compare the following groups:

adMIT, adMITTed, adMITTance	EDit, EDited, EDiting
forGET, forGETTing, forGETTable	BENefit, BENefited, BENefiting
beGIN, beGINNing, beGINNer	HARDen, HARDened, HARDening
overLAP, overLAPPing	deVELop, deVELoped, deVELoping
reGRET, reGRETTed, reGRETTable	proHIBit, proHIBited, proHIBitive
preFER, preFERRed, preFERRing	PREFerence, PREFerable
reFER, reFERRed, reFERRing	REFerence

NOTE: There is doubling after the single vowel *i* in *equip—equipped* (the *u* does not combine with *i* but is part of the consonant *qu*); there is no doubling of the final *x* in *mix—mixed* (*x* is a double consonant).

SP 3c   Y as a Vowel. *Y* is sometimes used as a consonant (*year, youth*), sometimes as a vowel (*my, dry; hurry, study*). As a single final vowel, it changes to *ie* before *s*, to *i* before all other endings except *ing*.

ie: family—families, fly—flies, study—studies, try—tries, quantity—quantities

i: beauty—beautiful, bury—burial, busy—business, copy—copied, dry——drier, lively—livelihood, noisy—noisily

y: burying, copying, studying, trying, worrying

When it follows another vowel, *y* is usually preserved: *delays, joys, played, valleys.* A few common exceptions are *day—daily, gay—gaily, lay—laid, pay—paid, say—said.*

SP 3d Final *E*.

(1) A silent *e* at the end of a word is dropped before an ending that begins with a vowel; it is preserved before an ending that begins with a consonant:

bore	boring	boredom
hate	hating	hateful
like	liking, likable	likely
love	loving, lovable	lovely

The following words do *not* fit into this pattern: *argue—argument, due—duly, dye—dyeing* (as against *die—dying*), *mile—mileage, true —truly, whole—wholly.*

(2) A final *e* may signal the difference in pronunciation between the final consonants in *rag* and *rage* or in *aspic* and *notice.* Such a final *e* is preserved not only before a consonant but also before *a* or *o*:

ge: advantage—advantageous, change—changeable, courage—courageous, outrage—outrageous

ce: notice—noticeable, peace—peaceable

SP 4 WORDS OFTEN MISSPELLED

Studies of the words most frequently misspelled in student writing have resulted in substantial agreement on words most likely to cause spelling difficulties. In addition to words listed in SP 1–3, the following list will repay careful study:

absence	across	already	applying
abundance	actuality	altogether	appreciate
accessible	address	always	approach
accidentally	adequate	amateur	appropriate
acclaim	admit	among	approximately
accommodate	adolescence	amount	area
accompanied	advantageous	analysis	argue
accomplish	advertisement	analyze	arguing
accumulate	afraid	annual	argument
accurately	against	anticipate	arising
accuses	aggravate	anxiety	arrangement
accustom	aggressive	apologize	article
achievement	alleviate	apology	artistically
acknowledgment	allotted	apparatus	ascend
acquaintance	allowed	apparent	assent
acquire	all right	appearance	athlete
acquitted	altar	applies	athletic

attendance
audience
authority
balance
basically
basis
beauty
becoming
before
beginning
belief
believe
beneficial
benefited
boundaries
breath
brilliant
Britain
business
buses
calendar
candidate
career
careless
carrying
category
ceiling
cemetery
challenge
changeable
character
characteristic
chief
choose
chose
clothes
coarse
column
comfortable
comfortably
coming
commission
committed
committee
companies
competition
competitive
completely

comprehension
conceivable
conceive
concentrate
condemn
confident
confidential
conscience
conscientious
conscious
considerably
consistent
continually
continuous
control
controlled
convenience
convenient
coolly
courageous
course
courteous
criticism
criticize
cruelty
curiosity
curriculum
dealt
deceit
deceive
decision
definite
definitely
definition
dependent
describe
description
desirability
desirable
despair
desperate
destruction
devastate
develop
development
device
difference
different

difficult
dilemma
dining
disappear
disappearance
disappoint
disastrous
discipline
disease
disgusted
dissatisfaction
dissatisfied
doesn't
dominant
due
during
ecstasy
efficiency
efficient
eighth
eliminate
embarrass
embarrassment
eminent
emphasize
endeavor
enforce
enough
entertain
environment
equipped
erroneous
especially
etc.
exaggerate
excellent
exceptionally
exercise
exhaust
exhilarate
existence
experience
explanation
extraordinary
extremely
familiar
families
fascinate

finally
financial
financier
foreign
forward
friend
fulfill
fundamentally
further
gaiety
generally
genius
government
governor
grammar
guaranteed
guidance
happily
happiness
height
heroes
heroine
hindrance
hopeful
huge
humorous
hundred
hurriedly
hypocrisy
hypocrite
ignorant
imaginary
imagination
immediately
immensely
incidentally
indefinite
independent
indispensable
inevitable
influence
ingenious
intellectual
intelligence
interest
interpret
interrupt
involve

irrelevant	occasion	possible	separate
irresistible	occasionally	practical	sergeant
itself	occurred	precede	shining
jealous	occurrence	prejudice	significance
knowledge	omit	prepare	similar
laboratory	operate	prevalent	sincerely
laid	opinion	privilege	sophomore
leisure	opponent	probably	speech
likelihood	opportunity	procedure	sponsor
literature	optimism	proceed	strength
livelihood	original	professor	stretch
loneliness	paid	prominent	strictly
losing	parallel	propaganda	subtle
magnificence	paralysis	prophecy	succeed
maintain	paralyze	psychology	successful
maintenance	particularly	pursue	summarize
manageable	passed	quantity	surprise
manufacturer	past	really	temperament
marriage	peace	recommend	tendency
mathematics	peculiar	regard	therefore
meant	perceive	relief	thorough
medieval	perform	relieve	together
merely	performance	religion	tragedy
mileage	permanent	repetition	transferred
miniature	persistent	representative	tries
minute	persuade	resource	undoubtedly
mischievous	pertain	response	unnecessary
muscle	phase	rhythm	useful
mysterious	phenomenon	ridiculous	using
naïve	philosophy	roommate	various
necessarily	physical	safety	vengeance
necessary	piece	satisfactorily	villain
ninety	pleasant	schedule	weird
noticeable	possess	seize	writing
obstacle	possession	sense	

EXERCISES

A. Insert the missing letter in each of the following words: accept-
___nce, attend___nce, brilli___nt, consist___ncy, defin___te, excell___nt, ex-
ist___nce, experi___nce, independ___nt, indispens___ble, occurr___nce, irre-
sist___ble, perform___nce, persist___nt, separ ·___te, tend___ncy.

B. Look up the plural of *cargo, Eskimo, hoof, mosquito, motto, piano,
solo, soprano, wharf, zero.*

(ex.)

C. Select the appropriate word in each of the numbered pairs:

1. After Jean-Pierre *(1)accepted/(2)excepted* our invitation to spend a month in the nation's *(3)capital/(4)Capitol*, he applied to the American *(5)consul/(6)counsel* for a visa. 2. The *(7)presence/(8)presents* of federal troops prevented further *(9)incidence/(10)incidents*. 3. The city's employees presented the members of the city *(11)council/(12) counsel* with a declaration of *(13)rights/(14)rites* and *(15)principals/ (16)principles*. 4. My moral *(17)principals/(18)principles* do not permit a *(19)personal/(20)personnel* appearance at a play depicting *(21) loose/(22)lose* behavior. 5. Though he can *(23)cite/(24)site* no precedent, the city *(25)council/(26)counsel* advises us to *(27)adapt/(28) adopt* a motion providing for the *(29)censoring/(30)censuring* of foreign films. 6. After our *(31)censor/(32)censure* of conditions at the plant, the owner *(33)affected/(34)effected* changes *(35)affecting/(36) effecting* most of his *(37)personal/(38)personnel*. 7. The teachers wanted to wait on the steps rather *(39)than/(40)then* enter the *(41) capital/(42)Capitol*, for all *(43)accept/(44)except* the *(45)principal/ (46)principle* had already been *(47)their/(48)there*.

D. What is the difference in meaning between the words in each of the following pairs? Aid—aide, causal—casual, complimentary—complementary, costume—custom, emigrant—immigrant, eminent—imminent, isle —aisle, key—quay, meet—mete, rational—rationale, stationary—stationery, straight—strait.

E. Insert *ei* or *ie:* ach__vement, bel__ver, dec__tful, f__ld, inconc__vable, misch__f, perc__ve, rec__ving, rel__f, s__ze, w__rd, y__ld.

F. Select the appropriate word in each of the numbered pairs: *(1) bared/(2)barred* from office; his *(3)bating/(4)batting* average; *(5)caned/(6) canned* meat; a *(7)hatful/(8)hateful* task; *(9)hoping/ (10)hopping* for the best; *(11)pined/(12)pinned* to the mat; a *(13)well-planed/(14)well-planned* outing; *(15)robed/(16)robbed* in white; a boy *(17)spiting/(18)spitting* his parents; *(19)taped/(20)tapped* him on the shoulder.

G. Combine the following words with the suggested endings: accompany—ed, advantage—ous, argue—ing, benefit—ed, carry—s, come—ing, confide—ing, differ—ing, excite—able, friendly—ness, lively—hood, occur —ing, prefer—ed, remit—ance, sad—er, satisfy—ed, shine—ing, sole—ly, study—ing, tragedy—s, try—s, use—ing, valley—s, whole—ly, write—ing.

SPECIAL MARKS AND CAPITAL LETTERS

Many spelling errors result from inaccurate or inappropriate use of special marks and of capital letters. Often you will have to rely on a college dictionary in deciding whether to hyphenate a compound word, whether to capitalize a word derived from a proper name, or whether to underline a foreign expression. At the same time, remembering a number of basic conventions will enable you to settle many questions without the dictionary, or to make intelligent use of the information it provides.

SP 5   THE APOSTROPHE

The **apostrophe**, like the other special marks discussed in this section, has no exact equivalent in speech and is therefore easily omitted or misplaced.

SP 5a   Contractions. *The apostrophe is used in contractions to indicate that one or more letters have been omitted* (*I'll* go now; *I'm* too tired; *we're* almost ready). It appears most frequently in contractions using a shortened form of *not: haven't, can't, wouldn't, won't, isn't.* Take care not to misspell *doesn't,* which is a shortened form of "*does* not."

A few contractions are easily confused with words of different spelling and different meaning. *It's,* meaning *it is,* differs from *its,* meaning "of it" or "belonging to it." *Who's,* meaning *who is,* differs from *whose,* which means "of whom" or "of which." *They're* means *they are* and differs from both *there* and *their:*

> *It's* time to give the cat *its* milk.
> *Who's* to say *whose* fault it is?
> If *their* lights are turned off, *they're* not *there.*

NOTE: Contractions are characteristic of informal conversation. Avoid them in formal reports, research papers, and letters of application. Use them cautiously in ordinary expository prose. Some readers approve of contractions only in distinctly informal writing.

SP 5b   Possessives. *The apostrophe designates a special form of nouns.* A person closely associated with something named by another noun often appears in the **possessive** form, usually produced by adding an apostrophe plus *s* to the plain form of a noun: *my sister's purse, Mr. Smith's garage, the student's notebook.* Often the possessive indicates where something belongs or who owns an article. However, it also indicates many other relationships between two closely associated nouns: *the boy's friends, the firemen's ball, a* *man's world, the child's innocence, the children's capers, the general's dismissal.* Possessives occur in many familiar expressions: *an hour's drive, the day's news, a moment's notice, a dollar's worth, tonight's paper.*

Note the following variations:

(1) Sometimes the plain form of a noun already ends in *s*. The possessive is then formed by adding an apostrophe only. This applies especially to plural forms. Compare the following pairs:

the Turk's wives (one Turk)	the Turks' wives (several Turks)
the girl's swimming pool (one girl)	the girls' swimming pool (several girls)
a week's pay	two weeks' pay

Names of individuals do not always follow this rule. The writer may or may not add a second *s*, depending on whether he would expect an extra syllable in pronunciation: *Mr. Jones' car—Mr. Jones's car; Dolores' hair—Dolores's hair; Charles Dickens' first novel—Charles Dickens's first novel.*

(2) The apostrophe is *not* used in the *possessive forms of personal pronouns*. No apostrophe appears in *his, hers, its, ours, yours,* or *theirs*. It does appear in the possessive forms of such indefinite pronouns as *one* (one's friends), *everyone* (to everyone's surprise), *someone* (at someone's suggestion; also, at someone else's house).

SP 5c Plurals of Letters and Symbols. *The apostrophe is often used to separate the plural s from the name of a letter or a symbol or from a word named as a word* (two large 7's; if's and but's):

> Those great big beautiful A's so avidly sought, those little miserly C's so often found, were meant for another time and another student body.—Oscar Handlin, "Are the Colleges Killing Education?" *Atlantic*

SP 6 THE HYPHEN

Use of the **hyphen** is the least uniform and the least stable feature of English spelling. In doubtful cases, the most recent edition of a reputable dictionary is the best available guide.

SP 6a Compound Words. *Treatment varies for words habitually used together as a single expression.* Some compound words are clearly distinguished from ordinary combinations by differences in both writing and pronunciation: *black bird* (black BIRD) but *blackbird* (BLACKbird), *dark room* (dark ROOM) but *darkroom* (DARKroom). Such unmistakable compounds are *bellboy, bridesmaid, headache, highway, newsstand, summertime,* and *stepmother.* In many similar compounds, however, the parts are conventionally kept separate: *bus boy, commander in chief, goose flesh, high school, labor union, second cousin.* Still other compound words conventionally require a hyphen: *able-bodied, bull's-eye, cave-in, great-grandfather, merry-go-round, mother-in-law.*

Be sure to spell *today, tomorrow, nevertheless,* and *nowadays* as single words. Be sure *not* to spell as single words *all right, a lot* (a lot of time), *be able,* and *no one.*

SP 6b   Prefixes. *Many hyphenated compounds consist of a prefix, or introductory qualifier, and the word it precedes.* All-, ex- (in the sense of "former"), *quasi-, self-,* and sometimes *co-* require a hyphen: *all-knowing, ex-husband, quasi-judicial, self-contained, co-author.* All prefixes require a hyphen before words beginning with a capital letter: *all-American, anti-American, pro-American, un-American.*

Often a hyphen prevents the meeting of two identical vowels: *anti-intellectual, re-election, semi-independent.* Less frequently, a hyphen distinguishes an unfamiliar use of a prefix from a familiar one: *recover—re-cover* (make a new cover), *recreation—re-creation* (creating again or anew).

SP 6c   Group Modifiers. *Several words may temporarily combine as a modifier preceding a noun.* They are then usually joined to each other by hyphens: *a flying-saucer hat, a middle-of-the-road policy, a question-and-answer period, a step-by-step account, a devil-may-care attitude.* No hyphens are used when the same combinations serve some other function in a sentence: *tend toward the middle of the road; explain a process step by step.*

No hyphen is used when a modifier preceding a noun is in turn modified by an adverb ending in *ly: a fast-rising executive, a well-balanced account* but *a rapidly growing city, a carefully documented study.* (See G 7 for borderline distinctions.)

SP 7   CAPITALS

Although practice varies on minor points, the following conventions of capitalization are widely observed.

SP 7a **Proper Names.** *Proper names are always capitalized.* For instance, we capitalize the names of persons, places, regions, historical periods, ships, days of the week, months (but not seasons), organizations, religions: *James, Brazil, the Middle Ages, S.S. Independence, Sunday, February, Buddhism.* Many other words are capitalized because they are derived from proper names: *English grammar, French pastry, German beer, Parisian fashions, Christian charity, Marxist ideas.* In some of these words the proper name involved has been lost sight of, and a lower-case letter is used: *guinea pig, india rubber, pasteurized milk.* When you are in doubt, consult your dictionary.

Note the following difficulties:

(1) The same word may apply to various examples of a kind or serve as a proper name for a person, an institution, a place. For instance, *democratic* means "related to popular representation," whereas *Democratic* means "related to a specific party that has made the term *democratic* a part of its official designation." Similarly, one can hold "republican" views without holding "Republican" views, "orthodox" views without being a member of the "Orthodox" church. A student of "history" studies a general subject; "History 31" is the name of a specific course. With a lower-case letter, "east," "west," or "south" is a general direction; "the Far East," "the Middle West," and "the South" are specific geographical areas. *My mother* identifies by reference to a common relationship; *Mother* names one specific person.

(2) Generally applicable descriptions of a title, a family relationship, an institution, or a geographical feature are capitalized when they combine with a proper name: *Major Brown, Aunt Augusta, Sergeant Barnacle, Campbell High School, Indiana University, Tennessee Valley Authority, Medora Heights, Lake Erie.* Some titles refer to only one person and can take the place of the person's name: *the Pope, the Queen* (of England), *the President* (of the United States).

SP 7b **Titles of Publications.** *A capital letter marks the first and all major words in the title of a book, other publication, or work of art.* The only words not counting as major are articles (*a, an,* and *the*), prepositions (*at, in, on, of, from, with*), and connectives (*and, but, if, when*). Prepositions and connectives are usually capitalized when they have five or more letters. Observe these conventions in writing the title of a theme:

> My First Day on Campus
> Life in a Dormitory
> Get Rich Through Hypnosis
> New Facts About the Common Cold

The same conventions apply to titles of publications cited in a sentence:

> Several generations of Americans read *Sink or Swim, Phil the Fiddler, Mark the Match Boy,* and *From Canal Boy to President,* records of achievement which rewarded personal goodness with happiness and goods.—Saul Bellow, "The Writer as Moralist," *Atlantic*

EXERCISES

A. Check for appropriate use of the apostrophe in choosing between the spellings in each of the following pairs.

1. When the mother and the father respect each *(1)other's/(2)others'* opinions, children learn to live harmoniously by following their *(3) elders/(4)elders'* example. 2. Since the *(5)chairmans/(6)chairman's* resignation, the *(7)members/(8)member's* have been speculating about *(9)whose/(10)who's* going to succeed him. 3. *(11)Mrs. Beattys/(12) Mrs. Beatty's* husband still sends her *(13)flowers/(14)flower's* on *(15) Valentines/(16)Valentine's* Day. 4. We were all overjoyed when my *(17)sister's/(18)sisters'* baby took *(19)its/(20)it's* first faltering steps. 5. A *(21)student's/(22)students'* lack of interest is not always the *(23) teachers/(24)teacher's* fault. 6. *(25)Its/(26)It's* the *(27)parents/(28) parents'* responsibility to provide for their *(29)children's/(30)childrens'* religious education. 7. *(31)Lets/(32)Let's* borrow *(33)someones/(34) someone's* car and go for an *(35)hour's/(36)hours'* drive. 8. *(37) Charles/(38)Charles's* father murmured audibly that the assembled *(39) relatives/(40)relative's* had consumed at least ten *(41)dollars/(42)dollars'* worth of food.

B. Insert hyphens or combine elements where appropriate.

1. The prospective son in law listened self consciously to Mother's praise of the bride to be. 2. Those who denounced the parking privileges for out of town students were obviously not from out of town. 3. Both pro British and anti British Arabs were united in their contempt for ex king Farouk. 4. The anti intellectual local news paper had called our candidate an absent minded ex professor and a tool of the labor unions; never the less he was re elected. 5. Now a days few self respecting candidates conduct old fashioned campaigns taking them into out of the way places. 6. Mr. Andrews and his co

author have written a well documented account of the un democratic procedures followed by quasi judicial agencies.

C. Revise the following passage to make it conform to the conventions governing the use of capitals.

Boris was a young american pianist. His father came from a calvinistic new england family. His mother, who had been born in the caucasus, spoke french, german, and russian, as well as english and her native armenian. She had studied classical music in european cities like paris and vienna. Before he was ten, boris could play everything from viennese waltzes to presbyterian hymns. In high school he read books like *the life of beethoven, all about wagner,* and *brahms through the eyes of a friend.* At east bloomingdale city college, he took a course in music appreciation as well as a course entitled "the great composers." After he graduated, he spent the summer in california and the winter giving concerts in the middle west.

Fame came to boris in march one year when, armed with his bible, he set off for a contest in a country dominated by marxist ideology but susceptible to capitalist music. Even orthodox socialists cheered wildly when boris was awarded the first prize. Back home, the united states senate promptly commended boris's achievement as a national triumph and a vindication of democratic principles. Only one democratic and two republican senators abstained. The national broadcasting company paid the back rent on boris's piano after he performed in a sunday morning concert given by the new york philharmonic orchestra and broadcast from carnegie hall. In june, *lifemanship* magazine had an article on boris in its section entitled "speaking of pianists." The article said: "So catholic is the appeal of music that it reconciles, for a time, yankees and southerners, protestants and catholics, russians and americans."

PUNCTUATION MARKS
Reference Chart

COMMA

before coordinating connectives	P 3d
with nonrestrictive adverbial clauses	P 4b
after introductory adverbial clauses	P 4c
with nonrestrictive modifiers (other than adverbial clauses)	P 5b–c
after introductory modifiers (other than adverbial clauses)	P 5c
with adverbial connectives	P 3c
with *especially, namely, for example,* etc.	P 2b
with *after all, of course,* and other sentence modifiers	P 5c
between items in a series	P 6a
in a series of parallel clauses	P 3b
between coordinate adjectives	P 6b
with dates and addresses, etc.	P 6c
with direct address and other light interrupters	P 7c
between repeated or contrasted elements	P 6d
with quotations	P 8a–b, d

SEMICOLON

between closely related sentences	P 3a
before adverbial connectives	P 3c
before coordinating connectives between clauses containing commas	P 3d
in a series with items containing commas	P 6a

COLON

to introduce a list or explanation	P 2b
to introduce a formal quotation	P 8a
between closely related sentences	P 3a

PERIOD

at end of sentence	P 1c, P 2
ellipsis	P 8c
with abbreviations	M 2

DASH

break in thought	P 2a, P 7a
before summary at end of sentence	P 7a

QUOTATION MARKS

with quotations	P 8a–d
quotation within quotation	P 8a
with terminal marks	P 8b
with slang or technical terms	P 8e
to set off titles	M 1e

EXCLAMATION MARK	P 1a
QUESTION MARK	P 1b
PARENTHESES	P 7b

15: PUNCTUATION

THE USES OF PUNCTUATION

When we speak, we do more than put the right words together in the right order. We pause at the right times, raise our voices for emphasis. To the structures and forms we study in the grammar of the written sentence, speech adds **intonation**: differences in timing, pitch, and stress that make our words mean what we want them to mean. Such differences are further supplemented by facial expressions and gestures: the knowing wink that indicates irony, the raised forefinger that signals emphasis. When writing, we use punctuation marks for similar purposes.

The English system of punctuation has relatively few ways of indicating differences in emotion or attitude. In speech, "George is an honor student" can express many different shades of meaning. Wide-eyed amazement and emphatic pronunciation indicate that we regard honor students with awe and respect; a shrill pitch of excitement indicates that we are surprised, happy, or angry; an incredulous raising of the voice indicates our doubt that George could have been selected. When we try to reproduce such differences in writing, we are soon reduced to devices frowned upon by conservative readers:

George is an honor student!
George is an honor student?
George is an honor student (!).
George is an honor (?) student.
George is an "honor" student.

English punctuation is best equipped to signal differences in structure. Punctuation marks may separate groups of words from each other. They may establish different kinds of connection between them. For instance, punctuation may show two closely related groups of words to be a question followed by an answer:

> When am I going to see him again? Perhaps never.

It may show them to be a general statement followed by detailed explanation:

> The room was full of noisy men: ranchers, merchants, and lawyers.

It may show them to be an important statement followed by incidental additional information:

> Richard inherited his uncle's estate, which had been in the family since 1632.

The conventional system of punctuation, like English spelling, developed in a somewhat haphazard fashion. However, it has the great advantage of being readily understood by all educated readers. With minor variations, certain ways of doing things are repeated over and over in most of what you read. Besides, like conventional spelling, conventional punctuation is generally accepted as a symptom of literacy. Unconventionally punctuated sentences, though to a lesser degree than misspelled words, invite disapproval and ridicule.

PUNCTUATING THE COMPLETE SENTENCE

P 1   END PUNCTUATION

End punctuation puts a stop to an utterance that is grammatically complete. Such utterances may have to become part of a coherent narrative or argument before their full meaning becomes clear. They do not need anything before them or after them to be complete as far as grammatical structure is concerned.

P 1a   Exclamations. The **exclamation mark** terminates an utterance that has an unusual amount of energy or emphasis behind it. Such utterances range from a groan, curse, or shout to an order or command. *The exclamation mark can signal excitement, insistence, surprise, indignation, or fear:*

> Ouch! Hurrah!
> Silence! Get up! Close the book!
> He loves me!
> And this man wants to be President!

•|

To preserve its usefulness, avoid using the exclamation mark as an easy way of making trivial things seem important. Avoid using more than one exclamation mark at a time.

P 1b   Questions. Whenever you raise your voice inquiringly at the end of something you say, you should terminate the written equivalent with a **question mark** (*Did you see my hat?*). However, not all questions are marked by intonation. *Use the question mark whenever an utterance is worded as a request for information:*

> Who are you?
> What did he want?

Many students forget to use question marks at the end of questions that are long or involved:

> How is the student who enters college as a freshman supposed to find his way through the maze of instructions and regulations printed in small print in the college catalogue?

(1) Use question marks even after *rhetorical questions*. Rhetorical questions do not really ask for an answer but already indicate what the correct answer is supposed to be by the way they are worded:

> Are you implying that our candidate is a liar?
> Am I, life-long servant of this great republic, going to betray the trust placed in me by my constituents?

(2) You are free to omit the question mark after *requests phrased as questions* for the sake of politeness:

> Will you please notify your clients of our decision?
> Will you please notify your clients of our decision.

P 1c   Statements. Statements are terminated by **periods**. *To use the period appropriately, you must be able to recognize the type of grammatically self-contained unit called a sentence.*[1] Some students use periods between units that are not complete sentences but merely **sentence fragments**. Others go to the opposite extreme by omitting the period between two complete sentences, thus producing what is called a **fused sentence**.

COMPLETE: He is gone. *He left for Alaska.*
FRAGMENT: He left yesterday. *For Alaska.*
FUSED: You won't find him *he left for Alaska.*

[1] See G 2 for discussion of sentence structure and common sentence patterns.

P 2 ELIMINATING FRAGMENTS

The type of sentence fragment most common in student writing is caused by afterthoughts added to the main statement. After making a statement (*I left home*), the writer adds some detail or explanation without realizing that the addition is not a second complete sentence (*To go to college*). He makes a statement (*These are my relatives*) and adds comment (*A fine group of people*). He makes a statement (*I kept my eyes open for suspicious characters*) and adds an example or illustration (*For example, policemen and store detectives*). Each of these afterthoughts is a sentence fragment when separated from the main statement by a period.

Grammatically, such fragments are of several common types:

APPOSITIVES:	A great man. My history teacher. Carts loaded with fruit.
ADJECTIVES, ADVERBS:	Beautiful in the morning sun. Carelessly as usual.
PREPOSITIONAL PHRASES:	For the last time. With great trepidation. On behalf of the management.
VERBALS, VERBAL PHRASES:	Leaving the car behind. Other things being equal.
DEPENDENT CLAUSES:	Because I did not study. Though nobody replied. Which came far too late. (See P 4a.)

Many such fragments can be joined to the main statement either without any punctuation at all (*I left home to go to college*) or by a comma (*These are my relatives, a fine group of people*). Whenever a fragment is pointed out to you in your writing, try first to connect it with the main idea to which it belongs in such a way that the sentence flows smoothly, without interruption:

FRAGMENT:	Be sure to be there. *At seven o'clock.*
REVISED:	Be sure to be there *at seven o'clock.*
FRAGMENT:	He bought a used car. *In spite of my warnings.*
REVISED:	He bought a used car *in spite of my warnings.*

If the fragment cannot become part of either the preceding or the following statement, you may have to develop the material it contains into a complete sentence:

FRAGMENT: He appealed to a higher court. *Being a futile effort.*
REVISED: He appealed to a higher court. *The effort was futile.*

P 2a **Breaks in Thought.** *At times, material added to the main statement is kept clearly separate as an afterthought.* To indicate the break in thought, use a **dash** instead of a period:

These are my relatives—*a motley crew.*
He would close his eyes and talk into the dictaphone—*a strange way to write an English theme.*

Dashes can suggest the casual rambling of conversation or the jerky movement of an improvised speech. On the other hand, they can emphasize a break for ironic or dramatic effect.[2]

P 2b **Explanation and Enumeration.** *To establish a definite connection between an explanatory afterthought and the preceding statement, use a colon or common transitional expression.*

(1) The **colon** serves to introduce a *list or description of* something that has already been mentioned in a more general way:

We have two excellent players this year: *Phil and Tom.*
She served an old-fashioned breakfast: *fishballs, brown bread, and baked beans.*
Your friend lacks an essential quality: *tact.*

The colon, like the period, ordinarily has a complete statement in front of it. Unlike the period, it may be followed by a group of words that is not a complete statement.

(2) Explanations or examples added to a complete statement are often introduced by expressions like *especially, such as, namely,* or *for example.* Like the colon, these expressions signal that something is to follow. When they introduce material that is not a complete sentence, they are usually preceded by a **comma:**

He took several courses in the humanities, *such as French Literature and Elementary Logic.*
Plato and Aristotle wrote in the same language, *namely Greek.*

In formal usage, another comma often keeps *namely, for example, for instance,* and *that is* separate from the explanations or examples they introduce:

Professor Miller objected to my system of punctuating, for example, my use of dashes.

[2] See P 7a.

Do not use another comma if the introductory expression is *especially* or *such as*.

P 2c Permissible Nonsentences. *Permissible fragments are common in speech and are used in writing for special effects.* Informal speech uses many fragmentary sentences whose meaning the listener can infer from gestures or from the context. When such fragmentary sentences occur in writing, they preserve a conversational quality and become a characteristic of a distinctly informal style. Most teachers and editors either consider them too informal for ordinary expository prose or simply take them as a sign of ignorance, if not of illiteracy. On the other hand, experienced writers use a number of permissible fragments, better called **nonsentences**, for special purposes. The following examples illustrate the most common of these:

(1) *Common transitional expressions.*

> *So much for* past developments. *Now for* a look at our present problems.

(2) *Answers to questions,* suggesting the give-and-take of conversation or the rhetorical question-and-answer technique of the orator.

> What did we gain? *Nothing.*

(3) *Descriptive passages,* especially when designed to give a static, pictorial effect.

> We stood in the hot dry night air at one in the morning, waiting for a train at an Arizona station. *Nothing but the purple arc of sky and at the end of the platform the silhouette of a cottonwood tree lapped by a hot breeze. The stars big as sunflowers.*—Alistair Cooke, *One Man's America*

(4) In narrative, *passages suggesting random, disconnected thought.*

> *Fifty dollars to Dorothy's piano teacher. His sister. Another plain girl.* She might as well learn how to play the piano.—Irwin Shaw, "Main Currents of American Thought"

(5) Transcripts of *conversation or dialogue.*

> In one part of the picture you see five young men in white coats conferring around a microscope. The voice on the sound track rings out

boldly, *"No geniuses here. Just a bunch of good Americans working together."*—William H. Whyte, Jr., "The New Illiteracy," *Saturday Review*

Most teachers discourage their students from experimenting with such incomplete sentences until they have learned to use complete sentences effectively and confidently.

EXERCISES

A. Check the following passages for conventional use of end punctuation. Label each passage S (satisfactory), F (unsatisfactory because containing a fragment), or U (unsatisfactory for some other reason).

1. Fred was collecting pictures of architectural marvels, such as Gothic cathedrals and Aztec pyramids. 2. The next summer I tried a new sales technique. With good results. 3. You will not be able to reach them. They left no address. 4. I remember the festive spirit of the Christmas season in my home town. The many colorful lights along the city streets. 5. When will parents realize that their children's education is not someone else's responsibility but their own. 6. He left school after two years. To take over his father's business. 7. The airline refused to transport his pet: a tame puma. 8. Rapidly growing housing tracts have created many problems. The most serious one being inadequate school facilities. 9. Why should I spend my time making excuses for an incorrigible liar. 10. He remembered his first glimpse of the United States. The Manhattan skyline. 11. Many of my friends were studying a foreign language, especially Spanish or French. 12. The club invited a well-known guest lecturer. An anthropologist from Cornell. 13. The osprey dives into the water to seize its prey. Plunging down from heights of up to one hundred feet. 14. Please stop at the post office. We need some stamps. 15. The gallery was showing the work of several French painters, especially Degas and Monet.

B. In the following passage, insert appropriate punctuation in the numbered spaces. Draw a diagonal line through inappropriate capitals (high/schools). Leave a blank space where no punctuation is required.

Have you been to the circus lately＿＿＿(1) What a change from old times＿＿＿(2) Only one thing seems the same＿＿＿(3) The tent＿＿＿(4) Most of the performers seem to have lost their zest＿＿＿(5) Especially the clowns and· acrobats＿＿＿(6) Where are the many hilariously funny clowns＿＿＿(7) Of days gone by ＿＿＿(8) One of them used to drag into the arena＿＿＿(9) A huge and complicated machine＿＿＿(10) To serve as a cigarette lighter＿＿＿(11) Acrobats used to fly from trapeze to trapeze＿＿＿

(12)   Without a net_____(13)   The modern circus is half tiresome floats_____(14)   And half commercials_____(15)   How can the spectators get into the true circus spirit_____(16).

C. From your current writing and reading, select ten sample sentences that illustrate the various conventions of punctuation discussed in the preceding section.

JOINING AND PUNCTUATING CLAUSES

P 3   JOINING INDEPENDENT CLAUSES

Your sentences will often contain not one subject-predicate group but several. The individual subject-predicate groups that can make up more complicated sentences are called **clauses**. Next to end punctuation, the most important kind of punctuation is that which joins two or more clauses.

P 3a   Closely Related Sentences. *A semicolon or colon may replace the period between two complete sentences.*

(1) The **semicolon** joins *complete sentences that are closely related.* Often two statements go together as related pieces of information, develop the same mood or point of view, line up related ideas for contrast:

> The door was locked; the windows were closed.
> Some librarians circulate books; others hoard them.
> The Queen is not allowed to wear a crown; nothing less than a halo will suffice.—Kingsley Martin, "Strange Interlude," *Atlantic*

When a semicolon replaces the period between two closely related statements, the first word of the second statement is *not* capitalized.

(2) In informal writing, a **colon** often replaces the semicolon when the second statement gives the reader information or explanation that helps him understand the first one. Formal usage prefers the semicolon unless the *first statement clearly introduces the second:*

> One thing was certain: he would never race again.

P 3b   Comma Splice. *Commas join complete sentences only under special circumstances.*

(1) The **comma** generally indicates a less significant break than the semicolon. Next to the sentence fragment, the most noticeable departure from conventional punctuation is the "comma fault," the

practice of rambling on from one complete statement to the other with only a comma to keep them apart. A group of statements spliced together by a comma is called a **comma splice** or, sometimes, a **run-on** sentence:

COMMA SPLICE: The doctor looked worn, he had stayed up all night.
REVISED: The doctor looked worn; he had stayed up all night.

(2) One permissible exception to the traditional rule against comma splices is a *sentence composed of three or more parallel clauses*. **Commas** may appear between clauses that are not only closely related in meaning but also similar in structure:

> He came, he saw, he conquered.
> The birds were chirping, the dogs were barking, the horses were neighing in the fields.

(3) When only two clauses are connected by a comma, the conventions of formal writing require the logical connection and similarity in structure to be especially close. This is often the case in clauses expressing a *carefully balanced contrast:*

> Now, of course, there are no more contractors, only developers. And *they no longer build houses, they build homes.* And *they no longer build one at a time, they scorn to undertake less than eight hundred at a crack.*—Gerald W. Johnson, "Baltimore: The City Nobody Knows," *Atlantic*

NOTE: Some reputable writers use the comma in less obviously balanced sentences. This practice is often condemned as careless:

> The grass is rich and matted, you cannot see the soil.—Alan Paton, *Cry, the Beloved Country*

> Across the holy river is the foundation of a companion tomb which Shah Jenan had wanted to build for himself, only this one was to be of black marble.—Leslie C. Stevens, "The Grand Trunk Road to Agra," *Atlantic*

P 3c   Adverbial Connectives. *Adverbial connectives overlap with other groups of connectives in meaning but differ from them in typically requiring a semicolon. A therefore, consequently,* or *hence* signals a logical conclusion from something that went before. *Furthermore* or *moreover* prepares the reader for additional details or arguments. These and similar connectives establish a definite and rather formal connection between two sentences.

(1) **Adverbial connectives** are *therefore, consequently, hence, accordingly, moreover, furthermore, besides, however, nevertheless, indeed,* and *in fact.* Since they show that two sentences are closely related, the sentences they join are typically separated by a **semicolon** rather than by a period. A period, nevertheless, would still be possible and acceptable:

> Business was improving; *therefore,* we changed our plans.
> Business was improving. *Therefore,* we changed our plans.
>
> The hall was nearly empty; *nevertheless,* the curtain rose on time.
> The hall was nearly empty. *Nevertheless,* the curtain rose on time.

(2) A connective of this group need not be placed at the point where the first statement ends and the second statement begins. You have to make sure that the *semicolon appears at the point where the two statements join,* regardless of the position of the connective:

> Attendance is compulsory; *therefore,* the students have no choice.
> Attendance is compulsory; the students, *therefore,* have no choice.
> Attendance is compulsory; the students have no choice, *therefore.*

This possibility of a shift in position is a test that you can employ to identify members of this group. They share their freedom of movement with adverbs, a characteristic that explains their description as adverbial connectives or connective adverbs.

(3) Adverbial connectives are often set off from the rest of the second statement by **commas**, as in the examples already given. You then have to make sure that there is a punctuation mark both before and after the connective. This means that a connective occurring in the middle of the second statement needs not one comma but two:

> The food, *however,* was impossible.

NOTE: Whether you set off an adverbial connective should depend partly on the amount of emphasis you would give it when reading the sentence aloud. It also depends on the level of formality of your writing. Informal and journalistic writing tend toward **open punctuation,** using fewer commas than formal writing does. Accordingly, the authors of popular books and magazine articles tend not to separate adverbial connectives from the rest of a clause.

P 3d Coordinating Connectives. *Coordinating connectives typically require a comma.* Instead of using *however* or *therefore,* you can establish a somewhat more immediate connection between two sentences by using *but* or *so.*

(1) *And, but, for, or, nor, so,* and *yet* establish a close relation between two clauses without making the one more important than the other. They are typically preceded by a **comma**:

> The bell finally rang, *and* George rushed out of the room.
> She saw me, *but* she did not recognize me.
> We went inside, *for* it had started to rain.
> You had better apologize, *or* she will not speak to you again.

Notice the reversal of subject and verb after *nor:*

> We cannot through the courts force parents to be kind, *nor can we force* men to be wise by the pressure of committees.—Dan Lacy, "Obscenity and Censorship," *The Christian Century*

Do not use the comma with these connectives when they join two words or two phrases rather than two clauses (came in *and* sat down, tired *but* happy, for cash *or* on credit).

(2) *And, but,* and *or* are often used without a comma when the clauses they join are short:

> The wind was blowing *and* the water was cold.

Yet and *so* are often used with a **semicolon**:

> The critics praised Oliver's work; *yet* no one bought his paintings.

Any coordinating connective may be used with a semicolon, especially if it joins *clauses that already contain commas* or that are unusually long:

> Previously the river has always been accompanied by mountains, near or far; *but* they lay generally parallel to its course. Now in the Big Bend the river encounters mountains in a new and extraordinary way; *for* they lie, chain after chain of them, directly across its way.—Paul Horgan, "Pages from a Rio Grande Notebook," *The New York Times Book Review*

(3) Unlike adverbial connectives, coordinating connectives do not change their position in the sentence; the *and* or the *for* always occurs at the beginning of the clause which it joins to the preceding

one. They are not set off from the rest of the clause they introduce; there is no comma after *and, but,* or *yet* unless it is required by some other convention of punctuation. Like adverbial connectives, however, coordinating connectives leave the clauses they join self-sufficient or independent grammatically. Thus, the clauses they connect may still be kept separate from each other by a **period**:

> I called your office twice. *But* nobody answered. *So* I left without you.

P 4 ADVERBIAL CLAUSES

Adverbial connectives and coordinating connectives leave the clauses which they join independent. A third type of connective subordinates the second clause to the main clause of the sentence. It changes a self-sufficient, independent clause into a **dependent clause**, which normally cannot stand by itself. "If I were a boy" does not become a complete sentence until you answer the question "If you were a boy, then what?"

P 4a Subordinating Connectives. *Because of characteristic differences in grammatical behavior and punctuation, subordinating connectives must be carefully distinguished from other types of connectives.* They normally introduce adverbial clauses, which tell us something about the circumstances of an action or event described in the main part of the sentence. *When, whenever, while, before, after, since, until, as long as,* and *where* introduce information about time and place. *Because, if, provided,* and *unless* introduce reasons or conditions. Subordinating connectives can turn a group of words into a sentence fragment even though the group has both a subject and a predicate. A complete sentence, in other words, normally contains a subject and a predicate *not* introduced by a subordinating connective. To put it more generally, *a complete sentence normally contains at least one independent clause.* Beware of dependent clauses added to a main statement as an explanatory afterthought:

FRAGMENT: He failed the test. *Because he did not study.*
REVISED: He failed the test *because he did not study.*

(2) To identify a subordinating connective, try to reverse the order of the two statements which it joins. *Subordinating connectives*

introduce material that may precede rather than follow the main clause:

> Vote for me *if you trust me.*
> *If you trust me,* vote for me.
>
> I drove more slowly *after I noticed the police car.*
> *After I noticed the police car,* I drove more slowly.

P 4b   Restrictive and Nonrestrictive Adverbial Clauses. *Restrictive adverbial clauses are typically not separated from the rest of the sentence; nonrestrictive ones are set off by a comma.*

(1) Adverbial clauses usually *restrict or qualify in a significant way the meaning of the clause to which they are joined.* Suppose a father tells his son, "I'll raise your allowance *after I strike oil.*" Without the proviso about striking oil, the sentence would sound like an immediate promise of more money. With the proviso, it means that the son will get more money only by a very remote chance. "After I strike oil," in other words, makes a great difference as far as the meaning of the complete sentence is concerned. When they *follow* the main clause, such **restrictive** clauses are not set off by punctuation:

> I consulted my notes *before I spoke.*
> Do not sign anything *until you hear from me.*
> We cannot keep you on the team *unless you improve.*

(2) Occasionally, the *time, place, or condition for an action or event is already indicated in the main clause.* In that case, the dependent clause may merely elaborate on the information already given. Such dependent clauses are called **nonrestrictive** and are separated from the main clause by a **comma**:

> Bats were well developed *as far back as the Eocene, when man's ancestors were still in the trees.*
>
> He was born *in California, where one can pick oranges during the Christmas holidays.*

A number of subordinating connectives usually introduce nonrestrictive material and as a result require a comma. The most important ones are *though, although,* and *whereas.* Rather than adding essential qualification, these words establish a *contrast between the statements they connect:*

> I like the work, *though the salary is low.*
> Her friend wore a .sports shirt and slacks, *whereas the other men wore tuxedos.*

Combinations like *whether or not* and *no matter how* indicate that the main statement is true or applicable regardless of possibilities mentioned in the dependent clause:

> We are canceling the lease, *whether you like it or not.*
> She will never forgive you, *no matter what you do.*

(3) Some subordinating connectives introduce *either restrictive or nonrestrictive material, depending on the meaning of the sentence.* Notice the comma that signals the difference between the members of each of the following pairs:

> Why are you going to town?
> I am going to town *because I want to do some shopping.*
> (The reason for your trip is the essential part of the sentence.)

> What are you going to do?
> *I am going to town,* because I want to do some shopping.
> (The reason for your trip is added, nonrestrictive explanation.)

> I am telling you this *so that* there will be no misunderstanding.
> (*So that* reveals purpose or intention.)
> The cafeteria was small, *so that* it was always overcrowded.
> (*So that* introduces an unintended result.)

NOTE: Some connectives belong to different groups of connectives depending on their meaning in the sentence. *However* is normally an adverbial connective and requires a semicolon. It sometimes takes the place of the subordinating connective *no matter how* and requires a comma:

> I cannot please him; *however, I am trying hard.*
> I cannot please him, *however hard I try.*

Though, normally a subordinating connective, is often used in informal English as an adverbial connective placed in the middle or at the end of a clause:

> I felt entitled to more freedom; *my parents, though, didn't agree with me.*

P 4c   Introductory Adverbial Clauses. *An adverbial clause that precedes rather than follows the main clause is usually set off.* After an introductory adverbial clause, a **comma** normally indicates where the main clause starts:

> *If you want to do well,* you will have to work hard.
> *Whenever there is a heavy rain,* the area is threatened by floods and slides.

(ex.)

After restrictive introductory material, this comma is optional. Some writers consider it unnecessary after an introductory clause that is fairly short, provided the sentence would be clear without the optional punctuation.

NOTE: Subordinating connectives are not the only way of relating a dependent clause to another clause. Two other types of dependent clauses are treated under P 5. (See P 5a for noun clauses, P 5d for adjective clauses.)

EXERCISES

A. Check the following passages for conventional use of punctuation marks in joining clauses. Label each passage S (satisfactory), C (unsatisfactory because of a comma splice), U (unsatisfactory for some other reason).

1. I asked my father for a car instead he gave me a bicycle. 2. I know the city very well; I used to live there, in fact. 3. In Europe family ties are close, the whole family does things together. 4. There is a growing audience for ballet, and the theater flourishes in half a dozen centers outside New York. 5. All the polls favored our candidate; the election, however, told a different story. 6. Previews consist of short selections from the movie being advertised, usually these are the most exciting or the most daring parts. 7. Children are like tape recorders; they repeat everything they hear. 8. We had planned to look for driftwood on the beach, but the rain kept us indoors. 9. The horses must have been frightened by the crowd, for they started rearing and tugging nervously at their bridles. 10. High costs make orchestra deficits perennial, yet almost everywhere performances are sold out. 11. I hurriedly went downstairs for breakfast was ready. 12. His landlady did not know his whereabouts, nor could she name his companions. 13. A teacher cannot do everything for his students they must meet him half way. 14. Classes are large, therefore few students have a chance to participate in discussion. 15. Our school annual was to give many students a chance to participate; the captain of the football team, consequently, became our sports editor.

B. Check the following passages for conventional use of punctuation marks with subordinating connectives. Label each passage S (satisfactory), F (unsatisfactory because of a sentence fragment), or U (unsatisfactory for some other reason).

1. Though his paintings were truly remarkable, few of them found buyers among museums or private collectors. 2. Cleaning pots and pans looks easy on television. Whereas at home it takes a lot of hard work. 3. Unless a man has an unusual fondness for teaching grade

school children are best taught by women. 4. Most of the animals were extremely shy, so that photographing them required much patience. 5. After the camera had followed the hero to his destination in the West, it switched back to the freshly plowed fields of Iowa. 6. The city is desperately short of hospital space because, most people don't appreciate the need for adequate facilities. 7. Myrna has been afraid of heights since she was a small child. 8. Mountain climbing does not appeal to me; however exciting it may be to others. 9. Because many educated people in India know English, foreign visitors seldom learn Hindu. 10. If we didn't know the teacher usually supplied the answers in class. 11. In Mexico architecture seemed to flourish, whereas at home it had seemed a lost art. 12. The city relinquished one hundred acres of city-owned land so that the local baseball team could build a new stadium there. 13. Ralph was suspended last year. After he put war paint on the bronze Indian decorating the principal's lawn. 14. Our house is a shambles, whenever my uncle's family pays us a visit. 15. Ask me when you need advice; ask your father when you need money.

C. In the following passages, insert appropriate punctuation in the numbered spaces. *Use no capitals or periods not already supplied in the text.* Leave a blank space where no punctuation is required.

1. If my own experience is typical__(1) high school students are reluctant readers__(2) because books play only a very minor role in their environment. Few teachers make their students explore the school library__(3) although it may contain everything from Chaucer to Sagan. The most popular students often read very little__(4) the newcomer__(5) therefore__(6) associates books with "longhairs" and intellectuals. When the student returns to his home__(7) the television set occupies the place of honor in the living room__(8) whereas__(9) the bookcase may stand as a dust catcher in a hidden corner.

2. Elia Kazan is best known as a director of motion pictures__(1) however__(2) he first became famous__(3) when he directed plays by Thornton Wilder__(4) and Arthur Miller. Kazan's life is an American success story__(5) of a familiar kind__(6) for he came to this country as the son of Greek immigrants__(7) when he was five. He first lived in Manhattan__(8) later his parents moved to New Rochelle__(9) where he attended high school. Because he was foreign-born__(10) young Kazan long felt an outsider__(11) nevertheless__(12) he graduated with honors from Williams College__(13) and was highly praised as an actor__(14) before he was thirty.

D. From your current writing and reading, select ten sample sentences that illustrate the various conventions of punctuation discussed in the preceding section.

USING INTERNAL PUNCTUATION

P 5 PUNCTUATING MODIFIERS

Internal punctuation becomes important when various kinds of material intervene between the basic elements of a sentence. Often nouns and verbs are accompanied by further material that develops, embroiders, or modifies the meaning they convey.

P 5a Unnecessary Commas. *Unless extraneous material intervenes, there is no punctuation between basic elements of a sentence.* Do not put a comma between a subject and its verb, between a verb and its object, between a verb and a description of the subject, or between the two or three basic elements and the various phrases added to the sentence to describe circumstances, reasons, or conditions:

Andrew	studies	his textbooks	in bed.
Gaston	had been	a mess sergeant	during the war.
Jones	left	his wife	to shoot elephants.

The rule against punctuation breaking up the basic sentence pattern applies even when the place of the subject, the object, or the description of the subject is taken by a clause within a clause. Such clauses, which appear in positions frequently occupied by nouns, are called **noun clauses**. They become *part* of another clause and should not be confused with clauses which are *joined* to another clause:

NOUN (Subject):	*The writer*	knew your name.
NOUN CLAUSE:	*Whoever wrote it*	knew your name.
NOUN (Object):	John announced	*his plans.*
NOUN CLAUSE:	John announced	*that he would retire.*
NOUN (Description):	Your net gain is	*a small sum.*
NOUN CLAUSE:	Your net gain is	*what little remains after taxes.*

Be careful not to put a comma before or after a noun clause, especially one introduced by *that:*

We knew *that he is unreliable.*
That he failed to answer your letter is a bad sign.

P 5b   Restrictive and Nonrestrictive Modifiers. *Restrictive modifiers are not separated from what they modify; nonrestrictive modifiers are set off by commas.* This convention applies especially to modifiers inserted after a noun (or noun equivalent) to clarify or develop its meaning:

> The student, *a freshman,*   studied the handbook.
> The student, *looking weary,*   studied the handbook.
> The student, *who had little time,*   studied the handbook.
>
> He studied the handbook, *a fascinating volume.*
> He studied the handbook, *a text required in the course.*

Modifiers become an essential part of the main statement if *used for the purpose of identification.* In that case, they are **restrictive**; they restrict or narrow down a generally applicable term like *student* to help the reader single out one particular student or one particular type of student. Restrictive modifiers become an integral part of the sentence and are *not* set off by punctuation:

> Which student studied the book?
> The student *wearing the red hunting cap* studied the book.
>
> Which man took the money?
> The man *dressed in the pink shirt* took it.
>
> What kind of course appeals to you?
> Courses *which require hard work* appeal to me.

Often information accompanying a noun is not necessary for the purpose of identification. It merely gives your reader *further information* about something on which he has already focused; it is **nonrestrictive**. Nonrestrictive material is set off from the rest of the sentence by a **comma,** or by a comma both before and after it if it occurs in the middle of the sentence:

> He talked to his lawyer, *a well-known Boston attorney.*
> His lawyer, *who is a very impatient man,* gathered up his papers and stalked out of the hall.

The commas used to set off nonrestrictive modifiers often make the difference between a very cautious and a very sweeping statement. "Americans *who do not speak French* need not apply" excludes only certain Americans, those that do not speak French. "Americans, *who do not speak French,* need not apply" excludes all Americans and at the same time makes a sweeping claim about their linguistic abilities. The commas used to signal the difference in meaning correspond to a

,/

break signaled in speech by a characteristic change in the tone of voice. You can train your ear to catch the distinction by going over the sample sentences already given and reading them out loud.

The following points should be noted:

(1) **Dashes** are occasionally used to set off a nonrestrictive *modifier that contains internal punctuation* and that would not be clearly marked without them:

> His lawyer—*a gruff, stubborn, impatient man*—stalked out of the hall.

(2) A *proper name* is usually adequate identification; a modifier following the name usually becomes nonrestrictive and is set off by commas. Several such modifiers may succeed each other:

> Mr. Smith, *my history teacher,* dismissed his class early.
>
> In 1942, he joined the Actors' Theater, *a repertory company with strong political views.*
>
> David Daiches, *English-born but Scottish-educated, formerly a professor at Chicago and Cornell, now at the University of Sussex,* chaired the meeting with the skill and courage of a lion-tamer.—Ralph W. Condee, "Bedlam at Edinburgh," *The Reporter*

Occasionally, a restrictive modifier is needed to help the reader distinguish between several people of the same name:

> I find it hard to distinguish between Holmes *the author* and Holmes *the Supreme Court justice.*

When your reader already knows whom you have in mind, even a proper name may be additional, nonrestrictive information:

> His oldest sister, *Martha,* has always helped him when he was in trouble.

(3) **Adjective clauses** modify a noun or noun equivalent and usually begin with *who, which,* or *that.* Clauses beginning with *when, where,* and *why* are also adjective clauses if they are used to modify a noun. Adjective clauses, like other modifiers, may be *either restrictive or nonrestrictive.* However, those beginning with *that* are always restrictive:

> The book *that you sent me* was very exciting reading.

Sometimes a noun is modified by a subject-predicate group from which a possible pronoun or connective has been omitted. Such abbreviated adjective clauses are always restrictive:

Most of the things [*that*] *I like to eat* are fattening.
She wrote a long passionate letter to the man [*whom*] *she loves.*

P 5c   **Sentence Modifiers.** *Many sentence modifiers are set off by commas.* Modifiers may modify sentence elements other than nouns. They may also modify the sentence as a whole rather than any part of it.[3]

(1) *Verbals and verbal phrases modifying a verb* may be either restrictive or nonrestrictive. Notice the **comma** indicating the difference:

RESTRICTIVE: He always came into the office *carrying a shirt box full of letters under his arm.*

NONRESTRICTIVE: Deadline newspaper writing is rapid because it cheats, *depending heavily on clichés and stock phrases.*

Verbal phrases modifying the sentence as a whole are always set off:

To tell you the truth, I don't even recall his name.
The business outlook being rosy, he invested his savings in highly speculative stocks.
Our new manager has done rather well, *considering his lack of experience.*

(2) If a *sentence is introduced by a long or substantial modifying phrase,* a **comma** usually indicates where the main sentence starts:

After an unusually solemn Sunday dinner, Father called me into his study.

Like all newspapermen of good faith, Mencken had long fumed at the low estate of the journalistic rank and file.—Philip M. Wagner, "Mencken Remembered," *The American Scholar*

Introductory verbals and verbal phrases are set off even when they are short:

Smiling, she dropped the match into the gas tank.
To start the motor, turn the ignition key.

The comma after an introductory modifier can be an important clue to the meaning of a sentence, and omitting it may cause serious misreading. Compare the following two sentences:

---

[3] Adverbial clauses, which can be classified as sentence modifiers, are treated under P 4.

,|

When hunting, lions stay away from wooded areas.
When hunting lions, stay away from wooded areas.

(3) Expressions like *after all, of course, unfortunately, on the whole, as a rule,* and *certainly* often do not modify the subject or the predicate of a sentence but establish a connection between one sentence and another. Depending on the amount of emphasis you would give such a modifier when reading, you can make it stand out from the rest of the sentence by a **comma**:

> *After all,* we are in business primarily for profit.
> *On the other hand,* the records may never be found.
> You will submit the usual reports, *of course.*

Sentence modifiers that are set off require two commas if they do not come first or last in the sentence:

> We do not, *as a rule,* solicit applications.
> A great many things, *to be sure,* could be said in his defense.

P 6 COORDINATION

A major convention governing internal punctuation applies to clauses where several elements of the same kind appear together.

P 6a Series. *Commas normally separate three or more items of the same kind appearing in a series.* The most common pattern separates the elements from each other by **commas**, with the last comma followed by a connective tying the whole group together:

> *Phil, Jim,* and *Harry* came to see me.
> After dinner, we *talked, laughed,* and *sang.*
> *The new students enter* after a rigid selective process, *they present* few disciplinary problems, and *they arrive* after good and uniform preparation.—Oscar Handlin, "Are the Colleges Killing Education?" *Atlantic*

This basic *A, B,* and *C* pattern can be expanded to accommodate any number of elements:

> The boys had spread out around them the homely tools of mischief— *the long wires, nails, hammers, pliers, string, flashlights, paraffin* saved from the tops of their mothers' jelly jars, *knives* for cutting a clothesline or carving out insults to the grown-up world, and *tin cans* filled with rocks for making a farewell noise after the damage was done. —Lois Phillips Hudson, "The Buggy on the Roof," *Atlantic*

Notice the following variations:

(1) Occasionally, you will want to arrange in a series *groups of words that already contain commas*. To prevent misreading, use **semicolons** instead of additional commas to indicate the major breaks:

> Three persons were mentioned in her will: *John, her brother; Martin, her nephew;* and *Helen, her faithful nurse.*

(2) The last comma in a series is often left out in *informal and journalistic writing:*

> *Segregation, farm income* and *foreign aid* are persistent issues in American politics.

More unusual is the practice of using commas only and leaving out the connective:

> The idea was to pool all the needs of all those who had in one way or another been bested by their environment—*the crippled, the sick, the hungry, the ragged.*—John Lear, "The Business of Giving," *Saturday Review*

P 6b   Coordinate Adjectives. *Adjectives are often separated by a comma corresponding to a characteristic break in speech.* Two adjectives describing different qualities of the same noun may be coordinated by a **comma** rather than by *and*. They are then called coordinate adjectives:

a *black* and *shaggy* dog	a *black, shaggy* dog
a *starved* and *exhausted* stranger	a *starved, exhausted* stranger
a *grand* and *awe-inspiring* sunset	a *grand, awe-inspiring* sunset

Not every sequence of adjectives falls into this pattern. Often an adjective combines with a noun to indicate a type of person or object (a *public* servant, a *short* story, a *black* market). An adjective preceding such a combination modifies the combination as a whole and should not be separated from it by a comma:

> a *secretive* public servant
> a *long* short story
> a *lively* black market

NOTE: Often the most reliable method of distinguishing between the two kinds of adjective is to read the sentence out loud. This method will help especially with combinations where the difference in meaning is not obvious (a *tired, weary old man* but *an old, tired, weary man; chattering, giggling little girls* but *tiny, anemic, undernourished children*).

P 6c **Dates and Addresses.** *Commas are needed with dates, addresses, page references, and similar information consisting of three or four different parts.* The different items are kept separate from each other by a **comma**; the last item is followed by a comma unless it is at the same time the last word of the sentence:

> The date was *Tuesday, December 16, 1952.*
> Please send my mail to *483 Tulane Street, Jackson, Oklahoma,* starting the first of the month.
> The quotation is from *Chapter V, page 43, line 7,* of the second volume.

Commas are also used to keep separate the different parts of *measurements* employing more than one unit of measurement, but the last item is usually not separated from the rest of the sentence:

> The boy is now *five feet, seven inches* tall.
> *Nine pounds, three ounces* is an unusual weight for this kind of fish.

P 6d **Repetition and Contrast.** *Commas are needed between expressions that either are identical or give two different versions of the same meaning.* Use the **comma** after a word or phrase to be repeated or to be followed by a definition or explanatory paraphrase:

> *Produce, produce!* This is a law among artists, or rather it is their inner compulsion.—Malcolm Cowley, "Artists, Conscience, and Censors," *Saturday Review*

> I am asking *whether you recall his exact language, whether you remember exactly what he said.*

Commas also separate words or groups of words that establish a *contrast:*

> *His wife, not his brother,* needs the money more.
> *The days were warm, the nights cool.*

P 7 INTERRUPTERS

To some extent the conventions of internal punctuation follow the rhythms of speech. This is true of the practice of setting off interrupters, elements that are not part of the main structure of the sentence in which they occur.

P 7a   Heavy Interrupters. *Some interrupters constitute a very definite break.* A speaker may realize in the middle of a sentence that he has omitted some preliminary detail or clarification. He may then interrupt his sentence, change his pace and tone of voice, and supply a hurried explanation. Or a speaker may pause to give special impact to a word or phrase. In writing, such material is set off from the rest of a sentence by **dashes.** Dashes tend to emphasize or dramatize the material they set off.

Four uses of such dashes are especially common:

(1) A *complete sentence is inserted into another sentence*, without a connective or relative pronoun to join them.

> Lady Macbeth—*has this been noted?*—takes very little stock in the witches.—Mary McCarthy, "General Macbeth," *Harper's*

(2) A *list enumerating details or examples* interrupts rather than follows a clause.

> Three of my friends—*Simp, Shnorkel, and Bip*—were waiting for me at the door.

(3) After a list of possible subjects, a sentence starts anew with a summarizing *all, these,* or *those.*

> *The visual essay, the rhythmic album, the invitation to drop in on a casual conversation*—these are the idiosyncratic traits by which television, as television, has come to be recognized.—Walter Kerr, "What Good Is Television?" *Horizon*

(4) A word or phrase is made to stand out for emphasis or for a *climactic effect.*

> After twenty-three years, he was leaving Newston jail—*a free man.*

P 7b   Parenthetic Material. *Some interrupters, though constituting a definite break, supply relatively unimportant data or are mere asides.* The place of dashes may then be taken by **parentheses,** which make the material they enclose seem secondary:

> Fatal accidents (*we had three of them last year in a town of 5,000 people*) can often be traced to excessive speed.

Kazan directed the rest of his considerable steam into studying English (*he graduated with honors*), waiting on tables, and joining as many extracurricular campus clubs as he could.—Thomas B. Morgan, "Elia Kazan's Great Expectations," *Harper's*

Parentheses are commonly used to enclose dates, addresses, page references, chemical formulas, and similar information if it might be of interest to some readers but is not an essential part of the text. Here are some typical examples: (*p. 34*) (*first published in 1910*) (*now called Market Street*).

NOTE: When inserted into another sentence, a sentence in parentheses, like a sentence set off by dashes, usually begins with a lower-case letter and has no end punctuation. When a sentence in parentheses begins *after* end punctuation, end punctuation is required inside the final parenthesis:

Select your purchases with care. (*No refunds are permitted.*)

P 7c   Light Interrupters. *Many interrupters blend into the sentence they interrupt, producing only a slight break.* Such interrupters are set off by **commas**.

(1) Use commas when you interrupt a statement to *address the reader* or to *comment* on the source, validity, or plausibility of what you are saying:

Marriage, *dear boy,* is a serious business.
Politicians, *you will agree,* were never popular in this part of the country.
Our candidate, *it seems,* is not very well known.

(2) Commas set off the *introductory greetings and exclamations,* as well as the introductory *yes* and *no,* which frequently precede a statement in conversation and in informal writing:

Why, I don't even know that man.
Yes, you can now buy Pinko napkins in different colors.
Well, you can't have everything.

(3) Commas set off the *shortened questions* often added to a statement to elicit agreement or confirmation:

You are my friend, *aren't you?*
So he says he is sick, *does he?*

(4) Commas may take the place of dashes to set off a word for

emphasis. They can suggest a *thoughtful pause* rather than a dramatic break:

> We should act, *and suffer,* in accordance with our principles.
> People cannot, *or will not,* put down the facts.

(5) Slight breaks corresponding to those caused by light interrupters are sometimes caused by *sentence elements that have changed their usual position in the sentence:*

> Laws, *to be cheerfully obeyed,* must be both just and practicable.
> Philip, *for no apparent reason at all,* got up and left the room.
> Marriage, *unless it is to be a failure,* must be completely voluntary.

EXERCISES

A. Check the following passages for conventional punctuation of modifiers. Label each passage S (satisfactory), F (unsatisfactory because of a sentence fragment), or U (unsatisfactory for some other reason).

1. With only a cautious enthusiasm, newspapers are giving a little extra Sunday space to culture.   2. Despite the opposition of a crooked sheriff, the hero, a handsome screen cowboy on a $5,000 horse, succeeded in straightening things out.   3. The proctor—a waspish, restless man—kept his eye on the whispering students.   4. Everyone, who is physically able, should have some exercise each day.   5. The kind of history that we were taught dealt mainly with the pageantry of princes and with the intrigues of empire.   6. Queen Victoria, brought from retirement by the skill of Disraeli, became the adored symbol of domestic virtue and imperial greatness.   7. Having swallowed enough water to last me all summer I decided to leave water skiing to those who had an aptitude for it.   8. My father who taught both in high school and in college gave me many helpful pointers on how to budget my time.   9. Major medical news—the discovery of a new surgical technique, the development of a cure for heart disease—is sometimes buried on the back pages.   10. Work after school can cut severely into study time, forcing the students to study late at night.   11. All kinds of opinion-makers—people who would never dream of insulting a Negro, Jew, Catholic, or Paiute Indian—delight in slipping their daily needle of sarcasm into the politician.   12. Usually a selfish person is a spoiled person. One who must have his way or else.   13. A good example of our neglect of public health problems, is the lack of hospital space for the mentally ill.   14. With print orders now running fourteen million monthly, the *Reader's Digest* faces no serious competition in its field.   15. Pontius Pilate, Procurator of Palestine, the highest judge and top administrator of the country, had few of the marks of greatness.

(ex.)

B. Check the following passages for conventional punctuation of co-ordinate or closely related elements. Label each passage S (satisfactory) or U (unsatisfactory).

1. Congress has the right to approve presidential appointments, to override presidential vetoes, and to impeach the President. 2. The old, the infirm and the widowed, are the most frequent victims of the confidence man's schemes. 3. While living there, I knew I was sharing a room with a friend, not just a roommate. 4. To my weary, apprehensive parents, November 12, 1939, was a momentous day. 5. More people than ever are painting pictures going to museums and listening to classical music. 6. The new hospital was faced partly with aluminum sun-breakers, partly with ceramic tile. 7. The alderman complained that the Henry E. Lee Memorial Library was a gigantic, white elephant. 8. Our editorial and executive offices are located in the Newsweek Building, Broadway and 42nd Street, New York 36, New York. 9. The ores of the Comstock Lode not the natural beauty of the sierras had brought my family to Nevada. 10. Henry had not been heard from since he went to a carnival party in Munich Germany. 11. Ex-senators, ex-governors, ex-cabinet members, and distinguished private citizens have at times made good ambassadors. 12. The miles upon miles of small houses are new, spick-and-span, and highly sanitary, but they are also indistinguishable from those in Kankakee, Illinois; Lincoln, Nebraska; or Oakland, California.

C. Check the following passages for conventional punctuation of interrupters. Label each passage S (satisfactory) or U (unsatisfactory).

1. Photography, you will agree, is not yet generally accepted as an art form. 2. For years, English Methodists have debated the merits of reunion with the Anglican Church (2,922,000 members). 3. Many fine programs though presented mainly for entertainment, supplement what the child learns in school. 4. Painter Du Bois—his work is represented in Manhattan's Metropolitan Museum of Art—resisted the modern trend toward abstraction. 5. The lone rider, the barroom fight, and the gingham-clad heroine—these are the indispensable ingredients of the third-rate cowboy movie. 6. At one time President Wilson was a university president wasn't he? 7. A dozen last-inning victories (six of them since July 4) have given hometown fans something to cheer about. 8. He reports that political independents—his term is the mugwumps—have ejected the old-line party hacks from the city government. 9. Why if I were you Alice I would see a lawyer first thing tomorrow morning. 10. Peter Minuit I am sure you remember bought Manhattan Island from the Indians for a handful of trinkets. 11. The government, many businessmen feel, should insure foreign investments against expropriation. 12. A trip abroad, to be truly enjoyable, should be carefully planned.

D. In the following passages, insert appropriate punctuation in the numbered spaces. *Use no capitals or periods not already supplied in the text.* Leave a blank space where no punctuation is required.

1. Good television plays___(1) which are not very numerous___(2) do not have a simple___(3) predictable___(4) ending. The viewer cannot tell___(5) what will happen___(6) until the play is over. *Arts Theater*___(7) which was discontinued last June___(8) was a good example of this type of program. The play___(9) that I remembered best___(10) dealt with a punch-drunk prizefighter___(11) who fell in love with an attractive___(12) well-educated___(13) girl. Until the very end of the play___(14) I did not know___(15) whether the fighter would win the girl.

2. In recent months___(1) senators___(2) ex-athletes___(3) and the clergy have added their voices to a mounting chorus of indignation. They agree with the many American___(4) physical___(5) education teachers___(6) who condemn Americans as flabby___(7) lazy___(8) and generally unfit. These people seem to fear___(9) that the Russians___(10) a race of tawny___(11) muscle-bound gymnasts___(12) will one day descend upon our shores and thresh each of us individually. My own fear is that the slender___(13) bony look in fashion among Americans today may be a handicap in the battle for the minds of men. How can the hungry___(14) human beings of other countries believe that a nation of gaunt___(15) emaciated people is as well off as it pretends to be?

3. My father___(1) the oldest child in a family with seven children___(2) grew up on a farm near Cleveland___(3) Ohio. My grandfather having died in an accident___(4) Father___(5) besides working on the farm___(6) helped out at the local post office___(7) to support his mother___(8) and the younger children. Being an unusually earnest___(9) studious___(10) young man___(11) he studied for an exam___(12) that would enable him to become an inspector. He took the exam___(13) passed it with excellent grades___(14) and went to work investigating the activities of swindlers___(15) who used the mails to defraud the public.

4. Now___(1) the purpose of a quick___(2) warm synthesis between research___(3) thinking___(4) and writing is to attain the three prime qualities of historical composition___(5) clarity___(6) vigor___(7) and objectivity. You must think about your facts___(8) analyze your material___(9) and decide exactly what you mean___(10) before you can write it___(11) so that the average reader will understand. Most of the facts that you excavate from the archives___(12) like all relics of past human activity___(13) are dumb things___(14) it is for you to make them speak by proper selection___(15) arrangement___(16) and emphasis.

E. From your current writing and reading, select ten sample sentences that illustrate the various conventions of punctuation discussed in the preceding section.

F. Show how each of the following (slightly abridged) passages employs but also varies the conventions of punctuation described in the preceding section. Read each passage out loud to show how punctuation corresponds to the rhythms of speech.

1. Often the students taught each other more effectively than the teachers could, gained more from extracurricular activities than from formal classwork. The experience of writing for the paper, or of managing a team, or of singing and playing, and, most of all, the undirected talk that swirled formlessly through the night have a value that cannot be recognized in grades or credits. (Oscar Handlin)

2. Always, in the past, war and the threat of war, whether aggressive or defensive, were usable instruments. Nations could enlarge their territories, acquire profitable colonies, change the religion of a vanquished population, all by means of war. Thus, in the old days before the nuclear age began, war was a usable—however horrible and expensive—instrument of national purpose. (Walter Lippmann)

3. The mark of my mother's character was not caution, which denotes a lack of imagination, but the opposite—an unrelenting remembrance of every hurt, betrayal, and sorrow. If, at any hour of the day or night—it did not matter whether she was feeding her children or had been awakened from a deep sleep—someone should mention a Mrs. Bernstein whom she had not seen since twenty years before, and of whom she knew nothing, not even her first name, my mother would immediately, like a spider, spin back and forth on the few threads that connected with Mrs. Bernstein; she would brood, brood, brood on her and absorb into the texture of her own present sorrow the life story of someone she had not thought of in years. (Alfred Kazin)

THE TECHNIQUE OF QUOTATION

P 8   QUOTATION

Often, you will need to indicate that you are reproducing information or ideas derived from a specific source, that you are quoting something first said or observed by someone else.

> **P 8a** **Direct Quotation.** *In repeating someone's exact words, distinguish them clearly from your own text.* Such direct quotations are enclosed in **quotation marks.** They are usually separated by a **comma** from the statement identifying the source:

> She said, "Leave me alone."
> "I don't care," he said.

Often the *credit tag* (or statement identifying the source) *interrupts the quotation* instead of introducing or concluding it. You then need **commas** both before and after the credit tag if it splits one complete sentence. You need a comma before and a period after the credit tag if it comes between two complete sentences:

> "All men," Aristotle wrote, "naturally desire knowledge."
> "All men are curious," Aristotle wrote. "They naturally desire knowledge."

The following variations from these basic conventions are important:

(1) No comma is required with extremely *short quotations* or with *quotations worked into the pattern of a sentence* that is not a mere credit tag:

> Your saying "I am sorry" was not enough to soothe his wounded pride.

> The clatter of dishes and tableware, mingled with lusty shouts of "Seconds here!" and "Please pass the butter!", will resound across the country.—John Crawford, "A Plea for Physical Fatness," *Atlantic*

No comma is required when the credit tag follows a question or an exclamation:

> "Is everybody all right?" he shouted at the top of his voice.

(2) *Long or formal quotations* are often introduced by a **colon** instead of a comma. Whether you use a comma or a colon, capitalize the first word of the quotation if it was capitalized in the original source (or if it would have been capitalized if written down).

> Saarinen's definition of architecture's purposes describes his work: "To shelter and enhance man's life on earth and to fulfill his belief in the nobility of his existence."

(3) *Long quotations* (more than ten typed lines) should be set off from the rest of a paper *not* by quotation marks but by indention and single-spacing. The same applies to quotations consisting of more

than a full line of poetry. See Section 8 and the sample paper that follows it for examples of such **block quotations.**

(4) Be sure to indicate when the person you are quoting is quoting someone else. In a quotation marked by the conventional set of double quotation marks, **single quotation marks** signal a *quotation within a quotation:*

> He said, "Our Congressman's constant cry of 'Cut that budget!' deceives no one."
>
> In the words of Chester Bowles, "In our national efforts to prove that we are 'realists' who do not 'go off half-cocked,' we have developed an appalling gap between the moral beliefs to which we subscribe and our day-to-day performance."

P 8b   Terminal Marks in Quotations. *Observe conventional sequence when quotation marks coincide with other marks of punctuation.*

(1) Commas conventionally precede the final quotation mark, whereas *semicolons and colons conventionally follow it.*

> As he said, "Don't worry about me," the ship pulled away from the quay.
> You said, "I don't need your sympathy"; therefore, I didn't offer any.

(2) End punctuation usually precedes the final quotation marks, as in all the examples given so far. Sometimes, however, you will have to use a *question mark or an exclamation mark after the quotation has formally ended.* This means that the quotation itself is not a question or an exclamation. Rather, you are asking a question or exclaiming about the quotation.

> Who said, "We are strangers here; the world is from of old"?
> Don't ever tell a girl, "There'll never be another woman like my mother"!

NOTE: *A terminal mark is not duplicated at the end of a quotation* even when logic might seem to require its repetition. For instance, use only one question mark even when you are asking a question about a question:

> Were you the student who asked, "Could we hold the class on the lawn?"

P 8c   Insertions and Omissions. *In direct quotation, any changes you make in the original text should be clearly indicated to your reader.*

(1) If for any reason you insert *explanations or comments of your own,* you should set them off from the quoted material by **square brackets:**

> As Dr. Habenichts observes, "Again and again, they [the Indians] saw themselves deprived of lands of whose possession they had been assured with solemn oaths."

> The note read: "Left Camp B Wednesday, April 3 [actually April 4]. Are trying to reach Camp C before we run out of supplies."

A comment sometimes inserted in a quotation is *sic,* the Latin word for "thus," which indicates that a passage that seems questionable or contains errors was transcribed exactly the way it occurred in the original source.

> The police records contained this short entry: "The accomplices of the suspect is [*sic*] unknown."

(2) If you want to *omit unnecessary or irrelevant material* from a quotation, you have to indicate the omission by three consecutive periods, adding up to a total of four if the omission occurs after a period in the original text:

> The report concluded on an optimistic note: "All three of the patients . . . are making remarkable progress toward recovery."

> "To be a bird is to be alive more intensely than any other living creature, man included. . . . They live in a world that is always present, mostly full of joy." So wrote N. J. Berrill, Professor of Zoology at McGill University.—Joseph Wood Krutch, "If You Don't Mind My Saying So," *The American Scholar*

To indicate extensive omissions (a line or more of poetry, a paragraph or more of prose), you may use a single typed line of spaced periods.

NOTE: Periods indicating an omission are called an **ellipsis.** An ellipsis can easily distort or falsify a quotation by omitting important details or qualifications. A testimonial reading "This might have been a good book if it had been more carefully planned" should not be shortened to read ". . . a good book."

P 8d   Indirect Quotation. *In indirect quotations, you reproduce someone else's ideas or thoughts but translate them into your own words.* Indirect quotations are *not* enclosed in quotation marks:

> Aristotle stated *that all men naturally desire knowledge.*
> General Grant replied *that he doubted the wisdom of such a move.*
> The artist asked me *which of the drawings I liked best.*

(1) Indirectly quoted statements often appear in the form of noun clauses introduced by *that*, indirectly quoted questions in the form of noun clauses introduced by words like *whether, why, how,* or *which.* Such clauses are *not* separated from the statement indicating the source by a comma or colon. The following passage, by contrast, shows ways of *working the source statement into the indirect quotation as an interrupter,* requiring **commas**:

> *As Gandhi remarked,* the first consequence of nonviolent action is to harden the heart of those who are being assaulted by charity. But, *he continued,* all the while they are being driven to a frenzy of rage, they are haunted by the terrible knowledge of how wrong they are.
> —Michael Harrington, "Whence Comes Their Passion," *The Reporter*

(2) Even in an indirect quotation, you may reproduce some words or phrases exactly as they were used by the person you quote. To indicate that you are *preserving part of the original wording,* you should enclose such directly quoted words and phrases—but not any other part of the quotation—in **quotation marks**:

> The author felt that students could not be "tricked or coerced into thinking."

> The government radio referred to the accused men as "bandits" and "murderers" and promised that justice would be upheld "regardless of the cost."

P 8e   Words Set Off from Context. *Quotation marks sometimes indicate that a writer is using words and phrases that are not part of the vocabulary he would normally employ.* In other words, he is using expressions that are not his own, even though he may not be quoting them from any specific source.

(1) **Quotation marks** may identify words that are employed for *local color or comical effect.* They enable a writer to show irony by holding an expression as it were at arm's length:

> At the school I attended, a girl who did not go on "dates" or take an interest in "fellows" was not accepted as a normal human being.

> It would seem that every modern child's pleasure must have its "constructive aspects."—Lois Phillips Hudson, "The Buggy on the Roof," *Atlantic*

> Shepley, Bulfinch, Richardson & Abbott were retained to design a "championship amphitheater."—Benjamin DeMott, "Suspended Youth," *The American Scholar*

Avoid using such quotation marks as a way of evading responsibility for undesirable or inappropriate expressions.

(2) Either quotation marks or italicized print—which corresponds to underlining in a typed manuscript—identifies *technical terms* presumably new to the reader and *words discussed as words,* as in a discussion of grammar or meaning.

> She wore a "Mother Hubbard," a loose, full gown long since out of fashion.
>
> In logic, the term *inference* refers to a conclusion or deduction arrived at by reasoning.
>
> The word *mob* was attacked as slang by some eighteenth-century writers.

(3) **Italics** rather than quotation marks identify *words that have been borrowed from foreign languages* and have not become part of the generally accepted vocabulary of the English language:

> Logrolling and back scratching are his exercises; *Quid pro quo* and *Cui bono?* are his mottoes.—William Lee Miller, "Confessions of a Conferencegoer," *The Reporter*

Many legal and scientific terms borrowed from Latin belong in this category:

> A writ of *certiorari* is issued by a superior court to obtain judicial records from an inferior court or quasi-judicial agency.
>
> The sperm whale, *Physeter macrocephalus,* is valuable for its oil and spermaceti.

EXERCISES

A. Check the following passages for conventional punctuation of quotations. Label each passage S (satisfactory) or U (unsatisfactory).

1. "Everything has already been said," wrote André Gide, "but since nobody ever listens we always have to start all over again."

2. "I am Grace Anders," she said, "do you mind if I come in?"

3. "Terrible!" the director shouted. "Let's take that passage again, starting from 'O, that this too too solid flesh would melt . . .' "

4. Newspaper veterans turned the phrases "culture beat" and "culture editor" over in their mouths with the gusto of a man biting into an unripe olive.

(ex.)

5. The lady from Buffalo kept asking the guide "what he meant by primitive?"

6. Wild applause and shouts of "Encore!" greeted us when the curtain parted.

7. Instead of congratulating me, John said, "Beauty contests—what a farce!"

8. According to one irate bystander, the murderer deserved no more sympathy than a "rabid dog."

9. "I'm all right," said my uncle, "just watch what you are doing the next time."

10. The speaker charged "that the television audience resembled the ancient Romans, who liked to see gladiators do battle to the death."

11. The speaker quoted Jefferson as saying that "our new circumstances" require "new words, new phrases, and the transfer of old words to new objects."

12. The constant war cry of my high school English teachers was give an example!

B. In the following passage, insert appropriate punctuation in the numbered spaces. Underline lower-case letters that should be replaced with capitals (english). Leave a blank space where no punctuation is required.

The article points out___(1) that many commercials are directed at the younger and more impressionable among television fans___(2) for instance___(3) a commercial might go like this___(4) Harry the Bat eats Bang Cereal every morning to grow big and strong___(5) so why don't you kiddies have your mom buy some today___(6) Mom is then plagued by the___(7) kiddies___(8) until she buys the cereal___(9) wasn't it Edgar Guest who said___(10) none but the hard of heart can resist the pleading look of a child___(11) this technique takes unfair advantage of the parents___(12) for___(13) as a friend of mine recently put it___(14) children are often even more gullible than adults___(15).

C. From your current writing and reading, select ten sample sentences that illustrate the various conventions of punctuation discussed in the preceding section.

D. (**Review of punctuation**) Explain the use of punctuation marks in each of the following passages. Point out sentences that you would have punctuated differently and explain why. Explain effects achieved by unconventional punctuation.

1. In recent years it has been possible to make motion-picture films of events on the surface of the sun, and by speeding them up

several hundred times to project on the screen the life story of cata-
clysmic solar events which may occupy hours of time and quadrillions
of cubic miles of space. Some of these films are awe-inspiring: they
show immense fountains of flame spurting to heights of a hundred
thousand miles from the sun's edge; bridges of fire, which could span
a dozen earths, forming and crumbling; exact replicas of A-bomb
bursts—but a thousand times as large—shooting up into space.—Arthur C. Clarke, "The Secret of the Sun," *Holiday*

2. Many of the greatest classics were written, assuredly, without children in mind, and were taken over by children who cheerfully
disregarded what they could not understand and cherished what they
could. Thus Defoe, old and cantankerous, did not mean to write for
children, but they adopted Robinson Crusoe and own him still; soon
Crusoe spread all over the globe; he was celebrated in every language;
he suffered one metamorphosis after another, most famously in "Swiss
Family Robinson," but in dozens of others as well. After two hundred
years he is read avidly by children in Montana and Tasmania and Nor-
way, and very little by their parents. Nor did the harsh and embittered
Jonathan Swift mean to write for the young, but he could not help
himself either, it seems. The children took over Gulliver and went with
him on his travels, they made him into a fairy-story character.—Henry
Steele Commager, "When Majors Wrote for Minors," *Saturday Review*

3. Men are brought to these conferences, regularly, in a sort of
balanced ticket: one Jew, one Catholic, one Protestant; one labor
leader to every businessman; one Republican to every Democrat; very
carefully, a Negro and a woman; an economist with the Economist's
View, a psychoanalyst with the Psychoanalytical View, a philosopher
with the Standpoint of Philosophy. In my earliest conferencegoing
days I myself was a College Student, attending as representative dec-
oration conferences composed mainly of older people. Invariably there
would come a golden moment when—since I then had sense enough
to keep my mouth shut and would not have spoken—the chairman
would pounce: "But let us hear from the Student Mind"; or "And
how does this sound to Young People?"—William Lee Miller, "Confessions of a Conferencegoer," *The Reporter*

4. There are thousands of other places calling for an artist's
skill—state buildings, municipal buildings, railway stations, restau-
ants, schools, hospitals, and even the places where our dead lie. Dec-
oration of these would keep artists going for a hundred years. When
I was in New York City I had to go to see the Federal taxing officer
in Battery Park, to settle accounts before departing. I came into a big
room filled with benches on which people were sitting, waiting their
turn to interview the officer. A big flag of the United States, tacked to
the back wall, almost stretched from side to side. Nailed, not to the

mast, but to the wall. No place for a flag to be, for a flag should always fly. Attached to its halyard, secured to its staff, a flag is active, a flag is alive. Stretched alone, and tacked to a wall, it is a dead thing. A flag crucified.—Sean O'Casey, "Always the Plough and the Stars," *The New York Times Book Review*

5. The major interest we have in the liberal arts is with man and his achievement. But it is not the abstraction "man" that concerns us. For it was not man that wrote *Hamlet,* but Shakespeare; not man that composed *Don Giovanni,* but Mozart; not man that painted the "View of Toledo," but El Greco; not man that completed the *Summa Theologica,* but Thomas Aquinas.—Neal W. Klausner, "The Humanities: Mirrors of Genius," *The American Scholar*

CHAPTER EIGHT

GLOSSARIES

16: GLOSSARY OF USAGE

NOTE: The following glossary reviews the status of words, word forms, and constructions that are frequently criticized as careless, illogical, excessively informal, or otherwise restricted in appropriateness and effectiveness. The glossary is limited to information that goes beyond the scope of the ordinary dictionary entry or that tends to be lost in the wealth of other information a dictionary provides.[1]

a, an.   The *a* should appear only before words that begin with a consonant *when pronounced: a desk, a chair, a house, a year, a* C, *a university.* The *an* should appear before words that begin with a vowel when pronounced (though in writing, the first letter may be a consonant): *an eye, an essay question, an honest man, an* A, *an* M, *an uninformed reader.* In the latter position, *a* is nonstandard.

above, above-mentioned, aforementioned, aforesaid.   Avoid the use of *above, above-mentioned, aforementioned,* and the like, to refer to something previously mentioned. These phrases suggest the wooden, bureaucratic style of some business letters, many government publications, and most legal documents. Use a less mechanical, less obtrusive expression like "this point," "this fact," "these considerations." If a *this* would not be clear, use a brief phrase restating or summarizing the point to which you wish to refer.

allusion, illusion.   An "allusion" is a hint or indirect reference (to call an athlete a "Goliath" is to use a Biblical allusion). An "illusion"

---

[1] For confusing words often included in a Glossary of Usage, see SP 2c; for a list of idiomatic prepositions, see D 1e.

is a deceptive sense impression or a mistaken belief. When an illusion is serious and persistent enough, it may become a "delusion."

amount, number. *Amount* is sometimes used loosely instead of *number* in reference to things counted individually and as separate units:

SATISFACTORY: A large *number* (not *amount*) of people were waiting.
SATISFACTORY: The *number* (not *amount*) of unsold cars on dealers' lots was growing steadily.

and and but at the beginning of a sentence. When *and* and *but* are used at the beginning of a sentence, or at the beginning of a paragraph, they have the effect of partly canceling out the pause signaled by the period or by the paragraph break. They can therefore suggest a sudden or important afterthought. But many modern writers start sentences with *and* or *but* merely to avoid heavier, more formal connectives like *moreover, furthermore, however,* and *nevertheless.*

and/or. *And/or* is an awkward combination sometimes necessary in commercial or official documents. Its use in ordinary expository prose is an annoying mannerism.

angle, approach, slant. *Angle, approach,* and *slant* are currently overused as snyonyms for "attitude," "point of view," "position," or "procedure."

apt, liable, prone. In informal speech and writing, *apt, liable,* and *prone* all appear in the sense of "likely." In formal usage, *apt* suggests that something is likely because of someone's aptitude ("he is apt to become a successful artist"); *liable* suggests that what is likely is burdensome or undesirable ("he is liable to break his leg"); *prone* suggests that something is almost inevitable because of strong habit or predisposition ("he is prone to suspect others").

as. *As* as a substitute for *that* or *whether* ("I don't know *as* I can come") or as a substitute for *who* ("Those *as* knew her avoided her") is nonstandard. As a substitute for *because* or *while, as* is often criticized as ambiguous, unemphatic, or overused (see D 7a).

attenuate, extenuate. Both *attenuate* and *extenuate* basically mean "to thin out." *Extenuate* is the legal term: "Extenuating circumstances" make a crime seem less serious or contemptible than it originally appeared.

attribute, contribute. *Contribute* means "to give one's share" or "to have a share" in something; *attribute* means "to trace or ascribe something to a cause or source" ("He *attributed* the crossing of the letters in the mail to the intervention of a supernatural power").

being as, being that. As substitutes for *because* or *since*, *being as* and *being that* ("*being that* I was ill") are nonstandard.

between, among. *Between* is historically related to *twain*, which in turn is a variant of *two*. As a result, grammarians have often restricted *between* to references to two of a kind (distinguish *between* right and wrong) and required *among* in references to more than two (distinguish *among* different shades of color). *Between* is also appropriate when more than two things can be considered in pairs of two:

> He had sand *between* his toes.
> Bilateral trade agreements exist *between* many European countries.

Indiscriminate substitution of *between* for *among* invites avoidable criticism.

blame for, blame on. There are two idiomatic uses of the word *blame:* "He blamed the passenger *for* the accident" or "He blamed the accident *on* the passenger." The first of these is preferred in formal English.

calculate, reckon, expect, guess. In formal written English, *calculate* and *reckon* usually imply computing or systematic reasoning; *expect* implies expectation or anticipation; *guess* implies conjecture. In the sense of "think," "suppose," or "consider," these verbs are colloquial or dialectal.

can and may. Formal English uses *can* in the sense of "be able to" or "be capable of," *may* to indicate permission. The use of *can* to indicate permission, increasingly common in speech and writing, is generally considered colloquial:

FORMAL: You *may* (have my permission to) take as much as you *can* (are able to) eat.
COLLOQUIAL: *Can* I speak to you for a minute?

cannot help but. Although occasionally found in writing, *cannot help but* is widely criticized as an illogical or confused variant of *cannot help:*

SATISFACTORY: I *cannot help* wishing that I had never met you.
SATISFACTORY: I *cannot but* wish that I had never met you.

childish, childlike. "Childish gesture" and "childlike gesture" both remind us of children; but the former suggests silliness or immaturity, the latter endearing innocence.

compare with, compare to. We compare two cities *with* each other to see what they have in common, but we compare a city *to* an anthill to show what a city is like.

continual, continuous. To be "continuous," something must extend without interruption in space or in time. People may keep up a "continual" conversation, interrupted because they have to pause for breath.

couple of. In formal writing, *couple* refers to two of a kind, a pair. Used in the sense of "several" or "a few," it is colloquial. Used before a plural noun without a connecting *of*, it is nonstandard.

COLLOQUIAL: We had to wait *a couple of* minutes.
NONSTANDARD: We had only *a couple* dollars left.

credible, credulous, creditable. Stories may be credible or incredible; the people who read them may be credulous or incredulous. An act that does someone credit is a creditable act.

cute, great, lovely, wonderful, swell. Words like *cute, great, lovely,* and *wonderful* so often express thoughtless or insincere praise that their use in formal writing can suggest immaturity. *Cute* is colloquial. *Swell* is slang.

different than. *Different from* is characteristic of formal written English. Nevertheless, *different than*, widely used in speech, is becoming acceptable in writing. Recent writers on usage point out that it is the more economical way of introducing a clause:

ECONOMICAL: We tried a different method *than* we had used last year.
LESS ECONOMICAL: We tried a different method *from the one* we had used last year.

disinterested, uninterested. In formal writing, *disinterested* usually means "unswayed by personal, selfish interest" or "impartial." The word is used especially to indicate the absence of a financial interest or of personal ambition: "We were sure he would be a *disinterested* judge." The use of *disinterested* in the sense of "uninterested" or "indifferent" is colloquial.

do form for emphasis. Verb forms with *do, does,* or *did* can serve as emphatic variants of the simple present and the simple past: "She may not wear the latest fashions, but she *does know* how to cook." In student writing, the emphatic *do* is sometimes overused:

OVERDONE: I really *did appreciate* the teacher's help an awful lot.
BETTER: I *appreciated* the teacher's help.

double comparative, double superlative. Short adjectives usually form the comparative by adding the suffix *er* (*cheaper*), the superlative by adding the suffix *est* (*cheapest*). Long adjectives and adverbs ending in *ly* usually employ the intensifiers *more* and *most* instead (*more expensive, most expensive*). Forms using both the suffix and the intensifier are nonstandard (*more cheaper, most cheapest*).

double negative. Double and triple negatives—the use of additional negative words to reinforce a negation already expressed—are nonstandard: "I *didn't* do *nothing.*" "*Nobody* comes to see me *no more.*"

due to as a preposition. *Due to* is generally accepted as an adjective: "His absence was *due to* ill health." "His absence, *due to* ill health, upset our schedule." As a preposition meaning "because of," *due to* is often criticized:

OBJECTIONABLE: He canceled his lecture *due to* ill health.
SAFE: He canceled his lecture *because of* ill health.

each other, one another. Careful writers distinguish between *each other* (referring to two persons or things) and *one another* (referring to more than two).

enthuse. *Enthuse* is a "back formation" from the noun *enthusiasm* and is used in colloquial English as a convenient short cut for "become enthusiastic" and "move to enthusiasm." Similar back formations, like *reminisce* from *reminiscence,* have become generally acceptable. *Enthuse* still has a long way to go.

etc. *Etc.,* the Latin abbreviation for "and so on" or "and the like," often serves as a vague substitute for additional details, examples, or illustrations. Furthermore, *ect.* is a common misspelling; "and etc." and "such as . . . etc." are redundant and unnecessarily reveal the writer's ignorance of Latin.

farther, further; all the farther. A traditional rule required *farther* in references to space and distance ("We traveled *farther* than we had expected"), *further* in references to degree and quantity ("We discussed it *further* at our next meeting") and in the sense of "additional" ("without *further* delay"). *Further* is now widely accepted as appropriate in all three senses.

All the farther in the sense of "as far as" ("This is *all the farther* we go") is variously classified as colloquial, nonstandard, or dialectal.

fortuitous, fortunate. "Fortuitous" changes are accidental, unplanned developments that often are, but don't have to be, fortunate.

full, fulsome. *Fulsome*, except when used by people who are confused by its similarity with *full*, means "offensive, disgusting." "Fulsome praise" is offensively exaggerated or insincere.

gentleman, lady, female. In nineteenth-century, and especially British, use, *gentleman* and *lady* identified people whose manners and social rank set them apart from the uneducated. Now both terms are usually used as polite equivalents of the blunter *man* and *woman*. Since they suggest refinement, they sometimes sound pretentious or ridiculous when used in comparatively unrefined situations. *Female* is biological and impersonal; it is overused as a condescending humorous term.

get, got, gotten. The verb *get* is used in many idiomatic expressions. Some of these are colloquial:

> *have got* (for "own," "possess," "have available")
> I *have got* ten dollars; she *has got* blue eyes; you *have got* ten minutes.
>
> *have got to* (for "have to," "must," "be obliged")
> I *have got to* leave now; we *have got to* think of our customers.
>
> *get to* (for "succeed")
> I finally *got to* see him.
>
> *get* (for "understand")
> *Get* it?
>
> *get* (for "arrest," "hit," "kill")
> The police finally *got* him.

get (for "puzzle," "irritate," "annoy")
What really *gets* me is that he never announces his tests.

Some grammarians commend the use of *get* in sentences like "He *got hit* by a truck" as an emphatic and unambiguous alternative to the ordinary passive, formed with *be, am, was, were* ("He *was hit* by a truck"). This use of *got* is still widely considered colloquial.

In American English, *have gotten* is an acceptable alternative to *have got*, except when the latter means *have* or *have to*.

hadn't ought to. *Ought,* unlike some other auxiliaries, has no form for the past tense. Forms like *had ought* or *hadn't ought* are nonstandard.

NONSTANDARD: You *hadn't ought* to ask him.
FORMAL: You *ought not to have* asked him.

human, humane. Not every human being is "humane"—that is, kind, compassionate, sensitive, or refined.

if, whether. Conservative readers object to *if* when used to express doubt or uncertainty after such verbs as *ask, don't know, wonder, doubt.* The more formal connective is *whether.*

FORMAL: I doubt *whether* his support would do much good.

in, into. Formal writing often requires *into* rather than *in* to indicate direction: "He came *into* (not *in*) the room."

infer, imply. In formal usage, *imply* means to "indicate or suggest a certain conclusion"; *infer* means "to draw a conclusion on the basis of what has been indicated or suggested." A statement can have various implications, which may lead to inferences on the part of the reader.

it's me, it is I. Traditional grammarians require *it is I* on the grounds that the linking verb *is* equates the pronoun *I* with the subject *it* and thus makes necessary the use of the subject-form. Modern grammarians recommend *it is me* on the grounds that usual English word order (he hit *me;* she asked *me*) makes the object-form natural. *It's me* is freely used in informal speech; other pronouns (*us, him, her*) preserve a more definitely colloquial flavor:

COLLOQUIAL: I thought it was *him*. It couldn't have been *us*.

judicial, judicious.   A "judicial" decision is a decision reached by a judge or by a court. A "judicious" decision shows sound judgment. Not every judicial decision is judicious.

kind.   Agreement requires "*this kind* of car" or "*these kinds* of fish." "*These kind* of cars" and "*those kind* of cars" are colloquial.

later, latter.   "Although both Alfred and Francis were supposed to arrive at eight, the former came earlier, the *latter later*."

learn, teach.   Except in nonstandard speech, the teacher *teaches* (rather than *learns*) the learner; the learner is *taught* (rather than *learned*) by the teacher.

leave, let.   In formal usage, *leave* does not mean "allow" or "permit"; you do not "leave" somebody do something. Nor does *leave* take the place of *let* in suggestions like "Let us call a meeting."

less, fewer.   *Less* is often used interchangeably with *fewer* before plural nouns. This use of *less* is widely condemned. The safe practice is to use *less* in references to extent, amount, degree (*less* friction, *less* money, *less* heat) but not in references to number (*fewer* people, *fewer* homes, *fewer* requirements).

like as a connective.   In informal speech, *like* is widely used as a connective replacing *as* or *as if* at the beginning of a clause:

INFORMAL: Do *like* I tell you.
FORMAL: Do *as* I tell you.

INFORMAL: The patient felt *like* he had slept for days.
FORMAL: The patient felt *as if* (or *as though*) he had slept for days.

However, *like* is generally acceptable as a preposition introducing a noun or a pronoun:

The girl looked *like* her mother.

luxuriant, luxurious.   A "luxurious" house may be surrounded by "luxuriant"—that is, profusely growing—vegetation.

moral, morale.   We talk about the "moral" of a story but about the "morale" of troops. People with good morale are not necessarily very moral, and vice versa.

most, almost.   *Most* is colloquial when used in the sense of "almost" or "nearly": "*Most* everybody was there" (for "*Nearly* everybody was there").

possessives with verbal nouns.   A traditional rule requires that a verbal noun (gerund) be preceded by a possessive in sentences like the following:

FORMAL: He mentioned *John's winning* a scholarship.
FORMAL: I am looking forward to *your mother's staying* with us.

This rule is widely observed in formal writing. In informal speech and writing the plain form is more common:

INFORMAL: Imagine *John winning* a scholarship!

practicable, practical.   A "practicable" plan seems capable of being put into practice. A "practical" plan, when put into practice, is workable or effective. Unlike things, people can be practical but not practicable.

preposition at the end of a sentence.   Many laymen remember a rule requiring a writer not to end a sentence with a preposition. This rule has been considerably modified by most teachers of grammar and of writing. The preposition that ends a sentence is idiomatic, natural English, though more frequent in informal than in formal use.

IDIOMATIC: I don't remember what we talked *about.*
IDIOMATIC: She found her mother-in-law hard to live *with.*
IDIOMATIC: You know very well what I hired you *for.*

On the other hand, placing a comparatively unimportant word at the end of a sentence can make a sentence sound unemphatic.

EMPHATIC: Let us not betray the ideals *for* which these men died.
EMPHATIC: Do not ask *for* whom the bell tolls.

prepositions often criticized.   *Inside of* (for *inside*), *outside of* (for *outside*), and *at about* (for *about*) are redundant.
     Back of for *behind* (*back of* the house), *inside of* for *within* (*inside of* three hours), *off of* for *off* (get *off of* the table), *outside of* for *besides* or *except* (no one *outside of* my friends), and *over with* for *over* (it's *over with*) are colloquial.
     As to, as regards, and *in regard to* are generally acceptable, but they can seem heavy-handed and bureaucratic when used as indiscriminate substitutes for briefer or more precise prepositions.

AWKWARD: I questioned him *as to* the nature of his injury.
PREFERABLE: I questioned him *about* his injury.

As to whether, in terms of, and *on the basis of* flourish in all varieties of jargon.

Per (a dollar *per* day), *as per* (*as per* your request), and *plus* (quality *plus* service) are common in business and newspaper English but inappropriate in a noncommercial context.

provided, provided that, providing. *Provided, provided that,* and *providing* are interchangeable in a sentence like "He will withdraw his complaint, *provided* you apologize." However, only *provided* has consistently escaped criticism and is therefore the safest form to use.

reason is because, reason why. In informal speech *the reason . . . is because* often takes the place of the more formal *the reason . . . is that.* The former construction is often criticized as redundant, since *because* repeats the idea of cause already expressed in the word *reason.* Either construction can make a sentence unnecessarily awkward.

INFORMAL: *The reason* that the majority rules *is because* it is strongest.
FORMAL: *The reason* that the majority rules *is that* it is strongest.
LESS AWKWARD: The majority rules *because* it is strongest.

Reason why, though equally open to the charge of redundancy, is less widely criticized.

respectfully, respectively. *Respectfully* means "full of respect"; *respectively* means "with respect or reference to each of several things in the order in which they were mentioned" ("*Un* and *deux* mean one and two respectively").

shall, will. In current American usage, *will* usually indicates simply that something is going to happen:

I *will* ask him tomorrow.
You *will* find it on your desk.
Mr. Smith *will* inform you of our plans.

The more emphatic *shall* often indicates that something is going to happen as the result of strong determination, definite obligation, or authoritative command:

I *shall* return.
We *shall* do our best.
Wages of common laborers *shall* not exceed twenty dollars a day.

Shall is also common in questions that invite the listener's approval or consent:

> *Shall* I wait for you?
> *Shall* we dance?

Formal English often reverses the relationship between *will* and *shall* in the first person; that is, after *I* and *we* but not after *you, he,* or *they.* "I *shall* see him tomorrow" then expresses simple, unemphatic future; "I *will* not yield" expresses determination. Questions would use the form expected in the answer: "*Shall* you see him tomorrow?" Current handbooks of grammar no longer require the observance of this convention.

should, would. In many uses, *should* and *would* are parallel to *shall* and *will.* "I *would* help you if I could" is parallel to "I *will* help you"; the formal alternative, "I *should* help you if I could," is parallel to "I *shall* help you." However, both *should* and *would* are also used with distinctive meanings of their own. *Should* may express obligation ("I *should* study more"), probability ("I *should* be able to finish it tonight"), or a hypothetical condition ("If he *should* resist, call me for help"). *Would* may express customary action ("He *would* listen patiently to my excuses").

split infinitives. Occasionally a modifier breaks up an infinitive; that is, a verbal formed with *to* (*to come, to promise, to have written*). The resulting split infinitive has long been idiomatic English and occurs in the work of many distinguished writers. However, a split infinitive can be awkward, especially if the modifier intervening after *to* consists of more than one word:

AWKWARD: He ordered us *to* with all possible speed *return* to our stations.
BETTER: He ordered us *to return* to our stations with all possible speed.

The words that most frequently split infinitives are overused intensifiers like *actually, definitely, literally, really,* and *virtually.* Omitting these altogether often improves the sentence:

> We expect the public *to* [literally] *overwhelm* us with orders.
> Education may be able *to* [virtually] *eliminate* race prejudice.

superlative in reference to two. In informal speech and writing, the superlative rather than the comparative frequently occurs in comparisons between only two things. This use of the superlative is widely considered illogical and generally labeled inappropriate to formal usage.

INFORMAL: Which of the two candidates is the *best* speaker?
FORMAL: Which of the two candidates is the *better* speaker?

take and, try and, up and. *Take and* in "I'd *take and* prune those roses" and *up and* in "He *up and* died" are dialectal. *Try and* for *try to* in "I'd *try and* change his mind" is colloquial.

titles: Dr., Prof., Reverend. In references to holders of academic degrees or titles, *Dr. Smith* and *Professor Brown* are courteous and correct. *Professor* is sometimes abbreviated when it precedes the full name: *Prof. Paul F. Brown*. In references to a clergyman, *Reverend* is usually preceded by *the* and followed by the first name, by initials, or by *Mr.* (*the Reverend William Carper; the Reverend W. F. Carper; the Reverend Mr. Carper*).

too. The use of *too* in expressions like "He isn't *too* well off" is often condemned as vague or overused.

type, type of, -type. The practice of omitting the *of* in expressions like "this *type* of plane" is colloquial. *Type* is increasingly used as a suffix to turn nouns into adjectives: "an escape-type novel," "a drama-type program." Such combinations strike many readers as barbarisms, foreign to idiomatic, natural English. Often they are used to turn simple ideas into fuzzy, wordy phrases: "a subsidy-type payment" says no more than "subsidy."

unique, perfect, equal. It is often argued that one thing cannot be *more unique, more perfect,* or *more equal* than another; either it is unique or it isn't. Formal English therefore often substitutes *more nearly unique, more nearly perfect, more nearly equal.*

up. *Up* is often criticized as redundant in expressions like *finish up, heat up, hurry up, rise up,* or *sober up.* In other expressions it modifies meaning or adds emphasis: *buy up, clean up, dress up, speak up, use up.* Most of these combinations have a colloquial flavor. *Beat up* is slang.

used to, didn't use to, used to could. Formal English does not employ *used to* in questions or negative statements with *did:*

INFORMAL: She *didn't use* to smoke.
FORMAL: She *used not to* smoke.

Used to could is nonstandard for *used to be able.*

very and much.   Formal usage prefers *much* or *greatly* to *very* before a verbal like *surprised* or *embarrassed* (past participle) if the verbal idea is still strong; that is, if the verbal has not yet become an ordinary adjective with little suggestion of action or process:

SOMETIMES CRITICIZED	SAFE
very surprised	*much* surprised
very embarrassed	*greatly* embarrassed
very astonished	*very much* astonished

where, where at, where to.   In formal English, *where* takes the place of *where to* ("*Where* was it sent?") and *where at* ("*Where* is he?"). Both *where to* and *where at* are generally condemned as redundant.
    Where used instead of *that* ("I read in the paper *where* a boy was killed") is colloquial.

-wise.   The practice of converting a noun into an adverb by tacking on *-wise* is characteristic of business or advertising jargon. Use *grammatically* for *grammar-wise,* *linguistically* for *language-wise.*

without, on account of.   *Without* and *on account of* are nonstandard or dialectal when they serve as connectives introducing a clause:

NONSTANDARD: The landlord won't let me stay *without* I pay the rent.
STANDARD: The landlord won't let me stay *unless* I pay the rent.
NONSTANDARD: Dr. X was unpopular *on account of* he was strict with his students.
STANDARD: Dr. X was unpopular *because* he was strict with his students.

you with indefinite reference.   Formal writing generally restricts *you* to the meaning of "you, the reader." Much informal writing uses *you* with indefinite reference to refer to people in general. Formal writing would substitute *one:*

INFORMAL: In ancient Rome, *you* had to be a patrician to be able to vote.
FORMAL: In ancient Rome, *one* had to be a patrician to be able to vote.
             (You, the reader, are definitely not a citizen of ancient Rome.)

17: GRAMMATICAL TERMS

NOTE: Use the index to locate fuller discussion of many of the grammatical terms listed in this glossary.

Absolute Construction.   A word or phrase that is grammatically independent of the rest of the sentence. Typically, a verbal or verbal phrase:

> *The guests having departed,* Arvin locked the door.

Active.   See VOICE.

Adjective.   A class of words that can point out a quality of a noun (or noun equivalent). They occur characteristically as modifiers of nouns ("the *happy* child") and as predicate adjectives ("The child was *happy*"). They normally have distinctive forms for use in comparisons (*happier, happiest; more reasonable, most reasonable*).

Adjective Clause.   A dependent clause serving an adjective function:

> The man *who had startled us* apologized.

Adverb.   A class of words used to modify verbs, adjectives, other adverbs, or a sentence as a whole:

> He ran *quickly.*
> He was *strangely* silent.
> He sang *moderately* well.
> *Surprisingly,* he did not answer.

Many adverbs show the distinctive *-ly* ending.

Adverb Clause. A dependent clause serving an adverbial function:

When the bell ceased to ring, I opened the door.

Agreement. Correspondence, mainly in number, between grammatically related elements. Use of matching forms of a subject and its verb (the *dog barks*—the *dogs bark*); choice of a pronoun matching its antecedent ("*Each* member must be aware of *his* responsibility").

Antecedent. The noun (or equivalent) for which a pronoun substitutes:

Aunt Hertha fell sick soon after *she* arrived.

Appositive. A noun (or equivalent) placed as a modifier next to —usually after—another noun:

Mr. Brown, *the registrar,* proved most helpful.

Article. *A* and *an* (the **indefinite** articles) and *the* (the **definite** article), used as noun markers:

a book, *an* honest man, *the* door

Auxiliary. Helping verbs used in forming complete verbs: *be* (*am, are, was,* etc.); *have; shall* (*should*); *will* (*would*); *can* (*could*); *may* (*might*); *must; ought.*

Case. Inflected forms of nouns and pronouns, signaling certain grammatical relationships within a sentence: the **possessive** of nouns (*George's* friend), the **subject-** and **object-forms** of pronouns (*I—me, he—him,* etc.).

Clause. A subject-predicate unit that may combine with other such units in a sentence. **Independent** clauses are grammatically self-contained and can be punctuated as complete sentences:

I think; therefore, I am.
I think. Therefore, I am.

Dependent clauses are grammatically subordinate to an independent clause (main clause):

Arvin had a dog, *which barked all night.*
After the rain stopped, we went home.

See ADJECTIVE CLAUSE, ADVERB CLAUSE, NOUN CLAUSE.

Collective Noun. Group nouns that are singular in appearance but may require a plural verb:

SINGULAR: The jury *votes* tomorrow. (thought of as a unit)
PLURAL: The jury *are* out to lunch. (thought of as individuals)

Comparative. The form of adjectives and adverbs that is used to indicate relative superiority:

Blood is *thicker* than water.

Complement. A sentence element completing the predication of the verb. The complements of action verbs are called **objects**:

Arvin called *the sheriff* (**direct** object).
She wrote *my father* (**indirect** object) *a letter* (**direct** object).

The complement of a linking verb is a noun or adjective describing the subject (**subjective complement**):

Her father was *a businessman* (**predicate noun**).
The girl looked *pale* (**predicate adjective**).

After some verbs, an object is followed by a description of the object (**objective complement**):

The editorial called the project *a failure.*
Arvin labeled the charges *ridiculous.*

Conjunction. See CONNECTIVE.

Conjunctive Adverb. See CONNECTIVE.

Connective. Words connecting sentence elements or clauses: **coordinating connectives** (*and, but, for, or, nor*); **subordinating connectives** (*if, when, because, though, whereas*); **adverbial connectives** (*however, therefore, consequently*).

Coordinate Adjectives. Two adjectives describing different qualities of the same noun, with a comma taking the place of *and:*

a *noisy, unruly* crowd

Correlatives. Pairs of connectives coordinating sentence elements or clauses: *either . . . or, neither . . . nor, not only . . . but also, whether . . . or.*

Elliptical Constructions.   Constructions in which missing elements are supplied to facilitate grammatical analysis:

> The paintings [*that*] he collected filled a large room.
> When [*she was*] interviewed, the actress denied rumors of an impending engagement.

Expletives.   The *it* or *there* used as mere introductory words in *it-is, there-is, there-are* sentences.

Finite Verb.   A term used to distinguish a complete verb from a verbal, which cannot by itself function as a predicate.

Function Words.   Words whose major function is to establish grammatical relationships within a sentence: articles, connectives, prepositions.

Gender.   The quality of nouns and pronouns that determines choice between *he, she,* or *it;* between *actor* and *actress, alumnus* and *alumna, fiancé* and *fiancée.*

Gerund.   See VERBAL.

Idiom.   An expression that does not conform to general grammatical patterns but is established by usage as the habitual way of conveying a given meaning:

> bear in mind, have a mind to, keep in mind

Infinitive.   See VERBAL.

Inflection.   Changes in the form of words to reflect changes in grammatical relationships. For instance, the plural *-s* of nouns; the *-s, -ed,* or *-ing* of verbs; the *-er* or *-est* of adjectives.

Intensifier.   Words that modify adjectives or adverbs and express degree; also called **intensive adverbs**:

> *very* hot, *quite* calm, *rather* young

Interjection.   A grammatically independent element used to express attitude or emotion: *Ah, oh, ouch,* etc.

Linking Verb.   See VERB.

Modifier. Words, phrases, or clauses that develop or restrict the meaning of other sentence elements or the sentence as a whole (see ADJECTIVE, ADVERB). **Restrictive** modifiers contribute to identification and need no punctuation; **nonrestrictive** modifiers provide additional information not essential to identification and are set off, normally by commas:

RESTRICTIVE: The man *who returned my wallet* was a complete stranger.

NONRESTRICTIVE: Mr. Norton, *who found my wallet,* is an old friend.

Mood. The classification of verb forms as **indicative** (plain or factual: *I am ready*); **imperative** (request or command: *Be quiet*); and **subjunctive** (hypothetical or contrary to fact: *I wish he were here!*).

Noun. A class of words that name or classify people, animals, things, ideas. They occur typically as subjects of clauses or as objects of verbs and prepositions. Their appearance is often signaled by noun markers like the articles (*a, an, the*). Many nouns add *-s* to the plain form to form the plural: *dogs, cars, houses, colleges.*

Noun Clause. A dependent clause taking the place of a noun:

That he was late does not surprise me.

Noun Equivalent. Sentence elements grammatically equivalent to nouns: pronouns, infinitives, gerunds, noun clauses.

Number. Choice of appropriate forms to express **singular** (one of a kind) or **plural** (more than one).

Object. See COMPLEMENT.

Object-Form. See CASE.

Participle. See VERBAL.

Passive. See VOICE.

Past. See TENSE.

Perfect. See TENSE.

Person. Choice of appropriate forms to express the person speaking (**first person:** *I know*); the person spoken to (**second person:** *you know*); or the person spoken about (**third person:** *he knows*).

Phrase. A group of related words, typically a preposition or a verbal accompanied by its object or other related material.

PREPOSITIONAL PHRASE: Irene sat *at the window.*
VERBAL PHRASE: Father gave up *smoking cigars.*

Predicate. The second basic element of the typical written sentence, making an assertion about the subject. The predicate consists of a complete (finite) verb and its possible complements and modifiers.

Preposition. A class of words that relate a noun (or equivalent) to the rest of the sentence:

Arvin left *after* dark.

Present. See TENSE.

Principal Parts. The basic forms of a verb: simple present (*know*), simple past (*knew*), past participle (*known*).

Progressive Construction. Verb forms expressing action in progress:

Fred *was lighting* a cigarette.

Pronoun. A class of words taking the place of nouns, classified as **personal** (*I, you, he*); **possessive** (*my, your, his*); **reflexive** or **intensive** (*myself, yourself, himself*); **demonstrative** (*this, that*); **relative** (*who, which, that*); **interrogative** (*who, which, what*); and **indefinite** (*one, anyone, everyone*). See CASE.

Relative Clause. A dependent clause related to the main clause by a relative pronoun:

The article *that I mentioned* begins on page five.

Restrictive. See MODIFIER.

Sentence. A grammatically complete and self-contained unit of thought or expression, set off from other such units by end punctuation. The typical written sentence contains at least a subject and a predicate (*Birds sing*). The most common exception is the subjectless request or command, in which the subject is said to be understood (*Show him in*).

Sentences combining two or more independent clauses are called **compound**. Sentences combining an independent and one or more dependent clauses are called **complex**. A combination of the two types is called **compound-complex**:

COMPOUND:	He hummed, and she sang.
COMPLEX:	He hummed when she sang.
COMPOUND-COMPLEX:	When they heard the news, he hummed and she sang.

Subject. The first basic element of the typical written sentence, about which the predicate makes an assertion.

Subject-Form. See CASE.

Subjunctive. See MOOD.

Superlative. The form of adjectives and adverbs used to express absolute (rather than relative) superiority:

Fred is the *fastest* runner on the team.

Tense. The system of verb forms expressing primarily different relationships in time:

PRESENT:	I know	PERFECT:	I have known
PAST:	I knew	PAST PERFECT:	I had known
FUTURE:	I will (shall) know	FUTURE PERFECT:	I will (shall) have known

Transitive. See VERB.

Verb. A class of words that signal the performance of an action, the occurrence of an event, or the presence of a condition. Verbs appear in typical verb positions ("Let's *leave*." "The boys *left* the scene"). They typically take an *s* in the third person singular of the present tense (*asks, leaves, condones*). They use characteristic **auxiliaries** in forms consisting of more than one word (*have left, was asked, will be leaving*). **Action verbs** are modified by adverbs; **linking verbs** are followed by adjectives:

ACTION VERB:	He *responded* quickly.
LINKING VERB:	His response *seemed* quick.

Regular verbs use the same form for the simple past and the past participle:

REGULAR:	I *laughed*	I have *laughed*
IRREGULAR:	I *knew*	I have *known*

Transitive verbs normally require an object:

TRANSITIVE:	He *raises* chickens.
INTRANSITIVE:	He *rises* early.

See TENSE, MOOD, VOICE.

Verbal. Forms that are derived from verbs but do not by themselves function as predicates: the **infinitive** (*to* form), **present participle** (*ing* form used as an adjective), **gerund** (*ing* form used as a verbal noun), **past participle** (*ed* form in regular verbs, irregular in others). Verbals appear as noun equivalents, modifiers, and *parts* of verbs.

INFINITIVE:	He liked *to dream.*
PRESENT PARTICIPLE:	Her *dreaming* look entranced him.
GERUND:	*Dreaming* got him nowhere.
PAST PARTICIPLE:	He had *dreamed* of childhood days.

Voice. The two sets of verb forms that show typically whether the subject is acting (**active**) or acted upon (**passive**):

ACTIVE:	Eileen *feeds* the children.
PASSIVE:	The children *are fed* by Eileen.

APPENDIX: LETTERS

Correspondence creates special problems of manuscript form. In writing or answering a formal invitation, you will do well to follow forms suggested in a book of etiquette. In writing a personal letter, you may allow yourself considerable freedom, as long as you observe the elementary courtesies of keeping your handwriting legible and using presentable stationery. Between these extremes of formality and informality is the kind of letter that you may have to write to a teacher, to a college official, or to a future employer. In applying for a scholarship or for a job, you will do well to follow a conventional letter form.[1]

The following specimen letter illustrates one of several styles widely used in business correspondence. You may use it as a model for spacing, indention, and punctuation. Notice especially the following points:

(1) Study the arrangement and relative position of the address of the sender and the address of the receiver, the former followed by the date. When you are writing to a group or to a firm rather than to one of its members, "Gentlemen" or "Dear Sirs" replaces the usual "Dear Mr. Brown" or the more formal "Dear Sir."

(2) The "complimentary close" may range from the formal "Respectfully yours" to the simple "Sincerely." A married woman may put (*Mrs.*) in front of her typed name.

(3) The letter should be typed on one side of standard typing paper, with ample margins. Balance the material on the page. Avoid crowding a short letter into the upper half of the page; double-space the body of a short letter for more balanced distribution of text.

---

[1] For advice on content and tone see Exercise A, Section 5.

138 South Third Street
San Jose, California
January 12, 1964

Mr. Ralph J. Clark, Jr.
Personnel Manager
San Rafael Independent-Journal
185 Washington Street
San Rafael, California

Dear Mr. Clark:

I should like to apply for a job with your newspaper.
My interest lies in general reporting, a field in which I
have had some working experience as well as college training.

During my last summer vacation I worked on the Santa
Clara Journal for thirteen weeks within the internship
program of the Journalism Department of San Jose State
College. I did general reporting and some photography.

As a student at San Jose State, I was a general
reporter and feature editor of the Spartan Daily, the
college newspaper. I will be graduated February 1 of this
year.

The following persons have consented to furnish
references:

> Dr. John Williams
> Associate Professor of Journalism
> San Jose State College
> San Jose, California
>
> Mr. Thomas Bigelow
> General Manager
> Santa Clara Journal
> Santa Clara, California
>
> Mr. Richard H. James
> Editor
> Los Angeles Examiner
> Los Angeles, California

I am available at your convenience for a personal
interview.

Yours truly,

Mary Ann Johnson

Mary Ann Johnson

EXERCISES

A. Write a letter of application for a position in which you have at one time or another taken an interest. Observe conventional letter form.

B. Find a project or recent development that merits publicity or support. Write a letter about it to the editors of a newspaper or magazine, to a legislator, or to a responsible official. Observe conventional letter form.

INDEX

Classification (continued)
    in organizing themes, O 2b:225–228
Clauses
    adjective, punctuation of, P 5b:443–444
    adverbial, punctuation of, P 4:436–439, Ex. 439–440
    definition and kinds of, G 2d:289–291; gt:478
    elliptical, G 2d:291
    independent (main), punctuation of, P 3:432–436, Ex. 439
    noun, punctuation of, P 5a:441
    relative, gt:482
    see also Sentence, Sentence style
Clichés, D 10c:371–372
    in description, 15–16
Climax
    in organizing themes, O 2b:228
    and sentence style, S 5b:394
Clipped forms, in colloquial English, D 3a:358
Coherence
    in autobiography, 41–43
    in description, 16–19
    in paragraphs, O 8a:271
    in research papers, 185–186
    see also Continuity, Organization, Transition
Colloquialisms, D 3a:357–358, Ex. 364–365
Colon
    between clauses, P 3a:432
    to introduce list or description, P 2b:429
    before quotations, P 8a:454
Commager, Henry Steele, 460
Commas
    adverbial connectives set off, P 3c:434
    for clarity, P 5c:444–445
    in comma splices, P 3b:432–433, Ex. 439
    between coordinate adjectives, P 6b:446–447
    with coordinating connectives, P 3d:435–436
    in dates, addresses, measurements, P 6c:447
    with direct address and other light interrupters, P 7c:449–450
    between independent clauses, P 3b:432–433, Ex. 439
    after introductory adverbial clauses, P 4c:438–439
    after introductory phrase or verbal, P 5c:444–445
    with namely, for example, that is, P 2b:429–430
    with nonrestrictive adverbial clauses, P 4b:437–439

Commas (continued)
    with nonrestrictive modifiers, P 5:442–445
    with quotations, P 8a:454–455
    for repetition and contrast, P 6d:447
    sentence modifiers set off, P 5c:444–445
    in series, P 6a:445–446
    unnecessary, P 5a:441
    verbal phrases set off, P 5c:444
Comparative, double, gl:468
Compare with, to, gl:467
Comparison
    of adjectives, G 2b:288; G 10b:325–326; G 10:479
    incomplete or illogical, G 10:325–326
Comparison and contrast
    in definition, 81
    in description, 19–20
    in organizing themes, O 2c:228–229
    in paragraph development, O 7c:268
Complement, G 2b:286–287; gt:479
    at beginning of sentence, S 1b:380
    objective, G 7b:317; gt:479
    subjective, G 7b:316; gt:479
Complex sentence, G 2d:290
Compound sentence, G 2d:290
Compound subject, G 3c:296–297
Compound words, SP 6a:419–420
Conant, James B., 181
Conclusions, O 3c:236–239, Ex. 253
Concrete detail
    in description, 13–16
    with generalizations, 94–95
Condee, Ralph W., 443
Conditional, G 12a:332
Confusing pairs
    spelling, SP 2c:410–412
    see also Glossary of usage
Conjunctions, see Coordinating connectives, Subordinating connectives
Conjunctive adverbs, see Adverbial connectives
Connectives
    correlative, G 11a:329; gt:479
    imprecise as, so, while, D 7b:366
    kinds and function, G 2d:289–290; gt:479
    overused and, S 3b:386–387
    pronoun form after as and than, G 6a:311
    punctuation of, P 3–4:432–440
Connotation
    in dictionary entries, D 1b:343–344
    in persuasion, 124–130
    variable, 128–129; D 1c:344
Consistency
    in diction, D 3a:357

Consistency (continued)
in logic, 110
of pronoun reference, G 12b:332–333
of tense forms, G 12a:330–332
Context
and meaning, 78; D 1c:344–345, Ex. 348–349
in note-taking and research, 185, 203
Continual, continuous, gl:467
Continuity
in paragraphs, O 6:261–264
through repetition and parallelism, S 5:392–396
in themes, O 4:239–243
Contraction
apostrophe in, SP 5a:418
of coordinate elements, G 10d:326–328
in informal style, SP 5a:418
Contrast, *see* Comparison and contrast
Convention
in autobiography, 39–40
as standard of correctness, 4–5
Cooke, Alistair, 265, 430
Coordinating connectives, G 2d:290
punctuation of, P 3d:435–436
Coordination, excessive, S 3b:386–387
Copula, *see* Verb, linking
Corrections
on final copy, M 1b:403
and revision, 5–6
Correctness, 4–5
Correlatives, G 11a:329
Could of, SP 2a:410
Couple of, gl:467
Cowley, Malcolm, 274, 303, 447
Crawford, John, 454
Credible, credulous, gl:467
Critical evaluation of student writing, 5–6
Crosby, John, 150
Cute, gl:467

Daiches, David, 67–68
Dash
for breaks in thought, P 2a:429
with heavy interrupters, P 7a:448
for modifier containing commas, P 5b:443
Data, G 3a:294
Davis, Elmer, 386
Deadwood, S 4a:389; *see also* Redundancy
Deduction, *see* Logic
Deductive order
in paragraphs O 7c:269–270
in themes, O 2d:231
Definition, 72–91, Ex. 85–90; Topics, 90–91

Definition (continued)
circular, 79
class and differentiation, 78–79
context considered in, 78
dictionary as source of, 77
in dictionary entries, D 1:340–341
examples with, 80–81
extended, 81
faulty or inadequate, 79–80
form of, 78–79
in introductions, O 3b:234–235
stipulated, 84
synonyms in, 80
in value judgments, 82–84
DeMott, Benjamin, 457
Denotation and connotation
in dictionary entries, D 1b:343–344
in persuasion, 124–130
Description, 12–32, Ex. 26–31; Topics, 31–32
comparison and contrast in, 19–20
figurative language in, 23–25
imaginative, 12
detail organized, 16–19; O 2b:225–228
detail selected, 13–15
dominant impression, 16
sensory detail, 14–15
specific words in, 20–21
stereotyped, 15–16
technical exposition, 12
technical terms in, 21–23
Detail
in description, 13–19
irrelevant, O 8a:270–271
in paragraph development, O 7a:264–265; O 8b:271–273
Development, *see* General and specific, Generalization, Paragraph
Dewey decimal system, 177
Dialects, D 4b:361–362
Dialogue, paragraphs in, 260
Diction, 339–377, Review Ex. 376–377
archaic and obsolete, D 5:362–363, Ex. 364–365
colloquial, D 3a:357–358, Ex. 364–365
context and meaning, D 1c:344–345, Ex. 348–349
denotation and connotation, 124–130; D 1b:343–344, Ex. 348
in description, 20–25
dialects, D 4b:361–362
fancy or ornate, D 3c:359–360
figurative, 23–25; D 10b:371
flowery, D 9c:370
in formal writing, 147
idiom, D 1e:346–347, Ex. 348
inaccurate, D 7:365–366, Ex. 372–373

HANDBOOK KEY